T0202611

Lecture Notes in Computer Science 13649

Founding Editors

Gerhard Goos
Karlsruhe Institute of Technology, Karlsruhe, Germany
Juris Hartmanis
Cornell University, Ithaca, NY, USA

Editorial Board Members

Elisa Bertino
Purdue University, West Lafayette, IN, USA
Wen Gao
Peking University, Beijing, China
Bernhard Steffen
TU Dortmund University, Dortmund, Germany
Moti Yung
Columbia University, New York, NY, USA

More information about this series at https://link.springer.com/bookseries/558

Wei Dong · Jean-Pierre Talpin (Eds.)

Dependable Software Engineering

Theories, Tools, and Applications

8th International Symposium, SETTA 2022
Beijing, China, October 27–29, 2022
Proceedings

Editors
Wei Dong 🆔
National University of Defense Technology
Changsha, China

Jean-Pierre Talpin
Inria
Rennes, France

ISSN 0302-9743   ISSN 1611-3349   (electronic)
Lecture Notes in Computer Science
ISBN 978-3-031-21212-3   ISBN 978-3-031-21213-0   (eBook)
https://doi.org/10.1007/978-3-031-21213-0

This Springer imprint is published by the registered company Springer Nature Switzerland AG
The registered company address is: Gewerbestrasse 11, 6330 Cham, Switzerland

Preface

This volume presents the proceedings of the 8th International Symposium on Dependable Software Engineering: Theories, Tools and Applications (SETTA 2022), held in Beijing during October 27–29, 2022, and co-located with ATVA 2022. This edition of the symposium received 29 submissions, from which 11 full papers and three short papers displaying promising work-in-progress were selected. Each submission was reviewed by at least 4 members of the Program Committee in a single-blind review process.

The purpose of the SETTA symposium is to bring international researchers together to exchange research results and ideas on bridging the gap between formal methods and software engineering. SETTA features research interests and results from different groups so as to initiate interest-driven research collaboration. It is aiming at academic excellence and its objective is to become a flagship conference on formal software engineering in China.

Formal methods emerged as an important area in computer science and software engineering about half a century ago. An international community has formed, researching, developing, and teaching formal theories, techniques, and tools for software modeling, specification, design, and verification. However, the impact of formal methods on the quality and improvement of software systems is, in practice, lagging behind. This is, for instance, reflected by the challenges in applying formal techniques and tools to engineering large-scale systems such as cyber-physical systems (CPS), the Internet of Things (IoT), enterprise systems, cloud-based systems, and so forth.

To achieve these goals and contribute to the sustainability of the formal methods research, it is important for the symposium to attract young researchers into the community. Thus, this symposium particularly encourages the participation of young researchers and students.

Topics of interest to SETTA include, but are not limited to:

- Requirements specification and analysis
- Formalisms for modeling, design, and implementation
- Model checking, theorem proving, and decision procedures
- Scalable approaches to formal system analysis
- Formal approaches to simulation, run-time verification, and testing
- Integration of formal methods into software engineering practice
- Contract-based engineering of components, systems, and systems of systems
- Formal and engineering aspects of software evolution and maintenance
- Parallel and multicore programming
- Embedded, real-time, hybrid, probabilistic, and cyber-physical systems
- Mixed-critical applications and systems
- Formal aspects of service-oriented and cloud computing
- Safety, reliability, robustness, and fault-tolerance
- Dependability of smart software and systems

- Empirical analysis techniques and integration with formal methods
- Applications and industrial experience reports
- Software tools to assist the construction or analysis of software systems

We would like to thank everyone who helped to make SETTA 2022 a success and we hope that you enjoy reading the selected papers.

Wei Dong
Jean-Pierre Talpin

Organization

General Chair

Huimin Lin — Institute of Software, Chinese Academy of Sciences, China

Program Co-chairs

Wei Dong — National University of Defense Technology, China
Jean-Pierre Talpin — Inria and Irisa, France

Publicity Chair

Bohua Zhan — Institute of Software, Chinese Academy of Sciences, China

Local Organization Committee

Andrea Turrini — Institute of Software, Chinese Academy of Sciences, China
Shuling Wang (Chair) — Institute of Software, Chinese Academy of Sciences, China
Bohua Zhan — Institute of Software, Chinese Academy of Sciences, China

Program Committee

Yamine Ait-Ameur — IRIT, INPT-ENSEEIHT, France
Richard Banach — University of Manchester, UK
Lei Bu — Nanjing University, China
Milan Ceska — Brno University of Technology, Czech Republic
Sudipta Chattopadhyay — Singapore University of Technology and Design, Singapore
Yu-Fang Chen — Institute of Information Science, Academia Sinica, Taiwan
Liqian Chen — National University of Defense Technology, China
Alessandro Cimatti — Fondazione Bruno Kessler, Italy
Florin Craciun — Babes-Bolyai University, Romania
Yuxin Deng — East China Normal University, China
Wei Dong — National University of Defense Technology, China
Hongfei Fu — Shanghai Jiao Tong University, China
Jan Friso Groote — Eindhoven University of Technology, The Netherlands

Dimitar Guelev	Bulgarian Academy of Sciences, Bulgaria
Thai Son Hoang	University of Southampton, UK
Chao Huang	University of Liverpool, UK
Yu Jiang	Tsinghua University, China
Sebastian Junges	Radboud University, The Netherlands
Yi Li	Nanyang Technological University, China
Guoqiang Li	Shanghai Jiao Tong University, China
Zhiming Liu	Southwest University, USA
Tiziana Margaria	Lero, Ireland
Dominique Mery	Loria, Université de Lorraine, France
Stefan Mitsch	Carnegie Mellon University, USA
Jun Pang	University of Luxembourg, Luxembourg
Dave Parker	University of Birmingham, UK
Yu Pei	Hong Kong Polytechnic University, China
Shengchao Qin	Teesside University, UK
Mickael Randour	F.R.S.-FNRS and Université de Mons, Belgium
Stefan Schupp	TU Wien, Austria
Zhiping Shi	Capital Normal University, China
Fu Song	ShanghaiTech University, China
Jeremy Sproston	University of Turin, Italy
Ting Su	East China Normal University, China
Meng Sun	Peking University, China
Jean-Pierre Talpin	Inria and IRISA, France
Andrea Turrini	Institute of Software, Chinese Academy of Sciences, China
Tarmo Uustalu	Reykjavik University, Iceland
Jim Woodcock	University of York, UK
Xiaofei Xie	Nanyang Technological University, China
Zhiwu Xu	Shenzhen University, China
Bai Xue	Institute of Software, Chinese Academy of Sciences, China
Chenyi Zhang	Jinan University, China

Advisory Board

Zhou Chaochen (Coordinator)	Institute of Software, Chinese Academy of Sciences, China
He Jifeng	East China Normal University, China
Cliff Jones	Newcastle University, UK
Deepak Kapur	University of New Mexico, USA
Li Wei	Beihang University, China

Steering Committee

| Zhenhua Duan | Xi'dian University, China |
| Martin Fränzle | University of Oldenburg, Germany |

Kim Larsen   Aalborg University, Denmark
Xuandong Li   Nanjing University, China
Zhiming Liu   Southwest University, USA
Sriram Rajamani   Microsoft Research, India
Ji Wang   NUDT, China
Kwangkeun Yi   Seoul National University, South Korea
Naijun Zhan (Chair)   Institute of Software, Chinese Academy of Sciences,
                              China

Keynotes Speakers

On SMT Solving for Multi-threaded Program Verification

Fei He [iD]

School of Software, Key Laboratory for Information System Security, MoE,
Beijing National Research Center for Information Science and Technology,
Tsinghua University, China
hefei@tsinghua.edu.cn

Abstract. Verifying multi-threaded programs is difficult because of the vast number of thread interleavings. Partial orders (called *happens-before orders*) can help with verification because they can represent many thread interleavings concisely. It is thus desired to efficiently handle happens-before order constraints for SMT-based multi-threaded program verification.

In this talk, I will report our recent work in this research line. We formalize a new *ordering consistency theory* for multi-threaded program verification that is applicable under various memory models (including sequential consistency, TSO and PSO). We develop two solvers for *ordering consistency theory*. The first solver checks consistency incrementally, generates minimal conflict clauses, and includes a custom propagation procedure. The second solver, based on preventive reasoning, has no requirement for consistency checking and conflict clause generation, and is thus more efficient. We implement our approaches in a prototype tool called DEAGLE which won *ConcurrencySafety* track in *SV-COMP 2022*.

Keywords: Program verification · Satisfiability modulo theory · Memory models · Concurrency

This work was supported in part by the National Natural Science Foundation of China (No. 62072267 and No. 62021002) and the National Key Research and Development Program of China (No. 2018YFB1308601).

Logic-Based Safety of Cyber-Physical Systems: Simultaneous Model Validation and Proof Transfer

Stefan Mitsch[iD]

Computer Science Department, Carnegie Mellon University, Pittsburgh PA,
USA
smitsch@cs.cmu.edu

Cyber-physical systems (CPS) are most prominently characterized by interaction between digital control and physical effects, and are operating increasingly often semi-autonomously or fully autonomously even in safety-critical domains. Strong correctness guarantees are needed for aviation, autonomous driving, railroad safety, robotics, factory automation, medical devices, and many other application areas. Formal methods promise to provide the much-desired rigorous correctness guarantees for cyber-physical systems: they make strong guarantees about the system behavior *if accurate models of the system can be obtained*. But any formal model we could possibly build, no matter how detailed, is necessarily an imperfect image of the real world. This gap between models and reality is fundamental and cannot be addressed with formal refinement techniques.

Light-weight formal methods, such as runtime verification and shielding, try to sidestep this challenge by replacing explicit models with monitors to flag and repair specification violations at runtime. In cyber-physical systems, however, predictive monitors are needed because safety-preserving interventions cannot be postponed until specification violations occur (e.g., collision avoidance systems need to engage brakes before a collision occurs). Encoding this predictive nature in the runtime-monitored properties puts the burden of deriving and justifying monitor conditions from models entirely on the user. As an alternative approach, online reachability analysis explicitly executes predictive models for runtime verification purposes. Any such attempts in disentangling modeling from verification when establishing formal guarantees about CPS are ill-fated because they make the predictive models a part of the trusted computing base.

The overall challenge of CPS safety presents a Gordion knot: we need models to analyze the correctness of safety interventions and to determine when to engage at runtime, but in order to ensure safety we need to scrutinize these very models for how accurately they represent reality, which can only be determined at runtime when the models are already operational.

This material is based upon work supported by the AFOSR under grant number FA9550-16-1-0288 and by the AFOSR and DARPA under Contract No. FA8750-18-C-0092. Any opinions, findings and conclusions or recommendations expressed in this material are those of the author(s) and do not necessarily reflect the views of the United States Air Force and DARPA.

This talk addresses a logic-based approach to cut this Gordion knot with simultaneous model validation and proof transfer. Crucially, we address the dichotomy between offline and online analysis while retaining both their benefits: results obtained offline in the theorem prover KeYmaeraX [4] provide provable guarantees about the running CPS by satisfying proof obligations at runtime with proof-generated monitors [10]. Advances in hybrid systems theorem proving establish confidence in the correctness of the produced artifacts (models, proofs, monitors, and code). The small trusted codebase of KeYmaeraX [12], formally verified real arithmetic quantifier elimination [13], verified compilation chains [2], and techniques for partial observability [11] not only pave the way towards establishing true safety and stability proofs [14] at the level of CPS operation at runtime, but also provide opportunity to develop a principled approach for safe learning-enabled control [1, 5, 8]. Advances in formalizing user-defined functions [6] and in proof management techniques [9] contribute to closing the gap between formal methods and engineering practice, as demonstrated with recent formal verification case studies in airborne collision avoidance [3] and railroad control [7].

References

1. Bayani, D., Mitsch, S.: Fanoos: multi-resolution, multi-strength, interactive explanations for learned systems. In: Finkbeiner, B., Wies, T. (eds.) VMCAI 2022. LNCS, vol. 13182, pp. 43–68. Springer, Cham (2022). https://doi.org/10.1007/978-3-030-94583-1_3
2. Bohrer, R., Tan, Y.K., Mitsch, S., Myreen, M.O., Platzer, A.: VeriPhy: verified controller executables from verified cyber-physical system models. In: PLDI, pp. 617–630. ACM (2018)
3. Cleaveland, R., Mitsch, S., Platzer, A.: Formally verified next-generation airborne collision avoidance games in ACAS X. ACM Trans. Embed. Comput. Syst.
4. Fulton, N., Mitsch, S., Quesel, J.D., Völp, M., Platzer, A.: KeYmaera X: an axiomatic tactical theorem prover for hybrid systems. In: Felty, A., Middeldorp, A. (eds.) CADE 2015. LNCS, vol. 9195, pp. 527–538. Springer, Cham (2015). https://doi.org/10.1007/978-3-319-21401-6_3
5. Fulton, N., Platzer, A.: Verifiably safe off-model reinforcement learning. In: Vojnar, T., Zhang, L. (eds.) TACAS 2019. LNCS, vol. 11427, pp. 413–430. Springer, Cham (2019). https://doi.org/10.1007/978-3-030-17462-0_28
6. Gallicchio, J., Tan, Y.K., Mitsch, S., Platzer, A.: Implicit definitions with differential equations for KeYmaera X. In: Blanchette, J., Kovács, L., Pattinson, D. (eds.) IJCAR 2022. LNCS, vol 13385, pp 723–733. Springer, Cham (2022). https://doi.org/10.1007/978-3-031-10769-6_42
7. Kabra, A., Mitsch, S., Platzer, A.: Verified train controllers for the federal railroad administration train kinematics model: balancing competing brake and track forces. IEEE Trans. Comput. Aided Des. Integr. Circuits Syst. (2022)
8. Kopylov, A., Mitsch, S., Nogin, A., Warren, M.: Formally verified safety net for waypoint navigation neural network controllers. In: Huisman, M., Păsăreanu, C., Zhan, N. (eds.) FM 2021. LNCS, vol. 13047, pp. 122–141. Springer, Cham (2021). https://doi.org/10.1007/978-3-030-90870-6_7

9. Mitsch, S.: Implicit and explicit proof management in KeYmaera X. In: FIDE@NFM, pp. 53–67 (2021)
10. Mitsch, S., Platzer, A.: ModelPlex: verified runtime validation of verified cyber-physical system models. Form. Methods Syst. Des. 49(1), 33–74 (2016)
11. Mitsch, S., Platzer, A.: Verified runtime validation for partially observable hybrid systems. CoRR abs/1811.06502 (2018)
12. Mitsch, S., Platzer, A.: A retrospective on developing hybrid system provers in the KeYmaera family. In: Ahrendt, W., Beckert, B., Bubel, R., Hähnle, R., Ulbrich, M. (eds.) Deductive Software Verification: Future Perspectives. LNCS, vol. 12345, pp. 21–64. Springer, Cham (2020). https://doi.org/10.1007/978-3-030-64354-6_2
13. Scharager, M., Cordwell, K., Mitsch, S., Platzer, A.: Verified quadratic virtual substitution for real arithmetic. In: Huisman, M., Păsăreanu, C., Zhan, N. (eds.) FM 2021. LNCS, vol. 13047, pp. 200–217. Springer, Cham (2021). https://doi.org/10.1007/978-3-030-90870-6_11
14. Tan, Y.K., Mitsch, S., Platzer, A.: Verifying switched system stability with logic. In: HSCC, pp. 2:1–2:11 (2022)

Abstraction-Based Training and Verification of Safe Deep Reinforcement Learning Systems (Extended Abstract)

Min Zhang

Shanghai Key Laboratory of Trustworthy Computing, East China Normal
University, Shanghai, China
zhangmin@sei.ecnu.edu.cn

Abstract. Deep Reinforcement Learning (DRL) systems shall be formally verified when they operate in safety-critical domains. However, their verification is a very challenging problem for two main reasons, i.e., the continuity and infinity of system state space and the inclusion of inexplicable decision-making deep neural networks (DNNs). We propose to first abstract the continuous and infinite state space into a finite set of *abstract states* and then train the system on these abstract states. This *abstract training approach* brings manifold benefits. First, we can build a verifiable formal model based on the same abstraction and verify whether it satisfies the expected safety and functional requirements using off-the-shelf model checkers. The verification results are then used to guide the abstraction refinement repeatedly for further training until all the requirements are satisfied. Second, we can perform a tight and scalable reachability analysis of the trained systems by treating the planted neural networks as black boxes, thus avoiding over-approximating them. Third, we can flexibly fine-tune the granularity in which the system states are abstracted for a better balance between robustness and performance.

Keywords: Abstraction · Deep reinforcement learning · Model checking · Probabilistic robustness · Reachability analysis

Background

Deep Reinforcement Learning (DRL) is an artificial intelligence technique for developing autonomous systems where deep neural networks (DNNs) are planted for decision-making. It has been developing quickly to solve those hard-specifiable systems such as robot control autonomous driving [9]. As some of those domains are safety-critical, their functionality, safety, and robustness shall be formally verified before deployment [4]. However, the verification problem is very challenging due to two main reasons. One is that the system state space is usually continuous and infinite, and the other is that the system is driven by an in-explicable and non-linear deep neural network. The two facts make it difficult to build an efficiently verifiable formal model. Existing verification approaches have to abstract the system state space and over-approximate the network after a system is trained. Such *ex post facto* verification has several limitations. One is that the abstraction and over-approximation introduce too much overestimation and consequently result in false positives in verification results. Another is that the verification results are hardly utilized to improve the system reliability as further training after verification may cause an unpredictable impact on system properties due to the inexplicability of neural networks [5].

Abstraction-Based Training and Verification

Verification-in-the-Loop Training [8]. As inspired by the importance of abstraction to the formal verification of infinite-state systems [7], we propose to abstract the infinite state space S of a DRL system into a finite set $\mathcal{S}$ of abstract states by defining the abstraction function $\mathcal{A} : S \to \mathcal{S}$ and train it on $\mathcal{S}$. At each training step t, we map the system state $s_t \in S$ to its corresponding abstract state $s = \mathcal{A}(s_t)$ and feed $\mathbf{s}$ into the planted neural network π to compute an action $a = \pi(\mathbf{s})$. A reward is then computed by a predefined reward function based on a and s_t, and the parameters in the neural network are updated correspondingly. The system proceeds to the successor state $s_{t+1} = f(s_t, a)$, where f is the system dynamics.

Under the same abstraction, we can build a state transition system $\mathcal{M}_{\mathcal{S}} = \langle \mathcal{S}, \mathcal{I}, \mathcal{T} \rangle$, where $\mathcal{I} = \{s | s \in \mathcal{S} \wedge \exists s_0 \in S_0.s = \mathcal{A}(s_0)\}$ and $(s, s') \in \mathcal{T}$ if $s' \in \hat{f}(s, \pi(s))$ for all $s, \mathbf{s}' \in \mathcal{S}$. Here, S_0 is the set of initial states of the system, and $\hat{f}(s, \pi(s)) = \{s' | \exists s \in \mathcal{C}(s).s' = \mathcal{A}(f(s, \pi(s)))\}$ denotes the set of successor abstract states from $\mathbf{s}$, where $\mathcal{C}$ is the corresponding concretization function of $\mathcal{A}$. $\mathcal{M}_{\mathcal{S}}$ is a simulation of the trained DRL system, i.e., for any transition from s_t to $s_{t+1} = f(s_t, a)$ and abstract state s, if $s = \mathcal{A}(s_t)$, then there exists $s' \in \mathcal{S}$ such that $s' \in \hat{f}(s, \pi(\mathbf{s}))$ and $s' = \mathcal{A}(s_{t+1})$. Since $\mathcal{S}$ is finite, we can leverage *off-the-shelf* model checkers to model check $\mathcal{M}_{\mathcal{S}}$ against the pre-specified properties defined in some temporal logic such as ACTL. When counterexamples are found, they could be spurious due to the abstraction. We then refine the abstract state $\mathcal{S}$ guided by the counterexamples and continue to train the system on the refined abstract state space. We repeat this *verification-in-the-loop* training process until all the properties are verified, and we finally obtain a verified safe DRL system.

Tight and Scalable Reachability Analysis [11]. Reachability analysis is an effective way to verify the safety properties of DRL systems [3, 6]. Given a DRL system with state space S, let R_S be the set of all the reachable states. We have $S_0 \in S$ and $s' \in R_S$ for all $s' \in S$ if there exists some state $s \in R_S$ such that $s' = f(s, N(s))$, where N is a neural network trained on S. Generally, it is an undecidable problem to check whether a state is reachable or not for a DRL system because the reachability problem of most nonlinear systems is undecidable [2]. Due to the infinity of S and the non-linearity of f, we have to over-approximate both N and f to overestimate R_S. This dual over-approximation results in too much overestimation and limited scalability to large neural networks.

By training the system on the abstract state space $\mathcal{S}$, we can over-approximate R_S more tightly and scalably via computing the set of reachable abstract states. Let the overestimated set be $\mathcal{R}_{\mathcal{S}}$, where $\mathcal{I} \in \mathcal{R}_{\mathcal{S}}$ and $s' \in \mathcal{R}_{\mathcal{S}}$ for all $s' \in \mathcal{S}$ if there exists some $s \in \mathcal{S}$ such that $(s, s') \in \mathcal{T}$. Because the neural network π is trained on $\mathcal{S}$, we can avoid over-approximating π and treat it as a black box when checking whether $(s, s') \in \mathcal{T}$ holds or not. It suffices to compute the corresponding action on s by $a = \pi(\mathbf{s})$ and determine the successor abstract states in $\hat{f}(s, a)$. The concretization of all the reachable abstract states constitutes an overestimated set of reachable actual states. In this process, we only need to over-approximate the dynamics f, which consequently yields a tight and scalable way to overestimate the set of reachable states for the DRL system.

Probabilistic Robustness Training and Evaluation [12]. Training on abstract states is also helpful in developing robust DRL systems. A DRL system is considered *robust* in a state with respect to some perturbation if it takes the same action on all the perturbed states. Under abstract training, a perturbed state may be mapped to the same abstract state and thus have the same action as the original state. The probability of mapping a perturbed state to the same abstract state as the original state can be estimated, yielding an analytical metric called *probabilistic robustness* to indicate the system robustness. The metric only depends on abstraction and thus can be computed analytically but not experimentally. We have proved that the probability increases monotonously with the granularity in which system states are abstracted. Consequently, we can achieve a flexible mechanism to balance the robustness and performance of trained DRL systems by fine-tuning the abstraction granularity of the system states.

The prototypes for the safe and robust training, verification and reachability analysis, and technical documents are available at https://github.com/aptx4869tjx/RL_verification.

Concluding Remarks

We believe that abstraction is a promising solution for connecting formal methods and deep reinforcement learning for developing provably reliable DRL systems. Following the work [1], which shows the feasibility of applying abstraction to the training phase, we demonstrate that abstraction can be utilized simultaneously in both verification and training. Introducing abstraction into both training and verification brings manifold benefits, e.g., simplifying the subsequent verification, utilizing the verification results for further training, computing tight sets of reachable states in a scalable and orthogonal manner to the size, architecture, and type of activation functions of neural networks, and balancing the robustness and performance by flexibly fine-tuning the abstraction granularity. All these benefits are necessary to develop safe and robust DRL systems.

Several problems remain ahead when the abstraction-based training and verification approach is applied to real-world complex DRL systems. One practical problem is extending it to high-dimensional systems, whose states require sophisticated abstractions defined particularly for neural network verification [10] to avoid state explosions in both training and verification phases. Another interesting direction is applying the proposed approaches to other variant DRL systems with non-deterministic and stochastic features, which could be verified using probabilistic and statistical model checking approaches. It is also interesting to explore the possibility of extending the training and verification approaches to classification tasks for training verifiable and robust deep neural networks.

Acknowledgments. The author thanks SETTA 2022 organizers for the invited talk. This work has been partially supported by National Key Research Program (2020AAA0107800), NSFC-ISF Joint Program (62161146001, 3420/21) and NSFC projects (61872146, 61872144), Shanghai Trusted Industry Internet Software Collaborative Innovation Center and "Digital Silk Road" Shanghai International Joint Lab of Trust-worthy Intelligent Software (Grant No. 22510750100).

References

1. Abel, D.: A Theory of Abstraction in Reinforcement Learning. Dissertation, Brown University (2020)
2. Asarin, E., Mysore, V.P., Pnueli, A., Schneider, G.: Low dimensional hybrid systems–decidable, undecidable, don't know. Inf. Comput. **211**, 138–159 (2012)
3. Fan, J., Huang, C., Chen, X., Li, W., Zhu, Q.: ReachNN*: atool for reachability analysis of neural-network controlled systems. In: Hung, D.V., Sokolsky, O. (eds) ATVA 2020. LNCS, vol. 12302, pp. 537–542. Springer, Cham (2020). https://doi.org/10.1007/978-3-030-59152-6_30
4. García, J., Fernández, F.: A comprehensive survey on safe reinforcement learning. J. Mach. Learn. Res. **16**, 1437–1480 (2015)
5. Henderson, P., Islam, R., Bachman, P., Pineau, J., Precup, D., Meger, D.: Deep reinforcement learning that matters. In: AAAI 2018, pp. 3207–3214. AAAI Press (2018)
6. Ivanov, R., Carpenter, T., Weimer, J., Alur, R., Pappas, G., Lee, I.: Verisig 2.0: verification of neural network controllers using Taylor model preconditioning. In: Silva, A., Leino, K.R. M. (eds.) CAV 2021. LNCS, vol. 12759, pp. 249–262 (2021). Springer, Cham. https://doi.org/10.1007/978-3-030-81685-8_11
7. Jackson, D.: Abstract model checking of infinite specifications. In: Naftalin, M., Denvir, T., Bertran, M. (eds.) FME 1994. LNCS, vol. 873, pp. 519–531. Springer, Heidelberg (1994). https://doi.org/10.1007/3-540-58555-9_113
8. Jin, P., Tian, J., Zhi, D., Wen, X., Zhang, M.: TRAINIFY: a CEGAR-driven training and verification framework for safe deep reinforcement learning. In: Shoham, S., Vizel, Y. (eds.) CAV 2022. LNCS, vol. 13371, pp. 193–218 (2022). Springer, Cham. https://doi.org/10.1007/978-3-031-13185-1_10
9. Kiran, B.R., et al.: Deep reinforcement learning for autonomous driving: a survey. IEEE Trans. Intell. Transp. Syst. pp. 4909–4926 (2021)
10. Singh, G., Gehr, T., Püuschel, M., Vechev, M.: An abstract domain for certifying neural networks. In: POPL 2019. pp. 1–30. ACM (2019)
11. Tian, J., Zhi, D., Wang, P., Liu, S., Katz, G., Zhang, M.: BBReach: tight and scalable black-box reachability analysis of deep reinforcement learning systems (2022, submitted)
12. Zhi, D., Tian, J., Wang, P., Liu, S., Wen, X., Zhang, M.: Probabilistic robustness for deep reinforcement learning with provable guarantees (2022, submitted)

Contents

Theorem Proving and SAT

Verification and Testing for Machine Learning

HashC: Making DNNs' Coverage Testing Finer and Faster

Weidi Sun, Xiaoyong Xue, Yuteng Lu, and Meng Sun[(✉)]

School of Mathematical Sciences, Peking University, Beijing, China
{weidisun,xuexy,luyuteng,sunm}@pku.edu.cn

Abstract. Though Deep Neural Networks (DNNs) have been widely deployed and achieved great success in many domains, they have severe safety and reliability concerns. To provide testing evidence for DNNs' reliable behaviors, various coverage testing techniques inspired by traditional software testing have been proposed. However, the coverage criteria in these techniques are either not fine enough to capture subtle behaviors of DNNs, or too time-consuming to be applied on large-scale DNNs. In this paper, we develop a coverage testing framework named HashC, which makes mainstream coverage criteria (e.g., NC and KMNC) much finer. Meanwhile, HashC reduces the time complexity of combinatorial coverage testing from polynomial time to linear time. Our experiments show that, 1) the HashC criteria are finer than existing mainstream coverage criteria, 2) HashC greatly accelerates combinatorial coverage testing and can handle the testing of large-scale DNNs.

Keywords: Neural networks · Testing · Coverage criteria

1 Introduction

Deep Neural Networks (DNNs) are gaining momentum for their ability in many industrial domain-specific tasks. The wide application of DNNs sets higher demands on their behavior reliability. Recently, the US transportation board's report [18] about unfortunate autonomous vehicles' accidents [3,31] also emphasizes that the improved assurance evaluation practices for deep learning systems are urgently needed. Among existing instruments for DNNs' assurance evaluation, testing is one of the best considering the balance between completeness and efficiency. However, it is impracticable to quantify DNNs' test adequacy by simply adopting software testing standards since the behavior of data-driven DNNs cannot be explicitly encoded into the control flow structures, i.e., the acceptable forms for these standards [23].

Actuated by the need for evaluating how well a test suite exercises a DNN, recent researches propose various coverage criteria. The first coverage criterion Neuron Coverage (NC) [21] is inspired by the code coverage in software testing. To measure the test adequacy, NC calculates the ratio of activated neurons, i.e., the neurons whose output values are above a predefined threshold during the execution of a test suite. Nevertheless, NC is not fine enough to distinguish the subtle differences between test suites. The finer coverage criteria are mainly developed in two ways. The bucket coverage criteria (BCCs) study individual neurons' outputs in detail. For example, IDC [4], NBC, SNAC and KMNC [13] partition the output value range of neurons into buckets and figure out the activated bucket ratio. The combinatorial coverage criteria (CCCs) analyze neurons' interactions. For example, 2-way coverage [12] inspired by combinatorial testing (CT) [17] combines each two neurons in one layer as a tuple and focuses on whether the so-called "neuron-activation configuration" of these tuples are covered. MC/DC neuron coverage [27] and 3-way coverage [24] go further than 2-way coverage by studying the interactions of neurons in adjacent layers. INC [26] investigates the transitive interaction among all neurons to make DNNs' combinatorial testing finer. In addition to BCCs and CCCs, TKNC [13] evaluates the ratio of top-k neurons and the surprise coverage (SC) [7] measures the relative novelty of the test inputs with respect to the training set.

However, all of these existing coverage criteria can hardly balance the quality and the efficiency of test adequacy evaluation. Both BCCs and CCCs have their own weakness. Most BCCs are not fine enough to capture test suites' subtle differences. In addition, BCCs lack the "scalability" regarding test suite size, their performance does not conform with DNN testing practice when the scale of evaluated test suite is too big or small. CCCs are too time-consuming for large-scale DNNs' testing. For example, k-way coverage testing has an $O(m2^k\binom{n}{k})$ running time[1] where n is the number of neurons in DNNs and m is the number of cases in a test suite and other CCCs are of polynomial time as well. Their time costs are unacceptable for evaluating the test adequacy of DNNs with millions of neurons. TKNC lacks the scalability regarding DNNs' scale. SC's weakness is that the quality of training set directly influences the evaluation result. Besides, SC cannot take all neurons into account for large-scale DNNs.

To measure DNNs' test adequacy more effectively and efficiently, we propose HashC, which is a coverage testing framework. HashC can make BCCs "combinatorial", while preserving their time complexity in $O(mn)$ which is linear in the number of neurons. The BCCs equipped with HashC can capture DNNs' overall behavior to become finer and scalable. Though the HashC criteria are combinatorial, they are markedly faster than existing CCCs because the "hashed activation analysis" of HashC greatly accelerates the test adequacy evaluation. More specifically, existing CCCs analyze each input in polynomial time, while HashC utilizes cryptographic hash functions to encode the activation states in $O(mn)$ and analyzes the activation digests (i.e., the encoding results) in $O(n)$. This "hashed activation analysis" also enables HashC to make up for CCCs' weakness of capturing the interactions among nonadjacent layers' neurons. Existing CCCs propagate interactions layer by layer to find nonadjacent layer interactions causing the loss of information during the transmission. HashC eliminates the loss by abandoning this common practice and studying all activation digests directly.

---

[1] The $\binom{n}{k}$ denotes $\frac{n!}{k!(n-k)!}$ which is the number of k-combinations from n elements.

We evaluate HashC criteria and other mainstream coverage criteria to show HashC's superiorities in test adequacy measurement and coverage testing acceleration. The comprehensive evaluation bases on two publicly available datasets (MNIST [10] and CIFAR-10 [8]) and 16 DNNs ranging from full-connected DNNs [5] with 300 neurons to GoogLeNet [28] with about 4 millions neurons.

Overall, the main contributions of this paper are as follows:

- The HashC coverage testing framework is designed for evaluating the adequacy of DNNs' test suites. It makes BCCs finer and scalable in linear time. It enables software engineers to tell the subtle differences between test suites regarding test adequacy.
- The hashed activation analysis consists of the hash encoding and the dependent relationship analysis. The utilizing of hash encoding compresses the activation states, which makes the activation states less space-consuming and easier to compare. The dependent relationship analysis reduces combinatorial coverage testing's time complexity from at least polynomial time to linear time and makes up for CCCs' weakness of capturing nonadjacent layers' interactions. The HashC criteria are able to handle large-scale DNNs.
- We comprehensively evaluate HashC criteria and other mainstream coverage criteria on two public datasets and 16 DNNs. The experimental result shows HashC's state-of-the-art performance in measuring test adequacy and accelerating coverage testing.

The rest of this paper is organized as follows. We firstly introduce this work's background including DNNs, cryptographic hash functions, and existing coverage criteria in Sect. 2. Then we present our coverage testing framework HashC in Sect. 3. In Sect. 4, we compare HashC with other mainstream coverage criteria in two aspects: the time cost and the performance in test adequacy evaluation. Finally, Sect. 5 concludes the paper.

2 Background

In this section, we briefly introduce the background of this work, including DNNs, cryptographic hash functions and existing coverage criteria evaluated in this paper.

2.1 Deep Neural Networks

A DNN is an artificial neural network which is formally defined as follows:

Definition 1 (Deep Neural Networks). *A* Deep Neural Network (DNN) *is defined as a triple $\mathcal{D} = (L, A, W)$ where*

- $L = \{L_k \mid k \in \{0, ..., l\}\}$ *is the set of layers in which L_0 is the* input *layer, L_ks $(0 < k < l)$ are the* hidden *layers, and L_l is the* output *layer. The neurons in these layers are represented as $n_{k,i}$, which means the i-th neuron in layer L_k. The output of $n_{k,i}$ is denoted as $x_{k,i}$.*

- *A is a set of activation functions.*
- *W includes the weights which connects the neurons in different layers and the biases.*

Then the forward-propagation can be defined as a function where input x is a vector, f_is are activation functions, W_is are weights and B_is are biases:

$$F(x) = f_l(W_l f_{l-1}(...f_1(W_1 x + B_1)...) + B_l)$$

In this work, we evaluate the coverage criteria on various DNN classifiers, e.g., FcNet [5], LeNet-5 [9], VGG16 [25], GoogLeNet [28], and ResNet34 [6].

2.2   Cryptographic Hash Function

Cryptographic hash function maps data of arbitrary size to a bit array (i.e., the message digest). Some cryptographic hash functions, such as SHA-1 [2], SHA-2 [29], SHA-3 [16], MD5 [22], and BLAKE2 [1], have been widely used in practice and become the basic tools of modern cryptography. We use the following main characteristics of an ideal cryptographic hash function:

- it is deterministic which means that the same input message results in the same digest;
- it can compute the hash value quickly;
- it is collision resistant.

The third characteristic of cryptographic hash function implies that:

1. For an input m_1, it is difficult to find a different m_2 satisfying

$$Hash(m_1) = Hash(m_2).$$

   This property is referred to as weak collision resistance.
2. It is difficult to find two different inputs m_1 and m_2 satisfying that

$$Hash(m_1) = Hash(m_2).$$

   This property is referred to as strong collision resistance.

The word "difficult" in these two properties means that finding such a pair m_1 and m_2 is essentially as difficult as solving a well-known and supposedly difficult (typically number-theoretic) problem, such as the computation of discrete logarithms or integer factorization [15]. Informally, the collision resistance is equivalent to that an adversary cannot modify or replace an input data without changing the corresponding digest. Thus, if two inputs have the same digest, we can be confident that they are identical. In this paper, we use cryptographic hash function to compress the activation states of neural networks and compare the digests to judge whether two states are identical.

2.3 Coverage Criteria

The evaluated coverage criteria are introduced as follows:

- **NC** is a typical BCC. To evaluate the test adequacy, NC quantifies the ratio of activated neurons. For a test suite I, a threshold t and a DNN N with n neurons, the activated neuron set can be defined as

$$A = \{x_{k,i} \mid \exists_{s \in S} \ x_{k,i}(s) > t\}$$

where $x_{k,i}(s)$ is the output of N's neuron $n_{k,i}$ with input s. The NC score of N on I is defined as $\frac{|A|}{n}$. As we need to update the activation states for every input, the time complexity of NC is $O(mn)$ where m is the size of test suite.
- **KMNC** is an extension of NC. It partitions the output value range of neurons into buckets and figures out the activated bucket ratio. For a test suite I, a set of buckets $\mathcal{B}$ and a DNN N, the activated buckets set can be defined as

$$A = \{B_{k,i,j} \mid \exists_{s \in I, B_{k,i,j} \in \mathcal{B}} \ x_{k,i}(s) \in B_{k,i,j}\}$$

where $B_{k,i,j}$ is the j-th interval belonging to $n_{k,i}$'s output range. The KMNC score of N on I is defined as $\frac{|A|}{|\mathcal{B}|}$. Similar to NC, KMNC's time complexity is $O(mn)$.
- **TKNC**, i.e., top-k neuron coverage records how many neurons have once been the most active k neurons on each layer. TKNC is denoted as $\frac{|T|}{n}$ where T is the set of top-k neurons. TKNC's time complexity is $O(mn)$.
- **2-way coverage** is a CCC inspired by combinatorial testing (CT) [11]. It combines the neurons in the same layer as pairs and examines the interactions in these pairs. Each pair of neurons $(x_{k,i}, x_{k,j})$ in L_k has four possible states:
  - $x_{k,i} > t$ and $x_{k,j} > t$,
  - $x_{k,i} > t$ and $x_{k,j} \leqslant t$,
  - $x_{k,i} \leqslant t$ and $x_{k,j} > t$,
  - $x_{k,i} \leqslant t$ and $x_{k,j} \leqslant t$,

  where t is a given threshold. A state is activated if at least one input makes the neurons satisfy the corresponding constraint. The 2-way coverage score is defined as $\frac{\sum_k |AS_k|}{\sum_k |CS_k|}$, where CS_k and AS_k denote the set of states and activated states of L_k, respectively. Supposing that the max number of neurons in a layer is n, if we select 2 neurons in this layer, the number of states is $\binom{n}{2}$. For each input, 2-way coverage needs to find the corresponding activated states. Therefore, the time complexity is $O(m2^k \binom{n}{k})(k = 2)$, i.e., $O(mn^2)$.
- **3-way coverage** is the extension of 2-way coverage. It is a CCC which focuses on the interactions among neurons in adjacent layers. Like the definition of states in 2-way coverage, each triple of neurons $(x_{k,i}, x_{k,j}, x_{k+1,i'})$ in adjacent layers has 8 possible states. The 3-way coverage score is defined as $\frac{\sum_k |AS'_k|}{\sum_k |CS'_k|}$, where CS'_k and AS'_k are states and activated states, respectively. The time complexity of 3-way coverage is $O(m2^k \binom{n}{k})$ in which $k = 3$, i.e., $O(mn^3)$.

- **INC** is a CCC designed to examine the interactions among all neurons of DNNs in acceptable duration. It is an approximation scheme of n-way coverage which has an $O(mn^2)$ running time.
- **Surprise Coverage** aims to measure the surprise (i.e., relative novelty) of the test suite with respect to the training set, by measuring the differences of activation states between inputs. Its time complexity is $O(mnM)$, where M is the size of training set. On large-scale DNNs, SC analyzes only one layer's activation states to reduce the time cost.

3   HashC Coverage Testing Framework

In this section, we present our HashC coverage testing framework. HashC measures the test adequacy by evaluating the diversity of features' combinations in test suites. The first coverage criterion NC holds the assumption that the outputs of neurons represent features. This assumption is supported by the recent feature visualization research [19] showing that the stimulated neurons (i.e., the neurons being highly activated by optimized inputs) represent some features like the cats, foxes, and cars in Fig. 1.

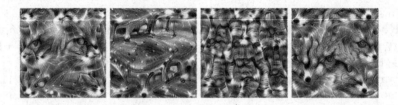

Fig. 1. Visualization of features represented by neurons

CCCs focus on the combination of these features and BCCs represent finer features by dividing the output value range of neurons into buckets. To take the advantages of both CCCs and BCCs, we define the dependent relationship among buckets to reflect the combination of BCCs' finer features:

Definition 2 (Dependent relationship of buckets). *Two buckets $B_{k,i,j}$ and $B_{k',i',j'}$ are dependent w.r.t. input set I (denoted by $B_{k,i,j} \sim_I B_{k',i',j'}$), if $x_{k,i}$ and $x_{k',i'}$ satisfy at least one of the following two constraints:*

- *The positive dependence: $(x_{k,i} \in B_{k,i,j}$ iff $x_{k',i'} \in B_{k',i',j'})$ and $(x_{k,i} \notin B_{k,i,j}$ iff $x_{k',i'} \notin B_{k',i',j'})$ for all inputs in I,*
- *The negative dependence: $(x_{k,i} \in B_{k,i,j}$ iff $x_{k',i'} \notin B_{k',i',j'})$ and $(x_{k,i} \notin B_{k,i,j}$ iff $x_{k',i'} \in B_{k',i',j'})$ for all inputs in I.*

The dependent buckets contain the features that always appear simultaneously. For example, $bucket_i$ and $bucket_j$ in Fig. 2 represent "cat" and "yellow" respectively. If these two buckets are positively dependent, "yellow" always comes

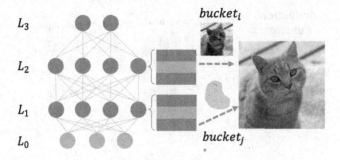

Fig. 2. Dependent buckets fix the combination of features

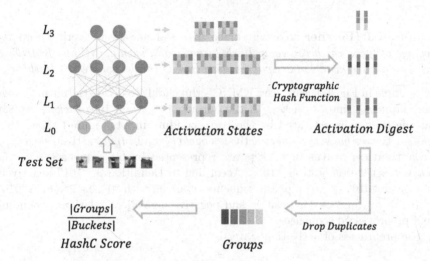

Fig. 3. Overview of HashC coverage testing framework

with "cat" causing the absence of other combinations like "yellow dog" or "black cat". Or if they are negatively dependent, the test suite lacks the combination "yellow cat". Thus, test suites with less dependence are more adequate. It is remarkable that, the dependence can also reflect the traditional BCCs' interest, as the absent features in BCCs satisfy HashC's dependent relationship.

The high-level workflow of HashC is shown in Fig. 3, which contains three parts:

- extracting and preprocessing the activation states of a DNN during the execution of the evaluated test suite;
- using cryptographic hash function to encode the activation states on-the-fly;
- grouping the activation digests and calculating the HashC score.

In the first part, we use the thresholds in the partner coverage criteria to partition the output value range of each neuron into buckets and record the activation states of these buckets.

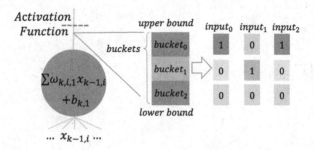

Fig. 4. KMNC based HashC uses the thresholds in KMNC to divide the output range of neurons into buckets and records the buckets' activation states

Definition 3 (Partner coverage criteria). Partner coverage criteria *are the coverage criteria which can equip HashC framework, such as NC and KMNC. A partner coverage criterion C equipped with HashC can be denoted as HashC-C.*

For example in Fig. 4, HashC uses KMNC's thresholds to divide the output range of a neuron $n_{k,i}$ into 3 buckets. If the output of $n_{k,i}$ falls into $bucket_i$, we say that the $bucket_i$ is activated by the corresponding input. Figure 4 shows that $input_0$ activates $bucket_0$, $input_1$ activates $bucket_1$, and $input_2$ activates $bucket_0$. The **activation states** of buckets are represented by bit sequences, e.g., the $bucket_0$'s activation state is "101". According to Definition 2, "101" negatively depends on "010". If we "flip" the sequences starting with "0", e.g., change "010" to "101", we can look for positive and negative dependent relations by finding equal preprocessed sequences.

The preprocess of activation states is:

$$Ac'_{k,i,j} = \begin{cases} Ac_{k,i,j} & \text{if } Ac_{k,i,j}[0] = 1; \\ \neg Ac_{k,i,j} & \text{otherwise} \end{cases}$$

where $Ac_{k,i,j}$ is the activation state of $B_{k,i,j}$, $Ac_{k,i,j}[0]$ is the first input's activation state of $B_{k,i,j}$, and $\neg Ac_{k,i,j}$ is the bitwise complement result of $Ac_{k,i,j}$. Two buckets are dependent if their activation states Ac'_0 and Ac'_1 satisfy $Ac'_0 = Ac'_1$.

In the second part, we use a cryptographic hash function[2] to extract the **activation digests**. This extraction can remarkably compress the huge amounts of activation states data which are hard to store and process. Cryptographic hash functions have strong collision resistance which means that if two inputs have the same digest, one can be very confident that they are identical. Thus, if the activation digests of two buckets are same, they are dependent.

This extraction runs in $O(mn)$ where m is the size of test suite and n is the number of neurons.

In the third part, we group the buckets by dropping the duplicate digests in $O(n)$. The realization of this $O(n)$ dropping is in Algorithm 1. The lookup/insert

---

[2] The function SHA-1 is used in this paper, because it is easier to compute than other cryptographic hash functions.

operation of a set is $O(1)$, and we repeat these two operations at most n times which leads to the final $O(n)$ time complexity.

Algorithm 1. Algorithm for dropping the duplicate digests

1: **Input:** digests D
2: **Output:** the distinct digests
3: $Dset = \varnothing$
4: **for** each *digest* in D **do**
5:     **if** *digest* not in *Dset* **then**
6:         $Dset$.add(*digest*)
7:     **end if**
8: **end for**
9: **Return** *Dset*

Each remaining digest represents a group which contains the buckets dependent upon each other. If a bucket is independent with all other buckets, it will be treated as a group which contains only one bucket. Obviously, the test suite with more groups has less dependence which means that they are more adequate. HashC score can be denoted as $\frac{\lambda}{\mu}$, where λ and μ are the numbers of groups and buckets, respectively. For test suites with multi-class inputs, the HashC score is:

$$HashC_{score} = \frac{1}{n} \sum_{i=1}^{n} \frac{\lambda_i}{\mu_i}$$

where λ_i and μ_i are the numbers of groups and buckets of each class, respectively. The time complexity of HashC is $\sum_i O(\mu_i n)$, i.e., $O(mn)$.

4   Evaluation

Experiments with different scales are designed to evaluate the coverage criteria of polynomial time and linear time, respectively. In these experiments, we compare HashC criteria with mainstream coverage criteria on two aspects: 1) the time cost, 2) the sensibility in distinguishing test suites with different adequacies. All these experiments are implemented on the Pytorch framework [20] and conducted on a GPU server. The server has 1 Xeon Gold 5118 2.30 GHz CPUs, 20 GB system memory and 1 NVIDIA Titan XP GPU.

4.1   Experiment Design

Experiment 1 is mainly designed for coverage criteria of polynomial time which cannot be applied to large-scale DNNs. It compares HashC-NC (i.e., the coverage criterion formed by NC equipped with HashC.) with SC, NC, and mainstream CCCs (i.e., polynomial time coverage criteria) including 2-way coverage, 3-way coverage, and INC. The hyper-parameters of these coverage criteria are as follows:

Table 1. Architecture of DNNs

DNNs	Fc$_i$ (i = 1,..,10)	LeNet-5*
Hidden neurons	i*300	36400
Hidden layers	3	6
Activation of hidden layers	ReLU	
Activation of output layers	Softmax	
Training set	MNIST	
Accuracy	at least 98.32%	99.17%

- The activation threshold t of NC, HashC-NC, 2-way coverage, 3-way coverage is set to 0.
- The surprise metric of SC is L_2 and other parameters are the same as in [7]. SC takes all neurons in DNNs into account in *Experiment 1*.

In the first part of *Experiment 1*, We use SC, CCCs, and HashC-NC to evaluate MNIST's test set on some DNNs with different number of neurons to show that: 1) the coverage criteria which takes polynomial time lack the scalability regarding DNN size; 2) HashC is markedly faster than CCCs. The details of the DNNs are shown in Table 1.

In the second part, we compare HashC-NC with SC and CCCs by evaluating two series of synthetic test suites with different adequacies to show that HashC-NC is more sensitive. In addition, we also compare HashC-NC with NC which demonstrates that HashC makes NC finer. These comparisons are based on a LeNet-5 with 5 hidden layers (6*12*12, 16*8*8, 16*4*4, 120, 84) and a FcNet with 3 hidden layers (512, 256, 64) whose accuracy are at least 98.71%.

The generation methods of two series of synthetic test suites are shown in Fig. 5. The first series of test suites are i-MNISTs with different sizes where $i = 1000, 2000, ..., 10000$. The i-MNIST represents some test sets and each test set has i samples. 10000-MNIST has only one set, i.e., MNIST's test set. Each i-MNIST ($i < 10000$) contains twenty sets which are denoted as i-MNIST$_k$s (k = 0,1,...,19). We generate i-MNIST$_k$s by selecting samples from their "fathers" randomly and evenly. For example, we firstly regard MNIST's test set as 10000-MNIST. The 9000-MNIST$_k$s select 900 inputs from each class of 10000-MNIST randomly (MNIST has ten classes), thus, 10000-MNIST is the father of 9000-MNIST$_k$s. Then 8000-MNIST$_k$ selects 800 inputs from each class of its "father" 9000-MNIST$_k$. We take twenty i-MNIST$_k$s' average coverage score to represent i-MNIST's score so as to eliminate the random error.

The second series of test suites are biased-j-MNISTs ($j = 10, 30, 50, 70, 90$) with the same size and different adequacies. Biased-j-MNISTs are generated in two steps:

- *Building 20 similar-feature-sets.* For each similar-feature-set, we select one seed from MNIST test set randomly and select 499 samples which are most "similar" to the seed from MNIST test set. To evaluate how "similar" two

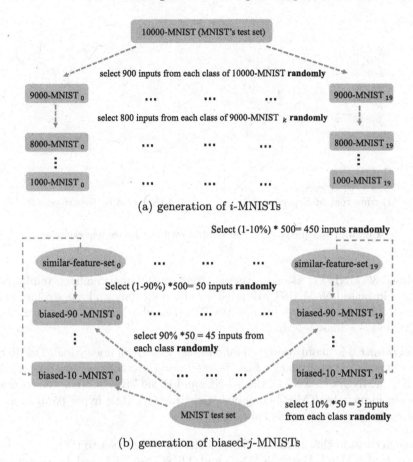

(a) generation of i-MNISTs

(b) generation of biased-j-MNISTs

Fig. 5. The generation of test suites

images are in a way coincides with human judgment, we utilize the perceptual similarity measurement LPIPS (Learned Perceptual Image Patch Similarity) [33]. Similarity measurements are designed to evaluate structured inputs' "perceptual distance", e.g., they can measure how similar are two pictures in a way coinciding with human judgment. There are many existing perceptually motivated distance metrics, such as SSIM [30], HDR-VDP [14], LPIPS [33], and FSIM [32].

- *Mixing the similar-feature-sets with MNIST test set.* We randomly select $(1 - j\%) * 500$ inputs from similar-feature-set$_k$ and $j\% * 50$ samples from each class of MNIST test set to form biased-j-MNIST$_k$ with 500 elements.

These test sets' adequacies are different. The adequacies of i-MNIST$_k$s are in ascending order of i. For example, 5000-MNIST$_k$ is more adequate than 4000-MNIST$_k$, because 4000-MNIST$_k$ is a subset of 5000-MNIST$_k$. The adequacies of biased-j-MNIST$_k$s are in ascending order of j, e.g., biased-50-MNIST$_k$ is superior

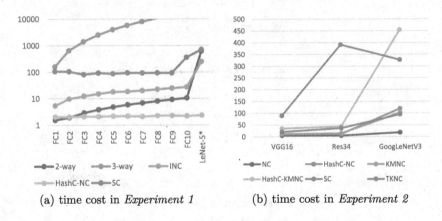

(a) time cost in *Experiment 1*   (b) time cost in *Experiment 2*

Fig. 6. The time cost (in seconds) of evaluated coverage criteria

to biased-30-MNIST$_k$. Because though they have same number samples, the samples in biased-50-MNIST$_k$ distribute more uniformly and can explore more features. The evaluation results of i-MNISTs (biased-j-MNISTs) are the average of i-MNIST$_k$s (biased-j-MNIST$_k$s).

Experiment 2 is mainly designed for coverage criteria of linear time. The design of this experiment is similar to *Experiment 1* and the compared coverage criteria are: NC, KMNC, SC, TKNC, HashC-NC, and HashC-KMNC (i.e., the coverage criterion formed by KMNC equipped with HashC.). The hyper-parameters of these coverage criteria are as follows:

– The activation threshold t of NC and HashC-NC are set to 0.
– The k of KMNC, HashC-KMNC, and TKNC are 4, 4, and 1, respectively. HashC-KMNC uses KMNC's buckets.
– The surprise metric of SC is L_2 and other parameters are the same as in [7]. SC analyzes the second to the last layer in VGG16, ResNet34, and GoogLeNet in *Experiment 2*.

In the first part, we use the compared coverage criteria to evaluate CIFAR10's test set on three DNNs which are much larger than the DNNs in experiment 1. We record the time cost to show that linear time coverage criteria can handle large-scale DNNs. These three typical DNNs, i.e., VGG16 (with 308746 neurons), ResNet34 (with 371210 neurons), and GoogLeNet (with 3948554 neurons) are trained by CIFAR10. In the second part, we reuse the VGG16, the ResNet34, and the GoogLeNet to compare the sensitivity of evaluated coverage criteria. We also build the synthetic test suites i-CIFAR10s and biased-j-CIFAR10s from CIFAR10's test set in the same way as *Experiment 1*.

Table 2. Coverage scores of polynomial time coverage criteria on i-MNISTs

		i-MNIST					
		1000	2000	4000	6000	8000	10000
NC	FcNet	0.607	0.6118	0.619	0.6225	0.6255	0.6283
2-way		0.5731	0.5784	0.5847	0.5877	0.5903	0.5924
3-way		0.4658	0.4736	0.4813	0.4851	0.488	0.4902
INC		0.6055	0.6112	0.6189	0.6225	0.6255	0.6283
HashC		0.1536	0.1596	0.3126	0.3208	0.3246	0.3292
SC		0.3207	0.384	0.437	0.4648	0.4858	0.503
NC	LeNet-5	0.9659	0.9716	0.9753	0.9769	0.9776	0.9779
2-way		0.9592	0.9668	0.9724	0.975	0.9766	0.9775
3-way		0.8933	0.9135	0.9289	0.9364	0.941	0.9439
INC		0.9638	0.9706	0.9753	0.9774	0.9785	0.9788
HashC		0.3641	0.3858	0.7586	0.7899	0.8031	0.8202
SC		0.3235	0.3844	0.4366	0.4637	0.4822	0.495

Table 3. Coverage scores of polynomial time coverage criteria on biased-j-MNISTs

		biased-j-MNIST				
		10	30	50	70	90
NC	FcNet	0.5675	0.5872	0.5932	0.5965	0.5993
2-way		0.5301	0.5506	0.5577	0.5616	0.5645
3-way		0.4056	0.434	0.4442	0.4499	0.4539
INC		0.5561	0.5845	0.5912	0.5949	0.5979
HashC		0.046	0.1132	0.1315	0.1327	0.1406
SC		0.1469	0.1893	0.221	0.2405	0.2517
NC	LeNet-5	0.9173	0.9421	0.9518	0.9566	0.9592
2-way		0.8784	0.9234	0.9378	0.9448	0.949
3-way		0.7236	0.8075	0.8385	0.8552	0.866
INC		0.8843	0.9288	0.9421	0.9494	0.9536
HashC		0.048	0.215	0.2787	0.3021	0.3211
SC		0.1621	0.2054	0.2369	0.2555	0.2588

4.2 Evaluation Results

The time cost evaluation results are shown in Fig. 6. Figure 6(a) shows the evaluation result of *Experiment 1*'s first part. The time cost of 2-way coverage, 3-way coverage, and INC explode along with the growth of DNN's scale. While HashC-NC's time cost is barely growing (2.0407 s on FC1 and 2.3166 s on LeNet-5*). The running time of 2-way coverage, SC, and INC on LeNet-5* are 265 times, 303 times and 107 times longer than HashC-NC's. Besides, 3-way coverage takes 24086.8 s (10909 times longer than HashC-NC's) on FC_{10} and more than 72 h on LeNet-5*. These evaluation results confirm that:

Table 4. Coverage scores of linear time coverage criteria on i-CIFAR10s

		i-CIFAR10s					
		1000	2000	4000	6000	8000	10000
NC	VGG16	0.9762	0.9764	0.9766	0.9767	0.9768	0.9768
HashC-NC		0.47632	0.4804	0.9573	0.963	0.9645	0.9653
KMNC		0.9995	0.9996	0.9996	0.9997	0.9997	0.9997
HashC-KMNC		0.4131	0.4329	0.7914	0.8739	0.8937	0.9203
SC		0.2194	0.3185	0.4254	0.4915	0.5323	0.565
TKNC		0.0451	0.0803	0.1361	0.18	0.2164	0.2474
NC	ResNet34	0.937	0.9401	0.9428	0.9439	0.9447	0.9452
HashC-NC		0.412	0.4356	0.8603	0.8906	0.9032	0.9145
KMNC		0.9994	0.9996	0.9999	1	1	1
HashC-KMNC		0.3985	0.4166	0.7762	0.8474	0.8656	0.8852
SC		0.4223	0.5041	0.5539	0.5778	0.5927	0.604
TKNC		0.0406	0.075	0.1339	0.1838	0.2269	0.2646
NC	GoogLeNet	0.9576	0.9595	0.9611	0.9618	0.9623	0.9627
HashC-NC		0.4382	0.4514	0.8863	0.9193	0.9313	0.938
KMNC		0.9529	0.9559	0.9581	0.9592	0.9599	0.9605
HashC-KMNC		0.278	0.3123	0.5577	0.7022	0.7497	0.7872
SC		0.3375	0.3904	0.4374	0.4651	0.4824	0.495
TKNC		0.0014	0.0027	0.0052	0.0076	0.01	0.0123

– the coverage criteria which take polynomial time lack the scalability regarding DNN size;
– SC cannot take the whole activation state of large-scale DNNs into account;
– HashC-NC is markedly faster than CCCs and SC.

Figure 6(b) shows the evaluation results of *Experiment 2*'s first part. It presents that, NC is the fastest coverage criteria and SC is slowest on average. However, all coverage criteria can finish in an acceptable duration (in 500 s) even on GoogLeNet with about 4 million neurons. So these coverage criteria can handle large-scale DNNs.

The coverage score evaluation results on i-MNISTs, biased-j-MNISTs, i-CIFAR10, biased-j-CIFAR10 are in Tables 2, 3, 4 and 5, respectively.[3] To draw an intuitive conclusion from the sensitivity evaluation results, we define the "sensitivity score". Sensitivity score measures the ability of coverage criteria for distinguishing test suites with different adequacies, or rather, shows how sensitive the coverage criteria score vary with test sets' adequacies.

Definition 4 (Sensitivity score). *A series of test suites $T_i s$' $(i = 0, 1, ..., N)$ adequacies are in ascending order of i. Evaluating $T_i s$ by a coverage criteria $\mathcal{C}$*

---

[3] Due to limited space, we only show the coverage scores of *i*-MNISTs $(i = 1000, 2000, 4000, 6000, 8000, 10000)$ in this paper.

Table 5. Coverage scores of linear time coverage criteria on biased-j-CIFAR10s

		biased-j-CIFAR10s				
		10	30	50	70	90
NC	VGG16	0.9747	0.9752	0.9754	0.9756	0.9757
HashC-NC		0.1761	0.2442	0.3814	0.422	0.4516
KMNC		0.9992	0.9993	0.9993	0.9994	0.9994
HashC-KMNC		0.1504	0.1619	0.257	0.309	0.3446
SC		0.097	0.1069	0.1172	0.1305	0.1436
TKNC		0.0223	0.0228	0.0233	0.0239	0.0243
NC	ResNet34	0.9288	0.9307	0.9318	0.9325	0.9331
HashC-NC		0.1459	0.1892	0.2636	0.3022	0.3445
KMNC		0.9995	0.9993	0.9995	0.9995	0.9991
HashC-KMNC		0.1541	0.1671	0.2416	0.2936	0.3329
SC		0.2914	0.2957	0.2989	0.3036	0.3068
TKNC		0.0213	0.0214	0.0215	0.0216	0.0216
NC	GoogLeNet	0.9534	0.9545	0.955	0.9552	0.9554
HashC-NC		0.1525	0.165	0.2955	0.3463	0.3957
KMNC		0.943	0.9457	0.9475	0.9483	0.9487
HashC-KMNC		0.093	0.0977	0.1264	0.1588	0.1922
SC		0.2464	0.2496	0.2542	0.2569	0.2585
TKNC		0.0007	0.0007	0.0007	0.0007	0.0007

on a DNN $\mathcal{N}$, the $\mathcal{C}$ score of T_i can be denoted as s_i. The sensitivity score SS of $\mathcal{C}$ on T_i and $\mathcal{N}$ is defined as $SS = (s_N - s_0) * \sum_{i=1}^{N}(1 - (\frac{s_{i-1}}{s_i})^2)$.

A coverage criterion with higher sensitivity score is finer, or rather, can separate the test suites with different adequacies more distinctly. For example, given two test suite T_0 and T_1, T_1 is more adequate than T_0. If the $\mathcal{C}_0$, $\mathcal{C}_1$, $\mathcal{C}_2$ score of T_0, T_1 are ($s_0 = 0.19$, $s_1 = 0.2$), ($s_0 = 0.18$, $s_1 = 0.3$), ($s_0 = 0.001$, $s_1 = 0.01$), the difference between T_0's and T_1's $\mathcal{C}_1$ scores is much greater than their $\mathcal{C}_0$ and $\mathcal{C}_2$ scores. Thus, the sensitivity score of $\mathcal{C}_0$, $\mathcal{C}_1$, and $\mathcal{C}_2$ are $9.75 * 10^{(-4)}$, 0.0768 and 0.00891, respectively, which means that $\mathcal{C}_1$ is finer than $\mathcal{C}_0$ and $\mathcal{C}_2$.

The sensitivity scores of all evaluated coverage criteria on i-MNISTs (i-CIFAR10s) and biased-j-MNISTs (biased-j-CIFAR10s) are in Table 6 where the cell with "*" means that evaluation of the corresponding score is not in our experiment design. These sensitivity scores show that HashC criteria perform better than NC, 2-way coverage, 3-way coverage, INC, and KMNC on all DNNs and test suites. SC is weaker than HashC criteria in all cases except i-CIFAR10-ResNet34 where TKNC's sensitivity score is 0.024 higher than HashC-KMNC's. TKNC's sensitivity score is higher than HashC criteria only in evaluating i-CIFAR10s on

Table 6. Sensitivity scores of all evaluated coverage criteria

	FcNet	LeNet-5	VGG16	ResNet34	GoogLeNet
	i-MNIST		i-CIFAR10		
NC	0.001	0.001	0.000	0.000	0.000
2-way	0.001	0.001	*	*	*
3-way	0.002	0.006	*	*	*.
INC	0.045	0.000	*	*	*
HashC-NC	0.172	0.500	0.419	0.577	0.515
SC	0.149	0.133	0.539	0.118	0.368
KMNC	*	*	0.000	0.00	0.008
HashC-KMNC	*	*	0.626	0.600	0.871
TKNC	0.118	0.143	0.520	0.624	0.035
	biased-j-MNIST		biased-j-CIFAR10		
NC	0.000	0.001	0.000	0.000	0.000
2-way	0.000	0.011	*	*	*
3-way	0.001	0.047	*	*	*
INC	0.006	0.010	*	*	*
HashC-NC	0.116	0.442	0.380	0.270	0.326
SC	0.095	0.076	0.033	0.002	0.001
KMNC	*	*	0.000	0.000	0.000
HashC-KMNC	*	*	0.242	0.217	0.117
TKNC	0.090	0.132	0.000	0.000	0.000

large-scale DNNs. However, TKNC is not a good choice for large-scale DNNs, as it is hard to satisfy. For example, our evaluation result shows that the highest TKNC score on GoogLeNet is just 0.0123. In addition, TKNC can hardly distinguish the test suites with same size and different adequacies on large-scale DNNs. Especially on GoogLeNet, TKNC is totally incapable of distinguishing biased-j-CIFAR10s, as its sensitivity score is zero. In conclusion, HashC criteria are finer than other evaluated criteria.

5 Conclusion

In this paper, we present a coverage testing framework named HashC which runs in linear time. It greatly accelerates the combinatorial coverage testing, and makes BCCs finer and scalable without increasing their time complexity. HashC criteria are finer than existing mainstream coverage criteria and can test large-scale DNNs in an acceptable duration. We believe that this effective and efficient framework can promote the application of coverage testing in the assurance evaluation practices for deep learning systems. In the future, we plan to refine the coverage criteria and utilize the coverage criteria to simplify the testing of DNNs further.

Acknowledgement. This research was sponsored by the National Natural Science Foundation of China under Grant No. 62172019, and CCF-Huawei Formal Verification Innovation Research Plan.

References

1. Aumasson, J.-P., Neves, S., Wilcox-O'Hearn, Z., Winnerlein, C.: BLAKE2: simpler, smaller, fast as MD5. In: Jacobson, M., Locasto, M., Mohassel, P., Safavi-Naini, R. (eds.) ACNS 2013. LNCS, vol. 7954, pp. 119–135. Springer, Heidelberg (2013). https://doi.org/10.1007/978-3-642-38980-1_8
2. Dang, Q.: Changes in federal information processing standard (FIPS) 180–4, secure hash standard. Cryptologia **37**(1), 69–73 (2013). https://doi.org/10.1080/01611194.2012.687431
3. Davies, A.: Google's self-driving car caused its first crash (2016). https://www.wired.com/2016/02/googles-self-driving-car-may-caused-first-crash/. Accessed 7 July 2021
4. Gerasimou, S., Eniser, H.F., Sen, A., Cakan, A.: Importance-driven deep learning system testing. In: Proceedings of 42nd International Conference on Software Engineering, ICSE 2020, 27 June - 19 July, 2020, Seoul, South Korea, pp. 702–713. IEEE (2020). https://doi.org/10.1145/3377811.3380391
5. Goodfellow, I.J., Bengio, Y., Courville, A.C.: Deep Learning. Adaptive Computation and Machine Learning, MIT Press, Cambridge (2016)
6. He, K., Zhang, X., Ren, S., Sun, J.: Deep residual learning for image recognition. In: Proceedings of 29th IEEE Conference on Computer Vision and Pattern Recognition, CVPR 2016, 27–30 June 2016, Las Vegas, NV, USA, pp. 770–778. IEEE Computer Society (2016). https://doi.org/10.1109/CVPR.2016.90
7. Kim, J., Feldt, R., Yoo, S.: Guiding deep learning system testing using surprise adequacy. In: Proceedings of the 41st International Conference on Software Engineering, ICSE 2019, Montreal, QC, Canada, 25–31 May 2019, pp. 1039–1049. IEEE/ACM (2019). https://doi.org/10.1109/ICSE.2019.00108
8. Krizhevsky, A., Hinton, G., et al.: Learning multiple layers of features from tiny images. Technical report (2009)
9. LeCun, Y., Bottou, L., Bengio, Y., Haffner, P.: Gradient-based learning applied to document recognition. Proc. IEEE **86**(11), 2278–2324 (1998)
10. LeCun, Y., Cortes, C., Burges, C.J.: The MNIST database of handwritten digits. https://yann.lecun.com/exdb/mnist/ (1998). Accessed 4 Jan 2020
11. Li, Z., Chen, Y., Gong, G., Li, D., Lv, K., Chen, P.: A survey of the application of combinatorial testing. In: Proceedings of 19th IEEE International Conference on Software Quality, Reliability and Security Companion, QRS Companion 2019, 22–26 July 2019, Sofia, Bulgaria, pp. 512–513. IEEE (2019). https://doi.org/10.1109/QRS-C.2019.00100
12. Ma, L., et al.: DeepCT: tomographic combinatorial testing for deep learning systems. In: Proceedings of 26th IEEE International Conference on Software Analysis, Evolution and Reengineering, SANER 2019, 24–27 February 2019, Hangzhou, China, pp. 614–618. IEEE (2019). https://doi.org/10.1109/SANER.2019.8668044

13. Ma, L., et al.: DeepGauge: multi-granularity testing criteria for deep learning systems. In: Proceedings of the 33rd ACM/IEEE International Conference on Automated Software Engineering, ASE 2018, 3–7 September 2018, Montpellier, France, pp. 120–131. ACM (2018). https://doi.org/10.1145/3238147.3238202
14. Mantiuk, R., Kim, K.J., Rempel, A.G., Heidrich, W.: HDR-VDP-2: a calibrated visual metric for visibility and quality predictions in all luminance conditions. ACM Trans. Graph. **30**(4), 40 (2011). https://doi.org/10.1145/2010324.1964935
15. Menezes, A., van Oorschot, P.C., Vanstone, S.A.: Handbook of Applied Cryptography. CRC Press, Boca Raton (1996). https://doi.org/10.1201/9781439821916
16. Morawiecki, P., Pieprzyk, J., Srebrny, M.: Rotational cryptanalysis of round-reduced KECCAK. In: Moriai, S. (ed.) FSE 2013. LNCS, vol. 8424, pp. 241–262. Springer, Heidelberg (2014). https://doi.org/10.1007/978-3-662-43933-3_13
17. Nie, C., Leung, H.: A survey of combinatorial testing. ACM Comput. Surv. **43**(2), 11:1–11:29 (2011). https://doi.org/10.1145/1883612.1883618
18. NTSB: Preliminary report: Highway hwy18mh010 (2018). https://www.ntsb.gov/investigations/AccidentReports/Reports/HWY18MH010-prelim.pdf. 'Accessed 7 July 2021
19. Olah, C., Mordvintsev, A., Schubert, L.: Feature visualization. Distillation **2**(11), e7 (2017). https://doi.org/10.23915/distill.00007
20. Paszke, A., et al.: Pytorch: an imperative style, high-performance deep learning library. CoRR abs/1912.01703 (2019)
21. Pei, K., Cao, Y., Yang, J., Jana, S.: DeepXplore: automated whitebox testing of deep learning systems. In: Proceedings of the 26th Symposium on Operating Systems Principles, SOSP 2017, 28–31 October 2017, Shanghai, China, pp. 1–18. ACM (2017). https://doi.org/10.1145/3132747.3132785
22. Rivest, R.L.: The MD5 message-digest algorithm. RFC. **1321**, 1–21 (1992). https://doi.org/10.17487/RFC1321
23. Salay, R., Czarnecki, K.: Using machine learning safely in automotive software: an assessment and adaption of software process requirements in ISO 26262. CoRR abs/1808.01614 (2018)
24. Sekhon, J., Fleming, C.: Towards improved testing for deep learning. In: Proceedings of the 41st International Conference on Software Engineering: New Ideas and Emerging Results, ICSE (NIER) 2019, 29–31 May 2019, Montreal, QC, Canada, pp. 85–88. IEEE (2019). https://doi.org/10.1109/ICSE-NIER.2019.00030
25. Simonyan, K., Zisserman, A.: Very deep convolutional networks for large-scale image recognition. In: Proceedings of 3rd International Conference on Learning Representations, ICLR 2015, 7–9 May 2015, San Diego, CA, USA. International Conference on Learning Representations (2015)
26. Sun, W., Lu, Y., Sun, M.: Are coverage criteria meaningful metrics for DNNs? In: Proceedings of 31st International Joint Conference on Neural Networks, IJCNN 2021, 18–22 July 2020, Virtual Event. IEEE (2021)
27. Sun, Y., Huang, X., Kroening, D.: Testing deep neural networks. CoRR abs/1803.04792 (2018)
28. Szegedy, C., et al.: Going deeper with convolutions. In: Proceedings of 28th IEEE Conference on Computer Vision and Pattern Recognition, CVPR 2015, 7–12 June 2015, Boston, MA, USA, pp. 1–9. IEEE Computer Society (2015). https://doi.org/10.1109/CVPR.2015.7298594
29. van Tilborg, H.C.A., Jajodia, S.: ISO 19790 2006 Security Requirements for Cryptographic Modules. In: van Tilborg, H.C.A., Jajodia, S. (eds.) Encyclopedia of Cryptography and Security, p. 648. Springer, Boston (2011). https://doi.org/10.1007/978-1-4419-5906-5_1038

30. Wang, Z., Bovik, A.C., Sheikh, H.R., Simoncelli, E.P.: Image quality assessment: from error visibility to structural similarity. IEEE Trans. Image Process. **13**(4), 600–612 (2004). https://doi.org/10.1109/TIP.2003.819861

31. Wiki: Death of elaine Herzberg (2018). https://en.wikipedia.org/wiki/Death_of_Elaine_Herzberg. Accessed 7 July 2021

32. Zhang, L., Zhang, L., Mou, X., Zhang, D.: FSIM: a feature similarity index for image quality assessment. IEEE Trans. Image Process. **20**(8), 2378–2386 (2011). https://doi.org/10.1109/TIP.2011.2109730

33. Zhang, R., Isola, P., Efros, A.A., Shechtman, E., Wang, O.: The unreasonable effectiveness of deep features as a perceptual metric. In: Proceedings of 31st IEEE Conference on Computer Vision and Pattern Recognition, CVPR 2018, 18–22 June 2018, Salt Lake City, UT, USA, pp. 586–595. IEEE Computer Society (2018). https://doi.org/10.1109/CVPR.2018.00068

MTUL: Towards Mutation Testing of Unsupervised Learning Systems

Yuteng Lu, Kaicheng Shao, Weidi Sun, and Meng Sun[✉]

School of Mathematical Sciences, Peking University, Beijing, China
{luyuteng,kevinskc,weidisun,sunm}@pku.edu.cn

Abstract. Unsupervised learning (UL) is one of the most important areas in artificial intelligence. UL systems are capable of learning patterns from unlabeled data and playing an increasingly critical role in many fields. Therefore, more and more attention has been paid to the security and stability of UL systems. Testing has achieved great success in ensuring the safety of traditional software systems and been gradually applied to supervised learning. However, UL is not in the consideration of most current testing methods. To fill this gap, we propose a novel mutation testing technique specific to UL systems. We design a series of mutation operators to simulate the unstable situations and possible errors that UL systems may encounter, and define corresponding mutation scores. Further, we combine the proposed technique with autoencoder for generating adversarial samples. In the evaluation phase, we demonstrate the practicability of the proposed technique based on three datasets.

Keywords: Mutation testing · Unsupervised learning · Cluster analysis · Autoencoder

1 Introduction

Unsupervised learning, which helps us infer patterns within unlabeled datasets, is an approach only relying on the understanding of data. Nowadays, UL has received more and more attention and been applied to various applications such as finance [1], compression [2], and software fault prediction [3]. Unfortunately, due to diverse possible risks that cluster analysis and generative adversarial network (GAN) may suffer [4], there exists a growing concern about the application of UL to safety-critical scenarios.

The testing approach has achieved great success in traditional software, where it can detect and fix abnormal behaviours of systems. In the past few years, the software engineering community mainly focused on investigating testing technologies to guarantee the trustworthiness of supervised learning (SL) systems. As a pioneer work on testing SL systems, DeepXplore [5] introduces neuron coverage and the first white-box testing framework for SL systems. Subsequently, [6–9] focus on testing criteria for SL systems. In another main stream of research, [10,11] design the mutation testing technique for SL systems to measure the quality of test suite. Meanwhile, [12,13] put forward testing specific to reinforcement learning (RL) systems. However, with the exception of [14], current researches on artificial intelligence (AI) safety do not consider testing techniques specific to UL.

Mutation testing [15], one of the most important testing techniques, has been successfully applied to SL and RL systems [10,11,13,16–18]. Whereas, different from SL, which relies on labeled data, and RL, which relies on the interaction between agents and corresponding environment, UL learns patterns from unlabeled data. Thus, the mutation testing approaches proposed in [10,11,13,16,18] are not suitable for UL.

To fill the aforementioned gap, we design *MTUL*, a mutation testing technology dedicated to unsupervised learning, which contains a family of mutation operators, mutation scores and the corresponding mutation testing frameworks. Different from [14], which designs a set of techniques based on metamorphic testing to help users select a specific clustering system according to their needs, *MTUL* is based on the idea of mutation testing. A rational approach to designing mutation operators is to simulate the situations that might cause clustering unstable or introduce adversarial attacks for GAN. In practice, we put forward mutation operators at the data level and algorithm level to imitate potential defects. Relying on operators, *MTUL* constructs the mutated datasets, which can be used as test suites, to assess the quality (*e.g.*, stability) enhancement of UL systems under test. Furthermore, *MTUL* can be combined with autoencoder [19] to help generate adversarial samples.

The main contributions in this paper are summarized as follows:

(1) We propose, implement and evaluate *MTUL*, a mutation testing approach specific to UL. *MTUL* can generate test suites and measure their quality. In addition, it enhances the stability of UL systems effectively.
(2) We introduce the data-level and algorithm-level mutation testing workflows for UL systems. A family of data-level and algorithm-level mutation operators are systematically designed to simulate UL faults. Further, the corresponding mutation scores are defined for quantitative evaluation.
(3) We combine *MTUL* with autoencoder to generate adversarial examples, and find out potential adversarial samples in given datasets.

The rest of the paper is organized as follows. We begin with a brief introduction on unsupervised learning and mutation testing in Sect. 2. Section 3 proposes the mutation testing framework for UL systems. Section 4 shows how to combine the mutation testing framework with autoencoder. Experiments are given in Sect. 5. Section 6 discusses related work. Finally, we conclude and discuss possible future work in Sect. 7.

2 Background

2.1 Unsupervised Learning

Basically, ML technology is usually categorized as supervised learning (SL), unsupervised learning (UL) and reinforcement learning (RL). Provided a labelled dataset, SL is able to learn a function that maps data to corresponding labels. RL is based on the interaction between a goal-oriented agent and the corresponding environment, with which the agent learns to achieve long-term goal.

However, in practice, many problems lack sufficient prior knowledge, which means that manual category labeling is difficult or even impossible. UL does not require labeled data and is capable of identifying latent patterns and structural information in unlabelled datasets on its own. UL mainly focuses on clustering, GAN [20], autoencoder [19], etc.

Cluster analysis, represented by K-means, is by far one of the most classic UL techniques and commonly used for statistical data analysis. By means of similarity criteria between data, clustering analysis assigns the given unlabeled data to different groups (*i.e.*, clusters). In an ideal situation, data in the same cluster have close properties, while data assigned to different clusters have low similarity or are not similar at all. Unfortunately, cluster analysis systems may suffer from various possible risks, such as noisy data in dataset, which might make clustering results unstable. Such instability always makes potential structural information in dataset indistinguishable.

GAN [20], which learns input data regularities, has a huge range of applications in diverse domains. It contains two neural networks (*i.e.*, Generator and Discriminator) gaming against each other to automatically predict plausible output examples drawn from the distribution of original dataset. Concretely, Generator strives to construct data regarded as real by Discriminator, and Discriminator attempts to distinguish whether the generated example is real or fake. Unavoidably, GAN may suffer from various issues, such as adversarial attacks [4], making it unstable. Simultaneously, since there is no standard to evaluate the model, GAN may be more unstable compared with other learning methods, which is one of the starting points of this work.

2.2   Mutation Testing

Mutation testing is a fault-based testing technique, spawned by three pioneering works [21–23] in the late 1970s.s. Nowadays, in the field of traditional software, mutation testing is a well-established technique for system security enhancement.

Mutation operators are used to simulate various faults that the system may encounter. The tester obtains a series of mutated programs (mutants) by injecting faults into the original program with the mutation operators. Comprehensibly speaking, mutants can simulate the corner cases that the original program may encounter. Therefore, by running the test dataset $\mathbf{D}$ on mutants, the quality of $\mathbf{D}$ can be assessed. If the result of running a test data $\mathbf{d} \in \mathbf{D}$ on mutant is different from the result of running $\mathbf{d}$ on the original program, the mutant is killed. Otherwise, the mutant is kept alive. Mutation score is the proportion of killed mutants in the corresponding mutant set. In other words, the more mutants are killed in the given mutant set, the higher the mutation score of the test data is. Since mutants simulate various errors that the original program may encounter, a test data with a higher mutation score has higher quality and is more likely to capture vulnerabilities within the program.

[10,11,16,18] pioneer the application of mutation testing technology to SL, design a series of mutation operators for SL systems to simulate potential faults, and introduce corresponding mutation scores. [24] investigates and conducts an evaluation of the mutation operators in [10,16]. A mutation testing technique for RL is proposed in [13], where a family of element-level and agent-level mutation operators are designed and implemented based on the characteristics of RL. The developments reveal the potential of mutation testing to enhance the security of AI systems. Below we introduce specific technical details about *MTUL*.

3 Mutation Testing Specific to Unsupervised Learning Systems

At the development level, UL is essentially different from traditional software, which contains units (*e.g.*, classes, branches) responsible for specific functions. Based on the predetermined control flows (*i.e.*, if-else statements, condition-controlled loops, etc.), the units coordinate and interact with each other.

Whereas, UL systems are driven by unlabeled data, which means that the learning process cannot be predetermined and is in fact random. So traditional mutation testing cannot be applied to UL systems. In this section, we introduce two general mutation testing workflows for UL systems[1], two sets of mutation operators and corresponding mutation scores.

3.1 Mutation Testing Workflow

In the following, we introduce the mutation testing workflows for UL systems. As shown in Fig. 1, data-level mutation operators mutate the original dataset to construct the mutated datasets in the initial stage. After that, both the generated datasets and corresponding original dataset are fed into the system under test. For cluster analysis, by calculating mutation scores based on clustering results, testers could find out high-quality mutated datasets, which may affect the stability of clustering. It is worth noting that the filtered high-quality datasets can enhance the stability of systems under test and avoid such datasets in advance. For GAN, since Discriminator manages to distinguish training data (*i.e.*, real data) from the data created by Generator, mutation will eventually be transmitted to generated data and cause perturbations to Discriminator. Similarly, we can calculate corresponding mutation scores corresponding to generated data for analysis. We emphasize that the proposed data-level technique is intended to chase down issues threatening the stability of UL systems and enhance stability.

Figure 2 shows the algorithm-level mutation testing workflow. For clustering, mutations are first performed on the original clustering system to obtain the corresponding mutated systems. Then, by executing both generated and original systems against test suite, testers can quantitatively measure whether the

---

[1] Due to the length limitation, we only discuss cluster analysis and GAN here. The design idea can be easily generalized to other UL systems.

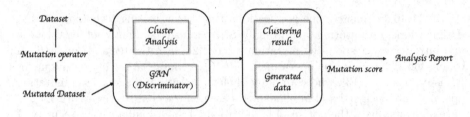

Fig. 1. Data-level mutation testing workflow

given suite is capable of finding system vulnerabilities. For GAN, by mutation operators proposed in Sect. 3.2 and the model-level operators in [18], we can directly mutate Generator or (and) Discriminator to generate mutated GANs. The mutated GANs cover diverse corner cases, making it possible to screen high-quality test suites.

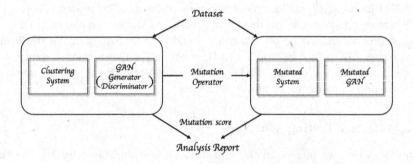

Fig. 2. Algorithm-level mutation testing workflow

3.2 Mutation Operators

For traditional software, control flows are predetermined and fixed. Consequently, mutation operators can be devised by directly modifying the control flows to introduce faults. As stated, UL systems are data-driven. Thus, we need to design mutation operators according to their characteristics.

Data-Level Mutation Operators. We consider simulating potential issues within unlabeled datasets in a targeted manner to design mutation operators for UL systems at the data level.

Data-Level Mutation Operators for Clustering. During cluster analysis, each sample is allocated to its matching cluster iteratively until convergence. As mentioned above, the main risk of this process stems from instability. To be specific, such instability refers to data with high similarity being misclassified into different clusters due to the concealed outlier data and noise data, etc.

Therefore, for datasets, we propose data-level mutation operators by introducing outlier data, noise data and mutation data, etc. Note that potential issues may originate from hacking, data pollution, or differences in data accuracy. In the following, six data-level mutation operators are specified in detail.

The first case is that the size of the dataset does not change before and after mutation (denoted as **Case 1**). Let $X = \{x_1, x_2, ..., x_n\}$ and $X' = \{x'_1, x'_2, ..., x'_n\}$ be the original and mutated dataset, respectively. In this case, we define three mutation operators: Mutation Point operator, Position Mutation operator and Dimensional Mutation operator.

Mutation Point Operator: The Mutation Point operator selects data in the original dataset and perturbs them one by one to get the corresponding mutated data. The number of mutated data can be preset, and it is also feasible to mutate only one original data. Such issue may happen when inputting certain data unintentionally or incorrectly.

Position Mutation Operator: Instead of implementing a series of independent perturbations, the Position Mutation operator selects a fixed perturbation method to inject faults. The selected perturbation is performed on a part of data in the dataset.

Dimensional Mutation Operator: The Dimensional Mutation operator brings the loss of dimension in cluster analysis. For example, for a dataset with data in three-dimensional space, data pollution or hacker attacks may cause some data to lose dimensional information. Data in the lost dimension are filled with 0 to simulate such errors.

The second case is that datasets are mutated by adding or deleting data (denoted as **Case 2**). Let $X = \{x_1, x_2, ..., x_n\}$ and $X' = \{x'_1, x'_2, ..., x'_{n'}\}$ be the original and mutated dataset, respectively, where $n' \neq n$. For this case, we define three mutation operators: Outlier operator, Noise Point operator and Density Mutation operator.

Outlier Operator: The Outlier operator simulates the error of one or more outliers existing in the dataset. Such error may destroy the original clustering result because the original similarity between data might be affected to accommodate the outliers.

Noise Point Operator: The Noise Point operator adds noise points to the original dataset to get the corresponding mutated dataset. We select a distribution based on which the operator constructs noise points.

Density Mutation Operator: The Density Mutation operator is achieved by adding or deleting data. There are two ways to implement this operator: (1) Randomly adding or deleting some data; (2) Selecting some data in the dataset, and adding or deleting data around them. Adding increases density and deleting decreases density.

Data-Level Mutation Operators for GAN. GAN is a combination of Generator and Discriminator. They game against each other to generate outputs

plausibly drawn from the original dataset. Discriminator attempts to distinguish the training data from samples constructed by generator. As we know,
GANs are data-driven. Ideally, data preparation, loading, and processing match
the expectation of the user. Unfortunately, potential errors in the dataset and
human factors (such as attacks) can lead to some edge cases. Due to the characteristics of GAN (*e.g.*, consisting of two gaming networks), in addition to the
operators proposed in [18] for a single network, we give the following four mutation operators.

Noise Injection Operator: The Noise Injection operator confuses discriminator by
(1) adding noise to training data or (2) mixing adversarial samples in the process
of loading data. Such error may occur during the data preparation phase. This
mutation is done by modifying the dataset before training.

Disturb Preprocessing Operator: Before the training process of GAN, data pre-
processing is sometimes required. Typically, preprocessing consists of procedures
that transform raw data into a format more adequate for further interpretability.
For instance, specific procedures can be shuffling the data, randomly selecting
parts of data from the training dataset or normalizing the data before training.
The operator adds, skips or changes some procedures in data preprocessing.

Randomness Reduction Operator: When training discriminator, it is necessary to
select a certain amount of real images randomly. Generator also requires random
points in the latent space as input. Failing to match the two demands above may
lead to potential problems. The Randomness Reduction operator accomplishes
such mutation by reducing randomness, which shields discriminator from the
overall perspective of real dataset or disables generator to map the entire latent
space to the data space, thereby simulating potential vulnerabilities.

Hyper-Parameter Operator: The hyper-parameter values have a definite impact
on the processing of data. The ways of implementing Hyper-parameter operator
includes: (1) changing the batch size; (2) changing the learning rate; (3) changing
the iterations of the training process. These mutations result in unstable data
training. The rationale for these designs is that when taking an after-trained
model as the original model in GAN training, the suitable hyper-parameters
may be different.

Algorithm-Level Mutation Operators. Next, we consider the issues that
the UL systems are likely to encounter from the perspective of algorithm, and
further give the corresponding mutation operators.

Algorithm-Level Mutation Operators for Clustering. The clustering process is carried out in an iterative manner, in which similarity criteria and preset
number of clusters are two crucial factors of clustering results. Thus, we modify
these factors to introduce potential errors.

Similarity Change Operator: The most commonly used similarity criterion is
Euclidean distance metric. The Similarity Change operator is implemented by

varying the similarity criterion, such as Manhattan distance metric, Chebyshev distance metric or Minkowski distance metric, in the clustering process.

Cluster Mutation Operator: When using K-means, the number of clusters is set in advance. The Cluster Mutation operator modifies the preset number of clusters to affect the clustering process.

Algorithm-Level Mutation Operators for GAN. The training of the GAN is driven by the game of two adversaries. We introduce three algorithm-level mutation operators below in detail.

Confusing Discriminator Operator: From the intent of training, discriminator intends to distinguish between real and fake data, assigning labels to real and fake data separately during training. However, wrong association confuses the discriminator, leading it to wrong target.

Change Sampling Operator: Discriminator and generator have downsampling and upsampling mechanisms respectively. The Change Sampling operator alters the downsampling or upsampling approach. For instance, the operator converts Conv2DTranspose into UpSampling2D when upsampling.

Mishandling Gradient Operator: The training process requires processing gradients. Common methods include BGD, SGD, MBGD, and gradient descent with Momentum. The Mishandling Gradient operator changes the gradient of model.

3.3 Mutation Scores

Mutation Scores for Clustering. Intuitively, a higher-quality mutated dataset is characterized by a lower difference from the original dataset and a more significant impact on clustering result. In order to synthetically evaluate the differences in datasets and clustering results before and after mutation, we define mutation scores as follows.

For **Case 1**, whether the selected operator is Mutation Point operator, Position Mutation operator or Dimensional Mutation operator, its essential function is to perturb part of data in the original dataset. Note that the clustering results of perturbed data and corresponding original data are very likely to be different. Thus, our main focus is whether perturbed data lead to changes in clustering results of unperturbed data. In addition, the extent of change is without doubt a matter of concern.

On account of the design intent mentioned above, mutation score for **Case 1** is expected to be able to measure changes in clustering results of the unchanged data. We name this mutation score as $MutationScore_{un}$, since it corresponds to the case where the dataset size remains *unchanged*.

Definition 1 ($MutationScore_{un}$). *Suppose m data within original dataset X have been mutated, then $n - m$ data remain untouched in mutated dataset X'. Among these untouched data, the number of data whose clustering results change* *against UL system T is denoted as* killed. *The MutationScore$_{un}$ for X, X' and T is defined as:*

$$MutationScore_{un}(X, X', T) = \frac{killed}{m} \tag{1}$$

For **Case 2**, whether the selected operator is Outlier operator, Noise Point operator, or Density Mutation operator, it is essential to add data to the original dataset or delete the selected data in the original dataset. Formally, let $X = \{x_1, x_2, ..., x_n\}$ and $X' = \{x'_1, x'_2, ..., x'_{n'}\}$ be mutated dataset and the corresponding original dataset, respectively. When $n' > n$, let $x'_{n+1}, x'_{n+2}, ..., x'_{n'}$ be the newly added data, then $x'_1, x'_2, ..., x'_n$ remain untouched. When $n' < n$, $x'_1, x'_2, ..., x'_{n'}$ are the remaining data that has not been deleted. We name mutation score for **Case 2** as *MutationScore$_c$* because it corresponds to the case where the dataset size *changes*.

Definition 2 (*MutationScore$_c$*). *Let n and n' be the size of original dataset X and mutated dataset X', respectively. Among the untouched data, the number of data whose clustering results change against UL system T is denoted as* killed. *The MutationScore$_c$ for X, X' and T is defined as:*

$$MutationScore_c(X, X', T) = \begin{cases} killed/(n'-n), & n' > n; \\ killed/(n-n'), & n' < n. \end{cases} \tag{2}$$

In line accordance with the above definitions, we can intuitively see that when the dataset suffers less perturbation but corresponding clustering results suffer a more prominent impact, the mutation score becomes higher.

When algorithm-level mutation is imposed on the parameters, we have the following mutation scores.

Definition 3 (*MutationScore$_p$*). *Let* killed *be the number of data whose clustering results change against original system T and the mutated system T', where parameters in T are $p_1, ..., p_k$ are replaced by $p'_1, ..., p'_k$ in T'. The MutationScore$_p$ for X, T and T' is defined as:*

$$MutationScore_p(X, T, T') = \frac{killed}{\Sigma_{i=1}^{k} log(max(p_i/p'_i, p'_i/p_i))} \tag{3}$$

Mutation Scores for GAN. Generally, a more dangerous mutation is likely to create a mutated GAN generating a set of images with a more explicit difference to that generated by the original GAN. To make quantification, we define *MutationScore$_G$* below, based on which we are able to assess potential danger in GAN and avoid the risks before and during training.

Definition 4 (*MutationScore$_G$*). *Let D be the standard discriminator (i.e., the discriminator of original GAN). Denote S and S' as image sets generated by the original generator and the mutated generator, respectively. Suppose that f and* *f′ are the proportions of images labelled as fake by D in S and S′, respectively. The MutationScore$_G$ for S, S′ and D is defined as:*

$$MutationScore_G(S, S', D) = \frac{|f - f'|}{f} \quad (4)$$

4   *MUAE*: The Combination of *MTUL* and Autoencoder

In this section, we propose *MUAE*, a framework for generating adversarial samples and detecting potential adversarial attacks within given dataset by combining *MTUL* with Autoencoder. Autoencoder is an artificial neural network learning how to perform efficient feature extraction and representation in an unsupervised manner, which means that training data are used as both input and target output. An autoencoder consists of two components: encoder and decoder. The encoder compresses and encodes input into code in low-dimensional space. The decoder attempts to reconstruct the input by mapping code back to high-dimensional space. Essentially, autoencoder uses a loss function (*e.g.*, *MSE*) during training to make the input and output as similar as possible.

To generate adversarial samples by modifying legitimate data in given dataset, *MUAE* first encodes and compresses all data in the dataset to two-dimensional space. In this way, feature set (*i.e.*, code in two-dimensional space) is obtained. Then, *MUAE* utilizes *MTUL* to mutate the feature set and pack the high-quality mutated feature set. By reconstructing high-dimensional data from the selected feature set, adversarial samples are possibly generated. For instance, testers could mutate the original feature set by feat of Outlier operator, and select the high-quality mutated set with *MutationScore$_c$*. After that, testers decode the added outliers back to high-dimensional space. Intuitively, if the outlier causes the clustering result unstable, the corresponding high-dimensional data is probably an adversarial sample.

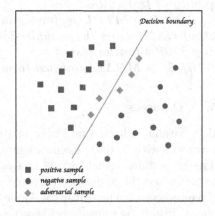

Fig. 3. An explanatory illustration of decision boundary.

The process of *MUAE* detecting whether dataset under test contains potential adversarial attacks or not is as follows. Note that our hypothesis is that there always exist a massive quantity of adversarial examples near the decision boundary (as shown in Fig. 3). First, *MUAE* compresses all data in the dataset except for suspicious data, and mutates the encoded feature set to obtain the corresponding mutated sets. After selecting those high-quality mutated sets, *MUAE* acquires the mutation points which cause more impact on the clustering result. Then *MUAE* decodes the corresponding points to generate the high-dimensional data. If the generated data contains adversarial examples, the corresponding points to these examples are likely to be near the boundary of feature set. By connecting multiple such points, approximate boundary can be found out. Afterwards, $MUAE$ encodes the suspicious data into two-dimensional plane and judges the relationship between the relevant two-dimensional points and boundary. If the point is near the boundary, the suspicious data is probably an adversarial sample and deserves further investigation. Thus, $MUAE$ helps avoid risks early on.

5   Experiment

We evaluate the effectiveness of $MTUL$ and derived technique $MUAE$ on two popular publicly available datasets (IRIS, MNIST) and a synthetic dataset. Implementation has been conducted on a MacBook Pro (2.6 GHz Intel Core i7 and 16 GB of memory) with numpy 1.19.4, matplotlib 3.3.3 and TensorFlow 2.1.0. The evaluation addresses three research questions for demonstrating how well $MTUL$ and $MUAE$ is consistent with its design objectives.

RQ1: Is MTUL able to chase down issues that interfere with the stability of clustering systems? Can MTUL quantitatively evaluate the quality of test suites?

RQ2: Can MTUL perform quantitative analysis on potential issues about GAN? Does the magnitude of mutation score correlate with the degree of potential issue?

RQ3: Is MUAE qualified to generate adversarial samples?

5.1   Datasets

IRIS dataset, collected by Fisher in 1936, is a multivariate dataset containing 3 categories with 50 data. Each category refers to a type of iris plant. The MNIST dataset contains 70000 28×28 images for 10 classes representing digits from 0 to 9. The synthetic dataset (denoted as Apple dataset) consists of 30 data for three categories. The feature of Apple dataset is that it can be stably separated into 3 clusters by k-means, as shown in Fig. 4(a).

5.2   Research Question 1

For humans, even if there are slight data perturbations in datasets with obvious boundaries, such as the Apple dataset, our judgment of corresponding clustering result will not produce huge deviations. However, even if difference between the mutated dataset and the original dataset is indistinguishable to human eyes, clustering results can be quite different. Regrettably, such situation is widespread.

To be more specific, general examples from the experiment are exhibited below. Figure 4(b), which corresponds to the Mutation Point operator, shows the mutated dataset constructed by selecting the data point (0.2, 0.2) in original dataset and mutating it to (0.415, 0.3). Figure 4(c), which corresponds to the Position Mutation operator, presents the mutated dataset generated by shifting the original data points with the subscript $3i + 1(0 \leq i \leq 9)$ 0.02 units to the left along the abscissa axis. The Dimensional Mutation operator corresponds to Fig. 4(d) where the data point (0.532, 0.472) is mutated to (0, 0.472), resulting in the loss of dimension. It is intuitive that the clustering results of the three mutation datasets are quite different from the original datasets. Quantitatively, the mutation scores corresponding to these three mutations are 18, 0.9 and 8 respectively. In addition, we observe that even though difference between the dataset mutated by Position Mutation operator and the corresponding original dataset is indistinguishable to human, there is a huge diversity in clustering results. It indicates that the Position Mutation operator is effective, which is in line with our expectations.

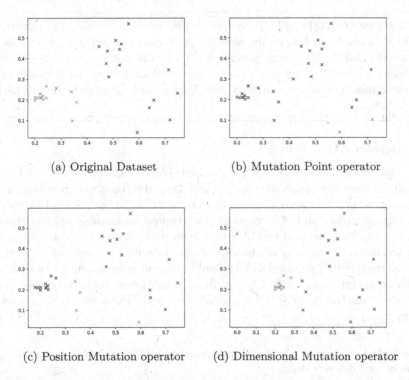

(a) Original Dataset   (b) Mutation Point operator

(c) Position Mutation operator   (d) Dimensional Mutation operator

Fig. 4. Comparison of clustering results. (a) is the original clustering result, (b) is the clustering result corresponding to the Mutation Point operator, (c) is the clustering result corresponding to the Position Mutation operator, (d) is the clustering result corresponding to the Dimensional Mutation operator.

The mutated datasets are capable of revealing potential instability of the system. Further, a mutated dataset with a higher mutation score is more likely to find potential vulnerabilities. Thus, we could adjust the system and patch the loopholes within system in a targeted manner. As an example, for the instability revealed by the mutated dataset shown in Fig. 4(b), the way to overcome it is to adjust the initial cluster centroid.

Due to space considerations, we just present specific examples of the Apple dataset here. Naturally, data-level mutation operators are available to handle the IRIS dataset. The number of clusters is expected to be 3 for the IRIS dataset. When the selection is correct, the clustering result is always satisfactory. However, the number of clusters can not be known in all scenarios. Therefore, algorithm-level loopholes are very likely to occur. In our experiment, the preset number of clusters is mutated by the Cluster Mutation operator. Specifically, the number of clusters is mutated to 4. Experiment shows that algorithm-level mutation is extremely harmful because even uncontaminated dataset (*i.e.*, the original dataset) has a very high mutation score. Thus, when conducting cluster analysis, it is of great importance to specify the preset number of clusters.

> **Answer to RQ1:** *MTUL* enables quantitative analysis on the quality of dataset. According to the feedback, it could help explore the reasons for instability and patch potential risks in the dataset. On the other hand, we see that by simulating diverse vulnerabilities, more possible error-related cases are covered, which ultimately improves the system security.

5.3 Research Question 2

GAN Mutant Model Generation: The original GAN we consider has seven layers, including a four-layer generator and a three-layer discriminator. See [25] for its specific structure. Through pre-experiments, we found that some of operators have a great impact on GAN, causing GAN to lose its learning ability. Specifically, the images generated by GAN that loses its learning ability are blank. In order to ensure the validity of the experimental results, we eliminate operators whose corresponding mutated GANs would fail, and generate mutants with the remaining operators to verify whether *MTUL* can assess potential errors. Note that we obtain the original GAN and the mutated GANs after 100 epochs of training.

Table 1. *M.S.* (*i.e.*, mutation scores) calculated under different *M.O.* (*i.e.*, mutation operators) and different degrees.

M.O.	fake	M.S.	M.O.	fake	M.S.
none (Original GAN)	73%	–	full-exponential-noise	100%	0.370
add	81.5%	0.116	5%-exponential-noise	76%	0.411
add-after	0%	1.0	1%-exponential-noise	70.5%	0.342
batch-down	99%	0.356	double-generator-lr	96%	0.315
batch-up	100%	0.370	confuse-discriminator-1/100	0%	1.0
full-gamma-noise	100%	0.370	confuse-discriminator-1/50	49.5%	0.322
5%-gamma-noise	86%	0.178	confuse-discriminator-1/10	70.5%	0.034
1%-gamma-noise	71.5%	0.021	confuse-discriminator-1	78%	0.068
full-gauss-noise	100%	0.370	confuse-discriminator-100	72.5%	0.007
5%-gauss-noise	87%	0.192	randomness-reduction	48.5%	0.336
1%-gauss-noise	82%	0.123	change-sampling	97%	0.329

Mutation Evaluation: After generating the mutants, we enter the execution phase, feeding the mutants with MNIST dataset. Table 1[2] summarizes the corresponding mutation scores to the mutants obtained by applying all available mutation operators. Mutated GANs are all based on the same original GAN. Calculations suggest that mutation score is indeed sensitive to potential errors. Additionally, we see that mutation score is positively correlated with degree of error. For instance, as the degree of injected gauss noise increases (from 1% to 100%), the mutation score increases.

Due to space limitations, a set of images generated by the generators of the original GAN and the mutated GANs (completely covers the mutation operators considered in the Table 1) are shown in *Figures Generated by Mutated GANs*.

> **Answer to RQ2:** *MTUL* can quantitatively analyze various potential errors about GAN. The mutation score is positively correlated with the degree of potential error. To be specific, as the degree of error deepens, the mutation score increases accordingly.

5.4 Research Question 3

Through the experiments for RQ1, we see what kind of mutation is likely to make the original stable clustering results change dramatically. Here, we implement *MUAE* for MNIST dataset. The trained autoencoder encodes the test dataset to a two-dimensional plane to obtain the corresponding feature set, as shown in Fig. 5. Autoencoder used in the experiment is an eight-layer network.

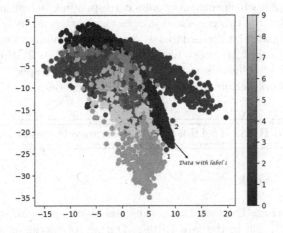

Fig. 5. MNIST-encoding

---

[2] See https://github.com/Yuteng-Lu/MT-GAN for relevant code and details of each operator.

Based on *MUAE*, we mutate the feature set to obtain the mutated feature sets and select the mutated set with high quality. Concretely, we use the Outlier operator to mutate the original feature set, generate and select the mutated set with high mutation score. Then we could decode the added outliers back to the high-dimensional space and obtain the corresponding data. Intuitively, if one outlier in the feature set causes the clustering result to be unstable, then the high-dimensional data corresponding to it is likely to be an adversarial sample.

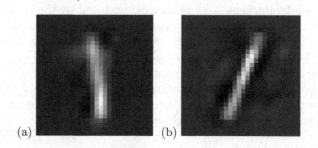

(a)   (b)

Fig. 6. Two generated adversarial examples

Two adversarial samples generated by *MUAE* are shown above. As shown in the Fig. 6(a) and Fig. 6(b), we present two generated images, which correspond to red points 1 and 2 in Fig. 5 respectively. These two points are exactly the outliers found that affect the clustering results. The coordinate of point 1 is $(8.28, -24.18)$ and the coordinate of point 2 is $(9, -17.5)$. These two points are near the cluster which contains points corresponding to legitimate data with label 1. Generally, the two generated images can be thought as being crafted by modifying legitimate data with label 1. According to human perception, these two generated images are most likely to be identified as 1. However, a well-trained network identifies these two images as 8 and 2, respectively. Note that the trained network performs well on the MNIST test dataset (Test accuracy = 0.981).

> **Answer to RQ3:** *MUAE* is able to generate adversarial samples.

6 Related Work

Mutation Testing. The mutation testing technique was spawned by three pioneering works [21–23] in the late 1970s.s. During its development, it has been applied to evaluate the quality of data and achieved great success. Nowadays, in the field of traditional software, mutation testing technique can be used to enhance system security. [26] proposes predictive mutation testing, which could predict the results of mutation testing without executing mutants. [27] divides 262 Android faults contained in 2,023 software artifacts from different sources into 14 categories to design 38 mutation operators. For Android apps, [28] designs an automated mutation testing framework. More than 8,000 mutants have been introduced based on the 38 operators proposed in [27]. In addition to the above applications, mutation testing could also be used in other fields, including aspect oriented programming, network-based protocols, etc. [10,11] pioneer the application of mutation testing technology to SL, design a series of mutation operators for feedforward neural network (FNN) and recurrent neural network (RNN). A testing framework is proposed in [10,11] and experiments have proved the technology effective. A mutation testing technique for RL is proposed in [13]. Based on the characteristics of RL, a set of element-level and agent-level mutation operators are proposed and implemented.

Autoencoder. [29] proposes an effective way of initializing weights, and allows Autoencoder to learn low-dimensional features of low-dimensional data to help reduce the dimension of data. [30] introduces a set of VAE-based hybrid frameworks that combine convolutional encoders and deconvolutional decoders with a recurrent language model to generate natural texts. [31] gives a junction tree variational Autoencoder to directly generate molecular graphs. The generation process is divided into two stages. First, a tree-structured scaffold is generated, and then a graph message passing network is used to obtain the molecule. [32] proposes an adversarial graph embedding framework for graph data. Two algorithms, named ARGA and ARVGA, for link prediction, node clustering, and graph visualization tasks are proposed. Based on a semantic Autoencoder, [33] proposes a zero-shot learning model.

7   Conclusion

This work proposes *MTUL*, a mutation testing technique for UL systems. Eleven data-level and five algorithm-level mutation operators are designed, and the corresponding mutation scores are introduced. Based on *MTUL*, we can evaluate the quality of dataset. We believe that *MTUL* can help testers find "malicious" data in unlabeled datasets. *MUAE*, the combination of *MTUL* and autoencoder, can assist in finding adversarial samples and the approximate boundaries between classes.

In the traditional software field, mutation testing is a mature technology to evaluate the quality of test data. We believe that mutation testing can also be more widely used in UL fields. Starting from cluster analysis and GAN, this work makes a preliminary exploratory attempt on the design of mutation testing specific to UL systems. In the future, we will further investigate more possible mutation operators for other UL systems.

Acknowledgement. This research was sponsored by the National Natural Science Foundation of China under Grant No. 62172019, 61772038, and CCF-Huawei Formal Verification Innovation Research Plan.

References

1. de Prado, M.L., Lewis, M.J.: Detection of false investment strategies using unsupervised learning methods. Quant. Finance **19**(9), 1555–1565 (2019)
2. Abbas, H.M., Fahmy, M.M.: Neural networks for maximum likelihood clustering. Signal Process. **36**(1), 111–126 (1994)
3. Liu, W., Liu, S., Qing, G., Chen, J., Chen, X., Chen, D.: Empirical studies of a two-stage data preprocessing approach for software fault prediction. IEEE Trans. Reliab. **65**(1), 38–53 (2016)
4. Kos, J., Fischer, I., Song, D.: Adversarial examples for generative models. In: 2018 IEEE Security and Privacy Workshops, SP Workshops 2018, San Francisco, CA, USA, 24 May 2018, pp. 36–42. IEEE Computer Society (2018)
5. Pei, K., Cao, Y., Yang, J., Jana, S.: Deepxplore: automated whitebox testing of deep learning systems. Commun. ACM **62**(11), 137–145 (2019)
6. Ma, L., et al.: Deepgauge: multi-granularity testing criteria for deep learning systems. In: Proceedings of the 33rd ACM/IEEE International Conference on Automated Software Engineering, ASE 2018, Montpellier, France, 3–7 September 2018, pp. 120–131. ACM (2018)
7. Sun, Y., Huang, X., Kroening, D., Sharp, J., Hill, M., Ashmore, R.: Structural test coverage criteria for deep neural networks. ACM Trans. Embed. Comput. Syst. **18**(5s), 94:1–94:23 (2019)
8. Kim, J., Feldt, R., Yoo, S.: Guiding deep learning system testing using surprise adequacy. In: Proceedings of the 41st International Conference on Software Engineering, ICSE 2019, Montreal, QC, Canada, 25–31 May 2019, pp. 1039–1049. IEEE/ACM (2019)
9. Gerasimou, S., Eniser, H.F., Sen, A., Cakan, A.: Importance-driven deep learning system testing. In: ICSE 2020: 42nd International Conference on Software Engineering, Seoul, South Korea, 27 June–19 July 2020, pp. 702–713. ACM (2020)
10. Ma, L., et al.: Deepmutation: mutation testing of deep learning systems. In: 29th IEEE International Symposium on Software Reliability Engineering, ISSRE 2018, Memphis, TN, USA, 15–18 October 2018, pp. 100–111. IEEE Computer Society (2018)
11. Hu, Q., Ma, L., Xie, X., Yu, B., Liu, Y., Zhao, J.: Deepmutation++: a mutation testing framework for deep learning systems. In: 34th IEEE/ACM International Conference on Automated Software Engineering, ASE 2019, San Diego, CA, USA, 11–15 November 2019, pp. 1158–1161. IEEE (2019)
12. Uesato, J., et al.: Rigorous agent evaluation: an adversarial approach to uncover catastrophic failures. In: 7th International Conference on Learning Representations, ICLR 2019, New Orleans, LA, USA, 6–9 May 2019. OpenReview.net (2019)
13. Lu, Y., Sun, W., Sun, M.: Mutation testing of reinforcement learning systems. In: Qin, S., Woodcock, J., Zhang, W. (eds.) SETTA 2021. LNCS, vol. 13071, pp. 143–160. Springer, Cham (2021). https://doi.org/10.1007/978-3-030-91265-9_8
14. Xie, X., Zhang, Z., Chen, T.Y., Liu, Y., Poon, P.-L., Xu, B.: METTLE: a metamorphic testing approach to assessing and validating unsupervised machine learning systems. IEEE Trans. Reliab. **69**(4), 1293–1322 (2020)
15. Jia, Y., Harman, M.: An analysis and survey of the development of mutation testing. IEEE Trans. Software Eng. **37**(5), 649–678 (2011)
16. Shen, W., Wan, J., Chen, Z.: Munn: mutation analysis of neural networks. In: 2018 IEEE International Conference on Software Quality, Reliability and Security Companion, QRS Companion 2018, Lisbon, Portugal, 16–20 July 2018, pp. 108–115. IEEE (2018)

17. Wu, H., Li, Z., Cui, Z., Zhang, J.: A mutation-based approach to repair deep neural network models. In: 8th International Conference on Dependable Systems and Their Applications, DSA 2021, Yinchuan, China, 5–6 August 2021, pp. 730–731. IEEE (2021)
18. Humbatova, N., Jahangirova, G., Tonella, P.: Deepcrime: mutation testing of deep learning systems based on real faults. In: ISSTA 2021: 30th ACM SIGSOFT International Symposium on Software Testing and Analysis, Virtual Event, Denmark, 11–17 July 2021, pp. 67–78. ACM (2021)
19. Vincent, P., Larochelle, H., Lajoie, I., Bengio, Y., Manzagol, P.-A.: Stacked denoising autoencoders: learning useful representations in a deep network with a local denoising criterion. J. Mach. Learn. Res. **11**, 3371–3408 (2010)
20. Goodfellow, I.J., et al.: Generative adversarial nets. In: Advances in Neural Information Processing Systems 27: Annual Conference on Neural Information Processing Systems 2014, 8–13 December 2014, Montreal, Quebec, Canada, pp. 2672–2680 (2014)
21. Lipton, R.: Fault diagnosis of computer programs. Ph.D. thesis, Carnegie Mellon University (1971)
22. DeMillo, R.A., Lipton, R.J., Sayward, F.G.: Hints on test data selection: help for the practicing programmer. Computer **11**(4), 34–41 (1978)
23. Hamlet, R.G.: Testing programs with the aid of a compiler. IEEE Trans. Software Eng. **3**(4), 279–290 (1977)
24. Jahangirova, G., Tonella, P.: An empirical evaluation of mutation operators for deep learning systems. In: 13th IEEE International Conference on Software Testing, Validation and Verification, ICST 2020, Porto, Portugal, 24–28 October 2020, pp. 74–84. IEEE (2020)
25. MTUL, August 2022. https://github.com/Yuteng-Lu/MT-GAN
26. Zhang, J., Zhang, L., Harman, M., Hao, D., Jia, Y., Zhang, L.: Predictive mutation testing. IEEE Trans. Software Eng. **45**(9), 898–918 (2019)
27. Vásquez, M.L., et al.: Enabling mutation testing for android apps. In: Proceedings of the 2017 11th Joint Meeting on Foundations of Software Engineering, ESEC/FSE 2017, Paderborn, Germany, 4–8 September 2017, pp. 233–244. ACM (2017)
28. Moran, K., et al.: MDroid+: a mutation testing framework for android. In: Proceedings of the 40th International Conference on Software Engineering: Companion Proceedings, ICSE 2018, Gothenburg, Sweden, 27 May–03 June 2018, pp. 33–36. ACM (2018)
29. Hinton, G.E., Salakhutdinov, R.: Reducing the dimensionality of data with neural networks. Science **313**(5786), 504–507 (2006)
30. Semeniuta, S., Severyn, A., Barth, E.: A hybrid convolutional variational autoencoder for text generation. In: Proceedings of the 2017 Conference on Empirical Methods in Natural Language Processing, EMNLP 2017, Copenhagen, Denmark, 9–11 September 2017, pp. 627–637. Association for Computational Linguistics (2017)
31. Jin, W., Barzilay, R., Jaakkola, T.S.: Junction tree variational autoencoder for molecular graph generation. In: Proceedings of the 35th International Conference on Machine Learning, ICML 2018, Stockholmsmässan, Stockholm, Sweden, 10–15 July 2018. Proceedings of Machine Learning Research, vol. 80, pp. 2328–2337. PMLR (2018)

32. Pan, S., Hu, R., Long, G., Jiang, J., Yao, L., Zhang, C.: Adversarially regularized graph autoencoder for graph embedding. In: Proceedings of the Twenty-Seventh International Joint Conference on Artificial Intelligence, IJCAI 2018, 13–19 July 2018, Stockholm, Sweden, pp. 2609–2615. ijcai.org (2018)

33. Kodirov, E., Xiang, T., Gong, S.: Semantic autoencoder for zero-shot learning. In: 2017 IEEE Conference on Computer Vision and Pattern Recognition, CVPR 2017, Honolulu, HI, USA, 21–26 July 2017, pp. 4447–4456. IEEE Computer Society (2017)

COOL-MC: A Comprehensive Tool for Reinforcement Learning and Model Checking

Dennis Gross[1(✉)], Nils Jansen[1], Sebastian Junges[1], and Guillermo A. Pérez[2]

[1] Radboud University, Nijmegen, The Netherlands
dgross@science.ru.nl
[2] University of Antwerp – Flanders Make, Antwerp, Belgium

Abstract. This paper presents COOL-MC, a tool that integrates state-of-the-art reinforcement learning (RL) and model checking. Specifically, the tool builds upon the OpenAI gym and the probabilistic model checker Storm. COOL-MC provides the following features: (1) a simulator to train RL policies in the OpenAI gym for Markov decision processes (MDPs) that are defined as input for Storm, (2) a new model builder for Storm, which uses callback functions to verify (neural network) RL policies, (3) formal abstractions that relate models and policies specified in OpenAI gym or Storm, and (4) algorithms to obtain bounds on the performance of so-called permissive policies. We describe the components and architecture of COOL-MC and demonstrate its features on multiple benchmark environments.

1 Introduction

Deep Reinforcement learning (RL) has created a seismic shift in how we think about building agents for dynamic systems [32,33]. It has triggered applications in critical domains like energy, transportation, and defense [4,13,34]. An *RL agent* aims to learn a near-optimal policy regarding some fixed objective by taking actions and perceiving feedback signals, usually rewards and observations of the *environment* [36]. Unfortunately, learned policies come with no guarantee to avoid *unsafe behavior* [14]. Generally, rewards lack the expressiveness to encode complex safety requirements [37] and it is hard to assess whether the training at a certain point in time is sufficient.

To resolve the issues mentioned above, verification methods like model checking [3,8] are used to reason about the safety of RL, see for instance [5,18,23,38]. However, despite the progress in combining these research areas, there is—to the best of our knowledge—no mature tool support that tightly integrates exact model checking of state-of-the-art deep RL policies. One of the reasons is that policies obtained on an OpenAI environment may be incompatible with a related

© The Author(s), under exclusive license to Springer Nature Switzerland AG 2022
W. Dong and J.-P. Talpin (Eds.): SETTA 2022, LNCS 13649, pp. 41–49, 2022.
https://doi.org/10.1007/978-3-031-21213-0_3

formal model (that can be used for model checking), and vice versa. These incompatibilities are often due to differences in their state or action spaces, or even their rewards. Another challenge is that verifying deep RL policies currently requires different algorithms, data structures, and abstractions depending on the architecture and size of a neural network (NN).

We present COOL-MC, an open-source tool that integrates the OpenAI gym with the probabilistic model checker Storm [11]. The purpose of the tool is *to enable training RL policies while being able to verify them at any stage of the training process.* Concretely, we focus on supporting the following methodology as main use case for COOL-MC. An RL expert is tasked with training an RL policy with formal guarantees. These guarantees are captured as formal specifications that hold on a well-defined formal model, formulated by the expert. At any stage of the learning, the RL expert wants to establish whether the policy has the desired properties as given by the formal model and specification.

Thus, the input of COOL-MC consists of two models of the environment: (1) an *OpenAI-gym compatible environment*, to train an RL policy; (2) an *Markov decision process (MDP)*, specified using the PRISM language [31], to verify the policy together with a formal specification e.g., a probabilistic computation tree logic (PCTL) formula. Only the MDP model of the environment is required: If no OpenAI-gym environment is given, COOL-MC provides a wrapper to cast the MDP as an OpenAI gym environment. The latter is done using a *syntax-based simulator* that avoids building the MDP explicitly in Storm. Training of an RL policy can be done using any RL agent available in the OpenAI gym. Any (trained) policy can then be formally verified via Storm using *callback functions* that query the NN and build the induced discrete-time Markov chain (DTMC) incrementally [7,10]. COOL-MC assumes no formal relation between the two given environment models. Of course, for the purpose of policy verification, the states of both have to be in some of relation. For this purpose, we support abstraction of models and policies. In particular, we employ a feature-based representation for MDPs [35]. Such features may, for instance, refer to concrete positions of agents in their environment, or to the fuel level of a car. We offer the user the option to *remap feature values* and to define *abstractions* of their feature domains [24] (see Sect. 2). This yields the opportunity to verify these formal abstraction and obtaining bounds on the actual policy.

Related Work. The recently developed MoGym [15] is built on top of the MODEST toolset [20], and it is related to our tool. The main difference is that our tool supports so-called permissive policies and feature remappings. Likewise, Bacci et al. tackle the problem of verifying stochastic RL policies for continuous environments via an abstraction approach [2] but they abstract the policy using mixed-integer LPs. This limits the NN architectures their tool can handle. In contrast, we take the trained policy exactly as is and are architecture-agnostic. Gu et al. propose a method called MCRL, that combines model checking with reinforcement learning in a multi-agent setting for mission planning to ensure that safety-critical requirements are met [17]. The difference in our approach is that we allow the post-verification of single RL policies in every kind of environment that can be modeled in the PRISM language. Mungojerrie uses RL to obtain an optimal policy w.r.t. a given ω-regular objective [19]. In [23], a similar approach is presented for objectives given in linear temporal logic (LTL). Shielded RL guides the RL agent during training to avoid safety violations [1,9,10,25]. We, on the other hand, do not guide the training process but verify the trained policy.

2   Core Functionality and Architecture of COOL-MC

We now present the core functionality and the architecture of COOL-MC.

Training. During RL training, interaction with the user-provided environment takes place as follows. Starting from the current state, the agent selects an action upon which the environment returns the next state and the corresponding reward to derive a near-optimal policy.

Verification. To allow model checking the trained policy (an RL agent) against a user-provided specification and formal model, we build the induced DTMC on the fly via Storm callback functions. For every reachable state by the policy, the policy is queried for an action. In the underlying MDP, only states that may be reached via that action are expanded. The resulting model is fully probabilistic, as no action choices are left open. It is, in fact, the Markov chain induced by the original MDP and the policy.

Policy Transformations. We extend the above-described on-the-fly construction with two abstractions. One of them relies on feature abstraction [12,28], while the other uses a coarser abstraction of the state variables [24]. In both cases, we obtain a new policy τ.

1. **Feature abstraction:** Assume the state space has some structure $S \subseteq Q \times I$ for suitable Q and I. Thus, states are pairs $s = (q, i)$ where q and i correspond to *features* whose values range over Q and I respectively. Let Act denote the actions in the MDP. Given a partition $K_1, \ldots, K_n$ of I, we abstract this feature from the policy π, by defining a *permissive* policy [12] $\tau \colon S \to 2^{\mathsf{Act}}$, i.e., a policy selecting multiple actions in every state. In particular, we consider $\tau(q, i) = \bigcup_{k \in K_n} \pi(q, k)$, with K_n is the unique set such that $i \in K_n$. This policy τ ignores the value of i in state (q, i) and instead selects any action that can be selected from states (q, k), with $k \in K_n$. Applying a permissive policy yields an induced MDP, which can be model checked to provide best- and worst-case bounds.
2. **Feature remapping:** In this case, we again assume $S \subseteq Q \times I$. Given a mapping $\mu : I \to Y$ with $Y \subseteq I$, we define the abstracted policy τ as follows. $\tau(q, i) = \pi(q, \mu(i))$ The feature values of i are effectively being transformed into values from a (possibly smaller) set of feature values $Y \subseteq I$ before being fed into the original policy.

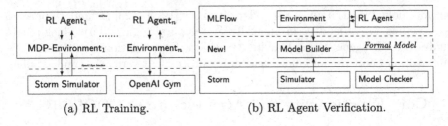

(a) RL Training.   (b) RL Agent Verification.

Fig. 1. COOL-MC architecture.

Architecture. COOL-MC is a Python toolchain on top of Storm and OpenAI gym. It also employs MLflow[1] as a file manager, which manages all the user experiments in the local file system, and allows the user to compare different experiments via the MLflow webserver. Furthermore, each task (for example, training or verification) is a separate MLflow component in the software architecture of COOL-MC and is controlled by the main script. COOL-MC also contains the *RL agent* component, which is a wrapper around the policy and interacts with the *environment*. Currently implemented agents include Q-Learning [39], Hillclimbing [30], Deep Q-Learning, and REINFORCE [40]. For training uses the Storm simulator or an OpenAI Gym (Fig. 1a). For verification, the model builder creates an induced DTMC which is then checked by Storm (Fig. 1b).

3   Numerical Experiments

Our experimental setup allows us to showcase the core features of COOL-MC. For clarity of exposition, in this paper, we focus on describing concise examples: In the *Frozen lake*, the agent has to reach a Frisbee on a frozen lake. At every step, the agent can choose to move "up", "down", "left", or "right". The execution of said movement is imprecise because of the ice: it is only as intended in 33.33% of the cases. In the remaining 66.66% of the cases, another movement is executed—the only restriction is that the agent cannot move in the direction opposite than its choice. The agent receives a reward of +1 if it reaches the Frisbee [6]. In the *Taxi* environment, the agent has to transport customers to their destination without running out of fuel; in the *Collision Avoidance* environment, it must avoid two obstacles in a 2D grid; the descriptions of the other environments (*Smart Grid, Stock Market, Atari James Bond, Atari Crazy Climber*)[2] can be found in the Appendix of our technical report [16]. We stress that the tool can handle several other benchmarks, e.g., PRISM-format MDPs from the *Quantitative Verification Benchmark Set* [21]. All experiments were executed on

---

[1] MLflow is a platform to streamline ML development, including tracking experiments, packaging code into reproducible experiments, and sharing and deploying models [41].

[2] We refer the interested reader to the repository https://github.com/LAVA-LAB/COOL-MC of the tool for more experiments with these and other environments.

a laptop with 8 GB RAM and an Intel(R) Core(TM) i7-8750H CPU@2.20 GHz
× 12.

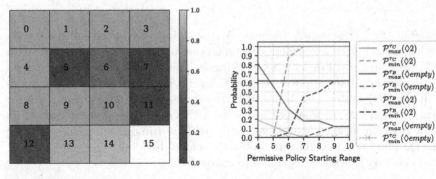

(a) Heatmap shows per state s the value $\mathcal{P}^{s,\pi_A}(\Diamond frisbee)$.

(b) Plot shows different permissive taxi policies "lumping" fuel levels.

Fig. 2. Frozen lake verification (a) and permissive taxi policies (b).

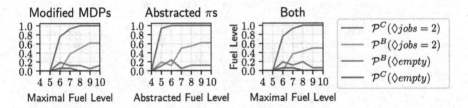

Fig. 3. Plots for the probabilities of running out of fuel on the road and finishing two jobs in three different settings for the trained policies π_B and π_C.

Policy Verification. The frozen lake environment is a commonly used OpenAI gym benchmark. Therefore, we trained a deep-neural-network policy π_A in this OpenAI gym for $100K$ episodes. For more information on the training process, see Appendix of our technical report [16]. After the learning process, we verified π_A in the frozen lake PRISM model (which describes the OpenAI environment). We investigate if the trained policy ultimately learned to account for the slippery factor. Figure 2a shows that the agent only falls into the water at the fifth position (from state 6 while selecting the action "left"). The agent reaches state 9 with a probability of $\mathcal{P}^{0,\pi_A}(\Diamond 9) = 1$. This indicates that the trained RL agent has learned to take the slippery factor into account since otherwise, it would not safely reach state 9. At state 9, we split the environment into an area in which the RL agent cannot fall into the water by following its policy and an unsafe area. If the agent successfully selects the action "down", it stays safe the rest of the trajectory to the Frisbee. Suppose the agent slips to state 10 while selecting "down", the probability of reaching the Frisbee declines to $\mathcal{P}^{10,\pi_A}(\Diamond frisbee) = 0.76$.

Scalability and Performance Analysis. A 10×10 instance of the collision avoidance benchmark with a slickness constant value of 0.1 results in an MDP with $1,077,628$ states and $118,595,768$ transitions. This already causes Storm to run out of memory. If we apply a policy (trained with COOL-MC), the induced DTMC has $1M$ states and $29,256,683$ transitions, and is now within reach for Storm, while the result may not be optimal. COOL-MC can handle sizes of up to 11×11 and a slickness assignment of 0.1 without running out of memory (see Table 1). The bottleneck of our tool is the model building time (see Table 1). Model checking times are negligible in comparison.

Table 1. Benchmarks for different environments and trained policies. Times are measured in seconds; *OOM* stands for out of memory.

Environment	MDP		DTMC						
	States	Trans.	Specification	Result	Build time	Check. time	States	Trans.
Frozen lake	17	152	$\mathcal{P}^{\pi_A}(\Diamond water)$	0.18	0.25	0	14	34
Taxi	8576	39608	$\mathcal{P}^{\pi_C}(\Diamond empty)$	0	4.78	0	252	507
Taxi	8576	39608	$\mathcal{P}^{\pi_C}(\Diamond 2)$	1	4.5	0	252	507
Collision 10 × 10	1077628	118595768	$\mathcal{T}^{\pi_D}(\Diamond collide)$	470.73	3106	226	1000000	29256683
Collision 11 × 11	1885813	211956692	$\mathcal{T}^{\pi_D}(\Diamond collide)$	546.18	3909	314	1771561	52433826
Collision 12 × 12	3148444	359797152	$\mathcal{T}^{\pi_D}(\Diamond collide)$	OOM	6619	OOM	2985984	89198366
Smart grid	271	10144	$\mathcal{P}^{\pi_E}_{<1000}(\Diamond black)$	0.02	0.48	0	40	176
Stock market	14760	89506	$\mathcal{P}^{\pi_F}(\Diamond loss)$	0	0.3	0	130	377
James bond	172032	3182592	$\mathcal{P}^{\pi_G}_{<15}(\Diamond done)$	0.23	1997	0.28	159744	1105920
Crazy climber	57344	499712	$\mathcal{P}^{\pi_G}_{<15}(\Diamond done)$	0	175	0	8193	32772

Feature Remapping. The policies π_B and π_C are trained in the taxi environment to transport passengers to their destinations. We are now interested in what happens if the taxi policies are deployed in cars with different maximal fuel-tank capacities. We can measure how well they perform for different such capacities using COOL-MC (left plot, Fig. 3). On the other hand, to reduce design or hardware costs, one might be interested in deploying a single policy with a "virtual" or abstracted maximal fuel-tank capacity. Feature remapping can obtain such policies from π_B or π_C. For example, an abstract fuel level of 6 means that all fuel levels 6–10 will be perceived as fuel level 6. The modified policy can then be evaluated in the original MDP (middle plot, Fig. 3). Perhaps more interestingly, one can choose a particular abstraction and evaluate its performance at different physical max fuel-tank capacities (right plot, Fig. 3).

Feature Abstraction. In Fig. 2b, we first transform the trained policies π_B, π_C into permissive ones τ_B, τ_C due to, for instance, the lack of exact fuel-level sensors in the deployment hardware. To counter this loss of precision, we can get a best- and worst-case analysis under τ_B, τ_C for different fuel-level ranges. For example, a starting range of 8 means that COOL-MC creates a permissive policy that "lumps" fuel-levels 8, 9, and 10 together. Permissive policies with larger starting ranges have min/max probabilities closer together.

4 Conclusion and Future Work

We presented the tool COOL-MC, which provides a tight interaction between model checking and reinforcement learning. In the future, we will extend the tool to directly incorporate safe reinforcement learning approaches [22,25–27] and will extend the model expressivity to partially observable MDPs [29].

References

1. Alshiekh, M., Bloem, R., Ehlers, R., Könighofer, B., Niekum, S., Topcu, U.: Safe reinforcement learning via shielding. In: AAAI, pp. 2669–2678. AAAI Press (2018)
2. Bacci, E., Parker, D.: Verified probabilistic policies for deep reinforcement learning. CoRR abs/2201.03698 (2022)
3. Baier, C., Katoen, J.P.: Principles of Model Checking. MIT Press, Cambridge (2008)
4. Boron, J., Darken, C.: Developing combat behavior through reinforcement learning in wargames and simulations. In: CoG, pp. 728–731. IEEE (2020)
5. Brázdil, T., et al.: Verification of Markov decision processes using learning algorithms. In: Cassez, F., Raskin, J.-F. (eds.) ATVA 2014. LNCS, vol. 8837, pp. 98–114. Springer, Cham (2014). https://doi.org/10.1007/978-3-319-11936-6_8
6. Brockman, G., et al.: OpenAI gym. CoRR abs/1606.01540 (2016)
7. Cassez, F., David, A., Fleury, E., Larsen, K.G., Lime, D.: Efficient on-the-fly algorithms for the analysis of timed games. In: Abadi, M., de Alfaro, L. (eds.) CONCUR 2005. LNCS, vol. 3653, pp. 66–80. Springer, Heidelberg (2005). https://doi.org/10.1007/11539452_9
8. Clarke, E.M., Henzinger, T.A., Veith, H., Bloem, R. (eds.): Handbook of Model Checking. Springer, Cham (2018). https://doi.org/10.1007/978-3-319-10575-8
9. David, A., et al.: On time with minimal expected cost! In: Cassez, F., Raskin, J.-F. (eds.) ATVA 2014. LNCS, vol. 8837, pp. 129–145. Springer, Cham (2014). https://doi.org/10.1007/978-3-319-11936-6_10
10. David, A., Jensen, P.G., Larsen, K.G., Mikučionis, M., Taankvist, J.H.: UPPAAL STRATEGO. In: Baier, C., Tinelli, C. (eds.) TACAS 2015. LNCS, vol. 9035, pp. 206–211. Springer, Heidelberg (2015). https://doi.org/10.1007/978-3-662-46681-0_16
11. Dehnert, C., Junges, S., Katoen, J.-P., Volk, M.: A Storm is coming: a modern probabilistic model checker. In: Majumdar, R., Kunčak, V. (eds.) CAV 2017. LNCS, vol. 10427, pp. 592–600. Springer, Cham (2017). https://doi.org/10.1007/978-3-319-63390-9_31
12. Dräger, K., Forejt, V., Kwiatkowska, M.Z., Parker, D., Ujma, M.: Permissive controller synthesis for probabilistic systems. Log. Methods Comput. Sci. **11**(2) (2015)

13. Farazi, N.P., Zou, B., Ahamed, T., Barua, L.: Deep reinforcement learning in transportation research: a review. Transp. Res. Interdisc. Perspect. **11**, 100425 (2021)
14. García, J., Fernández, F.: A comprehensive survey on safe reinforcement learning. J. Mach. Learn. Res. **16**, 1437–1480 (2015)
15. Gros, T.P., Hermanns, H., Hoffmann, J., Klauck, M., Köhl, M.A., Wolf, V.: MoGym: using formal models for training and verifying decision-making agents. In: Shoham, S., Vizel, Y. (eds.) CAV 2022. LNCS, vol. 13372, pp. 430–443. Springer, Cham (2022). https://doi.org/10.1007/978-3-031-13188-2_21
16. Gross, D., Jansen, N., Junges, S., Perez, G.A.: COOL-MC: a comprehensive tool for reinforcement learning and model checking. arXiv preprint arXiv:2209.07133 (2022)
17. Gu, R., Jensen, P.G., Poulsen, D.B., Seceleanu, C., Enoiu, E., Lundqvist, K.: Verifiable strategy synthesis for multiple autonomous agents: a scalable approach. Int. J. Softw. Tools Technol. Transfer **24**, 395–414 (2022). https://doi.org/10.1007/s10009-022-00657-z
18. Hahn, E.M., Perez, M., Schewe, S., Somenzi, F., Trivedi, A., Wojtczak, D.: Omega-regular objectives in model-free reinforcement learning. In: Vojnar, T., Zhang, L. (eds.) TACAS 2019. LNCS, vol. 11427, pp. 395–412. Springer, Cham (2019). https://doi.org/10.1007/978-3-030-17462-0_27
19. Hahn, E.M., Perez, M., Schewe, S., Somenzi, F., Trivedi, A., Wojtczak, D.: Mungojerrie: reinforcement learning of linear-time objectives. CoRR abs/2106.09161 (2021)
20. Hartmanns, A., Hermanns, H.: The modest toolset: an integrated environment for quantitative modelling and verification. In: Ábrahám, E., Havelund, K. (eds.) TACAS 2014. LNCS, vol. 8413, pp. 593–598. Springer, Heidelberg (2014). https://doi.org/10.1007/978-3-642-54862-8_51
21. Hartmanns, A., Klauck, M., Parker, D., Quatmann, T., Ruijters, E.: The quantitative verification benchmark set. In: Vojnar, T., Zhang, L. (eds.) TACAS 2019. LNCS, vol. 11427, pp. 344–350. Springer, Cham (2019). https://doi.org/10.1007/978-3-030-17462-0_20
22. Hasanbeig, M., Kroening, D., Abate, A.: Towards verifiable and safe model-free reinforcement learning. In: OVERLAY@AI*IA. CEUR WS, vol. 2509, p. 1. CEUR-WS.org (2019)
23. Hasanbeig, M., Kroening, D., Abate, A.: Deep reinforcement learning with temporal logics. In: Bertrand, N., Jansen, N. (eds.) FORMATS 2020. LNCS, vol. 12288, pp. 1–22. Springer, Cham (2020). https://doi.org/10.1007/978-3-030-57628-8_1
24. Jaeger, M., Jensen, P.G., Guldstrand Larsen, K., Legay, A., Sedwards, S., Taankvist, J.H.: Teaching stratego to play ball: optimal synthesis for continuous space MDPs. In: Chen, Y.-F., Cheng, C.-H., Esparza, J. (eds.) ATVA 2019. LNCS, vol. 11781, pp. 81–97. Springer, Cham (2019). https://doi.org/10.1007/978-3-030-31784-3_5
25. Jansen, N., Könighofer, B., Junges, S., Serban, A., Bloem, R.: Safe reinforcement learning using probabilistic shields (invited paper). In: CONCUR. LIPIcs, vol. 171, pp. 3:1–3:16. Schloss Dagstuhl - Leibniz-Zentrum für Informatik (2020)
26. Jin, P., Tian, J., Zhi, D., Wen, X., Zhang, M.: Trainify: a CEGAR-driven training and verification framework for safe deep reinforcement learning. In: Shoham, S., Vizel, Y. (eds.) CAV 2022. LNCS, vol. 13371, pp. 193–218. Springer, Cham (2022). https://doi.org/10.1007/978-3-031-13185-1_10
27. Jothimurugan, K., Bansal, S., Bastani, O., Alur, R.: Specification-guided learning of nash equilibria with high social welfare. In: Shoham, S., Vizel, Y. (eds.) CAV

2022. LNCS, vol. 13372, pp. 343–363. Springer, Cham (2022). https://doi.org/10.1007/978-3-031-13188-2_17

28. Junges, S., Jansen, N., Dehnert, C., Topcu, U., Katoen, J.-P.: Safety-constrained reinforcement learning for MDPs. In: Chechik, M., Raskin, J.-F. (eds.) TACAS 2016. LNCS, vol. 9636, pp. 130–146. Springer, Heidelberg (2016). https://doi.org/10.1007/978-3-662-49674-9_8

29. Junges, S., Jansen, N., Seshia, S.A.: Enforcing almost-sure reachability in POMDPs. In: Silva, A., Leino, K.R.M. (eds.) CAV 2021. LNCS, vol. 12760, pp. 602–625. Springer, Cham (2021). https://doi.org/10.1007/978-3-030-81688-9_28

30. Kimura, H., Yamamura, M., Kobayashi, S.: Reinforcement learning by stochastic hill climbing on discounted reward. In: ICML, pp. 295–303. Morgan Kaufmann (1995)

31. Kwiatkowska, M.Z., Norman, G., Parker, D.: PRISM 2.0: a tool for probabilistic model checking. In: QEST, pp. 322–323. IEEE Computer Society (2004)

32. Levine, S., Finn, C., Darrell, T., Abbeel, P.: End-to-end training of deep visuomotor policies. J. Mach. Learn. Res. **17**, 39:1–39:40 (2016)

33. Mnih, V., et al.: Human-level control through deep reinforcement learning. Nature **518**(7540), 529–533 (2015)

34. Nakabi, T.A., Toivanen, P.: Deep reinforcement learning for energy management in a microgrid with flexible demand. Sustain. Energy Grids Netw. **25**, 100413 (2021)

35. Strehl, A.L., Diuk, C., Littman, M.L.: Efficient structure learning in factored-state MDPs. In: AAAI, pp. 645–650. AAAI Press (2007)

36. Sutton, R.S., Barto, A.G.: Reinforcement Learning: An Introduction. MIT Press, Cambridge (2018)

37. Vamplew, P., et al.: Scalar reward is not enough: a response to Silver, Singh, Precup and Sutton (2021). Auton. Agents Multi Agent Syst. **36**(2) (2022). Article number: 41. https://doi.org/10.1007/s10458-022-09575-5

38. Wang, Y., Roohi, N., West, M., Viswanathan, M., Dullerud, G.E.: Statistically model checking PCTL specifications on Markov decision processes via reinforcement learning. In: CDC, pp. 1392–1397. IEEE (2020)

39. Watkins, C.J., Dayan, P.: Q-learning. Mach. Learn. **8**(3–4), 279–292 (1992). https://doi.org/10.1007/BF00992698

40. Williams, R.J.: Simple statistical gradient-following algorithms for connectionist reinforcement learning. Mach. Learn. **8**, 229–256 (1992). https://doi.org/10.1007/BF00992696

41. Zaharia, M., et al.: Accelerating the machine learning lifecycle with MLflow. IEEE Data Eng. Bull. **41**(4), 39–45 (2018)

Dependable Software Development

VM Migration and Live-Update for Reliable Embedded Hypervisor

Siran Li, Lei Wang$^{(\boxtimes)}$, Keyang Hu, Ce Mo, and Bo Jiang

Beihang University, Beijing 100191, People's Republic of China
{ohmrlsr,wanglei,hky1999,moce4917,jiangbo}@buaa.edu.cn

Abstract. With the development of hardware virtualization technology, more and more embedded hypervisors are being implemented. Traditional embedded hypervisors focus on resource utilization and real-time performance while neglecting the reliability requirements of embedded applications. In this paper, we implement two fault-tolerant mechanisms for an embedded hypervisor, which makes hypervisor more reliable without significant downtime. We apply VM migration to provide a runtime fault-tolerance mechanism to further enhance hypervisor reliability. To guarantee the regular operation of critical tasks during fault recovery, this paper implements a hypervisor live-update mechanism to complete fault recovery while avoiding migration network delays. Test results show that these mechanisms combine reliability and operational efficiency to meet the needs of embedded applications.

Keywords: Embedded hypervisor · Live-update · Migration · Reliability

1 Introduction

With the development of information systems and embedded technology, embedded software puts forward higher requirements for system reliability [16]. At the same time, many fault detection and fault-tolerant mechanisms have been proposed. The commonly used fault tolerance mechanism for embedded systems is dual-machine redundancy [21]. This mechanism can avoid hardware errors by hardware redundancy, which can effectively improve the reliability of embedded systems. However, this approach greatly reduces the resource utilization and causes a great waste of the limited hardware resources of the embedded platform. Software implementation of system reset is also one of the common fault tolerance solutions, such as the watchdog mechanism of Linux, which can record fault information and complete a reboot after a fault occurs. However, with the introduction of embedded virtualisation technology, it is difficult to replicate software fault tolerance at the system level for virtualised platforms, and software fault tolerance mechanisms can increase the complexity of the system code. How to ensure the reliability of the embedded hypervisor has become a challenge that needs to be addressed.

© The Author(s), under exclusive license to Springer Nature Switzerland AG 2022
W. Dong and J.-P. Talpin (Eds.): SETTA 2022, LNCS 13649, pp. 53–69, 2022.
https://doi.org/10.1007/978-3-031-21213-0_4

With the development of virtualization technology, more and more embedded hypervisors have been proposed and implemented. In order to meet the scenario requirements of mixed critical systems, existing embedded hypervisors often focus on attributes such as resource isolation and real-time performance [11], while ignoring the fault tolerance capability of hypervisor. Hypervisors such as ACRN [14] and Bao [15] have implemented many device models and can support multiple types of device virtualization, which can greatly improve resource utilization. At the same time, these hypervisors can also ensure the real-time performance of critical virtual machines (VM) and meet the real-time requirements of embedded applications by device pass-through mechanism. In terms of reliability, mainstream embedded hypervisors mainly focus on lightweight code implementation and formal verification, and often do not implement fault tolerance mechanisms and fault recovery functions. These hypervisors have smaller trusted computing bases (TCB) and are more reliable than hypervisors for cloud services [17]. However, lightweight code implementation cannot guarantee the safety and reliability of the hypervisor, and the lack of fault tolerance will make it difficult to meet the reliability requirement.

On the other hand, mainstream hypervisors usually use C language as the programming language. C has high operating efficiency with simple and flexible memory access logic, but it also causes many memory safety problems. C lacks strict syntax constraints and the assignment process can lose data precision. C can also access data at arbitrary addresses through pointer operations, which poses a significant threat to memory security [8]. Once these actions trigger vulnerabilities in embedded application scenarios, they will be difficult to remedy from the hypervisor level.

In order to solve these problems above, we designed and implemented a new type-1 embedded hypervisor. The contributions of this paper are as follows:

- We implement the VM migration and achieve fault tolerance through VM migration.
- We implement the hypervisor live-update and provide fault recovery capability.
- We provide differentiated services for different VMs, and provide good resource isolation capabilities and real-time performance.

2   Related Work

2.1   Embedded Hypervisor

KVM hypervisor [9] executes on Linux as a kernel module and provides a virtualized environment by QEMU [5]. KVM-QEMU makes full use of Linux device drivers and system services to provide more device modules, but it also expands the attack surface, which makes it difficult for KVM to meet the embedded requirement [2].

To solve this problem, various virtualization products (Jailhouse [19], Bao [15], ACRN [14]) have been proposed and implemented in recent years.

These hypervisors implement a variety of device models, have good resource isolation capabilities, and ensure the real-time performance of critical VMs. Compared with service-oriented hypervisors such as KVM and Xen [13], embedded hypervisors have a smaller code size, which can effectively reduce the number of possible code vulnerabilities. At the same time, due to the lightweight code of the embedded hypervisor, hypervisor reliability can be further guaranteed by means of formal verification.

These features ensure fewer software failures during operation, but due to the lack of fault tolerance mechanism, most embedded virtualization products do not have the ability to recover from failure. In the face of known code vulnerabilities, they can only be recovered by shutting down, updating the image, and restarting.

2.2   Virtual Machine Migration

Modern hypervisors are becoming increasingly complex, which often makes reliability difficult to guarantee. To circumvent hidden hypervisor bugs, administrators can periodically reset the service state through rebooting. This can alleviate possible problems in the short term, but some hidden bugs can still affect the system in the long term. On the other hand, an upgrade or reset of the hypervisor can cause an interruption during service, so there is a need to provide a mechanism to dynamically repair the hypervisor.

VM migration can migrate a running VM from the hypervisor on one hardware platform to another, or replace the hypervisor image without restarting the hypervisor and avoiding possible failures.

VM migration can be divided into three categories according to the timing of memory migration: pre-copy, post-copy [12] and hybrid-copy [3]. The main difference between these three migration strategies is the treatment of dirty pages, which are memory pages that have been transferred over the network but are written again by the virtual machine. Pre-copy is the most dominant migration method, which involves multiple rounds of memory copy and converging the number of dirty pages to a smaller data size before the VM is shut down for migration. Post-copy copies the VM state set to the target platform at the start of the migration and runs the VMs directly on the target platform. This mechanism further reduces downtime as the VM state set is much smaller than a dirty memory page. However, if the new VM accesses unmigrated memory data during runtime, an exception will be triggered and the corresponding memory data will need to be read from the source platform via network service. Hybrid-copy combines the two strategies by copying only the VM state set to the target platform once the dirty pages have converged to an acceptable size, leaving the remaining dirty pages to be handled in the same way as post-copy. This approach reduces the pressure on memory copies after the VM is started, but suffers from the same unreliability and low access performance.

Although pre-copy has significant downtime, it is still widely used in all types of hypervisors due to its reliability. Stefan Groesbrink and others tried to apply VM migration technology to hypervisor fault tolerance [10]. Through VM migration, hypervisor can migrate unaffected VMs to backup hardware when a failure occurs, ensuring the normal operation of VMs. This function does not require additional code support from the operating system or bare-metal applications, and can be implemented by the hypervisor's own function modules. However, VM migration relies on the network for data transmission, and high network transmission cost may harm the real-time performance of embedded applications.

2.3 Hypervisor Update

In order to solve the high cost of VM migration, Hardik Bagdi et al. used the nested virtualization technology of KVM to complete the local update of hypervisor, and named it HyperFresh [4]. HyperFresh uses the shared memory communication interface to transmit data, which avoids the cost of original network transmission and greatly improves the efficiency of VM migration. Nested virtualisation technology is also often used to improve fault tolerance. By introducing nested virtualisation, a more flexible mechanism for monitoring and recovering virtual machines can be implemented, further increasing system reliability [20]. However, as a hypervisor for cloud services, KVM cannot be directly applied to embedded scenarios. On the other hand, due to the resource constraints of the hardware platform, only a few embedded hypervisors support the nested virtualization.

In addition to type-2 hypervisor KVM, researchers have also experimented with introducing hypervisor live-update functionality for Xen [6]. By replacing image on the same hardware platform, the VMs continue to run in the new hypervisor environment, avoiding network transfers across hardware. From testing results, Xen's live-update has a performance advantage over VM migration. However, there is still millisecond-level downtime and live-update for multi-core VMs are not supported. Overall, replacing hypervisor images with memory copies is a viable option, but how to meet the needs of embedded systems remains a challenge.

3 The Design of Hypervisor

3.1 System Structure

The new hypervisor aims to be an efficient, scalable and real-time hypervisor. The design goals are as follows:

- We need to provide a small trusted computing base of hypervisor.
- We need to provide VM migration mechanism for fault tolerance.
- We need to provide hypervisor local live-update to respond more efficiently for hypervisor failures.
- We need to ensure isolation between different VMs.
- We need to be able to offer differentiated services for VMs.
- We need to guarantee the real-time performance of critical VMs.

The hypervisor implemented in this paper truly supports the following virtual machine types for different requirements. For management VM (MVM), we implement a dedicated Linux kernel module for MVM. Through this module, MVM can call the hypercall interface to realize functions such as VM migration and hypervisor live-update. For general-purpose VM (GVM), the computing tasks running on it do not have real-time characteristics. For soft real-time VM (SRTVM), we need to ensure its real-time performance. In the live-update process, the CPU assigned for SRTVMs needs to undertake less computing tasks, thereby shortening the VM-Exit [18] time and ensuring real-time performance. For hard real-time VM (HRTVM), we uses a completely exclusive resource allocation method to ensure its real-time performance. In the process of live-update, it is also necessary to prioritise the real-time performance of HRTVM.

Fault tolerance in traditional embedded systems usually requires additional support from the system, and this software support is only applicable to the current system and is not very versatile. In contrast, the hypervisor implemented in this paper supports multiple VM types, which means that the fault tolerance mechanism of the hypervisor should meet the needs of different VMs and be able to perform fault recovery for bare-metal applications. On the other hand, the hypervisor implements multiple device models such as passthrough devices, emulated devices, virtio devices, and so on, so fault tolerance requires the ability to maintain the state of each type of device. For generic GVMs, the hypervisor does not need to consider the time cost of fault tolerance, for SRTVM and HRTVM, the hypervisor needs to ensure that fault recovery does not affect the real-time performance of the task.

The VM migration and hypervisor live-update techniques implemented in this paper do not require additional support from the VM to update the hypervisor. The implementation of VM migration and hypervisor live-update can perform fault recovery within microsecond latency, thus ensuring the real-time requirements of SRTVM and HRTVM. This is described in Sects. 3.3 and 3.4.

3.2 Shared Memory

The shared memory mechanism is an efficient communication method, enabling high-speed data transfer between VMs and hypervisor, and is widely used in the VM migration and live-update mechanisms.

In the case of VM migration, for example, as the data transfer action is performed by the MVM, the MVM will frequently read the memory data of the GVM. Therefore, a shared memory mechanism is needed to enable the MVM to access the GVM's data without triggering any exceptions.

Based on ARMv8 virtualization, the physical address operated by the VM is called intermediated physical address (IPA), which is obtained by completing the address translation through the page table provided by the hypervisor. In order to achieve the effect of memory sharing between VMs, the hypervisor needs to maintain the range of IPAs currently occupied by MVMs, and then selects a section of IPA address space that has not yet been mapped, to create an address map for the GVM memory space. The hypervisor then informs the

MVM of the IPA address range and the MVM's kernel module establishes the mapping of the virtual address to the new IPA address space. Once the two-stage address mapping is established, the MVM is able to access GVM memory data via regular memory read and write instructions. In addition to sharing memory between VMs, we also enables memory sharing between MVMs and hypervisors. This feature will be used in live-update to assist the MVM with the loading of hypervisor images.

The hypervisor can specify address mapping permissions according to the use of shared memory. For example, in a VM migration scenario where the MVM only needs to read the memory data of the GVM, hypervisor can specify address translation permissions as read-only to prevent the MVM from causing damage to the GVM memory data and further guarantee memory isolation.

3.3 VM Migration

When a hardware failure occurs and has not affected the normal operation of the VM, hypervisor can perform fault recovery by means of VM migration. It is also possible to replace the hypervisor image to fix known vulnerabilities. VM migration requires memory dirty page tracking, memory copying, and device state migration etc. In addition to the migration service provided by the hypervisor, the MVM needs to provide the network service for migration between different hardwares.

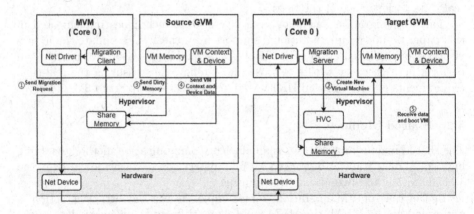

Fig. 1. VM migration process

The VM migration process is shown in Fig. 1. Firstly, MVM initiates a migration request through network to start VM migration. Then hypervisor on the target platform will allocate resources and create VM structure after receiving the request. If the target platform successfully creates a VM, the MVM network process reads the dirty page information of the source VM through the shared memory, and sends it to the target platform according to the dirty page bitmap.

During the migration process, the source VM can still access memory normally, while the hypervisor needs to intercept the memory write operation and record the dirty page corresponding to the address into the bitmap. After the in-memory data migration is complete, hypervisor needs to check whether the number of dirty pages exceeds the threshold. If so, hypervisor needs to transfer memory dirty pages again. When the number of dirty pages is below the threshold, the current platform will pause the source VM, and send the remaining dirty pages, VM context, and device data to the target platform. Eventually, the VM will continue to run on the target platform successfully.

VM migration is initiated and executed by the MVM. During this process, the MVM reads the target VM memory data several times via shared memory and sends the VM data to the target hardware platform via net request. The benefits are the following:

- We can reduce the disruption to the source VM by shifting the migration pressure from the source VM to the MVM.
- The source VM does not have to support net services, hypercall etc., to perform the migration which increase the applicability of the migration functionality.
- The MVM's physical network interface controller (NIC) provides better network transfer performance than the virtio NIC, further improving migration efficiency.

Due to the high network latency associated with large amounts of data copying, hypervisor does not send all of the VM memory data to the destination at once.

In order to reduce the impact of the migration on the VMs, hypervisor does not stop the source VMs during the data copying process of migration. While this is good for the performance of the VM, it introduces a new problem that the memory data which has been transferred can be modified by the running VM. Such pages are called dirty pages and need to be tracked by hypervisor and re-migrated during the next round of memory data transfers. This migration cost is considered acceptable to the VM when the number of dirty pages is less than a specified threshold. Only then does hypervisor terminate the VM and transfer the remaining dirty pages along with the VM state data to the target hardware, and completes the VM migration action. The time cost of a single exception handling has been tested to be $2\,\mu s$, with no serious impact on the performance of the VM computation.

The implementation of memory dirty page tracking relies on the ARMv8 memory management unit mechanism. When a migration request is initiated, hypervisor changes the stage-two page table permissions from read and write to read-only. Under this permission, the VM can still read data in memory, but when the VM attempts a memory write operation, an address translation exception is raised and caught by the hypervisor. During the exception handling process, hypervisor records the dirty page information in the bitmap and restores write access to the corresponding page. This can prevent unnecessary exceptions caused by VM writing the same page multiple times, further guaranteeing VM performance.

In addition to the memory accesses performed by the VM, some devices also perform write operations to memory. In the case of the virtio block, for example, when a VM initiates a block read request, hypervisor writes the block data to the specified VM memory. This hypervisor-initiated memory write operation does not trigger the address translation mechanism provided for the VM, thus circumventing the existing exception handling process. For such memory operations, if the VM is in a migrated state, hypervisor needs to track and process the memory write in virtio backend, log the dirty page information and restore the page table permissions.

Since the ARMv8 architecture doesn't provide dirty page tracking mechanism, the function of dirty page tracking is implemented by the hypervisor. On the other hand, hypervisor supports the migration of devices such as virtio net, virtio console, and virtual generic interrupt controller (vGIC). The types of VMs currently supported for migration include bare-metal application, ramdisk linux and network file system (NFS) linux, and the types of devices supported for migration include vGIC, virtio console and virtio net.

3.4 Hypervisor Live-Update

The implementation of VM migration is capable of handling most types of failures during the migration process while ensuring that the VMs are operational. However, like other mainstream hypervisor migrations implementations, we stop the VM before the last data transfer and do not resume until the remaining data has been transferred over the network to the target hardware platform. This process still introduces milliseconds of downtime, which has an impact on the execution of the VM's tasks.

To solve this problem, this paper designs and implements a live-update mechanism that can be used to fix known hypervisor vulnerabilities or update the hypervisor's code implementation. Compared with VM migration, live-update does not require data migration across devices and has lower migration costs. Live-update not only improves the fault tolerance of the hypervisor, but also ensures the real-time performance of cirtical VMs.

In live-update mechanism, the old hypervisor acts as a data provider, while the new hypervisor provides processing functions that accept and store data from the old hypervisor. The main process of live-update is shown in Fig. 2.

- MVM initiates a live-update request through hypercall, stores the new hypervisor image in the exception level 2 (EL2) heap space, and sends interprocessor interrupt (IPI) to other cores to inform that a new live-update action is in progress.
- After core 0 packs the data address, hypervisor calls the assembly function live_update to jump to the corresponding entry of the new image.
- Core 0 calls the live-update processing function to store the hypervisor data; other cores need to migrate the CPU private data after receiving IPI.

- Core 0 resets the exception vector table, and then returns to Exception Level 1 (EL1) to continue executing VM tasks.

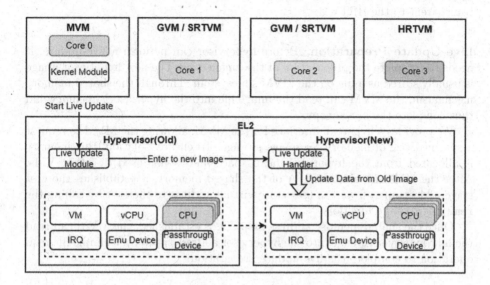

Fig. 2. Hypervisor live-update model

In the live-update process, data packaging is done by the old hypervisor, and data processing functions are implemented by the new hypervisor, which allows the new hypervisor to add or delete fields in the old data structure, or even completely modify the processing flow of exceptions and interruptions, so as to fix more types of code loopholes of the hypervisor.

In order to minimize the impact of live-update on other VMs, the core 0 owned by MVM will complete the copying of the data on the heap. However, the CPU structure is maintained by each core separately, and other cores cannot access this segment of data across cores, so the data must be migrated independently by each core.

The virtual address of the CPU structure is specified by the hypervisor. Through the memory mapping mechanism, different cores can get their own CPU structure by accessing the same virtual address. After triggering live-update, the new hypervisor can still access the original CPU structure through the same virtual address. This means that when the core updates the CPU structure, static properties such as CPUId do not need to be reassigned, and the core only need to focus on the update of the pointer. This design further reduces the workload of CPU structure update, thereby ensuring that the live-update will not have a great impact on the state of the VM.

For HRTVM, due to the use of generic interrupt controller (GIC) pass-through, device pass-through, ramdisk file system and other strategies, it never traps into the EL2 during its operation. Therefore, during the live-update process, hypervisor can temporarily not update the CPU structure where the HRTVM is located. The update operation is performed when it actively trap into EL2 or shut down. This ensures that the live-update action is completely transparent to the HRTVM.

Live-Update Preparation. Before hypervisor can perform a live-update, it needs to complete the preparation of the image copy. The new hypervisor image is usually stored as a file on the MVM's filesystem. Through the shared memory mechanism, the MVM can read the image file into the hypervisor's memory and thus complete the image copy.

We provides a hypercall interface for the MVM, allowing the MVM to request a specified size of memory for image storage. To ensure isolation, this memory is allocated from the hypervisor heap space and is not used by other VMs. After the MVM obtains the IPA of the shared memory, it establishes the first stage address map from the user state virtual address to the IPA by calling the remap_pfn_range function.

Once the shared memory address mapping is established, the MVM can read the new hypervisor image into the hypervisor address space via a simple file read operation to complete the live-update preparation.

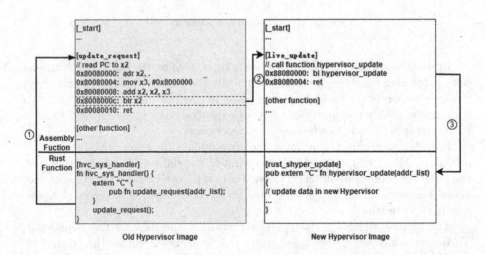

Fig. 3. Live-update image transfer

Live-Update Image Transfer. To implement the switch between the old and new hypervisor images, we implemented the live-update request and handler functions in assembly.

The hypervisor live-update image transfer flow is shown in Fig. 3. Firstly, as the live-update initiator, MVM triggers the hvc_sys_handler handler function via the hypercall, which actively calls the update_request assembly handler function. The live_update function for the new image has a fixed address deviation from the update_request function for the old image. So the address of the live_update function can be obtained by adding a fixed offset to the 'pc' value. Finally live_update actively calls the processing function hypervisor_update to complete the subsequent update action.

As the new image may make changes to some functions, this affects the layout of the code segment. To avoid this affecting the address offsets between the interfaces of the live-update functions, we implement this group of functions after the startup function, ensuring that there are no functions in the hypervisor code segment before the live-update assembly functions other than the startup function. The startup function is only called once during the startup process and is not called again during runtime, thus not triggering any possible security vulnerability, so there is no need to modify this part of the function. This ensures the address offsets of the live-update functions in the old and new image are not affected by other code changes.

Pre Update. Once the live-update has started, each core will trap into the hypervisor to make a copy of the data. There are dependencies between these data, e.g. there is an array of vCPU pointers in the CPU data structure, which needs to be updated after the vCPU update is complete. The CPU structure is private to each core and needs to be updated independently by each CPU, while the vCPU data is a public structure and is updated by core 0. This design may result in some cores entering the hypervisor and having to wait for core 0 to perform the preorder data update, affecting the performance of live-update.

To address this issue, hypervisor is pre-updated by core 0 before live-update. During this process, core 0 enters a new hypervisor image and completes the creation of the structure in the new runtime environment. The created structures are placeholder with default values and the assignment process will be completed during the live-update phase. Due to the presence of the placeholder structure, even though no assignment is performed, it is sufficient for other cores to support the pointer assignment required during the update process.

Final Update. After entering the live-update process, the runtime environment will switch to the new hypervisor image. The data structure of the old image can still be accessed via a pointer and the new system structure can be assigned by these data.

The update of the system structure can be divided into two steps: data parsing and data updating. The old hypervisor provides a list of data pointers to the new hypervisor. During the data parsing process, the new hypervisor dereferences the pointers in the list, keeping the data type the same as the old hypervisor, so that it can get the complete system structure data. During the data update process, hypervisor needs to call the data processing functions provided by the new image to complete the assignment of the system structure. In this mode, since the processing functions are provided by the new image, the data update can be completed even if the system structure has changed.

In addition to the data on the heap, live-updates also need to be concerned with changes to certain handling functions. In the case of exception handling functions, for example, hypervisor stores information about the exception vector table via the ARMv8 register vbar_el2. The live-update process requires resetting the value of this register to enable the exception handling functions provided by the new image.

On the other hand, hypervisor maintains a list of interrupt handling functions, including clock interrupts, IPIs, maintenance interrupts, etc. Hypervisor needs to actively update this list of functions during the live-update process to ensure that the hypervisor can index the correct interrupt handling function by interrupt number.

4   Evaluation

4.1   Environment

We deployed the hypervisor on an ARMv8 NVIDIA Jetson TX2 platform [1] for experiment and the hardware information shown in Table 1.

Table 1. Hardware information

CPU	HMP Dual Denver 2/2MB L2 Quad Arm Cortex-A57/2MB L2 @ 2.0 GHz
RAM	8 GB 128 Bit LPDDR4
INTC	GIC-400 (GICV2)
Storage	32 GB eMMC 5.1 Intel SSD 520 Series 240 GB
Network	10/100/1000 BASE-T Ethernet

In order to verify the effectiveness of the live-update implemented in this paper, this paper compares the performance difference between live-update and VM migration, whose performance is affected by network bandwidth, memory access frequency, dirty page threshold and other factors. In this paper, to ensure test fairness, no IO pressure is applied to GVM, and NFS rootfs is provided to avoid the cost of disk migration, further ensuring the performance of VM migration. The live-update implemented in this paper is not affected by VM memory access frequency and has no additional restrictions on file system types, which can better complete the update of hypervisor images.

In order to guarantee the reliability of the test results, we provided the VM with multiple device types and sufficient memory resources. The configuration information of the VMs under test is shown in Table 2.

Table 2. GVM information

VM type	Linux 4.9.140
RAM	2 GB 128 Bit LPDDR4
INTC	vGIC
Serial	Virtio Console
Network	Virtio Net
Root file system	NFS/Virtio Block

4.2 Impact on Real-Time Performance

The live-update is designed to address the serious impact of millisecond network delays caused by migration on real-time tasks. This paper uses cyclictest [7] to test the real-time performance of the VMs.

The cyclictest test results are shown in Fig. 4. For GVM, the average latency without live-update is $7\,\mu s$ and the maximum latency is $24\,\mu s$. When VM migration action is introduced, the average latency of rises to $12\,\mu s$ and the maximum latency reaches $7537\,\mu s$. such latency will have a serious impact on real-time tasks and is difficult to meet the requirements of embedded scenarios. When live-update is triggered during the cyclictest test, the average latency is still $7\,\mu s$ and the maximum latency rises to $36\,\mu s$. The live-update has little impact on the cyclictest results as the core is only responsible for the migration of CPU private data. Compared to the millisecond jitter caused by VM migration, the latency introduced by live-update is no more than $36\,\mu s$, which is a significant performance advantage for real-time tasks in embedded scenarios.

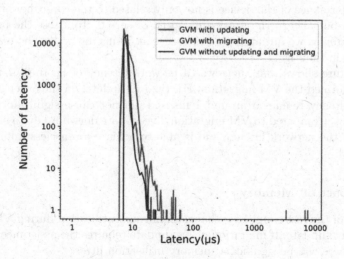

Fig. 4. Hypervisor migration and live-update real-time performance

4.3 Impact on Networking

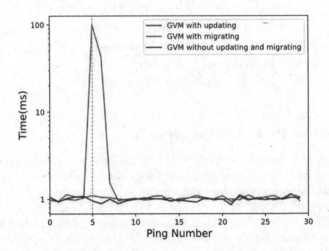

Fig. 5. Hypervisor migration and live-update net performance

The real-time test evaluates the performance of a single core live-update. Since most of the data is migrated by core 0, hypervisor guarantees the real-time performance of the VM by differentiating the workload. In addition to the real-time tests, this paper evaluates the impact of the live-update feature on network performance. As the migration of data from the emulated device is done by core 0, the performance of the device is not only related to the core where the GVM is located, but also to the processing speed of core 0. To assess the impact on network latency, we initiated ping messages at 50 ms intervals. The test results are shown in the Fig. 5.

The figure shows that there was a network latency of up to 99.7 ms when GVM performed the VM migration. For the live-update, on the other hand, the network latency remained around 1 ms and did not cause significant network fluctuations. Compared to VM migration, live-update does not have a significant impact on the network latency and is able to achieve a senseless update effect on the VM.

4.4 Impact on Memory

This part of the test counts the change in memory utilisation during VM migration and live-update. If migration or live-update requires the assistance of a VM process, there will be significant memory utilisation jitter.

The results are shown in Fig. 6. The data shows that there is no significant memory jitter during VM migration and live-update execution. For VM migration, the main part that requires VM participation is the linux network data

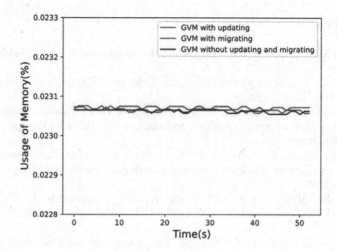

Fig. 6. Hypervisor migration and live-update memory usage performance

transfer. The VM migration designed and implemented in this paper shifts the pressure of data transfer from the GVM to the MVM, thus eliminating the need for the GVM to create and execute processes, and effectively ensuring the stability of the GVM. For live-update, the part that requires VM participation is the copy of the hypervisor image. This is usually done during the preparation phase of the live-update, and the image copy is initiated by the MVM, without affecting the GVM's operational state.

5   Conclusion

To deal with failure scenarios during operation, this article implements VM migration and hypervisor live-update. VM migration can cope with most failure scenarios. When a failure occurs, VM can be restored to the new hardware platform by means of VM migration.

Hypervisor live-update is a new fault-tolerant method proposed in this paper, which can effectively reduce the update delay without additional hardware redundancy and improve resource utilization. During the live-update, hypervisor can assign different update tasks according to the CPU type, thus ensuring the execution of critical tasks.

The results of our experimental evaluation confirms that the live-update implemented in this paper can ensure the real-time performance and meet the reliability requirements of embedded application. The performance of live-update is also independent of the network environment and task density of the VMs, providing better availability. Overall, these mechanisms can be used as the general solutions for embedded virtualization.

Acknowledgment. This work was partially supported by National Natural Science Foundation of China (No. 62077002) and Huawei Innovation Research Plan.

References

1. Jetson TX2 Module: NVIDIA Developer. developer.nvidia.com/embedded/jetson-tx2
2. Abeni, L., Faggioli, D.: Using Xen and KVM as real-time hypervisors. J. Syst. Archit. **106**, 101709 (2020)
3. Altahat, M.A., Agarwal, A., Goel, N., Kozlowski, J.: Dynamic hybrid-copy live virtual machine migration: analysis and comparison. Procedia Comput. Sci. **171**, 1459–1468 (2020)
4. Bagdi, H., Kugve, R., Gopalan, K.: HyperFresh: live refresh of hypervisors using nested virtualization. In: Proceedings of the 8th Asia-Pacific Workshop on Systems, pp. 1–8 (2017)
5. Bellard, F.: QEMU, a fast and portable dynamic translator. In: USENIX Annual Technical Conference. FREENIX Track, California, USA, vol. 41, pp. 10–5555 (2005)
6. Brasser, F.F., Bucicoiu, M., Sadeghi, A.R.: Swap and play: live updating hypervisors and its application to Xen. In: Proceedings of the 6th Edition of the ACM Workshop on Cloud Computing Security, pp. 33–44 (2014)
7. Cerqueira, F., Brandenburg, B.: A comparison of scheduling latency in Linux. PREEMPT-RT, and LITMUS-RT, July 2013
8. Cutler, C.: The benefits and costs of writing a POSIX Kernel in a high-level language. Ph.D. thesis, Massachusetts Institute of Technology (2019)
9. Dall, C., Nieh, J.: KVM/ARM: the design and implementation of the Linux ARM hypervisor. ACM SIGPLAN Not. **49**(4), 333–348 (2014)
10. Groesbrink, S.: Virtual machine migration as a fault tolerance technique for embedded real-time systems. In: 2014 IEEE Eighth International Conference on Software Security and Reliability-Companion, pp. 7–12. IEEE (2014)
11. Heiser, G.: The role of virtualization in embedded systems. In: Proceedings of the 1st Workshop on Isolation and Integration in Embedded Systems, pp. 11–16 (2008)
12. Hines, M.R., Deshpande, U., Gopalan, K.: Post-copy live migration of virtual machines. ACM SIGOPS Oper. Syst. Rev. **43**(3), 14–26 (2009)
13. Hwang, J.Y., et al.: Xen on ARM: system virtualization using Xen hypervisor for ARM-based secure mobile phones. In: 2008 5th IEEE Consumer Communications and Networking Conference, pp. 257–261. IEEE (2008)
14. Li, H., Xu, X., Ren, J., Dong, Y.: ACRN: a big little hypervisor for IoT development. In: Proceedings of the 15th ACM SIGPLAN/SIGOPS International Conference on Virtual Execution Environments, pp. 31–44 (2019)
15. Martins, J., Tavares, A., Solieri, M., Bertogna, M., Pinto, S.: Bao: a lightweight static partitioning hypervisor for modern multi-core embedded systems. In: Workshop on Next Generation Real-Time Embedded Systems (NG-RES 2020). Schloss Dagstuhl-Leibniz-Zentrum fuer Informatik (2020)
16. Narayanan, V., Xie, Y.: Reliability concerns in embedded system designs. Computer **39**(1), 118–120 (2006)
17. Pan, W., Zhang, Y., Yu, M., Jing, J.: Improving virtualization security by splitting hypervisor into smaller components. In: Cuppens-Boulahia, N., Cuppens, F., Garcia-Alfaro, J. (eds.) DBSec 2012. LNCS, vol. 7371, pp. 298–313. Springer, Heidelberg (2012). https://doi.org/10.1007/978-3-642-31540-4_23
18. Ramsauer, R., Kiszka, J., Lohmann, D., Mauerer, W.: Look mum, no VM exits! (Almost). arXiv preprint arXiv:1705.06932 (2017)
19. Sinitsyn, V.: Jailhouse. Linux J. **2015**(252), 2 (2015)

20. Tkachov, V., Hunko, M., Volotka, V.: Scenarios for implementation of nested virtualization technology in task of improving cloud firewall fault tolerance. In: 2019 IEEE International Scientific-Practical Conference Problems of Infocommunications, Science and Technology (PIC S&T), pp. 759–763. IEEE (2019)
21. Xu, Z., Liu, H., Liu, Y.: Fault tolerance technique based on state real-time synchronization. In: 2021 IEEE International Conference on Data Science and Computer Application (ICDSCA), pp. 61–65. IEEE (2021)

Mastery: Shifted-Code-Aware Structured Merging

Fengmin Zhu[1,4] , Xingyu Xie[1] , Dongyu Feng[1] , Na Meng[5],
and Fei He[1,2,3(✉)]

[1] School of Software, Tsinghua University, Beijing, China
hefei@tsinghua.edu.cn
[2] Key Laboratory for Information System Security, MoE, Beijing, China
[3] Beijing National Research Center for Information Science and Technology, Beijing, China
[4] Max Planck Institute for Software Systems, Saarbrücken, Germany
[5] Virginia Tech, Blacksburg, USA

Abstract. Three-way merging is an essential infrastructure in version control systems. While the traditional line-based textual methods are efficient, syntax-based structured approaches have shown advantages in enhancing merge accuracy. Prior structured merging approaches visit abstract syntax trees in a top-down manner, which is hard to detect and merge shifted code in the general sense. This paper presents a novel methodology combining a top-down and a bottom-up visit of abstract syntax trees, which manipulates shifted code effectively and elegantly. This merge algorithm is order-preserving and linear-time. Compared with four representative merge tools in 40,533 real-world merge scenarios, our approach achieves the highest merge accuracy and 2.4× as fast as a state-of-the-art structured merge tool.

Keywords: Version control systems · Three-way merging · Structured merging · Shifted code

1 Introduction

Thanks to the wide application of version control systems such as Git and SVN, *three-way merging* has become an indispensable task in contemporary software development. A *three-way merge scenario* (*base, left, right*) consists of three versions of a program, where the two *variants left* and *right* are both evolved independently, possibly by different developers, from their ancestor *base*. A three-way merge algorithm integrates the changes made by the variants and produces a merged version called a *target*. When the two variants (i.e., branches) introduce changes that are contradicted, according to *three-way merge principles*, a *conflict* shall be reported, leaving the developers to manually resolve them. The

---

Early revisions of this work were done when F. Zhu was in Tsinghua University.
F. Zhu and X. Xie—Contributed equally.

three-way merge principles conservatively describe whether the changes could be correctly integrated.

Unstructured Merge is a mature merging approach that regards programs as a sequence of lines of plain text. Since the context-free syntax is neglected, merge accuracy is yet unsatisfying—studies [16,17] have shown the presence of *false conflicts* (i.e., the conflicts that should have been avoided), which increases the user burden of manual resolution. To enhance merge accuracy, *structured merge*, representing programs as *abstract syntax trees* (ASTs), has gained significant research interest in recent decades [1,2,5,15,16,23,24]. A structured merge algorithm takes a set of mappings between different program versions as input and computes a merged version as output. The mappings are obtained by AST differencing (also known as AST matching) algorithms [6,7,9].

To compute a target AST, a structured merge algorithm needs to traverse the input ASTs (i.e., *base*, *left*, and *right*). Prior approaches [1,2,5,15,16,23,24] all use a *top-down* order, which is quite natural and intuitive as it follows the structure of ASTs. Such a top-down AST comparison is usually restricted to be *level-wise*—only AST nodes at the same level (or depth) get compared, which makes it hard to detect if one piece of code is shifted into another, namely *shifted code* [14]. To identify shifted code in a top-down manner, one could search for the *largest common embedded subtree*. This problem, however, is known to be $\mathcal{NP}$-hard and difficult to approximate for general cases [22]. A more scalable approach is to employ *syntax-aware looking ahead* matching [14], but: looking ahead is only enabled for a few types of AST nodes; the maximum looking-ahead distance is short for efficiency considerations. Their work focuses on the AST matching problem; how to correctly merge shifted code remains an issue.

Thinking oppositely, we find a *bottom-up* traversing order a better option. The key to detecting shifted code is to allow node mappings across AST levels, which is natural and easier via a bottom-up manner. Meanwhile, top-down merging cannot handle across-level mappings, which means bottom-up merging is needed as the follow-up of the matching phase. Sometimes, the bottom-up visit *alone* incurs redundant computations. As an extreme example, if *left* is the same as *base*, meaning no changes are introduced on *left*, then by three-way merge principles, *right* introduces unique changes and should be the target version— there is no need to further inspect any of their descendants as in a bottom-up manner. We fix this issue by bringing in top-down merging.

Combining a top-down pruning pass and a bottom-up pass, we present a novel three-way structured merge algorithm, where the trivial merge scenarios are processed in the former pass, and other nontrivial merge scenarios, which may involve shifted code, are carefully operated in the latter pass. Because our algorithm is non-backtracking, the time complexity is linear.

Like in JDime [16], we distinguish if the children of an AST node list can be "safely permuted" (i.e., the permutation preserves semantics). If not, the list is called *ordered* (e.g., a sequence of statements) and a good merge algorithm should preserve the original occurrence order of the children in the merged version, which we call *order-preservation*. We reduce this problem into computing a topological sort of a directed graph (that encodes required constraints), which is solvable by linear-time graph algorithms such as Kahn's algorithm [13].

We implemented our approach as a structured merge tool called Mastery[1]. To measure its usability and practicality in real scenarios, we extract 40,533 merge scenarios from 78 open-source Java projects. We identified that shifted code occurs in 38.54% merge scenarios, and conduct experimental comparisons with four representative tools: JDime (structured), jFSTMerge (tree-based semistructured), IntelliMerge (graph-based semistructured), and GitMerge (unstructured). Our results show: (1) Mastery achieves the highest merge accuracy of 82.26%; (2) Mastery reports the fewest 9.09% conflicts and the fewest 6,791 conflict blocks, excluding radical IntelliMerge; (3) Mastery is about 2.4× as fast as JDime, and about 1.3× as fast as jFSTMerge. Our tool and evaluation data are publicly available: https://github.com/thufv/mastery/.

To sum up, this paper makes the following contributions:

- We present a novel structured merge algorithm that visits ASTs in both a top-down and a bottom-up manner. The top-down pruning pass avoids a mass of redundant computations. The bottom-up pass makes it possible to handle shifted code elegantly and efficiently.
- We show that the proposed merging algorithm is linear-time and the ordered merging algorithm is order-preserving.
- We conduct comprehensive experiments on real-world merge scenarios. Results show that Mastery is competitive with state-of-the-art merge tools in the aspects of merge accuracy, the number of conflicts, and efficiency.

2   Preliminary

AST Nodes. In structured merging, programs are represented as *abstract syntax trees* (ASTs), parsed from source files. An AST is a labeled rooted tree with four types of nodes, each annotated with the name of its production rule in the grammar, called its *label* (*lbl*).

$$
\begin{array}{lll}
\text{Node } v ::= & \mathsf{Leaf}(lbl, x) & \text{(leaf)} \\
& | \ \mathsf{Ctor}_k(lbl, v_1, \ldots, v_k) & (k\text{-ary constructor}) \\
& | \ \mathsf{UList}(lbl, \{v_1, \ldots, v_n\}) & \text{(unordered list)} \\
& | \ \mathsf{OList}(lbl, [v_1, \ldots, v_n]) & \text{(ordered list)}
\end{array}
$$

A k-ary *constructor node* has exactly k children as its arguments. For instance, an if-statement—consisting of a Boolean condition, a true branch, and a false branch—is represented as a 3-ary constructor node. An arbitrary number of children is allowed in a *list node*, which is further divided into *unordered*—children can be safely permuted—and *ordered* (the opposite). For instance, a class member declaration list is unordered, while a statement list is ordered. In case of merge conflicts, we introduce conflicting nodes in target ASTs.

---

[1] Merging abstract syntax trees in a reasonable way.

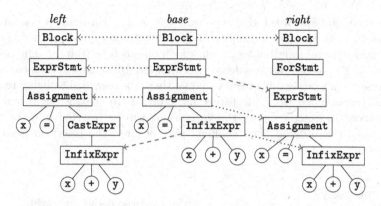

Fig. 1. A merge scenario with shifted code. (Shifted mappings are depicted as dashed arrows.)

AST Matching. A merging algorithm relies on a set of mappings between different versions of the programs to compute the merged version. The set of mappings between two ASTs T_1 and T_2 are represented by a *matching set* $\mathcal{M} = \{(u_i, v_i)\}_i$, where each pair (u_i, v_i) consists of two nodes $u_i \in T_1$ and $v_i \in T_2$. The mappings shall be *injective*—two nodes cannot be matched to the same node on the other AST simultaneously. Moreover, the matched nodes shall have the same label.

Table 1. Three-way merge principles (dual cases omitted).

Type	Version *base*	Version *left*	Version *right*	Target T	Explanation
1 Node	e	e	e'	e'	left-change
2 Node	e	e_L	e_R	conflict	inconsistent change
3 List	$e \in base$	$e \notin left$	$e \in right$	$e \notin T$	left-deletion
4 List	$e \notin base$	$e \in left$	$e \notin right$	$e \in T$ or conflict	left-insertion

Definition 1 (Shifted code). *Given two mappings $(u', v'), (u, v) \in \mathcal{M}$, if u is a child of u', whereas v is not a child (i.e., direct descendant) but a later descendant of v', then (u, v) is said a* shifted *mapping. Meanwhile, the code fragment corresponding to the subtree of v is called a* shifted code.

For example, on the merge scenario shown in Fig. 1: in *left*, the code fragment of `InfixExpr` is a shifted code and is shifted into a `CastExpr`; in *right*, the code fragment of `ExprStmt` is a shifted code and is shifted into a `ForStmt`.

Three-Way Merge Principles. A three-way merge algorithm must abide by a couple of principles, as presented in Table 1. To avoid repetition, the dual cases of rows 1, 3, and 4 are not displayed. The first two rules are applicable for all types of nodes. If a node is modified by exactly one of the variants, then the change is unique and itself gives the target (row 1). If a node is concurrently modified by both variants inconsistently, a conflict is reported, as the algorithm has no adequate information to decide which one to take (row 2). The last two rules are applicable for only (ordered and unordered) list nodes. If an element of *base* presents in exactly one of the variants, then it is regarded as being removed and will be excluded from the target list (row 3). In contrast, if a new node is introduced in exactly one of the variants, it will be inserted into the target list (row 4). For ordered lists, conflicts may occur if the insertion position is ambiguous.

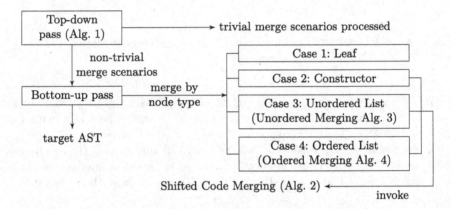

Fig. 2. High-level workflow of our merge algorithm.

3   Merge Algorithm

Given a three-way merge scenario (*base, left, right*), our merge algorithm accepts two matching sets (obtained by an AST matching algorithm) as input—$\mathcal{M}_L$ the matches between *base* and *left*, and $\mathcal{M}_R$ the matches between *base* and *right*. The algorithm generates a new tree, namely a *target AST*, as the merge result.

3.1   Algorithm Overview

Merging is performed on the matched nodes only, as unmatched nodes are assumed to have no relation. In the case of three-way merging, the two variants should match the base version. Formally, a merge scenario (b, l, r) is said *proper* if $(b, l) \in \mathcal{M}_L$ and $(b, r) \in \mathcal{M}_R$. The merge algorithm only needs to manipulate proper merge scenarios. Non-proper merge scenarios can be safely omitted because they are regarded as deletions and thus do not appear in the target.

Figure 2 presents the high-level workflow of our merge algorithm. It consists of a *top-down* pass followed by a *bottom-up* one. In the top-down pass (see Sect. 3.2 for details), input ASTs get traversed in pre-order, and any *trivial* merge

---

Algorithm 1: Top-down pruning pass

```
1  Function TopDownVisit(b: Node):
2  │   S ← [];
3  │   if ∃l ∈ left, r ∈ right : (b,l) ∈ M_L ∧ (b,r) ∈ M_R then
4  │   │   if b = r then R(b) ← l; return [];
5  │   │   if b = l or l = r then R(b) ← r; return [];
6  │   └   S += (b,l,r);
7  │   foreach child c of node b do
8  │   └   S ++= TopDownVisit(c);
9  └   return S;
```

---

scenario—any two of the three versions are equal—is processed immediately. Meanwhile, we collect other *non-trivial* proper merge scenarios in the list S.

In the bottom-up pass, the merge scenarios in S get processed in the reverse order, i.e., in post-order. Since matched nodes have the same label, the three versions in a proper merge scenario must be homogeneous—they must all be leaf nodes, constructor nodes, unordered list nodes, or ordered list nodes.

The first case, all nodes are leaf nodes, is the base case of our merge algorithm. This case is straightforward by three-way merge principles: We either take the only-changed variant as the target (by row 1 of Table 1) or report a conflict due to the inconsistent changes (by row 2).

The other cases are recursive cases where sub-scenarios need to be merged recursively. Merging constructor nodes of the same label and arity gives a constructor node of that label and arity too, and each child node is recursively merged from the sub-scenarios formed by the children at the corresponding index. Merging list nodes gives list nodes too, and it contains elements recursively merged from certain sub-scenarios drawn from the elements in the input lists (see Sect. 3.4 and Sect. 3.5 for details).

A challenging problem in solving the recursive cases is that: a sub-scenario (b,l,r) may *not be proper*, say b and l do not match. Even though it is rational to assume b matches *some descendant* of l (or else we simply report a conflict), which happens when l has shifted code. We encode this condition as a *relevant-to* relation: u is relevant to v, written $u \simeq v$, iff there exists a descendant $w \in v$ such that u matches w. With this notion, the assumption we make on a sub-scenario (b,l,r) is given by $b \simeq l \wedge b \simeq r$. Merging such a sub-scenario requires us to take shifted code into account. We will present this algorithm in Sect. 3.3.

The merge result of the merge scenario (b,l,r) is recorded in a map R so that the algorithm can query it later on demand. Instead of using the entire merge scenario (b,l,r) as the index (or key) for the map R, realizing that any node b of *base* appears in at most one merge scenario (by the injectivity of the matching sets), we simply use b as the index. In the end, the target AST of the top-most merge scenario (*base, left, right*) is obtained by querying $R(base)$.

Algorithm 2: Shifted Code Merging

---

1 **Function** IssueShifted(*b: Node, l: Node, r: Node*):
2   let l', r' be nodes s.t. $(b, l') \in \mathcal{M}_L, (b, r') \in \mathcal{M}_R$;
3   **if** $l' = l \wedge r' = r$ **then return** $\mathcal{R}(b)$;
4   **if** $l' \neq l \wedge r' = r$ **then return** $l[\mathcal{R}(b)/l']$;
5   **if** $r' \neq r \wedge l' = l$ **then return** $r[\mathcal{R}(b)/r']$;
6   **if** $l[\mathcal{R}(b)/l'] = r[\mathcal{R}(b)/r']$ **then return** $l[\mathcal{R}(b)/l']$;
7   **return** Conflict(l, r);

3.2 Top-Down Pruning Pass

In the top-down pass, we visit *base* in a descendant recursive manner by invoking TopDownVisit (Algorithm 1). This function returns all non-trivial merge scenarios that need processing later in the bottom-up pass. We use a list S to collect them. For short, we use two notations: $S += e$ for appending an element e to S, and $S ++= S'$ for appending all elements in S' to S. Upon traversing, if any trivial merge scenario is encountered, we immediately store the target AST in $\mathcal{R}$ and prune any further visit of its sub-scenarios by returning an empty list (lines 4–6). Otherwise, we proceed to collect merge scenarios recursively (lines 8–9).

3.3 Shifted Code Merging

Shifted code may exhibit in any type of node (except leaf node) in merge scenarios. Algorithm 2 presents a unified algorithm for dealing with shifted code. It requires $b \simeq l \wedge b \simeq r$. Merging is performed according to where the shifted code involves:

(no shifting) If (b, l, r) is proper, then we simply query $\mathcal{R}$ (line 3).
(left-shifting) If b matches r but not l, then there exists a l' such that it is shifted into l. To integrate this shifting, we first make a copy of l and replace l' with the merge result of (b, l', r') i.e., $\mathcal{R}(b)$ (line 4). The notation $u[w/v]$ gives an updated tree by replacing a subtree v with w on u.
(right-shifting) Line 5 is symmetric to the above case.
(consistent-shifting) If both variants involve shifted code, the only circumstance we can safely merge is when they yield the same result (line 6).
(inconsistent-shifting) Otherwise, report a conflict (line 7).

Consider the example in Fig. 1. When merging the merge scenario consisting of the three Assignments, CastExpr from *left*, InfixExpr from *base* and InfixExpr from *right* form the arguments b, l, r in Algorithm 2. The result is computed by taking the subtree of CastExpr and replacing its subtree of InfixExpr with the target one (by line 4). In merging the top-most merge scenario, the result is computed from the subtree of ForStmt by replacing its child ExprStmt with the target of ExprStmts (by line 5). In this way, the shifted changes made by the two variants are integrated.

Algorithm 3: Unordered merge

```
1  Function Unordered(B: Set, L: Set, R: Set):
2  │  T ← ∅;
3  │  foreach b ∈ B do
4  │  │  if ∃l ∈ L, r ∈ R : b ≃ l ∧ b ≃ r then
5  │  │  │  T ← T ∪ {IssueShifted(b, l, r)};
6  │  │  │  mark l, r as "visited";
7  │  │  else if ∃l ∈ L : b ≃ l then  // right case is symmetric
8  │  │  │  if b ≠ l then T ← T ∪ {Conflict(l, ε)};
9  │  │  │  mark l as "visited";
10 │  T ← T ∪ {e | e ∈ L ∪ R, e is not "visited"};
11 │  return T;
```

3.4 Unordered Merging

Let B, L, and R respectively be the set of elements of three unordered list nodes that form a merge scenario. The goal of unordered merging is to compute a set of elements T—without worrying about the order—that should appear in the target list. These elements are classified as follows:

(shifting) If an element $b \in B$ satisfies $b \simeq l \wedge b \simeq r$ for some $l \in L$ and $r \in R$, then the merge result is obtained by invoking IssueShifted(b, l, r).

(left/right-insertion) If an element of L or R is not related to any element of B, then by row 4 of Table 1 it is an insertion.

(left/right-deletion-change conflict) If an element b satisfies, for example (dual case is similar), $b \simeq r$ for some $r \in R$, then it is a left-deletion (thus not included in T) when $b = r$; and a left-deletion-change conflict when $b \neq r$.

The above is realized as Algorithm 3: First, traverse the elements in B and collect any shifting (line 4) or left-deletion-change conflict (line 7, right-deletion-change conflict is symmetric) in T. Meanwhile, mark every relevant left/right element as "visited" (lines 6 and 9). Then, all elements yet not marked must be left/right-insertions: thus insert them into T (line 10).

3.5 Ordered Merging

Merging ordered lists is more complex than merging unordered lists in that the elements of the target list must be in an order preserving the original occurrence order of associated elements in the merge scenario; and it is necessary to decide whether such an order uniquely exists—if not, to fit the merge algorithm into a conservative setting, conflicts shall be reported as well. For example, the conflicting scenario depicted in Fig. 3 is due to the ambiguity that whether Stmt2 should precede Stmt3 (note that both should be included in T as insertions).

Order-Preserving. Before presenting the merge algorithm, we first need a formal interpretation of "preserving the original occurrence order". Since the occurrence

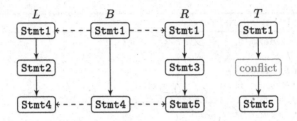

Fig. 3. A conflicting merge scenario of three statement-lists (B, L, R) with the target T. A dashed edge between two statements indicates they are matched.

order is a partial order relation, it is natural to regard the three ordered lists in the merge scenario (B, L, R) as three ordered sets $\langle B, \vartriangleleft_B \rangle$, $\langle L, \vartriangleleft_L \rangle$ and $\langle R, \vartriangleleft_R \rangle$. The occurrence order relation is denoted by $\vartriangleleft_X$ (for $X \in \{B, L, R\}$), formally defined as $X[i] \vartriangleleft_X X[j] \iff i < j$.

Let S be the set of elements that should appear in the target list T, computed by Unordered(B, L, R). We encode the relationship as partial functions $\pi_B : B \rightharpoonup T$, $\pi_L : L \rightharpoonup T$ and $\pi_R : R \rightharpoonup T$, associating an element in the input merge scenario with the corresponding element in the target list. For example, if $t^* \in S$ is a left-insertion, then t^* is a copy of some $l^* \in L$, thus we let $\pi_L(l^*) = t^*$.

Definition 2 (Order-preserving). *We say an ordered list T is an order-preserving w.r.t. (B, L, R) if T is a permutation of $S = $ Unordered(B, L, R) such that π_B, π_L, and π_R are monotone. A partial function $f : X \rightharpoonup Y$ is said monotone if for every $x_1, x_2 \in X$ such that $f(x_1)$ and $f(x_2)$ are both defined, $x_1 \vartriangleleft_X x_2$ entails $f(x_1) \vartriangleleft_Y f(x_2)$.*

In the above, the monotonicity condition precisely encodes our requirement of "preserving the original occurrence order".

Algorithm. The main goal of the algorithm (Algorithm 4) is to solve an order-preserving list and to decide the uniqueness of such lists. We compute an order-preserving list via constraint-solving—the constraints encode the monotonicity condition for the target list T by Definition 2. Technically each constraint has the form $e_1 \vartriangleleft e_2$, meaning "e_1 precedes e_2 in T". We propose an algorithm GenConstraints to produce them by traversing the elements of B, L, and R in their occurrence order, following the same structure of Algorithm 3, e.g., we generate the constraint "$\pi_B(b_1) \vartriangleleft \pi_B(b_2)$" for $b_1 \vartriangleleft_B b_2$.

Let Φ be the set of computed constraints (line 2). We represent the constraints as a directed graph (line 3) $G_\Phi = \langle V, E \rangle$, where: (1) the set of vertices are the elements of Unordered(B, L, R), i.e., $V = S$, and (2) for each constraint $(e_1 \vartriangleleft e_2) \in \Phi$, let $(e_1, e_2) \in E$ be an edge of G_Φ. It is well-known from graph theory that: there is a one-one correspondence between a topological sort of G_Φ and a satisfying solution of Φ, which further implies that: there is a one-one correspondence between an order-preserving list and a topological sort of G_Φ.

We compute an order-preserving list using classic topology sort algorithms such as Kahn's algorithm [13]. Following Kahn's algorithm, we facilitate a loop

---

Algorithm 4: Ordered merge

---

1 **Function** Ordered(*B: List, L: List, R: List*):
2    $\Phi \leftarrow$ GenConstraints(*B, L, R*);
3   Represent Φ as a directed graph $G_\Phi = \langle V, E \rangle$;
4    $Y \leftarrow []$;
5    $Z \leftarrow \{u \mid u \in V, indeg(u) = 0\}$;
6   **while** $Z \neq \varnothing$ **do**
7   **if** $|Z| \geq 2$ **then return** "conflict";
8   remove the sole vertex u from Z;
9       $Y +\!= u$;
10   **foreach** $(u, v) \in E$ **do**
11          $E \leftarrow E \setminus \{(u, v)\}$;
12   **if** $indeg(v) = 0$ **then**
13             $Z \leftarrow Z \cup \{v\}$;
14       $V \leftarrow V \setminus \{u\}$;
15   **if** $V \neq \varnothing$ **then return** "cyclic";
16   **return** Y;

(lines 6–14) to compute a topological sort and save it to a list Y. The auxiliary set Z (line 5) maintains all vertices with zero in-degree (i.e., without incoming edge). To further enable the uniqueness checking, we make the following extension: Each time the loop is entered, we check if Z has multiple elements. If so, choosing either vertex of Z gives a topological sort—in other words, the topological sort is not unique—so we report a conflict (line 7, highlighted). Otherwise, we follow the original Kahn's algorithm in lines 8–14. The loop repeats until Z is emptied. Suppose V is nonempty even when the loop exits, G_Φ must be cyclic and has no topological sort at all (based on the property of Kahn's algorithm), where a conflict exhibits as well.

The correctness of our ordered merge algorithm is stated as the following theorem:

Theorem 1. *Algorithm 4 returns an order-preserving list (without conflict) if and only if the order-preserving list w.r.t. input merge scenario uniquely exists.*

The ordered merge algorithm is linear because both Kahn's algorithm and the generation of constraints are linear. Moreover, the other algorithms mentioned before are also linear, thus:

Theorem 2. *The time complexity of the entire structured merge algorithm is linear (to the size of the input merge scenario).*

4 Implementation

We implemented the proposed approach as a structured merge framework, Mastery, written in Java. This framework consists of four modules:

1. a parser that translates input source files into ASTs;
2. a tree matcher that generates mappings between different program versions, using an adapted GumTree [7] algorithm;
3. a tree merger that computes the target AST, following the algorithms presented in Sect. 3;
4. a pretty printer that outputs the formatted code from the merged AST.

Mastery currently supports merging Java programs. We use JavaParser[2] to build ASTs from source code and pretty print source code from ASTs.

5   Evaluation

We extract 40,533 merge scenarios from 78 Java open-source projects hosted on GitHub, and then conduct a series of experimental evaluations to answer the following research questions:

RQ1: How often does shifted code occur in real-world merge scenarios?
RQ2: What is the merge accuracy of Mastery when compared to state-of-the-art merge tools?
RQ3: How many merge conflicts are reported by these tools?
RQ4: What is their performance from the perspective of runtime?

5.1   Experimental Setup

To select realistic and representative merge scenarios as our evaluation dataset, we seek the top-100 most popular open-source Java projects hosted on GitHub[3]; exclude any non-software-project (e.g., tutorials). On the remaining 78 projects, we extract merge scenarios via an analysis of their commit histories:

1. On all *merged commits*, we extract its two parents and their *base commit* from the Git history. The three source files with the same name extracted from the three commits each form a merge scenario (*base, left, right*), where *base* is from the base commit and the two variants are from the parent commits. The file (with the same name) in the merged commit is marked as the *expected* version, i.e., the *ground truth* of the merged result.
2. If any two of *base, left,* and *right* are equivalent, the target version of this merge scenario is obvious. To better examine the differences between the merge tools, we elide such trivial merge scenarios and instead only collect the merge scenarios where the three versions are pairwise distinct, judged by the `git diff` command.
3. Some source files cannot be correctly parsed, e.g., they include unresolved conflicts. We have to elide them too because structured approaches assume the input files to have valid syntax, checked by JavaParser.

---

[2] https://javaparser.org/.
[3] According to the following list, until July 12, 2021: https://github.com/EvanLi/Github-Ranking/blob/master/Top100/Java.md.

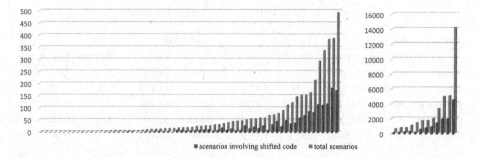

Fig. 4. Distribution of shifted code in each project. The projects are sorted by their number of merge scenarios in ascending order. We split them into two subfigures according to if the number of merge scenarios is less than 500 (left) or not (right).

4. In total, we collect 40,533 merge scenarios across 78 Java projects.

We compare Mastery with four state-of-the-art merge tools:

- JDime [16], a state-of-the-art structured merge tool,
- jFSTMerge [5], a well-known tree-based semistructured merge tool,
- IntelliMerge [20], a refactoring-aware graph-based semistructured merge tool,
- GitMerge, the default merging algorithm in Git.

All experiments were conducted on a workstation with AMD EPYC 7H12 64-Core CPU and 1 TB memory, running Ubuntu 20.04.3 LTS.

5.2 Frequency of Shifted Code (RQ1)

To calculate the frequency of shifted code, we use the state-of-the-art AST differencing tool, GumTree [7], to compute the matching sets among *base*, *left*, and *right*. Note that we don't need any merge tool for this evaluation. We detect shifted mappings from these matching sets according to Definition 1. Figure 4 presents how many merge scenarios in each studied project *involve* shifted code, meaning at least one shifted mapping is detected. Among the 40,533 merge scenarios, we find 15,620 merge scenarios involve shifted code—the frequency is 38.54%. In those merge scenarios, we detect 90,982 shifted mappings—on average 2.24 shifted mappings per merge scenario.

5.3 Taxonomy of Results

To understand the behavioral performance of the merge tools, we classify a merged result (for each merge scenario of each tool) into one of the following four categories:

Table 2. Distribution of the merged results.

Tool	Expected		Unexpected		Conflicting		Failed	
	Number	Accuracy	Number	Percentage	Number	Percentage	Number	Percentage
Mastery	**33342**	**82.26%**	3504	8.64%	3686	9.09%	1	0.00%
JDime	32789	80.89%	2446	6.03%	4610	11.37%	688	1.70%
jFSTMerge	30063	74.17%	3837	9.47%	6627	16.35%	6	0.01%
IntelliMerge	9774	24.11%	24555	60.58%	**3442**	**8.49%**	2762	6.81%
GitMerge	30643	75.60%	**791**	**1.95%**	9099	22.45%	**0**	**0.00%**

- *expected*: the merged file and the expected version (the ground truth) are *syntactically equivalent*, i.e., their ASTs are isomorphic to each other (allowing permutations of elements in an unordered list node);
- *unexpected*: the merged file is conflict-free and is nonequivalent to the expected version;
- *conflicting*: there is at least one conflict block in the merged file;
- *failed*: either the tool crashes or the execution exceeds the time limit 300 s.

Table 2 lists the merge results of the five tools. JDime and IntelliMerge failed on a considerable number of scenarios, mainly caused by their implementation bugs. IntelliMerge tends to produce more unexpected results because it adopts a radical merging algorithm that may violate the three-way merge principles when a deletion happens. For GitMerge, only 1.95% results are unexpected. To understand this phenomenon, we have to notice that all projects use GitMerge as default. If GitMerge does not report any conflict, the merged codes will usually become the *ground truth* in our evaluation, without being reviewed by the developers. Thus, the expected version is a kind of *biased* ground truth in favor of GitMerge. This finding is consistent with a previous work [20].

5.4 Merge Accuracy (RQ2)

The merge *accuracy* is calculated as the percentage of expected results. As shown in Table 2, Mastery achieves the highest accuracy of 82.26% among all tools. Comparing to JDime, Mastery gains 1.37% higher accuracy. Among the 1,398 scenarios where Mastery's results are expected whereas JDime's are not, we find 48.78% involves shifted code—10.25% higher than the overall frequency.

The scenarios where GitMerge produces unexpected or conflicting results are of special interest to us—in these merge scenarios, the expected versions (i.e., the merged versions in Git histories) must have been reviewed by the developers. If we consider only these 9,890 scenarios, the accuracy of the five tools except GitMerge are:

Mastery	JDime	jFSTMerge	IntelliMerge
32.17%	31.94%	17.26%	6.98%

Mastery still achieves the highest accuracy.

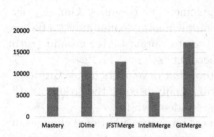

Fig. 5. Numbers of conflict blocks.

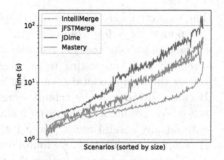

Fig. 6. Time cost of merging.

5.5   Reported Conflicts (RQ3)

In addition to the numbers of conflicting merge scenarios listed in Table 2, we also count the numbers of conflict blocks (or conflict hunks) as depicted in Fig. 5. Especially, IntelliMerge's radical strategy ignores three-way merge principles, making it achieve the lowest in both metrics. The other four tools all follow the three-way merge principles. Among them, Mastery reports the fewest 6,791 conflict blocks and the fewest 3,686 conflicting scenarios. Among the 1,650 scenarios where JDime's results are conflicting whereas Mastery's are not, we find 51.82% involves shifted code—higher than the overall frequency.

5.6   Runtime Performance (RQ4)

As unstructured GitMerge is inherent particularly efficient, we only compare the runtime performance among semistructured and structured tools. Ignoring the failed runs, Fig. 6 shows the runtime on merge scenarios sorted by the size (i.e., total file size in unit of byte) of merge scenarios in ascending order. Since the runtime of each tool has considerable ups and downs even on the merge scenarios of a similar size, for clearer illustrating, we plot each point as the average of adjacent 100 merge scenarios. The average times for the four tools are:

Mastery	JDime	jFSTMerge	IntelliMerge
10.33 s	24.06 s	13.21 s	4.34 s

Mastery is about 2.4× as fast as JDime, and about 1.3× as fast as jFSTMerge, which shows Mastery, as a structured merging tool, has competitive efficiency to semistructured merging tools.

5.7   Discussions

Threats to Validity. We find the following threats to our ground truth:

1. The expected version may not exactly be the merged version but the one postponed by a few commits, a.k.a. supplementary commits. Our dataset extraction process does not consider such supplementary commits. As a future direction, it is interesting to investigate how to obtain better ground truth taking the supplementary commits into account (such as [11,12]).
2. Because GitMerge is the default merging tool that developers use, if GitMerge reports no conflicts, its merging results will usually become the ground truth without any careful review, even if they are indeed wrong.
3. By empirical inspection, we found developers introduce additional changes in some merging scenarios, rather than only collaborating on the changes from *left* and *right*.

The ideal ground truth is to only merge changes in *left* and *right* correctly without introducing additional changes, and conflict blocks get reported if the changes are indeed semantically contradicted. Unfortunately, manual efforts seem inevitable approaching this ideality.

Limitations. Among the 438 merge scenarios where Mastery produces unexpected results while JDime produces expected results, we manually studied 10 random samples. We found that: In 4 merge scenarios, the expected versions introduce additional changes by developers or break three-way merge principles in other ways. Mastery produces the desired merge results w.r.t. three-way merge principles. The other 6 scenarios failed due to our limited support for *two-way merging*, where a merge scenario consists of only the two variants but not the base version. JDime realizes some heuristic two-way merging strategies, which can handle these merge scenarios better. These strategies can be realized in Mastery in the future.

6   Related Work

Structured Merge. Westfechtel [21] and Buffenbarger [3] pioneered in proposing merge algorithms that exploit structures of programs.

JDime [16] is a state-of-the-art tool for merging Java programs at AST level. In their AST representation, ordered and unordered lists are distinguished, and they propose distinct algorithms for merging them. We further distinguish ordered list nodes from constructor nodes (Sect. 2), as a list node can have an arbitrary number of children while a constructor node cannot. Their algorithm is in a top-down and level-wise manner, and is unable to merge shifted code.

Later, two extensions of JDime are proposed. One is an auto-tuning technique that switches between structured and unstructured merge algorithms for better efficiency [15]; the other is a syntax-aware looking ahead mechanism for identifying shifted code and renaming in the AST matcher [14]. To be scalable, the lookahead mechanism has restrictions on the types of nodes when lookahead is enabled (an if- or try-statement), and the maximum search distance of lookahead (3 or 4). Note that in their work, the lookahead mechanism is not applied to merging. Unlike them, our merge algorithm efficiently handles shifted code in a general sense (i.e., without the above restrictions).

Asenov et al. [2] propose an algorithm for matching and merging trees using their textual encoding, which enables the usage of standard line-based version control systems. To yield precise matching, external information, for example, unique identifiers across revisions, is required. Unfortunately, they are directly unavailable. Furthermore, they have to perform expensive tree matching algorithms.

Semistructured Merge. Apel et al. [1] invented *semistructured merge*—a novel way of combining unstructured and structured approaches—that aims to balance the generality of unstructured merge and the precision of structured merge. Since semistructured approaches represent only part of the programs (typically high-level structures) as ASTs and keep the rest (low-level structures, e.g., method bodies) as plain text, they are not as precise as fully-structured approaches. An empirical study [4] on over 40,000 merge scenarios reveals that semistructured merge reports more false positives than structured merge.

Shen et al. [20] propose a graph-based refactoring-aware semistructured merging algorithm for Java programs, which is implemented as a tool IntelliMerge. The major difference between refactoring and shifted code is that refactoring must preserve semantics while shifted code usually does not.

Conflict Resolution. Mens [17] thinks the resolution of conflicts caused by inconsistent changes made by variants is a major problem in version control. Since the resolutions of those conflicts are ambiguous, developers have the responsibility to resolve them manually. To alleviate manual efforts, Zhu and He [23] propose a synthesis-based technique that can automatically suggest candidate resolutions. In a real-time collaborative environment, it is also possible to simply prevent any presence of conflicts using locks [8,10,18,19].

7   Conclusion and Future Directions

We present Mastery, a three-way structured merge framework based on the methodology of combining the top-down and bottom-up visits of ASTs. This framework benefits from both the efficiency of handling trivial merge scenarios via a top-down pass and the effectiveness of handling non-trivial merge scenarios via a bottom-up pass, which makes it possible to handle shifted code elegantly. In the future, we plan to support more programming languages in our framework and further improve the tree matching and merging algorithms based on our evaluation findings.

Acknowledgement. This work was supported in part by the National Natural Science Foundation of China (No. 62072267 and No. 62021002) and the National Key Research and Development Program of China (No. 2018YFB1308601).

References

1. Apel, S., Liebig, J., Brandl, B., Lengauer, C., Kästner, C.: Semistructured merge: rethinking merge in revision control systems. In: Proceedings of the 19th ACM SIGSOFT Symposium and the 13th European Conference on Foundations of Software Engineering, ESEC/FSE 2011, pp. 190–200. ACM, New York (2011). https://doi.org/10.1145/2025113.2025141
2. Asenov, D., Guenat, B., Müller, P., Otth, M.: Precise version control of trees with line-based version control systems. In: Huisman, M., Rubin, J. (eds.) FASE 2017. LNCS, vol. 10202, pp. 152–169. Springer, Heidelberg (2017). https://doi.org/10.1007/978-3-662-54494-5_9
3. Buffenbarger, J.: Syntactic software merging. In: Estublier, J. (ed.) SCM 1993/1995. LNCS, vol. 1005, pp. 153–172. Springer, Heidelberg (1995). https://doi.org/10.1007/3-540-60578-9_14
4. Cavalcanti, G., Borba, P., Seibt, G., Apel, S.: The impact of structure on software merging: semistructured versus structured merge. In: 2019 34th IEEE/ACM International Conference on Automated Software Engineering (ASE), pp. 1002–1013, November 2019. https://doi.org/10.1109/ASE.2019.00097
5. Cavalcanti, G., Borba, P., Accioly, P.: Evaluating and improving semistructured merge. Proc. ACM Program. Lang. 1(OOPSLA), 59:1–59:27 (2017). https://doi.org/10.1145/3133883
6. Dotzler, G., Philippsen, M.: Move-optimized source code tree differencing. In: Proceedings of the 31st IEEE/ACM International Conference on Automated Software Engineering, ASE 2016, pp. 660–671. ACM, New York (2016). https://doi.org/10.1145/2970276.2970315
7. Falleri, J.R., Morandat, F., Blanc, X., Martinez, M., Monperrus, M.: Fine-grained and accurate source code differencing. In: Proceedings of the 29th ACM/IEEE International Conference on Automated Software Engineering, ASE 2014, pp. 313–324. ACM, New York (2014). https://doi.org/10.1145/2642937.2642982
8. Fan, H., Sun, C.: Dependency-based automatic locking for semantic conflict prevention in real-time collaborative programming. In: Proceedings of the 27th Annual ACM Symposium on Applied Computing, SAC 2012, pp. 737–742. Association for Computing Machinery, New York (2012). https://doi.org/10.1145/2245276.2245417
9. Fluri, B., Wuersch, M., PInzger, M., Gall, H.: Change distilling: tree differencing for fine-grained source code change extraction. IEEE Trans. Softw. Eng. 33(11), 725–743 (2007). https://doi.org/10.1109/TSE.2007.70731
10. Ho, C.W., Raha, S., Gehringer, E., Williams, L.: Sangam: a distributed pair programming plug-in for Eclipse. In: Proceedings of the 2004 OOPSLA Workshop on Eclipse Technology EXchange, Eclipse 2004, pp. 73–77. Association for Computing Machinery, New York (2004). https://doi.org/10.1145/1066129.1066144
11. Ji, T., Chen, L., Yi, X., Mao, X.: Understanding merge conflicts and resolutions in git rebases. In: 2020 IEEE 31st International Symposium on Software Reliability Engineering (ISSRE), pp. 70–80 (2020). https://doi.org/10.1109/ISSRE5003.2020.00016
12. Ji, T., Pan, J., Chen, L., Mao, X.: Identifying supplementary bug-fix commits. In: 2018 IEEE 42nd Annual Computer Software and Applications Conference (COMPSAC), vol. 01, pp. 184–193 (2018). https://doi.org/10.1109/COMPSAC.2018.00031

13. Kahn, A.B.: Topological sorting of large networks. Commun. ACM **5**(11), 558–562 (1962). https://doi.org/10.1145/368996.369025
14. Leßenich, O., Apel, S., Kästner, C., Seibt, G., Siegmund, J.: Renaming and shifted code in structured merging: looking ahead for precision and performance. In: 2017 32nd IEEE/ACM International Conference on Automated Software Engineering (ASE), pp. 543–553, October 2017. https://doi.org/10.1109/ASE.2017.8115665
15. Leßenich, O., Apel, S., Lengauer, C.: Balancing precision and performance in structured merge. Autom. Softw. Eng. **22**(3), 367–397 (2014). https://doi.org/10.1007/s10515-014-0151-5
16. Leßenich, O., Lengauer, C.: Adjustable syntactic merge of java programs. Master's thesis, Department of Informatics and Mathematics, University of Passau (2012)
17. Mens, T.: A state-of-the-art survey on software merging. IEEE Trans. Softw. Eng. **28**(5), 449–462 (2002). https://doi.org/10.1109/TSE.2002.1000449
18. Reeves, M., Zhu, J.: Moomba – a collaborative environment for supporting distributed extreme programming in global software development. In: Eckstein, J., Baumeister, H. (eds.) XP 2004. LNCS, vol. 3092, pp. 38–50. Springer, Heidelberg (2004). https://doi.org/10.1007/978-3-540-24853-8_5
19. Salinger, S., Oezbek, C., Beecher, K., Schenk, J.: Saros: an eclipse plug-in for distributed party programming. In: Proceedings of the 2010 ICSE Workshop on Cooperative and Human Aspects of Software Engineering, CHASE 2010, pp. 48–55. Association for Computing Machinery, New York (2010). https://doi.org/10.1145/1833310.1833319
20. Shen, B., Zhang, W., Zhao, H., Liang, G., Jin, Z., Wang, Q.: IntelliMerge: a refactoring-aware software merging technique. Proc. ACM Program. Lang. **3**(OOPSLA) (2019). https://doi.org/10.1145/3360596
21. Westfechtel, B.: Structure-oriented merging of revisions of software documents. In: Proceedings of the 3rd International Workshop on Software Configuration Management, SCM 1991, pp. 68–79. ACM, New York (1991). https://doi.org/10.1145/111062.111071
22. Zhang, K., Jiang, T.: Some MAX SNP-hard results concerning unordered labeled trees. Inf. Process. Lett. **49**(5), 249–254 (1994). https://doi.org/10.1016/0020-0190(94)90062-0
23. Zhu, F., He, F.: Conflict resolution for structured merge via version space algebra. Proc. ACM Program. Lang. **2**(OOPSLA) (2018). https://doi.org/10.1145/3276536
24. Zhu, F., He, F., Yu, Q.: Enhancing precision of structured merge by proper tree matching. In: 2019 IEEE/ACM 41st International Conference on Software Engineering: Companion Proceedings (ICSE-Companion), pp. 286–287. IEEE (2019)

KCL: A Declarative Language for Large-Scale Configuration and Policy Management

XiaoDong Duo, Pengfei Xu[✉], Zheng Zhang, Shushan Chai, Rui Xia, and Zhe Zong

Ant Group, Hangzhou, China
lingzhi.xpf@antgroup.com

Abstract. In recent years, the diversification, complexity, immediacy, and scale of delivery and operational requirements have increased exponentially. For example, delivering and managing complex service mesh and various cloud-native technologies, supporting a variety of operations on infrastructures, such as database, load balancer, dynamic configuration, etc, configuring monitoring for all types of applications, and arranging a range of variety of services and applications to regions across data centers or public clouds. These are just a glimpse of the leopard, and it is actually difficult to list them all. By summarizing and abstracting, we propose the KCL declarative language, development mechanism, and consistent workflow. Through the language model and constraint capabilities, we can improve the large-scale efficiency and liberate multi-team collaborative productivity of operational development and operation systematically while ensuring stability for large-scale configuration and policy management. KCL helps users of various roles to complete operational development and operation tasks in a simple, scalable, stable, efficient, divided-and-conquered manner. To date, the KCL has been used in more than 800 projects, and the average configuration writing and distributing time is shortened from more than 25 days to 2 days.

Keywords: Language · Delivery · Operation · Stability · Collaborative

1 Introduction

With the development of the Internet, the software deployment cycle has accelerated significantly. Every day, a large number of engineers perform frequent configuration and policy changes, and unavoidable human error leads to malfunctions [35]. For example, the nationwide network paralysis in South Korea was caused by incorrect network configuration [12]. In addition, there are many configuration and policy scenarios, such as application, monitoring, service authentication, and so on. It is difficult for automated systems to uniformly manage and configure

W. Dong and J.-P. Talpin (Eds.): SETTA 2022, LNCS 13649, pp. 88–105, 2022.
https://doi.org/10.1007/978-3-031-21213-0_6

the distribution of multiple configuration and policy scenarios using some simple variant data format.

Based on these problems, we designed and implemented Kusion Configuration Language (KCL)[1] for the large-scale configuration and policy management. KCL provides the following support:

Stability. Incorrect configuration codes can cause runtime failures. Some data formats and other configuration languages lack systematic validation and testing capabilities. KCL guarantees stability using a variety of methods, such as the type system [8,29], immutability, static validation, and testing, etc.

Engineering. KCL provides the necessary language abilities to make programming possible and absorb the code organization capabilities of Object-Oriented Programming (OOP), such as *schema*, *mixin*, and inheritance, to improve reusability and engineering. In addition, we use plugins to extend the domain capabilities of KCL. We implement a dynamic configuration in the form of top-level argument, use tools and KCL multilingual APIs to realize automatic configuration management.

Scalability. In a large-scale collaboration scenario, the configuration is defined by multiple teams with different professions. It is necessary to consider the impact of collaborative development on stability and engineering. KCL provides support of reuse and isolation of multiple tenants and multiple environments, and can merge these configurations into a complete one automatically. By KCL, the average configuration collaborative writing and deploying time is shortened to 2 h.

In the paper, we propose the KCL declarative language [20], development mechanism and consistent workflow to improve the large-scale efficiency and liberate multi-team collaborative productivity of operational development and operation systematically while ensuring stability for large-scale configuration and policy management.

2   Background and Related Work

In addition to the general configuration, the features of the cloud-native configuration include a large quantity and wide coverage. For example, Kubernetes provides a declarative Application Programming Interface (API) mechanism and the openness allows users to make full use of its resource management capabilities [23]; however, this also implies error-prone behaviors. (1) Kubernetes configuration lacks user-side validation methods and cannot check the validity of the data. (2) Kubernetes exposes more than 500 models, more than 2,000 fields, and allows users to customize the model without considering the configuration reuse of multiple sites, multiple environments, and multiple deployment topologies. Fragmentation configuration brings many difficulties to the collaborative writing and automatic management of large-scale configuration.

---

[1] https://github.com/KusionStack/KCLVM.

The cloud-native communities have made considerable attempts to advance their configuration technologies, which can be divided into three categories: (1) Low level data format based tools for templating, patching, and validation, which use external tools to enhance the reuse and validation; (2) Domain-Specific Languages (DSLs) and Configuration Languages (CLs) to enhance language abilities [10]; and (3) General Purpose Language (GPL)-based solutions, using GPLs' Cloud-Development Kit (CDK) or framework to define configuration [11].

Previous efforts do not meet all these needs. Some tools (e.g., [19,41]) verify configuration based on the Kubernetes API. Although it supports checking missing attributes, the validation is generally weak and limited to Open Application Programming Interface (OpenAPI) [5]. Some tools (e.g., [1,13,28,34]) support custom validation rules, but the rule descriptions are cumbersome. In terms of configuration languages, most (e.g., [9,15,25,31]) focus on reducing boilerplates, and only a few focus on type checking, data validation, testing, etc. [26].

Helm [18] and Kapitan [21] used parameterized template techniques to solve the problem of dynamic configuration. As the scale increases, parameterized templates tend to become complex and difficult to maintain; parameter substitution sites must be identified manually. However, it is tedious and error-prone, parameters will gradually erode the template, and any value in the template may gradually evolve into parameters (e.g., [30]). Compared with using the Kubernetes API directly, the readability of such a template combined with many parameters is often worse [22]. Kustomize uses code patching to realize the reuse of the multi-environment configuration code [33]. This inspired us to adopt similar designs and practices (Sect. 6.3 and Sect. 7).

3   Overview

KCL focuses on serving the configuration and policy system. We design KCL from the theory and technology of programming languages and the requirements of many scenarios. Figure 1 shows the subset of the KCL grammar. The core syntax of KCL is the definition of *schema* model (modeling) and the definition of type and *check* rules (constraints), because in large-scale configuration and strategy scenarios, there are a large number of basic capabilities of the runtime can be reused for resources such as Deployment and Service in Kubernetes. KCL enables direct reuse of user models, static type checking, and adds incremental constraint capabilities and automated integration capabilities on top of them. Figure 2 shows a KCL configuration. In KCL, we can use the *schema* to implement the configuration and policy capabilities. In Fig. 2, we have implemented a Kubernetes *deployment* instance [4].

Generally, KCL has the following characteristics:

Simple. The configuration of attributes in KCL usually meets the simple pattern

$$k \ op \ (T) \ v, \tag{1}$$

$$
\begin{aligned}
KCL &::= stmt^* \\
stmt &::= schema \mid assert \mid import \mid assign \mid ... \\
schema &::= [\textbf{schema}]\ id['('parent\_id')']\ ['['arguments']']'\ :\ 'schema\_body \\
schema\_body &::= [mixin\_stmt]\ [schema\_context] \\
&\quad\ \ [check\_block] \\
mixin\_stmt &::= \textbf{mixin}\ '['\ id^*\ ']' \\
schema\_context &::= [attr \mid if \mid assign \mid assert \mid expr]^* \\
attr &::= id['?']\ ':'\ Type\ ['='expr] \\
check\_block &::= \textbf{check}\ ':'\ check\_stmt^* \\
check\_stmt &::= expr[',' msg] \\
assign &::= id\ '='\ expr \\
assert &::= expr[',' msg] \\
&\quad ...\qquad ...
\end{aligned}
$$

Fig. 1. (Subset of) KCL grammar

where k is the attribute name, v is the attributes value, op is the operator defined in Sect. 6.3 and T is the type annotation. Since KCL has the ability of the type inference, T is usually omitted.

Stability. KCL is a statically typed [32] and compiled language. KCL allows developers to use the *schema* keyword to define static data structures and discover various problems at compile time. Besides, We can use the *check, requires* and *assert* keyword to define a series of validation rules and perform compile-time rule conflict checking and runtime verification.

Engineering. KCL provides many language features to meet programming development. Specifically, we can use language features such as comprehension, conditions, arithmetic, and logic to meet engineering needs. Besides, we can use *schema* to define structures, use *mixin* to define reusable code in schema, use *protocol* to define the constraints of mixin code blocks, and use inheritance to define reusable structure definitions, simplifying structure definition and reuse.

Scalability. A large number of features related to collaborative development are provided to satisfy developers' ability to meet the needs of expanding the configuration and policy. For example, we can use different configuration attribute operators defined in Sect. 6.3 to merge configuration of different environments.

4   Stability

Type System. Based on the user role division and ensuring semantics simplicity, the configuration type and data are separated in the KCL, which allows the definition of the type of variables, schema attributes, and arguments.

Suppose Γ is a well-formed environment [29], and all free variables of S are defined in Γ, $\Gamma \vdash S$. Assert that the well-formed type is $\Gamma \vdash \Diamond$. In the environment Γ, E has the type T. Table 1 shows the KCL type notions.

```
1   import kubernetes.core.v1
2
3   deployment = v1.Deployment {
4       metadata.name = "nginx-deployment"
5       metadata.labels.app = "nginx"
6       spec = {
7           replicas = 3
8           selector.matchLabels.app = "nginx"
9           template = {
10              metadata.labels.app = "nginx"
11              spec.containers = [{
12                  name = "nginx"
13                  image = "nginx:1.14.2"
14                  ports = [{ containerPort = 80 }]
15              }]
16          }
17      }
18  }
```

Fig. 2. Example of KCL configuration

Any and *Nothing* are the upper and lower bounds of the type, and satisfy

$$Nothing \subseteq T \subseteq Any. \tag{2}$$

Based on the type definition of KCL, we can construct the derivation rules for all KCL statements and expressions. For example, the derivation rules for the *list* expression can be written as

$$\frac{\Gamma \vdash E_1 : T_1 \; E_2 : T_2 \; ... \; E_n : T_n}{\Gamma \vdash [E_1, E_2, ..., E_n] : listof(sup(T_1, T_2, ..., T_n))}, \tag{3}$$

where E_n denotes the n-th expression of the *list*, T_n denotes the n-th expression type of the *list*, and *sup* denotes the type minimum supremum function [29], whose input parameter is a set of types, and the result is determined by the partial order relationship between different types.

The reason why we use the union type in KCL is that a configuration type is often diverse. For example, the *str—int* union type of string and integer is more suitable than the *any* type because it has a lower minimum type upper bound. In KCL, type checking at compile time is jointly determined by the type partial ordering relationship and derivation rules.

Immutability. The correct configuration may be incorrect because of the modifications of other teams. In some cases, we defined attribute values, which are uniquely determined and should not be modified. KCL is easy to find such errors through static checking.

Table 1. KCL type notions

Type notion	Notation
Boolean	$\dfrac{\Gamma \vdash \Diamond}{\Gamma \vdash boolean}$
Integer	$\dfrac{\Gamma \vdash \Diamond}{\Gamma \vdash integer}$
Float	$\dfrac{\Gamma \vdash \Diamond}{\Gamma \vdash float}$
String	$\dfrac{\Gamma \vdash \Diamond}{\Gamma \vdash string}$
Literal	$\dfrac{c \in \{boolean, integer, float, string\}}{\Gamma \vdash literal of(c)}$
List	$\dfrac{\Gamma \vdash T \quad T \neq Void}{\Gamma \vdash list of(T)}$
Dict	$\dfrac{\Gamma \vdash T_1 \quad \Gamma \vdash T_2 \quad T_1 \neq Void \quad T_2 \neq Void}{\Gamma \vdash dict of(T_k = T_1, T_v = T_2)}$
Structure	$\dfrac{\Gamma \vdash T_1 \ \dots \ \Gamma \vdash T_n \quad T_i \neq Void \quad K_i \neq K_j, \text{when } i \neq j}{\Gamma \vdash struct of(K_1 : T_1, \dots, K_n : T_n)}$
Union	$\dfrac{\Gamma \vdash T_1 \ \dots \ \Gamma \vdash T_n \quad T_i \neq Void}{\Gamma \vdash union of(T_1, \dots, T_n)}$
Void	$\dfrac{\Gamma \vdash \Diamond}{\Gamma \vdash Void}$
Any	$\dfrac{\Gamma \vdash \Diamond}{\Gamma \vdash Any}$
Nothing	$\dfrac{\Gamma \vdash \Diamond}{\Gamma \vdash Nothing}$

Validation. As a configuration language, KCL covers all the capabilities of OpenAPI in terms of validation. Because KCL can be regarded as a structure of data, more attention is paid to the schema object in OpenAPI [5].

Besides, KCL also proposes a check-block, which is defined in the schema and consists of a set of logical expressions and optional error messages. The advantages of check-block are as follows: (1) better readability, all constraints of the attributes can be found in check-block, avoiding scattering in various parts of the configuration code; (2) stronger expressive ability, check-block supports checking any logical expressions; (3) some check expressions can be statically analyzed at compile time. As shown in Fig. 3, we can check the *Resource* through the unit literal and the *requires* static check in KCL. Using a check-block provides a more flexible and

```
1   import units
2
3   type UnitType = units.NumberMultiplier
4
5   schema Resource:
6       cpu: int | UnitType = 1
7       memory: UnitType = 1024Mi
8       disk: UnitType = 10Gi
9
10      check:
11          requires cpu and 0 < cpu <= 64
12          requires memory and 0 < memory <= 64Gi
13          requires disk and 0 < disk <= 1Ti
```

Fig. 3. Validation in KCL

lighter validation method. Simultaneously, this is a strong immutable constraint
that avoids situations in which the configuration is modified after being defined
and does not meet expectations.

The KCL compiler will find code errors at compile time as much as possible
through static type checking and model checking. For errors that cannot be found
at compile time, KCL will perform error checking at runtime by calculating the
value of the corresponding variable.

Model Checking. In addition to writing check expressions in the KCL schema,
the KCL compiler can also perform static analysis at compile time thanks to the
declarative check expressions and the static type, such as checking and analyzing whether check logic expressions have occurred conflict through the formal
verification tool, e.g., SMT solver, namely Z3 [6,7].

Specifically, we define a series of constraints T for each attribute s, the constraint state of all attributes is

$$\mathcal{F} = T[s_1] \wedge T[s_2] \wedge ... \wedge T[s_N], \tag{4}$$

where N is the total number of attributes with constraints. What the model
checking needs to do is to calculate the *and* result of the schema construction
process φ and the given attribute constraint state $\mathcal{F}$.

$$\varphi \wedge \mathcal{F}. \tag{5}$$

When the solution of all the constraint attributes cannot be obtained, the verification fails, and the KCL compiler throws out the error and prompts users
to manually modify the configuration value and its constraints. By the above
method, we can find conflicts between constraints or conflicts between configuration values and constraints.

5   Engineering

In KCL, we effectively reduce the duplicate configuration code, and provide a
more flexible capability to define the configuration. KCL provides many capabilities related to engineering, taking into account that many codes are not only
written by developers, but also automatically modified through tools.

5.1   Structure

In KCL, to meet the requirements of model definition, abstraction, and templating, we can use *schema* to organize the configuration data. *Schema* is the core
feature of KCL, which defines attributes, operations, mixins, and check-blocks.
A complete schema definition can be written as

$$S = \Sigma_{i=1}^{N} \{s_i, T_i, T[s_i]\}, \tag{6}$$

where N is the total number of attributes, $\mathcal{T}$ is the attribute constraint mentioned in Sect. 4, s_i and T_i denotes the i-th attribute name and type. Simultaneously, to improve the reusability of the code and meet the needs of hierarchical definition, KCL draws on the experience of OOP and uses single inheritance to reuse and extend the schema. Schema inheritance can be regarded as a special type of partial order relationship mentioned in Sect. 4, and satisfies

$$unionof(T_1, T_2) = T_2 \Leftrightarrow T_1 \subseteq T_2, \tag{7}$$

where T_1 and T_2 are both schema types. When the above equation is not satisfied, the KCL compiler will throw a type check error.

```
1   mixin OverQuotaMixin:
2       overQuotaToleration = Toleration {
3           key = "sigma.ali/is−over−quota"
4           operator = "Equal"
5           value = "true"
6           effect = "NoSchedule"
7       } if data.overQuota else Undefined
8
9       overQuotaMatchExpression = NodeSelectorRequirement {
10          key = "sigma.ali/is−over−quota"
11          operator = "In"
12          values = ["true"]
13      } if data.overQuota else Undefined
```

Fig. 4. OverQuotaMixin.k

Besides, KCL provides the mechanism for *mixin*, which is used to define reusable code snippets and is introduced into the schema declaratively. We use *mixin* to define the mapping logic between models. As shown in Fig. 4, the case of *overQuota* in Sect. 2 is encapsulated as *OverQuotaMixin* with the KCL keyword *mixin*. Thus, we not only simplify the definition of models but also facilitate user understanding.

6   Scalability

6.1   Configuration Definition

As shown in Fig. 5, the KCL code generates two graphs during the compilation process corresponding to the schema model definition and the declared configuration. The schema model definition includes references, inheritances, and composition relationships between models, and the configuration data declared on the user side are the model instantiation. The overall compilation process can be divided into three steps:

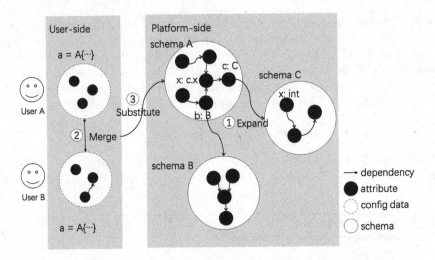

Fig. 5. KCL compilation process

1. Expand the model based on dependencies.
2. Merge different configuration codes.
3. Substitute the merged configuration into the platform model until all configuration attributes have certain values to obtain the final configuration.

6.2   Configuration Substitution

Algorithm 1 shows the configuration substitution process according to dependencies, and the main steps are:

1. Traverse all the key k and expression e of the input configuration C_i, and use the lookup function to substitute its dependent value recursively.
2. Store the calculated value in the output configuration and cache, which is used to avoid multiple calculations.
3. When all the key calculations are completed, we get the substitution completed configuration C_o.

6.3   Configuration Merge

After the configuration substitution is completed, KCL provides the ability to automatically merge configurations. As shown in Fig. 6a, the user defines two configurations for different environments. The KCL compiler recursively traverses and merges the same nodes and downstream nodes in the Abstract Syntax Tree (AST).

Algorithm 1: The configuration substitution process.

Input: the input configuration C_i
Output: the merged configuration C_o

1 $C_o \leftarrow \{\}$;
2 $cache \leftarrow \{\}$;
3 **foreach** $k,\ e\ in\ C_i$ **do**
4   **if** $k\ in\ cache$ **then**
5 | $\ C_o[k] = cache[k]$;
6   **else**
7 | $\ v = \mathrm{lookup}(k, e)$;
8 | $\ cache[k] = v$;
9   **end**
10 **end**
11
12 **function** $\mathrm{lookup}(k, e)$
13 $v \leftarrow \varnothing$;
14 **foreach** $k_d\ in\ \mathrm{dependence}(e)$ **do**
15   **if** $k_d\ in\ cache$ **then**
16 | $\ v = cache[k_d]$;
17   **else**
18 | $\ v = \mathrm{lookup}(k_d, C_i[k_d])$;
19   **end**
20 **end**
21 **return** v;
22 **end**

Besides, KCL provides configuration merge strategies including idempotent mergers, patch mergers, and unique configurations (Fig. 6b). The base and production configurations in idempotent merging satisfy the commutative law [37], and require developers to manually handle configuration conflicts between base and production. Patch merger as an overlay function including overwrite, delete and append that is similar to Kustomize. A unique configuration requires that the configuration block be globally unique and unmodified or redefined in any form. KCL simplifies the collaborative development on the user side through multiple merging strategies and reduces the coupling between configurations.

Specifically, the configuration usually consists of several key-value pairs. We assign a third dimension to the configuration entry in KCL e.g., the strategy of attribute merging, that is, the attribute operator. Suppose a configuration value is σ, then it can be expressed by

$$\sigma = \sum_{i=1}^{N} \{k_i, v_i, o_i\}, \tag{8}$$

where N denotes the number of all entries in the configuration value, i denotes the index of the configuration entry, k_i, v_i and o_i denotes the key, value and the attribute operation of the i-th configuration entry respectively. Besides, v_i

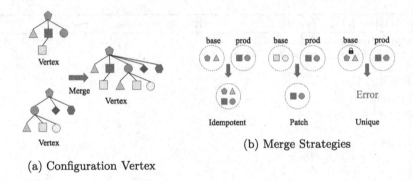

(a) Configuration Vertex

(b) Merge Strategies

Fig. 6. Configuration Merge

can be a KCL basic type value or a recursive configuration block. The merger operation of two different configuration value σ_u and σ_v can be expressed as

$$\sigma_u \cup \sigma_v = \sum_{j=1}^{N_u+N_v} \{k_j, v_j, o_j\}. \tag{9}$$

Considering there are same keys in the two configuration values and assuming that one of same keys is k_s and the number of same entries is M, then the merged result of key k_s can be expressed as

$$\sum_{k=1}^{M} \{k_s, v_k, o_k\} = \{k_s, \{v_1, o_1\} \oplus \{v_2, o_2\} \oplus \dots \oplus \{v_M, o_M\}\}, \tag{10}$$

where $\oplus$ denotes the entry value merge operator. Please note that o is one of the attribute operations including the unique merge operation, idempotent merge operation, the overwrite operation, and the append operation. $\oplus$ represents the operation between the two entries, which is left associative and has the following properties:

- When the operation o_1 is the unique configuration operation, the calculation is invalid.
- When the operation o_1 is not the unique configuration operation, the configuration entry on the right side of the $\oplus$ operator has a higher priority, so we can get $\{v_1, o_1\} \oplus \{v_2, o_2\} = \{v_1 \oplus v_2, o_2\}$
- When o_2 is an idempotent merge operation, there is a commutative law $\{v_2 \oplus v_1, o_2\} = \{v_1 \oplus v_2, o_2\}$ [37], and when the recursive partial order relationship $v_2 \subseteq v_1$ is satisfied, the calculation is valid. Besides, the partial order

```
1  appConfiguration: AppConfiguration {
2      mainContainer: {
3          name = "app_container"
4          env = [{name = "APP_NAME", value = "app"}]
5      }
6      resource: {cpu = 4, memory = 8Gi, disk = 20Gi}
7      image: "images.example/app:base"
8  }
```

(a) base.k

```
1   appConfiguration: AppConfiguration {
2       # Use the append attribute operator += to append a
3       # Env and there are two Envs in the dev environment.
4       mainContainer.env += [{name = "TEST_ENV", value = "true"}]
5       # Use the attribute operator =
6       # to overwrite the resource.cpu in the base.
7       resource.cpu = 8
8       # Overwrite the image.
9       image = "images.example/app:prod"
10      # Add a attribute overQuota with the value False
11      overQuota = False
12  }
```

(b) prod.k

Fig. 7. User side code of base and production environment

calculation of two values can be defined as

$$v_2 \subseteq v_1 \Leftrightarrow \begin{cases} v_2 == v_1 \ if \ v_1 \in \{Int, Float, Boolean, String\} \\ len(v_2) == len(v_1) \ and \ \forall \ i, \ item(v_2, i) \subseteq item(v_1, i) \\ \quad if \ v_1 \in List \ and \ if \ v_2 \in List \\ \forall \ k, item(v_2, k) \subseteq item(v_1, k) \\ \quad if \ v_1 \in \{Dict, Structure\} \ and \\ \quad if \ v_2 \in \{Dict, Structure\} \end{cases} \quad (11)$$

where i denotes the index of the list element, len denotes the length of the list element, k denotes the key of the dict and structure element, and item denotes the item of the list, dict and structure element.

– When the operation o_2 is an overwrite operation, $\{v_1 \oplus v_2, o_2\} = \{v_2, o_2\}$.
– When the operation o_2 is an append operation, it will try to add v_2 to the list of v_1, and stop the calculation when v_1 is not a list type.

Figure 7 shows an example of the configuration merge. For an application configuration, there is a basic configuration *base.k*. SRE and developers maintain the configuration *prod.k* of the production and development environment respectively, and their configuration does not affect each other. As shown in

```
1   appConfiguration: AppConfiguration {
2       mainContainer = {
3           name = "app_container"
4           env = [
5               {name = "APP_NAME", value = "app"}
6               {name = "TEST_ENV", value = "true"}
7           ]
8       }
9       resource = {cpu = 8, memory = 4Gi, disk = 20Gi}
10      # Overwrite the image.
11      image = "images.example/app:prod"
12      # Add a attribute overQuota with the value False
13      overQuota = False
14  }
```

Fig. 8. Equivalent merge code

Fig. 8, the KCL compiler merges them into the equivalent code. Besides, the schema *AppConfiguration* is the application configuration structure defined by the third-party platform layer, and it maps the user's configuration to Kubernetes resources such as *Deployment* and *Service* [3,4].

7 Workflow

In addition to the design of language ability, we solve some real problems using practical solutions.

In the long-term exploration, we summarized the use experience of KCL as the best practice. The workflow is divided into four steps, as shown in Fig. 9:

1. **Coded.** Use the KCL OpenAPI tool to generate KCL schemas from the Customer Resources Definitions (CRDs) or OpenAPI models [2,5]. These schemas define the atomic capabilities of the platform.
2. **Abstraction.** Based on these atomic capabilities, the platform abstracts user-oriented front-end models and provides a set of templates. These front-end models cannot work independently, and corresponding back-end models are required. These back-end models will eventually obtain an instance of the front-end model at runtime; it parses the input front-end model and converts it into Kubernetes resources.
3. **Configuration.** Developers or SREs describe the requirements of applications based on front-end models. Users can define the base and different environment configurations for different environments e.g., base, development and production and different localities. In most cases, defining configurations only requires declaring key-value pairs. For some complex scenarios, users can define the logic to generate configurations.

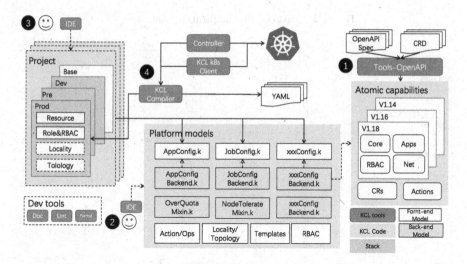

Fig. 9. Workflow

4. **Automation.** After defining the user's configuration, all components have been defined and are ready to be automated. The platform can compile, execute, output, modify, query, and perform other automatic works through the KCL CLI or GPL-binding APIs. Users can also deploy the KCL configuration to the Kubernetes cluster with tools.

8   Evaluation

We compared the language ability of KCL to other configuration languages (Sect. 8.1). In summary, KCL balances simplicity and functional comprehensiveness. In complex configuration scenarios, KCL provides better support.

For the second questions, we analyzed statistics of application of KCL. To date, we manage multi-ops scenarios in a unified way, saving 30,000+ manhours in total. Through code reuse, the compression ratio of configuration code information has reached 17.38% (Sect. 8.2).

8.1   Comparison with Other CLs

We compared the features of KCL with those of other configuration languages, and the results are presented in Table 2.

Generally, nearly all configuration languages support variables, references, data types, arithmetic, logics, conditionals, built-in functions, and imports. Following the declarative principle, these languages provide minimal or no support for function definitions and loops. KCL and some other languages provide a schema for defining data types that abstract the configuration. The difference is that KCL provides schema inheritance, whereas most configuration languages

Table 2. Features of configuration languages

	KCL	GCL	CUE	Jsonnet	HCL	Dhall
Variables	✓	✓	✓	✓	✓	✓
Reference	✓	✓	✓	✓	✓	✓
Data types	✓	✓	✓	✓	✓	✓
Schema	✓	✓	✓	✗	✗	✓
Inherited	Schema	Tuple	✗	obejct	data	data
Arithmetic&Logic	✓	✓	✓	✓	✓	✓
Loop	List/dict/schema comprehension	List comprehension	List comprehension	List/object comprehension	For splat (comprehension)	List generate function
Conditional	✓	✓	✓	✓	✓	✓
Built-in function	✓	✓	✓	✓	✓	✓
Function definition	✓	✗	✗	✓	✗	✓
Import	✓	✓	✓	✓	✓	✓
Type check	✓	✓	✓	✗	✗	✓
Testable	✓	✗	✗	✓	✗	✓
Mixin	✓	✗	✗	✗	✗	✗
Data integration	✓	✗	✗	JSON	✗	✗
Dynamic configuration	✓	✗	✗	✓	✗	✗
Policy	✓	✗	✗	✗	✗	✗
Merge	Idempotent merge/ patch/ unique configuration	Patch	Idempotent merge	Patch	✗	Idempotent merge/ patch

are inherited or merged directly based on the structured data. KCL has also been enhanced in terms of verification, mixing, dynamic configuration, and configuration merging to better facilitate developers to carry out efficient and stable collaboration.

Principally, KCL is better for engineers to use than other CLs because: (1) KCL has more features to define the configuration, which is widely needed by cloud-native applications in which the state-of-the-art modes fail to consider; (2) KCL provides stronger verification and collaboration capabilities; (3) KCL is a statically typed language that provides the type index needed for automation at compile time.

8.2   Benefits from KCL

To date, the KCL has been used in more than 800 projects (e.g., application, middleware, network, monitoring and database operations, etc.). These projects all use the design of the multi-site, multi-environment and multi-tenant as a best practice. Besides, the average configuration writing and distributing time is shortened from more than 25 days to 2 days.

As shown in Fig. 10, the KCL code for applications in multiple environments is reduced to approximately 17.38%. Moreover, for each application, the greater the number of environments, the lower information compression ratio, which means that the KCL configuration can be easily extended in different environments, but will not bring redundancy.

In addition, benefiting from KCL and support for automation, we automate some daily operations, such as modifying the configuration file when the image is updated. We analyzed the last 2000 commits, and 62.5% of which are submitted by robots. Administrators in repository maintain the scripts used for checking.

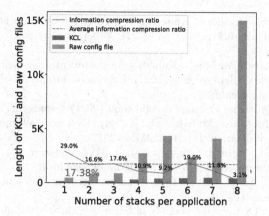

Fig. 10. Information compression ratio of KCL and raw config files

Developers and SRE develop models and define the configuration of new applications. Most of the code are submitted by bots responsible for operations and various scenarios. The number of codes automatically submitted by the system exceeds 21.24% that of users manually submitted, which keeps operations from tedious task of updating configuration.

9   Conclusion and Future Work

This paper presented KCL that serves the large-scale configuration and policy management scenario. KCL addresses three challenges: (1) stability, (2) engineering, and (3) scalability. We summarized the experiences of using the KCL and reported the best practices. Our future work includes the following:

Policy. We will better support policy capabilities such as logic writing and data query to satisfy scenarios such as service authentication.

Automation. We will provide a more complete KCL tool-set including create, retrieve, update and delete to meet more automation scenarios.

Security. We will improve language security through model checking and theorem proving and let more problems be exposed to compile time as much as possible. Besides, we will do static analysis through taint analysis and other methods.

References

1. Open-Policy Agent: conftest: write tests against structured configuration data using the open policy agent rego query language (2019). github.com/open-policy-agent/conftest
2. The Kubernetes Authors: Custom resources (2021). v1-20.docs.kubernetes.io/docs/concepts/extend-kubernetes/api-extension/custom-resources/

3. The Kubernetes Authors: Kubernetes documentation/concepts/services, load balancing, and networking/service (2021). kubernetes.io/docs/concepts/services-networking/service/
4. The Kubernetes Authors: Kubernetes documentation/concepts/workloads/ workload resources/deployments (2021). kubernetes.io/docs/concepts/workloads/ controllers/deployment/
5. The Swagger Authors: Openapi specification (2021). swagger.io/specification/
6. Beckett, R., Gupta, A., Mahajan, R., Walker, D.: A general approach to network configuration verification. In: SIGCOMM (2017)
7. Bjørner, N., de Moura, L., Nachmanson, L., Wintersteiger, C.: Programming z3 (2021). theory.stanford.edu/ nikolaj/programmingz3.html
8. Carpenter, B.: The Logic of Typed Feature Structures. Cambridge University Press, Cambridge (1992)
9. Bokharouss, I.: GCL viewer: a study in improving the understanding of GCL programs (2008)
10. Burns, B., Grant, B., Oppenheimer, D., Brewer, E., Wilkes, J.: Borg, Omega, and Kubernetes: Lessons learned from three container-management systems over a decade. Queue 14(1), 70–93 (2016)
11. Campbell, B.: The AWS CDK and Pulumi. In: Campbell, B. (ed.) The Definitive Guide to AWS Infrastructure Automation, pp. 237–272. Apress, Berkeley (2020). https://doi.org/10.1007/978-1-4842-5398-4_6
12. Da-sol, K.: KT suffers major network outage nationwide (2021). www.koreaherald.com/view.php?ud=20211025000650
13. Fairwindsops: polaris: Validation of best practices in your kubernetes clusters (2018). github.com/FairwindsOps/polaris
14. Giannarakis, N., Loehr, D., Beckett, R., Walker, D.: NV: an intermediate language for verification of network control planes. In: Proceedings of the ACM SIGPLAN Conference on Programming Language Design and Implementation (PLDI), pp. 958–973, June 2020. https://doi.org/10.1145/3385412.3386019
15. Google: Jsonnet: A data templating language for app and tool developers (2014). jsonnet.org/
16. Google: What is site reliability engineering (SRE) (2021). sre.google/
17. Grafana: Beautiful metric & analytic dashboards (2021). grafana.org/
18. Helm: The package manager for kubernetes (2021). helm.sh/
19. Instrumenta: kubeval: validate your kubernetes configuration files, supports multiple kubernetes versions (2019). kustomize.io/
20. Jääger, J., Pankova, A.: PrivaLog: a privacy-aware logic programming language. Association for Computing Machinery, New York (2021). https://doi.org/10.1145/3479394.3479410
21. Kapicorp: Generic templated configuration management for kubernetes, terraform and other things (2017). github.com/kapicorp/kapitan
22. Kubernetes: Declarative application management in kubernetes (2019)
23. Kubernetes: Managing resources for containers (2021). kubernetes.io/docs/concepts/configuration/manage-resources-containers/
24. Kubernetes: Understanding kubernetes objects (2021). kubernetes.io/docs/concepts/overview/working-with-objects/kubernetes-objects/
25. dhal-lang: dhall-haskell: Maintainable configuration files (2016). github.com/dhall-lang/dhall-haskell
26. cue-lang: CUE: Validate and define text-based and dynamic configuration (2020). cuelang.org/

27. Loeliger, J., McCullough, M.: Version Control with Git: Powerful Tools and Techniques for Collaborative Software Development. O'Reilly Media, Inc. (2012)
28. cloud66-oss: copper: a configuration file validator for kubernetes (2018). github.com/cloud66-oss/copper
29. Pierce, B.C., Benjamin, C.: Types and Programming Languages. MIT Press, Cambridge (2002)
30. The Example of Helm (2017). artifacthub.io/packages/helm/jenkinsci/jenkins
31. Riti, P., Flynn, D.: Terraform HCL (2021)
32. Sarkar, A., Sheeran, M.: Hailstorm: a statically-typed, purely functional language for IoT applications. In: Proceedings of the 22nd International Symposium on Principles and Practice of Declarative Programming, PPDP 2020. Association for Computing Machinery, New York (2020). https://doi.org/10.1145/3414080.3414092
33. kubernetes-sig: Kustomize: Kubernetes native configuration management (2019). kustomize.io/
34. stelligent: config-lint: Command line tool to validate configuration files (2018). github.com/stelligent/config-lint
35. Tang, C., et al.: Holistic configuration management at Facebook. In: Proceedings of the 25th Symposium on Operating Systems Principles, vol. 15, no. 1, pp. 328–343 (2015). https://doi.org/10.1145/2815400.2815401
36. cdk8s-team: CDK for kubernetes: Define kubernetes apps and components using familiar languages (2021). cdk8s.io/
37. Tomabechi, H.: Quasi-destructive graph unification. In: 29th Annual Meeting of the Association for Computational Linguistics, pp. 315–322 (1991)
38. Verma, A., Pedrosa, L., Korupolu, M.R., Oppenheimer, D., Tune, E., Wilkes, J.: Large-scale cluster management at Google with Borg. In: Proceedings of the European Conference on Computer Systems (EuroSys), Bordeaux, France (2015)
39. Wiki: Cloud native computing foundation Wiki (2021)
40. Wiki: Role-based access control (2021)
41. zegl: kube-score: Kubernetes object analysis with recommendations for improved reliability and security (2018). github.com/zegl/kube-score

EqFix: Fixing LaTeX Equation Errors by Examples

Fengmin Zhu[1,4] and Fei He[1,2,3(✉)]

[1] School of Software, Tsinghua University, Beijing, China
hefei@tsinghua.edu.cn
[2] Key Laboratory for Information System Security, MoE, Beijing, China
[3] Beijing National Research Center for Information Science and Technology, Beijing, China
[4] Max Planck Institute for Software Systems, Saarbrücken, China

Abstract. LaTeX is a widely-used document preparation system. Its powerful ability in mathematical equation editing is perhaps the main reason for its popularity in academia. Sometimes, however, even an expert user may spend much time fixing an erroneous equation. In this paper, we present EqFix, a synthesis-based repairing system for LaTeX equations. It employs a set of fixing rules and can suggest possible repairs for common errors in LaTeX equations. A domain-specific language is proposed for formally expressing the fixing rules. The fixing rules can be automatically synthesized from a set of input-output examples. An extension of relaxers is also introduced to enhance the practicality of EqFix. We evaluate EqFix on real-world examples and find that it can synthesize rules with high generalization ability. Compared with a state-of-the-art string transformation synthesizer, EqFix solved 37% more cases and spent less than half of their synthesis time.

Keywords: Domain-specific languages · Program synthesis · Program repair · Programming by examples

1 Introduction

LaTeX is a text-based document preparation system widely used in academia to publish and communicate scientific documents. The powerful typesetting of mathematical equations makes it a universal syntax for expressing mathematical equations. This syntax has been integrated into text-based markup languages like Markdown[1], and WYSIWYG (i.e., "What you see is what you get") document

---

This work was supported in part by the National Natural Science Foundation of China (No. 62072267 and No. 62021002) and the National Key Research and Development Program of China (No. 2018YFB1308601).

F. Zhu—Early revisions of this work were done when this author was in Tsinghua University.

[1] https://daringfireball.net/projects/markdown/.

W. Dong and J.-P. Talpin (Eds.): SETTA 2022, LNCS 13649, pp. 106–124, 2022.
https://doi.org/10.1007/978-3-031-21213-0_7

processors like MS Word[2]. Even on the web, one can display LATEX equations beautifully by MathJax[3].

Since the syntax of LATEX equations is quite *complex, non-expert* users may find it challenging to use. For example, one may expect "x^{10}" by typing "$\texttt{\$x\^{}10\$}$". This equation indeed compiles; however, its actual output is "$x^{1}0$", which goes against the user's expectation. When such an error occurs, one may resort to online help forums. However, this process is *never trivial*. First, the user has to provide several keywords (for searching) that well describe the error. Second, even if the user is fortunate to obtain some solutions, they may not necessarily work for the user's problem—the user still has to adapt the answers to that specific problem. The whole process—especially the adaption of the solutions to one's own problem—requires not only intelligence but also patience.

Programming by examples (PBE) is believed to be a revolutionary technique for end-user programming [1,7,8,10,12]. In recent decades, PBE has been adopted in the area of *program repair* [14,17]. NoFAQ [2] is a tool that employs *error messages* to assist the PBE-based repairing. This tool aims to fix common errors in Unix commands, from an input-output example that consists of an erroneous Unix command, an error message prompted by Shell, and a rectified command specified by experts. Note that the error messages prompted by Unix Shell are usually instantiated from a set of predefined templates; the stored information in the messages can thus be easily extracted by patterns.

Inspired by NoFAQ and other PBE techniques, we present EqFix, a system for automatically fixing erroneous LATEX equations by examples. Note that NoFAQ cannot be applied to our problem setting for two reasons: First, an equation error is not necessarily a compilation error, such as "$\texttt{\$x\^{}10\$}$" indeed compiles but produces an unexpected result. For such errors, one needs to specify the error message on their own. Thus, we cannot assume this message has a fixed structure (i.e., is instantiated from a template) as in NoFAQ. Second, the Unix command can be directly *tokenized* into a sequence of strings (using whitespaces as the delimiters), which makes it straightforward (by comparing the tokenized strings in turn) to locate the error position in the text of the Unix command. However, it is not the same case for equation text. Instead, we have to collaborate the corresponding *error message* to tokenize an equation.

To the best of our knowledge, EqFix is the first attempt at equation repair using PBE techniques. Novice users can use it to automatically fix common errors in LATEX equations; expert users can contribute corrections for erroneous equations. We design a *domain-specific language* (DSL) for formally defining the fixing rules for erroneous LATEX equations (Sect. 3). Intuitively, a fixing rule consists of an *error pattern*, which specifies what error messages this rule is applicable, and a *transformer* which performs the actual fixing via string transformation. We propose an algorithm for synthesizing fixing rules expressed by our DSL from input-output examples (Sect. 4). We also introduce *relaxers* to describe the *generalization* of equation patterns, with which the search space

---

[2] https://products.office.com/en-us/word.
[3] https://www.mathjax.org.

relating to the faulty parts is expanded so that we can handle more repairing problems.

We evaluated EqFix on a dataset containing 89 groups of real-world examples (Sect. 5). Note that NoFAQ is limited to repairing buggy Unix commands; we instead took the state-of-the-art PBE tool FlashFill as our baseline. We selected the longest example in each group as our test case. We found that EqFix solved 72 (80.9%) of the test cases in less time, whereas FlashFill solved only 39 (43.82%). Our prototype implementation and experiment artifact are publicly available: https://github.com/thufv/EqFix.

The main technical contributions of this paper are summarized as follows:

- We present EqFix, a PBE-based system for automatically fixing erroneous LATEX equations.
- We design a DSL for formally expressing fixing rules. We rely on equation patterns to extract and transfer relevant information between error messages and equations. The patterns can be generalized by relaxers when necessary.
- We conducted experiments on real-world examples. Results reveal the high effectiveness and applicability of our approach.

2   EqFix by Examples

We use several real-world examples (in Table 1) to showcase how EqFix repairs LATEX equations. All of the examples were extracted from an online LATEX forum[4]. To be clear and short, we neglect the unchanged substrings of long equations. Each example consists of three components – the input equation eq, the error message err, and the fixed equation fix. For convenience of reference, we number these examples from 1 to 8 and refer their components as eq_i, err_i, fix_i, for $1 \leq i \leq 8$, respectively. The LATEX output on each equation (if it compiles) is displayed below the equation text.

Examples #1 – #4 present a scene where a user expects a superscript but forgets to parenthesize the superscript expression. As shown in #1, given the input equation "\$x^10\$" (eq_1), LATEX treats only "1" but not the entire number "10" as the superscript. In this way, it outputs "x^10", which is against the user's intent. Note that the input equation eq_1 itself is syntactically correct because the LATEX compiler did not report any error. In this way, the user must specify an error message by hand to express their intent. To express the error type conveniently, a set of predefined *keywords* (Table 2 presents a selected subset) are provided for selection. In a future direction, via natural language processing, we may simply accept a natural language sentence as the error message for even better practicality. Then, the user needs to point out a substring of the erroneous input equation to show the error location. The error message is a combination of the keywords and substring of the input equation. Here, in err_1, "superscript" is a predefined keyword indicating some substring of the input equation is expected to be the superscript, and "10" gives the error location.

---

[4] https://tex.stackexchange.com.

Table 1. Motivating examples.

#	eq	err	fix
1	`$x^10$` x^10	`superscript 10`	`$x^{10}$` x^{10}
2	`$y^123+x$` $y^123 + x$	`superscript 123`	`$y^{123}+x$` $y^{123} + x$
3	`$f^(k)$` $f^(k)$	`superscript (k)`	`$f^{(k)}$` $f^{(k)}$
4	`$y=x+\ldots+x^10$` $y = x + \ldots + x^10$	`superscript 10`	`$y=x+\ldots+x^{10}$` $y = x + \ldots + x^{10}$
5	`${1,2,3$`	`Missing } inserted`	`${1,2,3}$` $1, 2, 3$
6	`$S={x_1,\ldots,x_n$`	`Missing } inserted`	`$S={x_1,\ldots,x_n}$` $S = x_1, \ldots, x_n$
7	`$2\^x$`	`Command \^ invalid` `in math mode`	`$2^x$` 2^x
8	`$\sum\limits_{i=1}\^N t_i$`	`Command \^ invalid` `in math mode`	`$\sum\limits_{i=1}^N t_i$` $\sum\limits_{i=1}^N t_i$

Then, an expert may fix[5] the input equation as "`$x^{10}$`", i.e., surrounding "10" with a pair of curly brackets. The three components, i.e., (eq_1, err_1, fix_1), compose an *input-output example*, with which we can synthesize a *(fixing) rule*. Each rule consists of an *error pattern* for matching the error message and a *transformer* that will be applied to the input equation to produce a fix. Intuitively, the underlying fixing strategy of this rule would be "surrounding the superscript with a pair of curly brackets".

EqFix can switch between the *training mode* for synthesizing rules and the *applying mode* for repairing erroneous equations, based on a *rule library* that saves all the learned rules so far. In the training mode, EqFix takes user-given examples (typically by expert users) as input. It first searches in its rule library to obtain a rule that can be *refined* to be *consistent* with the new examples. For instance, the example #2 can be added by refining the fixing rule synthesized merely by #1. If it is not the case (for instance, consider the examples #5 to #8), a new rule is synthesized and the rule library gets enlarged.

In the applying mode, EqFix attempts to solve an *equation repair problem*— an erroneous equation together with an error message—typically provided by an end user. To do so, it searches in its rule library for all applicable rules, i.e., those whose error patterns can match against the error message, and attempts to apply them (the transformer of the rule) to the input equation. For instance, the rule synthesized from examples #1 and #2 is applicable to equation repair problems #3 and #4: applying this rule on (eq_3, err_3) and (eq_4, err_4) gives fix_3 and fix_4 respectively. Since there can be more than one applicable rule, users are asked to review the suggested fixes and approve one that meets the intent. If no rule is applicable, or all suggested fixes are rejected by the user, EqFix fails on this equation repair problem. In that situation, we expect an expert user to

---

[5] As another option, we may get the fix by online search.

Table 2. Selected keywords supported by EqFix.

Keywords	Interpretations
Superscript	Expected as a superscript
Subscript	Expected as a subscript
Set	Expected as a set
Function	Expected as a math function/operator
Greek letter	Expected as a greek letter
Fraction numerator	Expected as the numerator of a fraction
Fraction denominator	Expected as the denominator of a fraction
Operator sum	Expected as a sum operator
Operator product	Expected as a product operator
Long arrow	Expected as a long arrow

figure out a correction, which, in association with the erroneous equation and the error message, forms a new example for synthesis under the training mode. The newly synthesized rule will be recorded in the rule library so that it can apply (under the applying mode) to future equation repair problems in this category.

Sometimes, an erroneous equation contains multiple errors. One needs to interact with EqFix in multiple rounds to fix them all. The user feeds the erroneous equation together with one of the error messages in the initial round and iteratively corrects the other errors using the fixed equation of the last round.

The rest examples in Table 1 showcase two LaTeXcompile errors: unmatched brackets (#5 – #6) and invalid superscript operator (#7 – #8). The error messages prompted by the LaTeXcompiler are instantiated from some templates defined by LaTeX. Both compiler-prompted and keywords-based error messages are handled in a unified way (we will explain that in Sect. 3.1). Back to the examples, a possible correction for #5 (#6 is similar) suggested by an expert is "${1,2,3}$", which inserts the missing right curly bracket ('}') at the end of the equation. A possible correction for #7 (and #8) is to use '^" in place of the erroneous "\^". Note that #8 is more complicated than #7, while it can be automatically fixed using the rule synthesized from #7.

In summary, EqFix facilitates an automated approach for fixing common errors in editing LaTeX equations. Our approach is rule-based (Sect. 3) and the synthesis by input-output examples (Sect. 4) is automated. One benefit of our system is that we may collect many examples and train a set of fixing rules from them in advance that covers many common problems end users meet. Another benefit is that the manual efforts of adapting the searched correction to their cases, which might be the most challenging part to end users, are saved.

3   Rules in EqFix

EqFix is a rule-based system. Rules are formally defined by a DSL as shown in Fig. 1. Each *rule* $\mathcal{R}$ is a pair $\langle EP, \mathcal{T} \rangle$, where EP is an *error pattern* describing the

$$\text{(Fixing) rule } \mathcal{R} ::= \langle EP, \mathcal{T}\rangle$$
$$\text{Transformer } \mathcal{T} ::= \{v_1 \mapsto \tau_1, \dots, v_k \mapsto \tau_k\}$$
$$\text{Error pattern } EP ::= [M_1, \dots, M_k]$$
$$\text{Matcher } M ::= s \mid v$$
$$\text{Equation pattern } P ::= [M_1, \dots, M_k]$$

Fig. 1. Syntax of fixing rules.

template of the error message and which problem-specific information needs to be extracted from that message, and $\mathcal{T}$ is a *transformer* specifying the required transformation on the erroneous equation to fix the equation repair problem.

3.1 Error Pattern

An error message either comes from the LᴬTEX compiler (e.g., #5 – #8 of Table 1) or the user (e.g., #1 – #4). For the latter case, we assume the error message starts with one or more predefined *keywords* (as in Table 2) that mention the error type and then followed by a substring of the erroneous equation which locates the error. In either case, we represent the error message as a natural language sentence that can be split into a list of *tokens* $[e_1, \dots, e_k]$ by delimiters (whitespaces, commas, etc.). EqFix is unaware of the resource of the error messages and employs a unified *error pattern* to match against them. Users are allowed to customize their keywords because EqFix regards them as normal tokens.

An *error pattern* $EP = [EM_1, \dots, EM_k]$ contains a list of *matchers*, where each of them is either: (1) a string matcher s that only matches against s itself, or (2) a variable matcher v that matches against any token and binds the matched token to v. An error message $[e_1, \dots, e_{k'}]$ matches EP if they have the same length ($k = k'$), and that every token e_i ($1 \leq i \leq k$) matches the corresponding matcher M_i. The matching result (if succeeds) is a mapping from variables to the bound string values $\{v_1 \mapsto s_1, \dots, v_k \mapsto s_k\}$.

Example 1. Consider $err_2 = [\text{"superscript"}, \text{"123"}]$ from Table 1. Let $EP_1 \triangleq [\text{"superscript"}, v_1]$ be an error pattern. Matching err_2 against EP_1 succeeds with $\{v_1 \mapsto \text{"123"}\}$, i.e., "123" is bound to v_1.

3.2 Equation Pattern

Unlike an error message, an equation text usually involves complicated syntax and thus cannot be directly tokenized by commonly seen delimiters. To extract the problem-specific information from an equation (e.g., to find the cause of the error), we propose the notion of an *equation pattern*.

An *equation pattern* $P = [M_1, \dots, M_k]$ consists of a list of matchers. Especially, the string and variable matchers in P must appear *alternately*, that is, if M_i is a string, then M_{i+1} must be a variable and vice versa. Intuitively, the string matchers in an equation pattern are indeed used as "delimiters" to tokenize the equation into a list of "tokens". Each "token" of the equation matches a variable matcher and may convey some *problem-specific* information which may be useful later in generating a corrected equation. Oppositely, if we allow consecutive variable matchers to appear in an equation pattern, the split would be *ambiguous*. For instance, consider a string "alpha" and an equation pattern $[v_1, v_2]$, we could either let v_1 match against "a" (and v_2 match against "lpha"), or let v_1 match against "al" (and v_2 match against "pha"), etc.

Pattern Matching. Given that string and variable matchers appear alternately, we pattern match an equation pattern P against an equation *eq* by simply locating the occurrences of the string matchers in *eq* (failure if we cannot)—the variable matchers then match against the substrings in between. For example, matching $[v_1, \text{"foo"}, v_2]$ against "(foo)" yields the bindings $\{v_1 \mapsto \text{"("}, v_2 \mapsto \text{")"}\}$, because the equation is split into three parts "(" $\cdot$ "foo" $\cdot$ ")".

Pattern Instantiation. Equation patterns can be regarded as "templates" of equation text where the variable matchers are "placeholders". Thus it is natural to define pattern *instantiation*—the reverse of pattern matching—to obtain a (concrete) equation by replacing the variable matchers with the bound strings.

Example 2. Consider example #2 of Table 1, where $eq_2 = \text{"\$y\^123+x\$"}$. Let $P_2 \triangleq [\text{"\$y\^"}, v_1, \text{"+x\$"}]$ be an equation pattern. Matching eq_2 against P_2 gives $\sigma = \{v_1 \mapsto \text{"123"}\}$. Further, instantiating P_2 with σ gives back eq_2.

Pattern Generation. In EqFix, equation patterns are not explicitly presented in the rule. They are only *intermediate* during rule application. To construct an equation pattern P from an erroneous equation *eq* with the matching result $\sigma = \{v_1 \mapsto s_1, \ldots, v_k \mapsto s_k\}$ from an error pattern, we substitute all the occurrences of $s_1, \ldots, s_k$ in *eq* with $v_1, \ldots, v_k$, respectively.

Example 3. Given $\sigma = \{v_1 \mapsto \text{"123"}\}$ and $eq_2 = \text{"\$y\^123+x\$"}$, applying the above process yields $[\text{"\$y\^"}, v_1, \text{"+x\$"}]$.

3.3 Transformer

Our DSL achieves an underlying repairing strategy via string transformation. Since string matchers express the *problem-unspecific* information, the substrings in the erroneous equation matched by them should be kept in the corrected equation. The substrings matched by variable matchers, on the other hand, need to be transformed by *string transformers*—functions that map a string into a new one. The string transformer we employ in EqFix is expressed by a variant of FlashFill's DSL [7] but possesses a more restricted syntax for better efficiency. Technical details can be found in our extended version [29]. In EqFix, we define a *transformer*—a mapping from the variable matchers into string transformers—to collect all necessary string transformations.

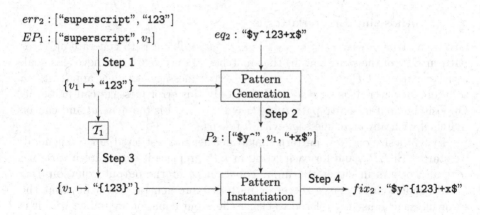

$err_2 :$ ["superscript", "123"]

$EP_1 :$ ["superscript", v_1] $eq_2 :$ "\$y^123+x\$"

Step 1

$\{v_1 \mapsto$ "123"$\}$ ⟶ Pattern Generation

Step 2

T_1 $P_2 :$ ["\$y^", v_1, "+x\$"]

Step 3

$\{v_1 \mapsto$ "{123}"$\}$ ⟶ Pattern Instantiation — Step 4 → $fix_2 :$ "\$y^{123}+x\$"

Fig. 2. Application of the rule $\mathcal{R}_1 = \langle EP_1, T_1 \rangle$ to the input (eq_2, err_2).

Example 4. Let τ_1 be a string transformer that inserts a pair of curly parentheses surrounding the input. Let $T_1 \triangleq \{v_1 \mapsto \tau_1\}$ be a transformer. Applying T_1 to $\sigma = \{v_1 \mapsto$ "123"$\}$ yields $\sigma' = \{v_1 \mapsto$ "{123}"$\}$.

3.4 Rule Application

Putting the above operations together, we now present how a rule $\mathcal{R} = \langle EP, T \rangle$ is applied to an equation repair problem (eq, err):

1. match EP against err to extract problem-specific information recorded in a mapping σ;
2. generate an equation pattern P (from σ), regarded as an "template" of eq;
3. perform the underlying repairing strategy expressed by the set of string transformers in T on σ to obtain a new σ';
4. obtain the corrected equation by instantiating P with σ'.

Example 5. Let rule $\mathcal{R}_1 \triangleq \langle EP_1, T_1 \rangle$, where EP_1 is defined in Example 1 and T_1 is defined in Example 4. Following the above steps, we apply $\mathcal{R}_1$ to the equation repair problem (eq_2, err_2) (depicted by Fig. 2):

1. matching EP_1 against err_2 gives σ (as in Example 1);
2. generate P_2 from eq_2 and σ (as in Example 3);
3. transform σ into σ' by T_1 (as in Example 4);
4. instantiating P with σ' gives fix_2 (as in Example 2).

4 Rule Synthesis

The rule synthesis algorithm takes a set of input-output examples $\mathcal{E}$ as the specification, and generates a fixing rule $\mathcal{R} = \langle EP, T \rangle$ consistent with the examples. The synthesis consists of two passes: (1) an error pattern EP is synthesized from the examples $\mathcal{E}$, and (2) a transformer T is synthesized from $\mathcal{E}$ and EP.

4.1 Synthesizing Error Patterns

Given an error message $err = [e_1, \ldots, e_k]$, our problem is to generate an error pattern EP (of the same length) that matches against err. To achieve this goal, a naive pattern $EP_\perp = [e_1, \ldots, e_k]$, the error message itself, is apparently a solution. However, it is so *restricted* that only this error message can match it. Oppositely, another naive pattern $EP_\top = [v_1, \ldots, v_k]$ is too *general* and can be matched with any error message with k tokens.

To synthesize an error pattern that is neither too restricted nor too general, we start with $EP_\perp$, and for each string in $EP_\perp$, replace it with a fresh variable; if it also occurs in either the input equation eq or the output equation fix. Such a replacement makes the error pattern more general. Realizing that the error message is usually related to either the input equation by telling why it is erroneous or the output equation by explaining how to repair it, the introduced variables, in either case, will capture such important information.

4.2 Synthesizing Transformers

The essential problem of synthesizing a transformer $\{v_1 \mapsto \tau_1, \ldots, v_k \mapsto \tau_k\}$ is to synthesize the underlying string transformers $\tau_1, \ldots, \tau_k$. This problem has been well-studied in previous literature, and a well-known approach could be the PBE approach invented by FlashFill [7]. To adopt their approach in our setting, we must extract a set of *input-output string examples*, each is a pair (s, s') packed the input string s and the expected output string s', as the specification for synthesizing each string transformer τ_i.

Let us first consider the situation where the generated pattern (using the pattern generalization process mentioned in Sect. 3.2) matches against both the input and output equations for all examples $\mathcal{E}$. This condition implies that we can always compute two mappings by matching the generated pattern against the input and output equation. Thus, to synthesize τ_i, we are able to extract an input-output string example $(\sigma(v_i), \sigma'(v_i))$ for each example in $\mathcal{E}$ (so the complete specification is their union), where σ and σ' are the two mappings computed as above.

Example 6. Given examples #1 and #2 from Table 1, to synthesize a transformer τ_1, we extract ("10", "{10}") from example #1, and ("123", "{123}") from example #2 (see Example 3 for the generated pattern). Thus, the complete specification for synthesizing τ_1 is $\varphi_1 = \{("10", "\{10\}"), ("123", "\{123\}")\}$.

Suppose the generated pattern only matches against the input equation but not the output; we must generalize this pattern so that it matches against the output equation. The generalization process is an extension to EqFix, and we will discuss it later in Sect. 4.3. Once this is done, the synthesis method we have just introduced works again. So far, we have adequate mechanism to synthesize a rule from example #1 of Table 1 (depicted in Fig. 3):

1. synthesize an error pattern EP_1 by comparing err_1 with eq_1 and fix_1, respectively, $\sigma_1 = \{v_1 \mapsto "10"\}$ records the values of the matched variable;

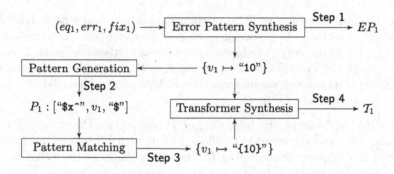

Fig. 3. Synthesis a rule $\mathcal{R}_1 = \langle EP_1, \mathcal{T}_1 \rangle$ by example (eq_1, err_1, fix_1).

2. generate the equation pattern P_1;
3. match P_1 against fix_1, yielding $\sigma'_1 = \{v_1 \mapsto \text{"}\{10\}''\}$;
4. synthesize τ_1 from $\{(\text{"}10'', \text{"}\{10\}'')\}$, which gives rise to the transformer $\mathcal{T}_1 = \{v_1 \mapsto \tau_1\}$.

4.3 Extension: Pattern Generalization via Lazy Relaxation

Let us study some examples to get a sense of how to generalize patterns.

Example 7. Consider example #5 of Table 1, where

- $eq_5 = \text{"\${1,2,3\$}''$,
- $fix_5 = \text{"\${1,2,3}\$}''$, and
- $err_5 = \text{"Missing } inserted}''$.

Let $EP_2 \triangleq [\text{"Missing}'', v_1, \text{"inserted}'']$ be the error pattern. Matching EP_2 against err_5 gives $\sigma_5 = \{v_1 \mapsto \text{"}\}''\}$. From eq_5 and σ_5, an equation pattern $P_5 = [\text{"\${1,2,3\$}'']$ is generated. We see that P_5 cannot be matched by fix_5. However, a more general pattern such as $[v]$ (where v is a fresh variable) matches with fix_5.

Example 8. Consider $eq = s_1 \cdot s_2 \cdot s_3 \cdot s_4$, $fix = s_1 \cdot s'_2 \cdot s'_3 \cdot s'_4$, and $\sigma = \{v_1 \mapsto s_2, v_2 \mapsto s_4\}$. Note that s_2, s_3 and s_4 are all modified in fix compared to eq, however s_3 is not bound to a variable in σ. From eq and σ, an equation pattern $[s_1, v_1, s_3, v_2]$ is generated, which apparently does not match against fix. However, a more general pattern like $[s_1, v]$ (v is a fresh variable) can match fix, where v is matched against $s'_2 \cdot s'_3 \cdot s'_4$.

We learn from the examples that if the generated equation pattern cannot match the output equation, we can always replace several string matchers with fresh variables until it matches against the output equation – we call this process *pattern relaxation*. As the relaxation goes on, the pattern becomes more and more general. In the worst case, it gives $P_\top = [v]$ that consists of a single variable v and can be matched by any string (as in Example 7). To find a relaxed pattern that is as strict as possible, the relaxation should be *lazy*.

Lazy Relaxation Process. Let P be an equation pattern, and s be a string (i.e., the output equation). As a special case, if P is a constant (i.e., contains no variables), $P_\top$ is the only possible relaxed pattern. Otherwise, since P cannot match against s, there must be some string s' in P that is not a substring of s. Three kinds of relaxations are performed on P depending on the relative position (left, right, or binary) of s' in P:

(left) If s' appears at the beginning of P, we replace the subpattern that consists of s' and the variable V followed by it, with a fresh variable $\mathsf{LVar}(V)$.
(right) If s' appears in the end of P, we replace the subpattern that consists of s' and the variable V before it, with a fresh variable $\mathsf{RVar}(V)$.
(binary) If s' appears in the middle of P, we replace the subpattern that consists of s' and the adjacent variables V_1 and V_2, with a fresh variable $\mathsf{BVar}(V_1, V_2)$.

The above repeats until the current pattern already matches against s.

Example 9. Pattern P_5 in Example 7 is relaxed to $P_\top$.

Example 10. Pattern $[s_1, v_1, s_3, v_2]$ in Example 8 is relaxed to $[s_1, \mathsf{BVar}(v_1, v_2)]$.

Example 11. Consider a pattern $[s_1, v_2, s_3, v_4, s_5, v_6, s_7]$ and an output equation $s_1' \cdot s_2 \cdot s_3 \cdot s_4 \cdot s_5' \cdot s_6 \cdot s_7'$. It takes several steps to obtain a relaxed result. In the following, we highlight the relaxed subpattern with an underline and annotate the unmatched string with an asterisk:

$$[\underline{s_1^*, v_2}, s_3, v_4, s_5, v_6, s_7] \rightarrow [\mathsf{LVar}(v_2), s_3, \underline{v_4, s_5^*, v_6}, s_7]$$
$$\rightarrow [\mathsf{LVar}(v_2), s_3, \underline{\mathsf{BVar}(v_4, v_6), s_7^*}]$$
$$\rightarrow [\mathsf{LVar}(v_2), s_3, \mathsf{RVar}(\mathsf{BVar}(v_4, v_6))]$$

Relaxers and Synthesis. We extend the rule DSL (Fig. 1) to include *relaxers* that syntactically encode the three kinds of relaxations, with id for no relaxation:

$$\text{Rule } \mathcal{R} ::= \langle EP, \{r_1, \ldots, r_k\}, \mathcal{T} \rangle$$
$$\text{Relaxer } r ::= \mathsf{id}(v) \mid \mathsf{LRelax}(r) \mid \mathsf{RRelax}(r) \mid \mathsf{BRelax}(r_1, r_2)$$
$$\text{Variable } V ::= v \mid \mathsf{LVar}(V) \mid \mathsf{RVar}(V) \mid \mathsf{BVar}(V_1, V_2)$$

In applying a rule with relaxers, one or more subpatterns of the generated equation pattern will be substituted with fresh variables according to the relaxers. For synthesis, the above lazy relaxation process is performed, and the relaxations that have been applied are recorded as corresponding relaxers. For more technical details, please refer to our extended version [29].

5   Evaluation

We prototyped the proposed approach as a tool EqFix, written in a combination of F# and C#, running on the .NET core platform. Rule application, synthesis algorithms, and relaxer extensions were built following the approaches proposed in the paper. We developed the synthesizer for string transformation under the PROSE framework (proposed in [22]), in which we specified the syntax and semantics of our DSL, a set of witness functions for guiding PROSE's synthesis engine, and a bunch of scoring functions for ranking candidate programs.

To measure the performance of EqFix, we conducted an experimental comparison with FlashFill [7], a state-of-the-art synthesizer for string manipulation, on a dataset that consists of 89 input-output *example groups* collected from the web (online help forums, tutorials, and technical blogs), each reveals one type of common mistake that users make, such as mismatch of delimiters and misuse of commands. Unlike the machine learning approaches, PBE techniques usually only need a few (2–5) examples. The lengths of the erroneous equations vary from 5 to 166, with an average of 18.

5.1 Experimental Setup

The baseline tool FlashFill was initially designed for string manipulation in spreadsheets (such as Excel), so an input-output example comprises a column of strings as input and a single string as output. To adapt FlashFill to our problem domain, we regarded an erroneous equation and an error message as two *indistinguished* input columns.

Another difference between FlashFill and EqFix is that FlashFill does not maintain a rule library. To make a fair comparison, we made the following adaption to avoid the usage of rule libraries: both tools were tested on an equation repair problem immediately after the rules were synthesized using the examples under the same example group. Since the number of consistent string transformers with a given specification is usually multiple, our synthesis algorithm will produce multiple candidate rules as well for one group of input-output examples. The candidate rules were ranked with heuristics, and we only attempted the top-10 candidate rules for each test case for fixing. If any rule gives a fixed equation that equals the expected correction of that test case, the test case is said "solved" (otherwise "failed"). In each example group, we left the one with the longest erroneous equation as the test case and the others as training examples. We set four training configurations C1, ..., C4, where Ci ($i = 1, ..., 4$) means the first i shortest (by the length of the erroneous equation) examples in the training set are used for synthesis. There were, in total, 356 training runs of EqFix (and also for FlashFill).

The experiments were conducted on an Intel(R) Core(TM) i5 laptop with 2.3 GHz CPU and 8 GB memory, running Mac OS 11.6 and .NET core 2.2.207.

5.2 Results

The overall number of solved test cases is presented in Fig. 4. EqFix outperformed FlashFill under all configurations. When training with only one example (C1), EqFix solved 67 (75.2%) test cases, whereas FlashFill failed to solve any. Both

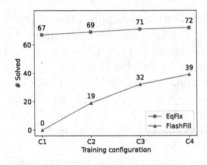
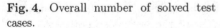

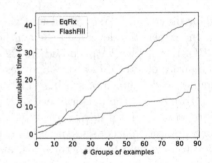

Fig. 4. Overall number of solved test cases.

Fig. 5. Cumulative synthesis time (s) with an increasing number of training example groups (C4).

EqFix and FlashFill performed better when more training examples were given—this is well-understood, as more training examples eliminate spurious rules and lead to more general rules. With the entire training set (C4), EqFix solved 72 (80.9%) while FlashFill solved less than half of the test cases. Therefore, EqFix has a more vital learning ability in our problem domain.

Impact of Ranking. To understand how ranking affects the ability to solve the test cases, we list the numbers of attempted rules[6] in Table 3. A cross mark "✗" indicates that no (top-10) rules produced the expected fix. Among the solved test cases by EqFix, at most 5 rules were attempted (#81), and 57 – 68 test cases were solved by the top-ranked rule. In contrast, FlashFill attempted at most 8 rules (#48), and 0 – 33 test cases were solved by the top-ranked rule. We also recognize that providing more training examples helps to decrease the number of attempts, e.g., in #4 and #82.

Generalization Ability. Thanks to the dynamic generation of equation patterns, the rules learned by EqFix are *insensitive* to where errors locate. In example #1 of Table 1, the erroneous part "10" appears at the end of the input equation, whereas in example #2, "123" appears before "+x" in the input equation. Although their positions are distinct, the rule synthesized by example #1 is general enough to fix problem #2, as the generated equation pattern P_2 (in Fig. 2) replaces "123" with v_1. In contrast, the rules learned by FlashFill are less general—in many cases, they are position-*sensitive* because FlashFill does not support extracting problem-specific information from error messages, which is a major difference between the two. As a result, the rule learned from #1 by FlashFill cannot generalize to solve #2 while EqFix can.

Efficiency. Figure 5 depicts the cumulative synthesis time when the number of training example groups increases under C4. The average time was 201 ms for EqFix and 476 ms for FlashFill. EqFix spent less time on 78 out of 89 runs.

---

[6] Rules were attempted in the order of the rank list.

Table 3. Numbers of attempted rules for solving each test case, EqFix (E) v.s. FlashFill (F).

#	C1 E	C1 F	C2 E	C2 F	C3 E	C3 F	C4 E	C4 F
1	1	✗	1	✗	1	✗	1	✗
2	1	✗	1	✗	1	✗	1	✗
3	✗	✗	✗	✗	✗	✗	✗	1
4	2	✗	2	✗	2	✗	1	1
5	1	✗	1	✗	1	✗	1	✗
6	1	✗	1	✗	1	✗	1	✗
7	1	✗	1	✗	1	✗	1	✗
8	✗	✗	✗	2	✗	2	✗	2
9	1	✗	1	✗	1	✗	1	✗
10	1	✗	1	1	1	1	1	1
11	1	✗	1	✗	1	✗	1	✗
12	✗	✗	✗	1	✗	1	✗	1
13	1	✗	1	1	1	1	1	1
14	1	✗	1	✗	1	✗	1	✗
15	✗	✗	✗	✗	✗	✗	✗	✗
16	1	✗	1	2	1	1	1	1
17	✗	✗	✗	✗	✗	✗	✗	✗
18	✗	✗	✗	✗	✗	✗	✗	✗
19	1	✗	1	✗	1	✗	1	✗
20	1	✗	1	✗	1	✗	1	✗
21	1	✗	1	1	1	1	1	1
22	1	✗	1	2	1	2	1	1
23	1	✗	1	2	1	✗	1	✗
24	1	✗	1	✗	1	✗	1	✗
25	1	✗	1	✗	1	✗	1	✗
26	2	✗	1	✗	1	1	1	1
27	1	✗	1	1	1	1	1	1
28	1	✗	1	2	1	2	1	1
29	1	✗	1	2	1	2	1	2
30	1	✗	1	✗	1	✗	1	✗
31	1	✗	1	1	1	1	1	1
32	2	✗	1	✗	1	✗	1	✗
33	2	✗	1	✗	1	✗	1	2
34	2	✗	2	✗	1	2	1	1
35	3	✗	2	✗	1	✗	1	✗
36	✗	✗	✗	✗	1	2	1	2
37	1	✗	1	✗	1	✗	1	✗
38	1	✗	1	✗	1	1	1	1
39	1	✗	1	✗	1	✗	1	✗
40	1	✗	1	✗	1	✗	1	✗
41	1	✗	1	✗	1	✗	1	1
42	✗	✗	✗	✗	✗	✗	✗	✗
43	1	✗	1	✗	1	1	1	1
44	1	✗	1	✗	1	✗	1	✗
45	1	✗	1	✗	1	1	1	1
46	✗	✗	✗	✗	1	1	1	1
47	1	✗	1	✗	1	4	1	✗
48	✗	✗	✗	8	✗	8	✗	8
49	✗	✗	3	2	3	2	3	2
50	1	✗	1	✗	1	✗	1	✗
51	1	✗	1	✗	1	✗	1	✗
52	1	✗	1	✗	1	✗	1	✗
53	1	✗	1	✗	1	✗	1	1
54	1	✗	1	✗	1	1	1	1
55	✗	✗	✗	✗	✗	✗	✗	✗
56	1	✗	1	✗	1	✗	1	✗
57	1	✗	1	✗	1	✗	1	✗
58	1	✗	1	✗	1	✗	1	✗
59	✗	✗	✗	✗	✗	✗	✗	✗
60	1	✗	1	✗	1	✗	1	✗
61	3	✗	3	2	3	2	3	1
62	1	✗	1	1	1	1	1	1
63	✗	✗	✗	✗	✗	✗	✗	✗
64	1	✗	1	2	1	✗	1	✗
65	1	✗	1	✗	1	✗	1	✗
66	1	✗	1	2	1	1	1	1
67	✗	✗	✗	✗	✗	✗	1	1
68	✗	✗	✗	✗	✗	✗	✗	✗
69	1	✗	1	✗	1	✗	1	1
70	✗	✗	✗	✗	1	1	1	1
71	1	✗	1	✗	✗	✗	✗	✗
72	1	✗	1	✗	1	✗	1	✗
73	1	✗	1	✗	1	1	1	✗
74	2	✗	1	✗	1	✗	1	✗
75	1	✗	1	✗	1	✗	1	1
76	1	✗	1	✗	1	4	1	1
77	✗	✗	✗	✗	✗	1	✗	1
78	✗	✗	✗	✗	✗	1	✗	1
79	✗	✗	✗	✗	✗	✗	✗	✗
80	1	✗	1	✗	1	1	1	1
81	5	✗	5	✗	5	✗	5	✗
82	3	✗	2	1	2	1	2	1
83	✗	✗	✗	✗	✗	✗	✗	✗
84	1	✗	1	✗	1	✗	1	✗
85	1	✗	1	✗	1	✗	1	✗
86	1	✗	1	✗	1	✗	1	✗
87	1	✗	1	✗	1	1	1	1
88	1	✗	1	✗	1	✗	1	✗
89	✗	✗	1	✗	1	✗	1	✗

Relaxer Extension. We also noticed that in 17 (19.1%) of the 89 synthesized rules under configuration C4, relaxers exhibited in the synthesized rule. This reveals that the relaxer extension is necessary and improves our tool's practicality.

Failure Cases. EqFix failed on 17 test cases under C4. Manually inspecting these cases, we classified the cause of failure into three categories:

- Inconsistent examples (7 cases): The provided examples are *inconsistent* with each other, so our synthesizer failed to give any consistent rule.
- Insufficient error message (6 cases): The provided error messages are *insufficient*, and EqFix could not generate a useful equation pattern.
- Restricted DSL expressiveness (4 cases): The test case is *deviated far* from the training examples of the same group, and due to the restricted expressiveness of our DSL, the learned rule could not generalize to that test case.

Testing the Rule Library. Additionally, we conducted another evaluation on the same dataset, but only for EqFix, that fitted a more realistic setting where equation repair problems are solved by trying the initial rules saved in a rule library. We obtained the initial rule library by learning from the entire training set examples (C4) under the training mode. Then, under the applying mode, we tested all 89 test cases. Interestingly, compared with the results shown in Table 3, one more test case (#71) was solved (by the top-ranked rule synthesized from the example group #69).

6 Related Work

Program Repair. Automated program repair aims to automatically correct programs so that they satisfy the desired specification [5]. Heuristic-based repair tools such as GenProg [4,15,26] employs an extended form of genetic programming with heuristics. However, it is shown that these techniques produce patches that overfit the test suite [25]. Ranking techniques have been studied to address the problem. ACS [27] produces precise patches with a refined ranking technique for condition synthesis. PAR [13] mines bug fix patterns from the history and gives frequently occurring fixes high priority. Prophet [17] outperforms the previous works by learning a probabilistic model for ranking the candidate patches.

Semantics-based repair techniques generate repairs via symbolic execution [18,21] and program synthesis [16]. Such techniques, however, are also suspected of overfitting the test suite. Recently, a new repair synthesis engine called S3 is proposed [14]. It leverages *Programming by Examples* (PBE) methodology to synthesize high-quality bug repairs, elaborating several ranking features.

Technically, EqFix belongs to the semantics-based family. To avoid overfitting, we also rely on the ranking technique for promoting rules with a high generality. Furthermore, syntactic errors are common and must be tackled in equation repair, while it is usually neglected in program repair, as people concern more about bugs [19]. HelpMeOut [9] aids developers to debug compilation and run-time error messages by suggesting past solutions. Unlike EqFix, it only provides related examples and cannot create repairs for new problems.

NoFAQ [2] is a system for fixing buggy Unix commands using PBE. Although the problem domain is similar to ours, due to its lazy synthesis algorithm, it only can synthesize a practical fixing rule when at least two examples are provided. In contrast, in many cases, one example is sufficient for EqFix. The DSL of NoFAQ can only accept tokenized strings (separated by spaces) as input. However, there is no direct way to tokenize an erroneous equation in our problem domain. We thus introduce the equation patterns and propose a mechanism for synthesizing them. These equation patterns help to pattern match against an equation and extract the variant parts, which need to be transformed later.

Text Transformation. FlashFill [7] pioneered in text transformation via program synthesis and was later extended for semantic transformation [24]. A similar technique is put into a live programming environment by StriSynth [6]. FlashExtract [12] automates data extraction by highlighting texts on web pages. String transformation is performed at a high level in these techniques, but it is unsuitable for repairing equations. We realize that error messages guide the repairing process. By pattern matching the error messages, we only perform the transformation on a few variables instead of the entire equation, which takes less time.

VSA-Based Program Synthesis. *Version space algebra* (VSA) has been widely adopted in PBE applications [1,10,11,22,23,28]. In those applications, VSA is critical as the set of candidate programs is possibly very large. In EqFix, the synthesized rules are represented compactly with VSA.

VSA-based program synthesis has also been applied in program transformation. Refazer [23] is a framework that automatically learns program transformations at an abstract syntax tree level. Feser et al. [3] propose a method for example-guided synthesis of recursive data structure transformations in functional programming languages. Nguyen et al. [20] present a graph-based technique that guides developers in adapting API usages.

7   Conclusion and Future Directions

We present EqFix, a system for fixing both compilation and typesetting errors in LATEX equations. We design a DSL for expressing fixing rules and propose a synthesis algorithm to learn rules from user-provided examples. In the future, our tool can be improved by leveraging data from various sources like LATEX online forums via crowdsourced learning. When a large rule library is established, it would be interesting to develop an EqFix plugin in modern editors for practical use. Furthermore, because adding more data does not require any change in EqFix but simply needs more input-output examples to construct synthesis rules, our approach can potentially be applied to other string and mathematical equation systems.

References

1. Barman, S., Chasins, S., Bodik, R., Gulwani, S.: Ringer: web automation by demonstration. In: Proceedings of the 2016 ACM SIGPLAN International Conference on Object-Oriented Programming, Systems, Languages, and Applications, pp. 748–764. ACM (2016)
2. D'Antoni, L., Singh, R., Vaughn, M.: NoFAQ: synthesizing command repairs from examples. In: Proceedings of the 2017 11th Joint Meeting on Foundations of Software Engineering, ESEC/FSE 2017, pp. 582–592. ACM, New York (2017). https://doi.org/10.1145/3106237.3106241
3. Feser, J.K., Chaudhuri, S., Dillig, I.: Synthesizing data structure transformations from input-output examples. In: Proceedings of the 36th ACM SIGPLAN Conference on Programming Language Design and Implementation, PLDI 2015, pp. 229–239. ACM, New York (2015). https://doi.org/10.1145/2737924.2737977
4. Goues, C.L., Nguyen, T., Forrest, S., Weimer, W.: GenProg: a generic method for automatic software repair. IEEE Trans. Software Eng. **38**(1), 54–72 (2012). https://doi.org/10.1109/TSE.2011.104
5. Goues, C., Forrest, S., Weimer, W.: Current challenges in automatic software repair. Software Qual. J. **21**(3), 421–443 (2013). https://doi.org/10.1007/s11219-013-9208-0
6. Gulwani, S., Mayer, M., Niksic, F., Piskac, R.: StriSynth: synthesis for live programming. In: 2015 IEEE/ACM 37th IEEE International Conference on Software Engineering, vol. 2, pp. 701–704, May 2015. https://doi.org/10.1109/ICSE.2015.227
7. Gulwani, S.: Automating string processing in spreadsheets using input-output examples. In: Proceedings of the 38th Annual ACM SIGPLAN-SIGACT Symposium on Principles of Programming Languages, POPL 2011, pp. 317–330. ACM (2011). https://doi.org/10.1145/1926385.1926423
8. Gulwani, S., Esparza, J., Grumberg, O., Sickert, S.: Programming by examples (and its applications in data wrangling). Verification and Synthesis of Correct and Secure Systems (2016)
9. Hartmann, B., MacDougall, D., Brandt, J., Klemmer, S.R.: What would other programmers do: suggesting solutions to error messages. In: Proceedings of the SIGCHI Conference on Human Factors in Computing Systems, CHI 2010, pp. 1019–1028. ACM, New York (2010). https://doi.org/10.1145/1753326.1753478
10. Kini, D., Gulwani, S.: FlashNormalize: programming by examples for text normalization. In: Proceedings of the 24th International Conference on Artificial Intelligence, pp. 776–783. AAAI Press (2015)
11. Lau, T.A., Domingos, P., Weld, D.S.: Version space algebra and its application to programming by demonstration. In: Proceedings of the Seventeenth International Conference on Machine Learning, San Francisco, CA, USA, ICML 2000, pp. 527–534. Morgan Kaufmann Publishers Inc. (2000)
12. Le, V., Gulwani, S.: FlashExtract: a framework for data extraction by examples. In: Proceedings of the 35th ACM SIGPLAN Conference on Programming Language Design and Implementation, PLDI 2014, pp. 542–553. ACM (2014). https://doi.org/10.1145/2594291.2594333
13. Le, X.B.D., Lo, D., Goues, C.L.: History driven program repair. In: 2016 IEEE 23rd International Conference on Software Analysis, Evolution, and Reengineering (SANER), vol. 1, pp. 213–224, March 2016. https://doi.org/10.1109/SANER.2016.76

14. Le, X.B.D., Chu, D.H., Lo, D., Le Goues, C., Visser, W.: S3: syntax- and semantic-guided repair synthesis via programming by examples. In: Proceedings of the 2017 11th Joint Meeting on Foundations of Software Engineering, ESEC/FSE 2017, pp. 593–604. ACM, New York (2017). https://doi.org/10.1145/3106237.3106309

15. Le Goues, C., Dewey-Vogt, M., Forrest, S., Weimer, W.: A systematic study of automated program repair: fixing 55 out of 105 bugs for $8 each. In: Proceedings of the 34th International Conference on Software Engineering, ICSE 2012, Piscataway, NJ, USA, pp. 3–13. IEEE Press (2012)

16. Long, F., Rinard, M.: Staged program repair with condition synthesis. In: Proceedings of the 2015 10th Joint Meeting on Foundations of Software Engineering, ESEC/FSE 2015, pp. 166–178. ACM, New York (2015). https://doi.org/10.1145/2786805.2786811

17. Long, F., Rinard, M.: Automatic patch generation by learning correct code. In: Proceedings of the 43rd Annual ACM SIGPLAN-SIGACT Symposium on Principles of Programming Languages, POPL 2016, pp. 298–312. ACM, New York (2016). https://doi.org/10.1145/2837614.2837617

18. Mechtaev, S., Yi, J., Roychoudhury, A.: Angelix: scalable multiline program patch synthesis via symbolic analysis. In: Proceedings of the 38th International Conference on Software Engineering, ICSE 2016, pp. 691–701. ACM, New York (2016). https://doi.org/10.1145/2884781.2884807

19. Monperrus, M.: Automatic software repair: a bibliography. ACM Comput. Surv. 51(1), 17:1–17:24 (2018). https://doi.org/10.1145/3105906

20. Nguyen, H.A., Nguyen, T.T., Wilson, Jr., G., Nguyen, A.T., Kim, M., Nguyen, T.N.: A graph-based approach to API usage adaptation. In: Proceedings of the ACM International Conference on Object Oriented Programming Systems Languages and Applications, OOPSLA 2010, pp. 302–321. ACM, New York (2010). https://doi.org/10.1145/1869459.1869486

21. Nguyen, H.D.T., Qi, D., Roychoudhury, A., Chandra, S.: SemFix: program repair via semantic analysis. In: Proceedings of the 2013 International Conference on Software Engineering, ICSE 2013, pp. 772–781. IEEE Press, Piscataway (2013)

22. Polozov, O., Gulwani, S.: FlashMeta: a framework for inductive program synthesis. ACM SIGPLAN Not. 50(10), 107–126 (2015)

23. Rolim, R., et al.: Learning syntactic program transformations from examples. In: Proceedings of the 39th International Conference on Software Engineering, ICSE 2017, pp. 404–415. IEEE Press, Piscataway (2017). https://doi.org/10.1109/ICSE.2017.44

24. Singh, R., Gulwani, S.: Learning semantic string transformations from examples. Proc. VLDB Endow. 5(8), 740–751 (2012). https://doi.org/10.14778/2212351.2212356

25. Smith, E.K., Barr, E.T., Le Goues, C., Brun, Y.: Is the cure worse than the disease? Overfitting in automated program repair. In: Proceedings of the 2015 10th Joint Meeting on Foundations of Software Engineering, ESEC/FSE 2015, pp. 532–543. ACM, New York (2015). https://doi.org/10.1145/2786805.2786825

26. Weimer, W., Nguyen, T., Goues, C.L., Forrest, S.: Automatically finding patches using genetic programming. In: 2009 IEEE 31st International Conference on Software Engineering, pp. 364–374, May 2009. https://doi.org/10.1109/ICSE.2009.5070536

27. Xiong, Y., Wang, J., Yan, R., Zhang, J., Han, S., Huang, G., Zhang, L.: Precise condition synthesis for program repair. In: Proceedings of the 39th International Conference on Software Engineering, ICSE 2017, pp. 416–426. IEEE Press, Piscataway (2017). https://doi.org/10.1109/ICSE.2017.45

28. Yaghmazadeh, N., Klinger, C., Dillig, I., Chaudhuri, S.: Synthesizing transformations on hierarchically structured data. In: Proceedings of the 37th ACM SIGPLAN Conference on Programming Language Design and Implementation, PLDI 2016, pp. 508–521. ACM (2016). https://doi.org/10.1145/2908080.2908088
29. Zhu, F., He, F.: Eqfix: fixing latex equation errors by examples (2022). https://doi.org/10.48550/ARXIV.2107.00613. https://arxiv.org/abs/2107.00613

Dependable CPS and Concurrent Systems

Translating CPS with Shared-Variable Concurrency in SpaceEx

Ran Li[1], Huibiao Zhu[1(✉)], and Richard Banach[2]

[1] Shanghai Key Laboratory of Trustworthy Computing, East China Normal University, Shanghai, China
hbzhu@sei.ecnu.edu.cn
[2] Department of Computer Science, University of Manchester, Oxford Road, Manchester M13 9PL, UK

Abstract. Cyber-physical systems (CPS), combining continuous physical behavior and discrete control behavior, have been widely utilized in recent years. However, the traditional modeling languages used to specify discrete systems are no longer applicable to CPS, since CPS subsume the combination of the cyber and the physical. To address this, a modeling language for CPS based on shared variables is proposed. In this paper, we present an implementation of this language in SpaceEx. Thus, a bridge between our language and hybrid automata is established.

Keywords: Cyber-physical system (CPS) · Hybrid automata · SpaceEx

1 Introduction

Cyber-physical systems (CPS) [5] are dynamical systems composed of discrete behaviors of the cyber and continuous behaviors of the physical. In CPS, computer programs can influence physical behaviors, and vice versa. The interdependency and integration between the cyber and the physical is useful in many fields, such as aerospace, automotive, healthcare and manufacturing [2].

However, the complexity of this combination can complicate the design of systems. Therefore, it is of primary importance to propose specification languages for CPS. For instance, Hybrid CSP (HCSP) [8] is an extension of Communicating Sequential Processes (CSP) by introducing differential equations in hybrid systems. He et al. presented a hybrid relational modeling language (HRML) in [4], where a signal-based interaction mechanism is adopted to synchronize activities of hybrid systems. In contrast, we proposed a language whose parallel mechanism in CPS is based on shared variables, [1]. We provided its denotational semantics and algebraic semantics in [6], and developed its proof system in [7]. Based on our previous work [1,6], in this paper, we connect the language with hybrid automata in SpaceEx. Through this transformation, we can build

---

This work was partially supported by the National Natural Science Foundation of China (Grant Nos. 61872145, 62032024).

W. Dong and J.-P. Talpin (Eds.): SETTA 2022, LNCS 13649, pp. 127–133, 2022.
https://doi.org/10.1007/978-3-031-21213-0_8

a bridge between our language and hybrid automata in SpaceEx, so that CPS specified by our language can be verified in SpaceEx.

The remainder of this paper is as follows. In Sect. 2, we introduce the model checker SpaceEx and recall the syntax of our modeling language. In Sect. 3, the translation from the language to models in SpaceEx is given. Finally, we conclude our work and discuss some future work in Sect. 4.

2   Background

In this section, we first briefly introduce the model checker SpaceEx. Moreover, we recall the syntax of our modeling language to describe CPS.

2.1   SpaceEx

SpaceEx [3] is a verification platform for hybrid systems. A model in SpaceEx contains one or several components. There are two kinds of components: **Base Component** (a single hybrid automaton) and **Network Component** (a parallel composition of several hybrid automata).

To be specific, in a base component, a vertex is called a location. A location is associated with an invariant and a flow. The automaton remains in the current location while the invariant is satisfied. A flow contains a set of differential equations that describe the evolution of continuous variables in this location. The edges between locations are called transitions. By defining transitions, the system can jump between locations. A transition can be associated with a synchronization label, a guard and an assignment. If the guard of this transition is satisfied, the related assignment can take effect and thus changes the values of variables instantaneously. The synchronization label is used to implement synchronization between different automata. By connecting base components via their variables and labels, a network component constructs a parallel composition of base components.

2.2   Syntax of Our Modeling Language

The syntax of our language is summarized in Table 1. This language was proposed in our previous work [1] and we elaborated it by detailing the guard conditions of the continuous behaviors in [6]. Here, x is a discrete variable, e is a discrete or continuous expression, v is a continuous variable and b stands for a Boolean condition.

Discrete Behavior. This language contains two kinds of discrete behaviors, i.e., discrete assignment $x := e$ and discrete event guard @gd.

- $x := e$ is a discrete assignment, which is an atomic action. It evaluates the expression e and assigns the value to the discrete variable x.
- @gd is a discrete event guard. It can be triggered when the discrete guard gd is satisfied. Otherwise, it waits until gd is triggered by the environment. Here, the environment consists of the other programs in the parallel composition.

Table 1. Syntax of our modeling language

Process	$P, Q ::= Db$	(Discrete behavior)
	$\| \ Cb$	(Continuous behavior)
	$\| \ P; Q$	(Sequential Composition)
	$\|$ **if** b **then** P **else** Q	(Conditional Construct)
	$\|$ **while** b **do** P	(Iteration Construct)
	$\| \ P \parallel Q$	(Parallel Composition)
Discrete behavior	$Db ::= x := e \mid @gd$	
Continuous behavior	$Cb ::= R(v, \dot{v})$ **until** g	
Guard Condition	$g ::= gd \mid gc \mid gd \vee gc \mid gd \wedge gc$	
Discrete Guard	$gd ::= true \mid x = e \mid x < e \mid x > e \mid gd \vee gd \mid gd \wedge gd \mid \neg gd$	
Continuous Guard	$gc ::= true \mid v = e \mid v < e \mid v > e \mid gc \vee gc \mid gc \wedge gc \mid \neg gc$	

Continuous Behavior. We employ differential relations to describe continuous behaviors in our language.

- $R(v, \dot{v})$ **until** g defines continuous behaviors. It denotes that the continuous variable v evolves as the differential relation $R(v, \dot{v})$ specifies until the guard condition g is met. Four kinds of guard condition g are allowed in our language, including discrete guard gd, continuous guard gc, mixed guards $gd \wedge gc$ and $gd \vee gc$.

Composition. Further, a process can be comprised of the above commands in the following way.

- $P; Q$ is sequential composition. The processes P and Q execute sequentially.
- **if** b **then** P **else** Q is a conditional construct. If the Boolean condition b is true, then the process P will be performed. Otherwise, Q is executed.
- **while** b **do** P is an iteration construct. The process P is executed repeatedly each time the Boolean condition b is true.
- $P \parallel Q$ is parallel composition. It represents that the processes P and Q run in parallel, and the parallel mechanism is based on shared variables.

3 Translation in SpaceEx

In this section, we convert our language to the form of hybrid automata in SpaceEx. We explain how to define variables. Then, we present the detailed transformation of basic commands and compound constructs in turn.

3.1 Variables

As the foundation of the translation, we first describe how to define variables in SpaceEx and introduce some vital variables that we used in our transformation.

Discrete Variables and Continuous Variables. There are only continuous variables (local or global) and constants in SpaceEx. Thus, to define discrete variables of our language in SpaceEx, we can consider them as a special kind of continuous variables whose derivative is always 0.

Crucial Variables. In our transformation, a global clock variable needs to be defined, so that it captures the real-time feature of CPS. Therefore, we define a continuous variable t which is controlled by a *Clock* automaton that simulates the real time clock. Moreover, we define *tert* as a local discrete variable controlled by the respective independent automaton. The terminal value of *tert* stands for the time when the program terminates.

3.2   Discrete Behavior

For discrete behaviors, there are two statements in our language, including discrete assignment $x := e$ and discrete event guard @gd.

Discrete Assignment. As introduced in Subsect. 2.1, the edges of the graph can allow the system to jump between locations [3]. It can change values of variables with the assignment. Hence, we can simply realize the discrete assignment by adding the corresponding assignment statement to the edge.

Discrete Event Guard. For discrete event guard, it can be triggered by the program itself or by the environment. In this formalization, we apply a synchronization label *change* to let the program observe the environment's action. Note that the observation through the label *change* means that the program can perceive all changes on shared variables, no matter whether this change can really trigger gd. To formalize the behavior of @gd, we set the following four locations.

- *init*: It is the initial location of @gd. One special point is that we set all initial states as instantaneous in our model. According to the initial data state, the automaton of @gd moves from the *init* location to the *term* location or the *wait* location.
- *term*: When the discrete guard gd is triggered, the program runs to the terminate location *term*. As mentioned before, the trigger action can be done by the program itself (i.e., gd is satisfied at the *init* location) or by the environment (i.e., the environment changes the corresponding variables and triggers gd).
- *wait*: This location represents that gd has not been triggered and the program is waiting for the environment. If the initial state cannot activate gd, the automaton jumps from the *init* location to the *wait* location. The automaton stays stuck in this location until the environment changes the variables in gd, and then reaches the *im* location.
- *im*: We introduce this intermediate location to determine whether the newly changed value by the environment can trigger gd. If gd is satisfied, the program moves to the *term* location. Otherwise, it returns to the *wait* location and waits for the environment again.

Example 1. We take @$x > 1$ as an example to illustrate the detailed formalization of @gd, and Fig. 1 presents its automaton in SpaceEx.

Here, x is the shared variable controlled by the environment. It can be changed by the environment and these changes can be perceived by @gd. As introduced in Subsect. 3.1, t is a global continuous variable which represents the global clock. $tert$ is a local discrete variable and it records when @$x > 1$ terminates. For @gd, it moves from the $init$ location to the $term$ location, if gd is satisfied (i.e., $x > 1$) at the beginning. If the current data state cannot meet gd (i.e., $x \leqslant 1$), the process jumps to the $wait$ location where the process waits for the environment to change x. Once the environment changes x, the environment automaton synchronizes with the @$x > 1$ automaton through the $change$ label. Consequently, the automaton reaches at the im location. Further, it moves to the $term$ location if the current value of x meets $x > 1$. Otherwise, the automaton returns to the $wait$ location.

3.3   Continous Behavior

For the continuous behavior $R(v, \dot{v})$ **until** g, we formalize the models according to the types of the guard g, including gc, gd, $gd \vee gc$ and $gd \wedge gc$. Due to the space limitations, we take $R(v, \dot{v})$ **until** $gd \vee gc$ as an example.

$g \equiv gd \vee gc$. If the guard condition is a hybrid one with the form of $gd \vee gc$, the program evolves until gd or gc is satisfied. As a result, we need to pay attention not only to when the evolution of the program makes gc hold, but also to when the behavior of the environment makes gd hold. Four locations (i.e., $init$, $evolve$, im and $term$) are defined to portray this statement.

- $init$: It stands for the initial location. As mentioned before, we assume that it is an instantaneous location and nothing needs to change at this location.
- $evolve$: Similar to the $wait$ location in the @gd automaton, the $evolve$ location implies that neither gd nor gc is satisfied. When the automaton is in the $evolve$ location, it means that the continuous behavior is evolving as the differential relation specifies.
- im: Considering that changes on gd from the environment need to be noticed, we introduce this intermediate location in a similar way as before.
- $term$: Once gd or gc is satisfied, the automaton moves to this location which indicates the continuous behavior terminates.

Example 2. $\dot{v} = 1$ **until** $x > 1 \vee v \geqslant 10$ is employed as an example and the corresponding model is given in Fig. 1(b).

If the initial state meets $x > 1$ or $v \geqslant 10$, the program terminates and the automaton jumps from the $init$ location to the $term$ location. Otherwise, it implies neither gd nor gc can be triggered. Then, the automaton reaches the $evolve$ location where the continuous variable v evolves as $\dot{v} = 1$. During this evolution, as soon as $v \geqslant 10$ is satisfied, the automaton reaches the $term$ location and the terminal time $tert$ is assigned to the current time point. Also, during this period, once the environment changes x, the automaton runs into the im location and checks whether the newly updated value of x caters to $x > 1$.

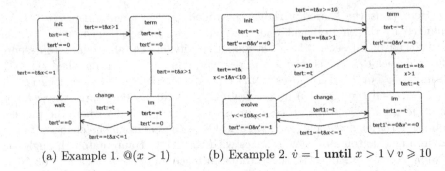

(a) Example 1. @($x > 1$)   (b) Example 2. $\dot{v} = 1$ **until** $x > 1 \vee v \geqslant 10$

Fig. 1. Models of examples in SpaceEx

3.4 Composition

Based on the models of discrete behaviors and continuous behaviors, we now translate the composition of the above commands into models in SpaceEx.

For the **sequential composition** $P; Q$, we can simply connect the two automata P and Q with a transition. This transition is from P's terminal location to Q's initial location, and it assigns P's terminal time to Q's initial time.

As for the **conditional construct** if b then P else Q, we need to determine whether to execute P or Q. If the Boolean condition b is true in the current state (i.e., in the *init* location), then P is selected to execute. Otherwise, Q is executed. We connect the *init* location to the initial location of the program (i.e., P or Q) to be executed with a transition whose guard is b or $\neg b$.

For the **iteration construct** while b do P, if the Boolean condition b is false at the very beginning (i.e., in the *init* location), the process terminates at once without executing P. Consequently, the automaton moves from the *init* location to the *term* location. If b is true, P will be executed repeatedly until b is false. We accomplish it by adding a transition from P's terminal location to P's initial location. After executing P several times, if b is false, the automaton can jump out the loop and enter the *term* location.

For the **parallel composition** $P \parallel Q$, we can first construct automata for parallel components (in their respective base components) and then connect them as a whole parallel program (in the network component).

4 Conclusion and Future Work

In [6], we elaborated our language for cyber-physical systems, based on our previous work [1]. In this paper, we transformed this language into automata in SpaceEx [3]. Therefore, under the guidance of the conversion, any CPS specified by our language can be modeled and verified in SpaceEx. In the future, the automatic translation of our language to models in SpaceEx will be explored.

References

1. Banach, R., Zhu, H.: Language evolution and healthiness for critical cyber-physical systems. J. Softw. Evol. Process. **33**(9) (2021)
2. Bu, L., Wang, J., Wu, Y., Li, X.: From bounded reachability analysis of linear hybrid automata to verification of industrial CPS and IoT. In: Bowen, J.P., Liu, Z., Zhang, Z. (eds.) SETSS 2019. LNCS, vol. 12154, pp. 10–43. Springer, Cham (2020). https://doi.org/10.1007/978-3-030-55089-9_2
3. Frehse, G., Le Guernic, C., Donzé, A., Cotton, S., Ray, R., Lebeltel, O., Ripado, R., Girard, A., Dang, T., Maler, O.: SpaceEx: scalable verification of hybrid systems. In: Gopalakrishnan, G., Qadeer, S. (eds.) CAV 2011. LNCS, vol. 6806, pp. 379–395. Springer, Heidelberg (2011). https://doi.org/10.1007/978-3-642-22110-1_30
4. Jifeng, H., Qin, L.: A hybrid relational modelling language. In: Gibson-Robinson, T., Hopcroft, P., Lazić, R. (eds.) Concurrency, Security, and Puzzles. LNCS, vol. 10160, pp. 124–143. Springer, Cham (2017). https://doi.org/10.1007/978-3-319-51046-0_7
5. Lanotte, R., Merro, M., Tini, S.: A probabilistic calculus of cyber-physical systems. Inf. Comput. **279**, 104618 (2021)
6. Li, R., Zhu, H., Banach, R.: Denotational and algebraic semantics for cyber-physical systems. In: ICECCS, pp. 123–132. IEEE (2022)
7. Li, R., Zhu, H., Banach, R.: A proof system for cyber-physical systems with shared-variable concurrency. In: Riesco, A., Zhang, M. (eds) Formal Methods and Software Engineering. ICFEM 2022. LNCS, vol 13478. Springer, Cham (2022). https://doi.org/10.1007/978-3-031-17244-1_15
8. Chaochen, Z., Ji, W., Ravn, A.P.: A formal description of hybrid systems. In: Alur, R., Henzinger, T.A., Sontag, E.D. (eds.) HS 1995. LNCS, vol. 1066, pp. 511–530. Springer, Heidelberg (1996). https://doi.org/10.1007/BFb0020972

A Contract-Based Semantics and Refinement for Simulink

Quan Sun[1], Wei Zhang[2], Chao Wang[2], and Zhiming Liu[2,3](✉)

[1] College of Computer Science and Technology, Nanjing University of Aeronautics
and Astronautics, Nanjing, China
quansun@nuaa.edu.cn

[2] College of Computer and Information Science, Southwest University, Chongqing,
China
{swuzhangwei,wangch1}@swu.edu.cn

[3] School of Software, Northwestern Polytechnical University, Xi'an, China
zliu@nwpu.edu.cn

Abstract. Simulink is a widely used tool for modelling, simulating, and
analyzing cyber-physical systems using block diagrams. Such diagrams
contain both discrete-time and continuous-time blocks. To analyze complex block diagrams, a semantics to support compositional reasoning and
verification is required. Contract-based modelling provides good compositional reasoning about complex systems. In this paper, we present a
contract-based semantic model for Simulink to formalise the semantics of
both discrete-time and continuous-time blocks. In our semantic formali-
sation, the semantics of a block is defined as a contract, and we define five
operations on contracts, which are sequential composition, parallel composition, feedback composition, variable renaming, and variable hiding.
We then define the *refinement* relation among the Simulink diagrams.

Keywords: Contract-based semantics · Compositional reasoning ·
Refinement · Simulink

1 Introduction

Simulink [16] is a well-known tool for the simulation and design of cyber-physical
systems (CPS). It offers a library of blocks, each of which is a basic block for
building block diagrams. Such diagrams consist of blocks connected by wires.
The wires describe the communications between the blocks. In a block diagram,
a block is either a basic block or a subsystem which is composed of other subsystems and basic blocks. We refer to basic blocks and subsystems as blocks.

This work was funded in part by the Chongqing Graduate Research and Innovation
Project (grant No. CYB20098), the National Natural Science Foundation of China
(No. 62032019, 61732019, 61672435, 62002298), and the Capacity Development Grant
of Southwest University (SWU116007).

W. Dong and J.-P. Talpin (Eds.): SETTA 2022, LNCS 13649, pp. 134–148, 2022.
https://doi.org/10.1007/978-3-031-21213-0_9

A block diagram contains both discrete-time and continuous-time blocks. A discrete-time block represents a system of difference equations, while a continuous-time block represents a system of differential equations. These equations define the behaviour of these two kinds of blocks, respectively. As for any complex and hierarchical models, a semantics to support compositional reasoning and verification is important for Simulink diagrams.

Contract-based semantic models provide good specification, compositional reasoning, verification and correct system design by refinement. In a contract-based semantic model, a contract [1] is to specify the behaviour of the system in terms of the *assumption* about the behaviour of the environment and the behaviour of the system to *guarantee* under the assumption. The about the environment assumption and the guarantee of the behaviour of the system are both specified by predicate formulas on the variables of the system and environment, which define sets of behaviours. Here, a behaviour is a sequence of states which assign values to the variables in an execution of a system interacting with its environment. Contract-based models are defined and used for various systems, e.g. software specification [17], reactive systems [14], and CPS [20].

In this paper, we propose a *contract-based semantic model* for Simulink, which contain both discrete-time and continuous-time blocks. First, we define a formal syntax for Simulink. This syntax consists of blocks and five operations on blocks, including sequential composition, parallel composition, feedback composition, variable renaming, and variable hiding. The syntax allows a Simulink diagram to be represented as an algebraic expression, inductively, similar to the style of CCS [18] and CSP [15]. This syntax also allows us to give a syntax-guided definition for the semantics of the expressions.

We then define the *contract* (V, A, G) for each expression representing a Simulink diagram by induction on the syntactic structure of the expression, where V is the set of free variables of the expression, A represents the *assumption*, and G represents the *guarantee*. We will consider both discrete-time and continuous-time blocks in our semantics, and the behaviour of a discrete-time block is also defined in the real-time domain. However, unlike the behaviour of continuous-time blocks, a discrete-time behaviour is a step function on the continuous-time domain. Moreover, we define the refinement relation between algebraic expressions.

The contributions of this paper are as follows:

1. We propose an inductively defined syntax to represent Simulink diagrams as algebraic expressions, and define a contract-based semantics for the expressions.
2. Our contract model captures not only the semantics of discrete-time blocks but also continuous-time blocks.
3. We formalise the refinement relation among Simulink diagrams.

This paper is organized as follows. In Sect. 2, we introduce the related work. In Sect. 3, we propose the syntax of the algebraic expression of Simulink diagrams. In Sect. 4, we define contract-based semantics for Simulink. In Sect. 5, we define the refinement relation between the algebraic expressions. In Sect. 6, we draw our conclusions and discuss future work.

2 Related Work

There exist a number of works on the formal semantics of Simulink. Chapoutot et al. [10] presented an abstract simulation method for the static analysis of Simulink block diagrams using abstract interpretation. Bouissou et al. [5] presented an operational semantics for Simulink, including continuous-time and discrete-time blocks. In comparison to the work [5], we present a contract-based semantics for Simulink in a denotation style. Rajhans et al. [19] presented a formal definition for Simulink blocks. Compared to the work [19], we consider not only the formal definition of Simulink blocks but also five operations on blocks.

There exist some works on translating Simulink block diagrams into other formal modelling languages for the semantics of Simulink. Cavalcanti et al. [8,9] presented a semantics and the refinement relation for discrete-time Simulink block diagrams. In [8], a discrete-time Simulink block diagram was translated to Circus, a combination of Z and CSP. In [9], a discrete-time Simulink block diagram was translated to CircusTime, a timed version of the Circus notation. Dragomir et al. [13] presented a compositional semantics and analysis framework for hierarchical block diagrams by translating discrete-time Simulink block diagrams into predicate transformers. Tripakis et al. [7] presented a method of translating discrete-time Simulink block diagrams to the synchronous language Lustre, for which there are many formal validation tools. For all the works mentioned above, continuous-time Simulink block diagrams are not considered. Chen et al. [11,12] presented an approach that translates both continuous-time and discrete-time Simulink block diagrams to Timed Interval Calculus (TIC), which is a real-time specification language. Zou et al. [24] presented a method of translating Simulink block diagrams into Hybrid CSP, which is a formal modelling language for hybrid systems. Zhou et al. [23] presented a recursive method for translating a subset of Simulink diagrams to input/output-entended finite automata. Bourke et al. [6] presented a method to translate a set of Simulink block library into the synchronous language Zélus, which extends a language Lustre with ordinary differential equations and zero-crossing events. Compared to the works discussed above, we define the refinement relation for Simulink, including discrete-time and continuous-time blocks.

The contract-based approach to analysis and verification of Simulink is investigated in the literature. Boström et al. [2–4] presented a contract-based approach and the refinement relation for verifying discrete-time Simulink block diagrams. Ye et al. [21,22] presented a compositional assume-guarantee reasoning framework for discrete-time Simulink diagrams using Unifying Theories of Programming (UTP). Compared to these works, our contract model captures not only the semantics of discrete-time blocks but also continuous-time blocks.

3   Syntax of Algebraic Expression of Simulink Diagrams

Simulink [16] is a graphical extension to MATLAB for the modelling, analyzing, and simulation dynamic systems. It offers a library of blocks, called the Simulink block library, each of which is a basic block for building block diagrams. Such block diagrams consist of blocks and wires. The wires describe the communications between the blocks. In a block diagram, a block is either a basic block or a subsystem which is composed of other subsystems and basic blocks. From now on, we will use a block to represent a basic block and a subsystem when there is no confusion. The block represents a system of equations. In particular, a discrete-time block represents a system of difference equations, while a continuous-time block represents a system of differential equations. These equations define the behaviour of these two kinds of blocks, respectively.

3.1   Signals

In Simulink, a *signal* is a function from time to values. The values can either be real numbers or complex numbers. For simplicity, we assume that these values are real numbers. We use the set $\mathbb{R}^+$ of non-negative real numbers to represent the time domain. The signal can either be a continuous-time signal or a discrete-time signal. A continuous-time signal s is a function from $\mathbb{R}^+$ to $\mathbb{R}$, where $\mathbb{R}$ represents the set of real numbers. An n-dimensional continuous-time signal $\mathbf{s}$ is a function from $\mathbb{R}^+$ to $\mathbb{R}^n$ such that for all $t \in \mathbb{R}^+$, $\mathbf{s}(t) = (s_1(t), \ldots, s_n(t))$, where $s_i(t)$ is the i-th component of the vector of $\mathbf{s}(t)$. A discrete-time signal s is a piece-wise constant continuous-time signal updated only at $k\tau$, where k is a natural number and τ is a positive real number. That is, for all $t \in [k\tau, (k+1)\tau)$, $s(t) = s(k\tau)$ and $\bigcup_{k \in \mathbb{N}} [k\tau, (k+1)\tau) = \mathbb{R}^+$. Note that we use bold lowercase letters to denote vectors.

3.2   Blocks

A block represents a system of equations, which define the relationship between the *input signals*, *output signals*, and the *internal state variables*. In this paper, we are interested in both discrete-time and continuous-time blocks, because such blocks are widely used to model dynamic systems. We formalise a block as follows.

Definition 1 (Block). *A block* B *is a tuple* $(U, X, Y, f, g, Init)$, *where:*

1. $U = \{u_1, \ldots, u_n\}$ *is the set of input variables (more precisely, variable names) and each variable denotes a signal,*
2. $X = \{x_1, \ldots, x_p\}$ *is set of internal state variables and each internal state variable denotes a function over time,*
3. $Y = \{y_1, \ldots, y_m\}$ *is the set of output variables and each variable denotes a signal,*

4. *f is the internal state transition function such that $\triangle \mathbf{x}(t) = f(\mathbf{x}(t), \mathbf{u}(t))$, where $t \in \mathbb{R}^+$ denotes the time variable, the operator $\triangle$ is either a derivative operator: $\dot{\mathbf{x}}(t) = f(\mathbf{x}(t), \mathbf{u}(t))$ in the case of continuous-time, or a difference operator: $\bar{\mathbf{x}}(t) = f(\mathbf{x}(t), \mathbf{u}(t))$ in the case of discrete-time. We write $\mathbf{x}(t) = (x_1(t), \ldots, x_p(t))$ for internal states vector, $\mathbf{u}(t) = (u_1(t), \ldots, u_n(t))$ for input vector. We write the difference operator $\bar{\mathbf{x}}(t)$ for the discrete-time internal states vector $(x_1(t+\tau), \ldots, x_p(t+\tau))$, where τ is a positive real number,*
5. *g is the output function such that $\mathbf{y}(t) = g(\mathbf{x}(t), \mathbf{u}(t))$, where we write $\mathbf{y}(t) = (y_1(t), \ldots, y_m(t))$ for output vector,*
6. *Init $\subset \mathbb{R}^p$ is the initial condition of $\mathbf{x}$ such that $\mathbf{x}(0) = \mathbf{x}_0 \in Init$.*

In the above definition, when the operator $\triangle$ is a derivative operator, we assume that function f is the Lipschitz function and $\mathbf{u}(t)$ is continuous. Under these assumptions, the equation $\dot{\mathbf{x}}(t) = f(\mathbf{x}(t), \mathbf{u}(t))$ has a unique solution $\mathbf{x}(t)$ satisfying $\mathbf{x}(0) = \mathbf{x}_0$.

Note that we allow U, Y, and X can be empty sets: if U is empty then the block is a *source block*; if Y is empty then the block is a *sink block*; if X is empty then the block is called *stateless*, Otherwise, such block is called *stateful*. For a stateless block, we use the notation – to indicate that it has no internal state transition function. Because the outputs of a block depend on its inputs and internal states, and the outputs of a block cannot be used to compute its outputs, we assume that U, Y, and X are pair-wise disjoint, i.e. $U \cap Y = U \cap X = Y \cap X = \emptyset$.

Example 1. Consider a stateful block **Integrator** and two stateless blocks **Gain** and **Subtract**. The block **Integrator** has an input u, an internal state x, and an output y. It represents the following system of equations:

$$\dot{x}(t) = u(t) \quad \text{with} \quad x(0) = x_0, \tag{1a}$$
$$y(t) = x(t). \tag{1b}$$

where $t \in \mathbb{R}^+$ denotes the time variable and x_0 is the initial value of x. By Definition 1, the **Integrator** is defined as follows:

$$\text{Integrator} = (\{u\}, \{x\}, \{y\}, \dot{x}(t) = u(t), y(t) = x(t), Init_1),$$

where $x(0) = x_0 \in Init_1 \subseteq \mathbb{R}$.

The block **Gain** has an input u and an output y. It represents the following equation:

$$y(t) = Ku(t), \tag{2}$$

where K is a constant. By Definition 1, the **Gain** is defined by:

$$\text{Gain} = (\{u\}, \emptyset, \{y\}, -, y(t) = Ku(t), true),$$

The block **Subtract** has two inputs u_1, u_2 and an output y. It represents the following equation:

$$y(t) = u_1(t) - u_2(t). \tag{3}$$

By Definition 1, the **Subtract** is defined by:

$$\text{Subtract} = (\{u_1, u_2\}, \emptyset, \{y\}, -, y(t) = u_1(t) - u_2(t), true).$$

3.3 Algebraic Expressions of Simulink Diagrams

As mentioned above, a block diagram is a graphical model of a dynamic system. Such a block diagram consists of blocks and wires hierarchically connecting them. In this subsection, we define block diagrams as algebraic expressions.

Before defining the syntax, we need the following notations and assumptions. Let Z_1 and Z_2 be sets, then the set difference $Z_1 - Z_2$ is a set of all elements in Z_1 but not in Z_2, i.e. $Z_1 - Z_2 = \{x \mid x \in Z_1 \text{ and } x \notin Z_2\}$. We use $|Z_1|$ to represent the size of the set Z_1. Let $\mathsf{B} = (U, X, Y, f, g, Init)$ be a block. For simplicity, we define $V = U \cup Y$. We shall use W and L to denote subsets of V. To change the names of input and output variables, we need to introduce a *renaming function*. The *renaming function* γ is a one-to-one function from W to W', where W is a subset of V and W' is the set of fresh variables.

In block diagrams, to ensure that only one block is responsible for controlling its output, we assume that two blocks have disjoint sets of names of the output variables. We also assume that there are no conflicts between the internal state names of different blocks.

The syntax of algebraic expression of Simulink diagrams is defined as follows.

Definition 2 (Syntax of Simulink). *Let* $\mathsf{B} = (U, X, Y, f, g, Init)$ *be a block. We define the syntax for Simulink by the following BNF rules:*

$$\mathsf{B} ::= \mathsf{B} \mid \mathsf{B}[\gamma] \mid \mathsf{B}\backslash L \mid \mathsf{B} ; \mathsf{B} \mid \mathsf{B} \parallel \mathsf{B} \mid \mathrm{Fb}(\mathsf{B}, \mathsf{B})$$

where L is a subset of V.

Informally, we can understand the above syntax in the following way:

1. A block B is a block diagram, where B is either a discrete-time block or a continuous-time block. To model block diagrams easier, we need to introduce two blocks, including $\mathsf{Id} = (\{u\}, \emptyset, \{y\}, -, y(t) = u(t), true)$ and $\mathsf{Split(n)} = (\{u\}, \emptyset, \{y_1, \ldots, y_n\}, -, \bigwedge_{i=1}^{n} y_i(t) = u(t), true)$, where $n \geq 2$. We use Id to model a wire which has an input and an output, $\mathsf{Split(n)}$ to model a wire which has a input and n output.

2. Let B be a block. Let V be a set of input and output variables for B. Suppose W is a subset of V. Then $\mathsf{B}[\gamma]$ is also a block with a set V' of input and output variables, where $\gamma : W \mapsto W'$ is a renaming function, W' is the set of fresh variables, and $V' = (V - W) \cup W'$. We write $[w'_{i_1}/w_{i_1}, \ldots, w'_{i_j}/w_{i_j} : w'_{i_{j+1}}/w_{i_{j+1}}, \ldots, w'_{i_n}/w_{i_n}]$ for renaming function γ, where $w'_{i_j} = \gamma(w_{i_j})$, for $j = 1, \ldots, n$. Here, we use a colon to denote the separation of input variables and output variables. Note that a renaming function only changes the names of the input and output variables, and does not change the meaning of a block.

3. The *hiding operation* $\backslash L$ makes some input and output variables internal to the block, so that those variables are used only for the interaction of the blocks, and are no longer be connected to other blocks. If B is a block, V is a set of input and output variables for B, and L is a subset of V, then $\mathsf{B}\backslash L$ is also a block with a set V' of input and output variables, where $V' = V - L$.

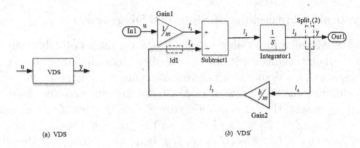

(a) VDS

(b) VDS′

Fig. 1. (a) The block VDS represents the vehicle dynamics system. (b) The block diagram VDS′ represents an implementation of the subsystem VDS.

4. The *parallel composition operation*, denoted by ∥, combines two blocks into a block. Let B_1 and B_2 be blocks. Suppose that V_1 and V_2 are sets of input and output variables for B_1 and B_2, respectively. Then $B_1 \parallel B_2$ is also a block with a set V of input and output variables, where $V_1 = U_1 \cup Y_1$, $V_2 = U_2 \cup Y_2$, $V = U \cup Y$, $Y = Y_1 \cup Y_2$ and $U = U_1 \cup U_2$. Note that in the analysis before we have assumed that $Y_1 \cap Y_2 = \emptyset$ and $U_i \cap Y_i = \emptyset$, for $i = 1, 2$.

5. The *sequential composition operation*, denoted by ;, combines two blocks into a block by identifying the output variables of one block which have the same name as the input variables of another block. Let B_1 and B_2 be blocks. Suppose that $V_1 = U_1 \cup Y_1$ and $V_2 = U_2 \cup Y_2$ are, respectively, sets of input and output variables for B_1 and B_2, such that the output variables of B_1 are the same as the input variables of B_2, i.e. $Y_1 = U_2$. Then, B_1 ; B_2 is also a block with a set U_1 of input variables and a set $Y_1 \cup Y_2$ of output variables, i.e. $V = U_1 \cup Y_1 \cup Y_2$. Note that if $|Y_1| \neq |U_2|$, this can always be fulfilled by using Id and Split(n).

6. The *feedback composition operation*, denoted by Fb, combines two blocks B_1 and B_2 into a block $Fb(B_1, B_2)$ by directed cycles, where some output variables of B_1 have the same name as some input variables of B_2, and some output variables of B_2 have the same as some input variables of B_1. To ensure that block diagrams are algebraic-loop-free, we assume that each block diagram must normally include at least one stateful block in every directed cycle. By 'algebraic-loop' we mean a feedback loop resulting in instantaneous cyclic dependencies.

   Let B_1 and B_2 be blocks, where at least one of B_1 and B_2 must be a stateful block. Suppose that $V_1 = U_1 \cup Y_1$ and $V_2 = U_2 \cup Y_2$ are, respectively, sets of input and output variables for B_1 and B_2 such that $U_2 \subseteq Y_1$, $Y_2 \subset U_1$. Then, $Fb(B_1, B_2)$ is also block with a set V of input and output variables, where $V = U \cup Y$, $U = U_1 - Y_2$, and $Y = Y_1 \cup Y_2$.

Example 2. Consider the block diagrams shown in Fig. 1. Each box is a block in the block diagrams. A label on a wire indicates the input and output variable name of the block. Those blocks can be connected by the wires if the output variable names of one block have the same input variable names of another block. The input and output of a system are described by rounded boxes with numbers. The subsystem VDS represents a vehicle dynamics system. Under the power given by the engine, the function of this system is to change the speed of the vehicle such that it reaches the desired speed. The subsystem VDS is given by the following equation:

$$\dot{y}(t) = \frac{1}{m}(u(t) - by(t)), \tag{4}$$

where u is the power given by the engine, m is the mass of the vehicle, b is the friction of the road, and y is the speed of the vehicle. By Definition 1, the VDS is defined by:

$$\text{VDS} = (\{u\}, \emptyset, \{y\}, -, g, true),$$

where the output function g represents the ordinary differential Eq. (4).

The block diagram VDS′ that implements the subsystem VDS consists of six blocks Id1, Split$_1$(2), Gain1, Gain2, Subtract1, and Integrator1. We have previously defined the blocks Id, Split(2), Gain, Subtract, and Integrator, where the block Split(2) is defined by Split(n) when $n = 2$, i.e. Split(2) = $(\{u\}, \emptyset, \{y_1, y_2\}, -, y_1(t) = u(t) \wedge y_2(t) = u(t), true)$. To compose those blocks, we first rename their input and output variable names. Then by Definition 2, we have Id1 = Id$[l_5/u : l_6/y]$, Split$_1$(2) = Split(2)$[l_3/u : y/y_1, l_4/y_2]$, Gain1 = Gain$[l_1/y]$, Gain2 = Gain$[l_4/u : l_5/y]$, Subtract1 = Subtract$[l_1/u_1, l_6/u_2 : l_2/y]$, and Integrator1 = Integrator$[l_2/u : l_3/y]$. Moreover, we have

$$\text{VDS}' = \text{Fb}((((\text{Gain1} \parallel \text{Id1}); \text{Integrator1}); \text{Split}_1(2)), \text{Gain2}) \backslash L,$$

where $L = \{l_1, l_2, l_3, l_4, l_5, l_6\}$. In Example 6, we will show that VDS′ is a refinement of VDS.

4   Contract-Based Semantics of Simulink

In this section, we first give the basic definitions that are used to model the evolution of a block over an interval of time, including a well-defined block and a state of variables. We then introduce the notion of a *contract* and define five operations on contracts. Finally, we define contract-based semantics for Simulink.

Definition 3 (Well-defined block). *Let* B $= (U, X, Y, f, g, Init)$ *be a block. We say that* B *is well-defined if the following conditions hold:*

1. *for all $t \in \mathbb{R}^+$, $(\mathbf{u}(t), \mathbf{x}(t)) \in \text{dom}(f)$, where the predicate $\text{dom}(f)$ represents evolution domain of function f,*
2. *for all $t \in \mathbb{R}^+$, $(\mathbf{u}(t), \mathbf{x}(t)) \in \text{dom}(g)$, where the predicate $\text{dom}(g)$ represents evolution domain of function g.*

We use the predicate $\mathcal{D}(\text{B})$ to represent the conjunction of the above condition for a block B. Note that if a block is stateless, we assume that $\text{dom}(f) = true$.

Let $\mathcal{V} = U \cup X \cup Y$ be a set of variables. We define a state of $\mathcal{V}$ as a function $\sigma : \mathcal{V} \mapsto \mathbb{R}$, where $\mathbb{R}$ is the set of all real numbers. We use Σ to denote the set of all states of $\mathcal{V}$. Let $V = U \cup Y$. We define the restriction of Σ to V as the set Σ_V.

We next define a trajectory of a block to represent the evolution of a block over an interval of time. Let τ be a positive real number. A trajectory of time $\mathcal{T}$ is a finite or infinite sequence of intervals I_k such that $I_k = [k\tau, (k+1)\tau)$ and $\bigcup_{k \in \mathbb{N}} [k\tau, (k+1)\tau) = \mathbb{R}^+$. We define a trajectory of a block as follows.

Definition 4 (Trajectory of block). *Let* B $= (U, X, Y, f, g, Init)$ *be a well-defined block. Let* $\mathcal{T}$ *be a trajectory of time. For all* $I_k \in \mathcal{T}$, *a trajectory of* B *is a function* $\rho \colon I_k \mapsto \Sigma$ *such that:*

1. *initial condition:* $\rho(0)(\mathbf{x}) \in Init$,
2. *internal state transition evolution: for all* $\eta \in I_k$,
   - *continuous-time:* $\frac{d\rho(t)(\mathbf{x})}{dt}(\eta) = f(\rho(\eta)(\mathbf{x}), \rho(\eta)(\mathbf{u}))$,
   - *discrete-time:* $\rho(\eta + \tau)(\mathbf{x}) = f(\rho(k\tau)(\mathbf{x}), \rho(k\tau)(\mathbf{u}))$,
3. *output evolution: for all* $\eta \in I_k$, $\rho(\eta)(\mathbf{y}) = g(\rho(\eta)(\mathbf{x}), \rho(\eta)(\mathbf{u}))$.

An observable trajectory of B is a function $ob(\rho) \colon I_k \mapsto \Sigma_V$, where $I_k \in \mathcal{T}$. We use $Tr(V)$ to denote the set of all observable trajectories of block B. A predicate whose free variables are from V is a function $P \colon Tr(V) \mapsto$ Bool, where Bool $= \{true, false\}$. Then, a predicate specifies a subset of $Tr(V)$. Given an observable trajectory $ob(\rho) \in Tr(V)$, we say that $ob(\rho)$ satisfies a predicate P, denote $ob(\rho) \models P$, if P is true in state $\sigma \in \Sigma_V$ for all $t \in \mathbb{R}^+$.

Definition 5 (Contract). *A contract C is a triple (V, A, G), where:*

1. $V = U \cup Y$, *in which U, Y are two finite and disjoint sets of input and output variables,*
2. A *is a predicate whose free variables are from V, and is called an assumption on the environment, and*
3. G *is a predicate whose free variables are from V, and is called a guarantee under the environment assumption.*

Here, we informal give an example that may help to understand contract-based semantics for Simulink.

Example 3. Consider a block `Divide` which has an input variable u and an output variable y. The output signal $y(t)$ of the `Divide` is equal to the input signal $u(t)$ divided by 1, for all $t \in \mathbb{R}^+$. Then by Definition 1, we have

$$\texttt{Divide} = (\{u\}, \emptyset, \{y\}, -, y(t) = 1/u(t), true),$$

where $t \in \mathbb{R}^+$. Hence, we define the semantics of such block as follows.

$$C_{\texttt{Divide}} = (\{u, y\}, u \neq 0, y = 1/u),$$

where the predicate $u \neq 0$ denotes $\forall t \in \mathbb{R}^+ : u(t) \neq 0$, and characterizes the assumption on the environment of the `Divide`. The predicate $y = 1/u$ denotes $\forall t \in \mathbb{R}^+ : y(t) = 1/u(t)$, and characterizes the guarantee of the `Divide` whenever the environment satisfies the assumption.

As mentioned in Sect. 3.3, we defined five syntactic operators for Simulink. For defining the semantics of Simulink, we shall define five operations on contracts, including variable renaming, parallel composition, variable hiding, sequential composition, and feedback composition.

Before composing two contracts, we shall consider renaming of contract variables. This operation allows us to change the name of its variables so that different contracts have no variable name conflicts, and the shared names of the input and output variables denote the required input and output connections. We formalise the renaming of contract variables in the following definition.

Definition 6 (Renaming of contract variables). *Let $C = (V, A, G)$ be a contract. Suppose that W is a subset of V and γ is a renaming function from W to W', where W' is the set of fresh variables. Then, rename $C[\gamma]$ is the contract (V', A', G'), which obtained by substituting the variable name w_i by $w'_i \in W'$ in predicates A and G, i.e. $V' = (V - W) \cup W'$, $A' = A[w'_1/w_1, \cdots, w'_n/w_n]$, and $G' = G[w'_1/w_1, \cdots, w'_n/w_n]$.*

We use $C[w'_1/w_1, \ldots, w'_j/w_j : w'_{j+1}/w_{j+1}, \ldots, w'_n/w_n]$ to represent the renaming function of contract C, where $w'_i = \gamma(w_i)$, for $i = 1, \ldots, n$. Here, we use a colon to denote the separation of input and output variables. Note that the renaming of contract variables only changes the names of its variables, and does not change the meaning of the contract.

Given two contracts $C_1 = (V_1, A_1, G_1)$ and $C_2 = (V_2, A_2, G_2)$, we say that C_1 and C_2 are disjoint if they have disjoint sets of output variables, i.e. $Y_1 \cap Y_2 = \emptyset$. Note that if $Y_1 \cap Y_2 \neq \emptyset$, then we can rename them such that $Y_1 \cap Y_2 = \emptyset$. When two contracts are disjoint, we define their parallel composition as follows.

Definition 7 (Parallel composition of contracts). *Let $C_1 = (V_1, A_1, G_1)$ and $C_2 = (V_2, A_2, G_2)$ be two disjoint contracts. Then, parallel composition $C_1 \parallel C_2$ is the contract (V, A, G), where $V = V_1 \cup V_2$, $A = A_1 \wedge A_2$, and $G = G_1 \wedge G_2$.*

The assumption of parallel composition of contracts is the conjunction of the assumptions A_1 and A_2, because of the environment satisfies both the assumptions A_1 and A_2, while the guarantee of parallel composition of contracts is the conjunction of the guarantees G_1 and G_2. For parallel composition of contracts, we have the following theorem.

Theorem 1. *Let C_1, C_2, and C_3 be disjoint contracts. Then we have*

1. $C_1 \parallel C_2 = C_2 \parallel C_1$;
2. $(C_1 \parallel C_2) \parallel C_3 = C_1 \parallel (C_2 \parallel C_3)$.

Sequential composition of contracts is defined as follows.

Definition 8 (Sequential composition of contracts). *Let $C_1 = (V_1, A_1, G_1)$ and $C_2 = (V_2, A_2, G_2)$ be contracts. Suppose that $V_1 = U_1 \cup Y_1$, $V_2 = U_2 \cup Y_2$, and $Y_1 = U_2$. Then sequential composition $C_1; C_2$ is the contract (V, A, G), where $V = U_1 \cup Y_1 \cup Y_2$, $A = A_1 \wedge (G_1 \Rightarrow A_2)$, and $G = G_1 \wedge G_2$.*

This definition says that if $A_1 \wedge (G_1 \Rightarrow A_2)$ holds, then $G_1 \wedge G_2$ holds. To ensure that $|Y_1| = |U_2|$, we need to introduce two contracts, $C_{\text{Id}} = (\{u, y\}, true, y = u)$ and $C_{\text{Split(n)}} = (\{u, y_1, \ldots, y_n\}, true, \bigwedge_{i=1}^{n} y_i = u)$, where $n \geq 2$. Then if $|Y_1| \neq |U_2|$, this can always be fulfilled by using C_{Id} and $C_{\text{Split(n)}}$. Let us illustrate sequential composition of contracts by means of an example.

Example 4. Consider two contracts C_{Sin} and C_{Divide}, where

$$C_{\text{Sin}} = (\{u, y\}, true, y = \sin u),$$
$$C_{\text{Divide}} = (\{u, y\}, u \neq 0, y = 1/u).$$

We want to describe the sequential composition of the contracts C_{Sin} and C_{Divide}, i.e. $C_{\text{Sin}}; C_{\text{Divide}}$. To this end, we first rename output variables of C_{Sin} and input variables of C_{Divide} such that the output variable name of C_{Sin} are the same as the input variable name of C_{Divide}. Thus by Definition 6, we have

$$C_{\text{Sin}}[l/y] = (\{u, l\}, true, l = \sin u),$$
$$C_{\text{Divide}}[l/u] = (\{l, y\}, l \neq 0, y = 1/l).$$

Hence by Definition 8, we get the sequential composition of C_{Sin} and C_{Divide}

$$C_{\text{Sin}}[l/y]; C_{\text{Divide}}[l/u] = (\{u, l, y\}, A, G),$$

where

$$A = true \wedge (l = \sin u \Rightarrow l \neq 0) \tag{5}$$
$$= (l \neq \sin u) \vee (l \neq 0)$$
$$G = l = \sin u \wedge y = 1/l \tag{6}$$

For sequential composition of contracts, we have the following theorem.

Theorem 2. *Let C_1, C_2, and C_3 be contracts. Then, we have*

$$(C_1; C_2); C_3 = C_1; (C_2; C_3).$$

Now, we define feedback composition of contracts.

Definition 9 (Feedback composition of contracts). *Let $C_1 = (V_1, A_1, G_1)$ and $C_2 = (V_2, A_2, G_2)$ be contracts. Suppose that $V_1 = U_1 \cup Y_1$, $V_2 = U_2 \cup Y_2$, $U_2 \subseteq Y_1$, and $Y_2 \subset U_1$. Then feedback composition $C_1 \otimes C_2$ is the contract (V, A, G), where $V = V_1 \cup V_2$, $A = A_1 \wedge (G_2 \Rightarrow A_1) \wedge (G_1 \Rightarrow A_2)$, and $G = G_1 \wedge G_2$.*

This definition asserts that if $A_1 \wedge (G_2 \Rightarrow A_1) \wedge (G_1 \Rightarrow A_2)$ holds, then $G_1 \wedge G_2$ holds. For defining the semantics of Simulink, we need to hide variables, so that hidden variables are used only for internal interaction of the contracts and cannot be used for external interaction of other contracts. We formalise the hiding of contract variables in the following definition.

Definition 10 (Hiding of contract variables). *Let $C = (V, A, G)$ be a contract and $L = \{l_1, l_2, \ldots, l_n\}$ be a subset of V. Then, hide $C \backslash L$ is the contract (V_1, A_1, G_1), where $V_1 = V - L$, $A_1 = (\forall L)A$, and $G_1 = (\exists L)G$.*

In the definition above, we use the shorthand $(\forall L)A$ for $(\forall l_1)(\forall l_2)\ldots(\forall l_n)A$, the shorthand $(\exists L)G$ for $(\exists l_1)(\exists l_2)\ldots(\exists l_n)G$. We use existential quantification to indicate that the variables of the guarantee G are hidden, while we use universal quantification to indicate that the variables of assumption A are hidden because we require that all outputs of one contract are appropriate inputs for another contract.

We now define the contract-based semantics of Simulink as follows.

Definition 11 (The semantics of Simulink). *Let* $\mathrm{B} = (U, X, Y, f, g, Init)$ *be a block. We define the contract-based semantics for Simulink by induction on the structure of* B:

$$\llbracket \mathrm{B} \rrbracket = (V, A, G) \qquad\qquad \llbracket \mathrm{B} \; ; \; \mathrm{B} \rrbracket = \llbracket \mathrm{B} \rrbracket \; ; \; \llbracket \mathrm{B} \rrbracket$$

$$\llbracket \mathrm{B} \backslash L \rrbracket = \llbracket \mathrm{B} \rrbracket \backslash L \qquad\qquad \llbracket \mathrm{B} \parallel \mathrm{B} \rrbracket = \llbracket \mathrm{B} \rrbracket \parallel \llbracket \mathrm{B} \rrbracket$$

$$\llbracket \mathrm{B}[\gamma] \rrbracket = \llbracket \mathrm{B} \rrbracket [\gamma] \qquad\qquad \llbracket \mathrm{Fb}(\mathrm{B}, \mathrm{B}) \rrbracket = \llbracket \mathrm{B} \rrbracket \otimes \llbracket \mathrm{B} \rrbracket$$

where $V = U \cup Y$, *an assumption predicate* $A = (\exists X)(\mathcal{D}(\mathrm{B}))$, *and a guarantee predicate* $G = (\exists X)(\mathbf{y} = g(\mathbf{x}, \mathbf{u}) \wedge \triangle \mathbf{x} = f(\mathbf{x}, \mathbf{u}) \wedge Init)$.

In the above definition, the assumption predicate specifies a set of observable trajectories for the environment of a block, while the guarantee predicate specifies a set of observable trajectories for the block under the environment assumption. The environment of a block consists of the other blocks in the system which the block interacts with, and external entities of the system which provide input to the block. Note that we use an equation $\triangle \mathbf{x} = f(\mathbf{x}, \mathbf{u})$ to denote either a differential equation $\dot{\mathbf{x}} = f(\mathbf{x}, \mathbf{u})$ or a difference equation $\bar{\mathbf{x}}(t) = f(\mathbf{x}, \mathbf{u})$. These two equations are considered as a special kind of predicates over variables set $U \cup X$.

We illustrate the semantics of Simulink by giving an example.

Example 5. Consider blocks `Integrator`, `Gain`, and `Subtract` from Example 1, and blocks `Id` and `Split(n)`, where

$$
\begin{aligned}
\texttt{Id} &= (\{u\}, \emptyset, \{y\}, -, y(t) = u(t), true), \\
\texttt{Gain} &= (\{u\}, \emptyset, \{y\}, -, y(t) = Ku(t), true), \\
\texttt{Integrator} &= (\{u\}, \{x\}, \{y\}, \dot{x}(t) = u(t), y(t) = x(t), Init_1), \\
\texttt{Subtract} &= (\{u_1, u_2\}, \emptyset, \{y\}, -, y(t) = u_1(t) - u_2(t), true), \\
\texttt{Split(n)} &= (\{u\}, \emptyset, \{y_1, \ldots, y_n\}, -, \textstyle\bigwedge_{i=1}^{n} y_i(t) = u(t), true).
\end{aligned}
$$

Then by Definition 11, we have

$$
\begin{aligned}
\llbracket \texttt{Id} \rrbracket &= (\{u, y\}, true, y = u), \\
\llbracket \texttt{Gain} \rrbracket &= (\{u, y\}, true, y = Ku), \\
\llbracket \texttt{Subtract} \rrbracket &= (\{u_1, u_2, y\}, true, y = u_1 - u_2), \\
\llbracket \texttt{Split(n)} \rrbracket &= (\{u, y_1, \ldots, y_n\}, true, \textstyle\bigwedge_{i=1}^{n} y_i = u), \\
\llbracket \texttt{Integrator} \rrbracket &= (\{u, y\}, true, (\exists x)(y = x \wedge \dot{x} = u \wedge Init_1)),
\end{aligned}
$$

where K is a constant and the predicate $Init_1$ is a subset of $\mathbb{R}$.

5 Refinement of Simulink

In this section, we define the refinement relation for Simulink.

Definition 12 (Refinement of blocks). *Let* B_1 *and* B_2 *be blocks. Let* $[\![B_1]\!] = (V, A_1, G_1)$ *and* $[\![B_2]\!] = (V, A_2, G_2)$. *We say that* B_2 *is a refinement of* B_1, *denoted by* $B_1 \sqsubseteq B_2$, *if* $A_1 \Rightarrow A_2$ *and* $G_2 \Rightarrow G_1$ *are valid.*

From the definition of the refinement relation on blocks, we find that the refinement relation $\sqsubseteq$ is a preorder relation, and we define the relation $B_1 \equiv B_2$ if $B_1 \sqsubseteq B_2 \wedge B_2 \sqsubseteq B_1$.

Example 6. Continuing Examples 2 and 5, we now show that the block diagram VDS' is a refinement of the block diagram VDS, i.e. VDS $\sqsubseteq$ VDS'. The block diagrams VDS and VDS' described in Example 2:

$$\text{VDS} = (\{u\}, \emptyset, \{y\}, -, g, true),$$
$$\text{VDS}' = \text{Fb}(((\text{Gain1} \parallel \text{Id1}); \text{Integrator1}; \text{Split}_1(2)), \text{Gain2})\backslash L,$$

where $\text{Id1} = \text{Id}[l_5/u : l_6/y]$, $\text{Split}_1(2) = \text{Split}(2)[l_3/u : y/y_1, l_4/y_2]$, $\text{Gain1} = \text{Gain}[l_1/y]$, $\text{Gain2} = \text{Gain}[l_4/u : l_5/y]$, $\text{Subtract1} = \text{Subtract}[l_1/u_1, l_6/u_2 : l_2/y]$, $\text{Integrator1} = \text{Integrator}[l_2/u : l_3/y]$, $L = \{l_1, l_2, l_3, l_4, l_5, l_6\}$, and the output function g represents the ordinary differential Eq. (4).

The power u is controlled between 0 and M by a controller such that the vehicle speed reaches desired speed. That is evolution domain of the output function g is the formula $0 \le u(t) \le M$ for all $t \in \mathbb{R}^+$. Then by Definition 11, we have

$$[\![\text{VDC}]\!] = \left(\{u, v\}, (0 \le u) \wedge (u \le M), \dot{y} = \frac{1}{m}(u - by) \right).$$

In Example 5 we obtained contract semantics for blocks Id, Split(2), Gain, Subtract, and Integrator. Then by Definition 11, we have $[\![\text{Id1}]\!] = [\![\text{Id}]\!][l_5/u : l_6/y]$, $[\![\text{Gain1}]\!] = [\![\text{Gain}]\!][l_1/y]$, $[\![\text{Gain2}]\!] = [\![\text{Gain}]\!][l_4/u : l_5/y]$, $[\![\text{Subtract1}]\!] = [\![\text{Subtract}]\!][l_1/u_1, l_6/u_2 : l_2/y]$, $[\![\text{Split}_1(2)]\!] = [\![\text{Split}(2)]\!][l_3/u : y/y_1, l_4/y_2]$, and $[\![\text{Integrator1}]\!] = [\![\text{Integrator}]\!][l_2/u : l_3/y]$, where

$$
\begin{aligned}
[\![\text{Id}]\!][l_5/u : l_6/y] &= (\{l_5, l_6\}, true, l_6 = l_5), \\
[\![\text{Gain}]\!][l_1/y] &= (\{u, l_1\}, true, l_1 = \tfrac{1}{m}u), \\
[\![\text{Gain}]\!][l_4/u : l_5/y] &= (\{l_4, l_5\}, true, l_5 = \tfrac{b}{m}l_4), \\
[\![\text{Subtract}]\!][l_1/u_1, l_6/u_2 : l_2/y] &= (\{l_1, l_6, l_2\}, true, l_2 = l_1 - l_6), \\
[\![\text{Split}(2)]\!][l_3/u : y/y_1, l_4/y_2] &= (\{l_3, v, l_4\}, true, l_4 = l_3 \wedge y = l_3), \\
[\![\text{Integrator}]\!][l_2/u : l_3/y] &= \left(\{l_2, l_3\}, true, (\exists L')(l_3 = x_1 \wedge \dot{x}_1 = l_2 \wedge Init_1') \right) \text{ where } L' = L \cup \{x_1\}.
\end{aligned}
$$

We write $Init_1'$ for the predicate $(0 \le x_0) \wedge (x_1 = x_0) \wedge (x_0 \le M)$. Moreover, we have

$$[\![\text{VDS}']\!] = (((([\![\text{Gain1}]\!] \parallel [\![\text{Id1}]\!]); [\![\text{Integrator1}]\!]; [\![\text{Split}_1(2)]\!]) \otimes [\![\text{Gain2}]\!])\backslash L$$
$$= \left(\{u, y\}, true, (\exists x_1) \left(\dot{x}_1 = \frac{1}{m}(u - bx_1) \wedge (y = x_1) \wedge Init_1' \right) \right).$$

Obviously, the following formulas are valid

$$((0 \leq u) \wedge (u \leq M)) \Rightarrow true,$$
$$(\exists L') \left(\dot{x}_1 = \frac{1}{m}(u - bx_1) \wedge (y = x_1) \wedge Init'_1 \right) \Rightarrow \dot{y} = \frac{1}{m}(u - by). \tag{7}$$

Hence by Definition 12, we conclude that VDS $\sqsubseteq$ VDS'.

6 Conclusion and Future Work

In this paper, we presented a contract-based semantic model for Simulink, including both discrete-time and continuous-time blocks. To formalise the semantics of Simulink, the semantics of a block was defined as a contract, and we proposed five operations on contracts. Moreover, we defined the refinement relation between Simulink diagrams.

There are several interesting directions for future work. We plan to mechanize the contract-based semantics of Simulink in Isabelle/HOL. Formalising multirate Simulink block diagrams using the contract-based semantic model. We also plan to propose a contract-based semantics for Stateflow.

References

1. Benveniste, A., et al.: Contracts for system design (2018)
2. Boström, P.: Contract-based verification of Simulink models. In: Qin, S., Qiu, Z. (eds.) ICFEM 2011. LNCS, vol. 6991, pp. 291–306. Springer, Heidelberg (2011). https://doi.org/10.1007/978-3-642-24559-6_21
3. Boström, P., Morel, L., Waldén, M.: Stepwise development of Simulink models using the refinement calculus framework. In: Jones, C.B., Liu, Z., Woodcock, J. (eds.) ICTAC 2007. LNCS, vol. 4711, pp. 79–93. Springer, Heidelberg (2007). https://doi.org/10.1007/978-3-540-75292-9_6
4. Boström, P., Wiik, J.: Contract-based verification of discrete-time multi-rate Simulink models. Softw. Syst. Model. **15**(4), 1141–1161 (2016)
5. Bouissou, O., Chapoutot, A.: An operational semantics for Simulink's simulation engine. In: Wilhelm, R., Falk, H., Yi, W. (eds.) SIGPLAN/SIGBED Conference on Languages, Compilers and Tools for Embedded Systems 2012, LCTES 2012, Beijing, China, 12–13 June 2012, pp. 129–138. ACM (2012)
6. Bourke, T., Carcenac, F., Colaço, J., Pagano, B., Pasteur, C., Pouzet, M.: A synchronous look at the Simulink standard library. ACM Trans. Embed. Comput. Syst. **16**(5s), 176:1–176:24 (2017)
7. Caspi, P., Curic, A., Maignan, A., Sofronis, C., Tripakis, S.: Translating discrete-time Simulink to Lustre. In: Alur, R., Lee, I. (eds.) EMSOFT 2003. LNCS, vol. 2855, pp. 84–99. Springer, Heidelberg (2003). https://doi.org/10.1007/978-3-540-45212-6_7
8. Cavalcanti, A., Clayton, P., O'Halloran, C.: Control law diagrams in *Circus*. In: Fitzgerald, J., Hayes, I.J., Tarlecki, A. (eds.) FM 2005. LNCS, vol. 3582, pp. 253–268. Springer, Heidelberg (2005). https://doi.org/10.1007/11526841_18

9. Cavalcanti, A., Mota, A., Woodcock, J.: Simulink timed models for program verification. In: Liu, Z., Woodcock, J., Zhu, H. (eds.) Theories of Programming and Formal Methods. LNCS, vol. 8051, pp. 82–99. Springer, Heidelberg (2013). https://doi.org/10.1007/978-3-642-39698-4_6

10. Chapoutot, A., Martel, M.: Abstract simulation: a static analysis of Simulink models. In: Chen, T., Serpanos, D.N., Taha, W. (eds.) International Conference on Embedded Software and Systems, ICESS 2009, Hangzhou, Zhejiang, P.R. China, 25–27 May 2009, pp. 83–92. IEEE Computer Society (2009)

11. Chen, C., Dong, J.S.: Applying timed interval calculus to Simulink diagrams. In: Liu, Z., He, J. (eds.) ICFEM 2006. LNCS, vol. 4260, pp. 74–93. Springer, Heidelberg (2006). https://doi.org/10.1007/11901433_5

12. Chen, C., Dong, J.S., Sun, J.: A formal framework for modeling and validating Simulink diagrams. Formal Aspects Comput. **21**(5), 451–483 (2009)

13. Dragomir, I., Preoteasa, V., Tripakis, S.: Compositional semantics and analysis of hierarchical block diagrams. In: Bošnački, D., Wijs, A. (eds.) SPIN 2016. LNCS, vol. 9641, pp. 38–56. Springer, Cham (2016). https://doi.org/10.1007/978-3-319-32582-8_3

14. Foster, S., Cavalcanti, A., Canham, S., Woodcock, J., Zeyda, F.: Unifying theories of reactive design contracts. Theor. Comput. Sci. **802**, 105–140 (2020)

15. Hoare, C.A.R.: Communicating Sequential Processes, vol. 178. Prentice-Hall, Englewood Cliffs (1985)

16. MathWorks: Simulink user's guide (2021)

17. Meyer, B.: Applying "design by contract". Computer **25**(10), 40–51 (1992)

18. Milner, R.: Communication and Concurrency, vol. 84. Prentice Hall, Englewood Cliffs (1989)

19. Rajhans, A., Avadhanula, S., Chutinan, A., Mosterman, P.J., Zhang, F.: Graphical modeling of hybrid dynamics with Simulink and Stateflow. In: Prandini, M., Deshmukh, J.V. (eds.) Proceedings of the 21st International Conference on Hybrid Systems: Computation and Control (part of CPS Week), HSCC 2018, Porto, Portugal, 11–13 April 2018, pp. 247–252. ACM (2018)

20. Sangiovanni-Vincentelli, A., Damm, W., Passerone, R.: Taming Dr. Frankenstein: contract-based design for cyber-physical systems. Eur. J. Control **18**(3), 217–238 (2012)

21. Ye, K., Foster, S., Woodcock, J.: Compositional assume-guarantee reasoning of control law diagrams using UTP (2018). https://eprints.whiterose.ac.uk/129640/15/Compositional_Assume_Guarantee_Reasoning_of_Control_Law_Diagrams_using_UTP_Tech_Report.pdf. Accessed 3 Apr 2022

22. Ye, K., Foster, S., Woodcock, J.: Compositional assume-guarantee reasoning of control law diagrams using UTP. In: Adamatzky, A., Kendon, V. (eds.) From Astrophysics to Unconventional Computation. ECC, vol. 35, pp. 215–254. Springer, Cham (2020). https://doi.org/10.1007/978-3-030-15792-0_10

23. Zhou, C., Kumar, R.: Semantic translation of Simulink diagrams to input/output extended finite automata. Discret. Event Dyn. Syst. **22**(2), 223–247 (2012)

24. Zou, L., Zhan, N., Wang, S., Fränzle, M., Qin, S.: Verifying Simulink diagrams via a hybrid Hoare logic prover. In: Ernst, R., Sokolsky, O. (eds.) Proceedings of the International Conference on Embedded Software, EMSOFT 2013, Montreal, QC, Canada, 29 September–4 October 2013, pp. 9:1–9:10. IEEE (2013)

Decidability of Liveness for Concurrent Objects on the TSO Memory Model

Chao Wang[1], Gustavo Petri[2], Yi Lv[3,6], Teng Long[4], and Zhiming Liu[1,5(✉)]

[1] Centre for Research and Innovation in Software Engineering, Southwest University, Chongqing, China

[2] Arm Research, Cambridge, UK

[3] State Key Laboratory of Computer Science, Institute of Software, CAS, China

[4] China University of Geosciences, Wuhan, China

[5] Centre for Intelligent and Embedded Software, Northwest Polytechnical University, Xi'an, China

zhimingliu88@swu.edn.cn

[6] University of Chinese Academy of Sciences, Beijing, China

Abstract. An important property of concurrent objects is whether they support progress – a special case of liveness – guarantees, which ensure the termination of individual method calls under system fairness assumptions. Liveness properties have been proposed for concurrent objects. Typical liveness properties include *lock-freedom*, *wait-freedom*, *deadlock-freedom*, *starvation-freedom* and *obstruction-freedom*. It is known that the five liveness properties above are decidable on the Sequential Consistency (SC) memory model for a bounded number of processes. However, the problem of decidability of liveness for finite state concurrent programs running on relaxed memory models remains open. In this paper we address this problem for the Total Store Order (TSO) memory model, as found in the x86 architecture. We prove that lock-freedom, wait-freedom, deadlock-freedom and starvation-freedom are undecidable on TSO for a bounded number of processes, while obstruction-freedom is decidable.

1 Introduction

A concurrent object provides a set of methods for client programs to access the object. Given the complexity of writing efficient concurrent code, it is recommended to use mature libraries of concurrent objects such as *java.util.concurrent* for Java and *std::thread* for C++11. The verification of these concurrent libraries is obviously important but intrinsically hard, since they are highly optimized to avoid blocking – thus exploiting more parallelism – by using optimistic concurrency in combination with atomic instructions like compare-and-set.

Various liveness properties (progress conditions) have been proposed for concurrent objects. Lock-freedom, wait-freedom, deadlock-freedom, starvation-freedom and obstruction-freedom [11, 15] are five typical liveness properties. A liveness property describes conditions under which method calls are guaranteed to successfully complete in an execution. Intuitively, clients of a wait-free library can expect each method call to return in finite number of steps. Clients using a lock-free library can expect that at

W. Dong and J.-P. Talpin (Eds.): SETTA 2022, LNCS 13649, pp. 149–165, 2022.
https://doi.org/10.1007/978-3-031-21213-0_10

any time, at least one library method call will return after a sufficient number of steps, while it is possible for methods on other processes to never return. Deadlock-freedom and starvation-freedom require each fair execution to satisfy lock-freedom and wait-freedom, respectively. Clients using an obstruction-free library can expect each method call to return in a finite number of steps when executed in isolation.

Programmers often assume that all accesses to the shared memory are performed instantaneously and atomically, which is guaranteed only by the sequential consistency (SC) memory model [13]. However, modern multiprocessors (e.g., x86 [8], ARM [16]), and programming languages (e.g., C/C++ [4], Java [17]) do not implement the SC memory model. Instead they provide *relaxed memory models*, which allow subtle behaviors due to hardware and compiler optimizations. For instance, in a multiprocessor system implementing the Total Store Order (TSO) memory model [3], each processor is equipped with a FIFO store buffer. In this paper we follow the TSO memory of [3] (similarly to [5,6,19]). Although in every realistic multiprocessor system implementing the TSO memory model, the buffer is of bounded size, to describe the semantics of *any* TSO implementing system it is necessary to consider unbounded size FIFO store buffers associated with each process, as in the semantics of [3]. Otherwise, TSO implementations with larger store buffer will not be captured by this theoretical TSO memory model. Any write action performed by a processor is put into its local store buffer first and can then be flushed into the main memory at any time. Some libraries are optimized for relaxed memory models. For example, some work-stealing queue implementations [14,18] are specifically written to perform well on TSO.

To address the problem of decidability of liveness properties, we remark that concurrent systems with a bounded number of processes on SC can be expressed as finite state *labelled transition systems* (LTS). Lock-freedom, wait-freedom and obstruction-freedom can be expressed as LTL formulas, as shown in [20]. We show that deadlock-freedom and starvation-freedom can be expressed as CTL* formulas. Given that LTL and CTL* model checking is decidable [7], it is known that lock-freedom, wait-freedom, deadlock-freedom, starvation-freedom and obstruction-freedom are decidable in this case. However, their decidability problem on TSO memory model for a bounded number of processes remains open.

In this paper, we study the decision problem of liveness properties on TSO. Our work covers the five typical liveness properties of [11], which are commonly used in practice. Our main findings are:

- Lock-freedom, wait-freedom, deadlock-freedom and starvation-freedom are *undecidable on TSO*, which reveals that the verification of liveness properties on TSO is intrinsically harder when compared to their verification on SC.
- Obstruction-freedom is *decidable on TSO*.

To the best of our knowledge, ours are the first decidability and undecidability results for liveness properties on relaxed memory models. Let us now present a sketch of the techniques used in the paper to justify our findings.

Undecidability Proof. Post proposes the post correspondence problem [21], a famous known undecidable problem. Ruohonen proposes the cyclic post correspondence problem (CPCP) [22], a variant of post correspondence problem and is also undecidable.

Abdulla *et al.* [2] reduce CPCP to checking whether a specific lossy channel machine has an infinite execution that visits a specific state infinitely often. Our undecidability proof of lock-freedom and wait-freedom is obtained by reducing the checking of the lossy channel machine problem to checking lock-freedom and wait-freedom for a specific library, based on a close connection of concurrent programs on TSO and lossy channel machines [3,23].

We generate a library template that can be instantiated as a specific library for each instance of CPCP. The collaboration between methods simulates lossy channel machine transitions. Each execution of the lossy channel machine contains (at most) two phases. Each *accepting* infinite execution of the lossy channel machine loops infinitely in the second phase. Thus, we make each method of the library work differently depending on the phase. Our library has the following features: if an infinite library execution simulates an accepting infinite execution of the lossy channel machine, then it violates lock-freedom, and thus, it also violates wait-freedom; if an infinite library execution does not simulate an accepting infinite execution of the lossy channel machine, then it satisfies wait-freedom, and thus, it also satisfies lock-freedom. This is because any execution that satisfies wait-freedom also satisfies lock-freedom. Therefore, we reduce checking whether the lossy channel machine has an accepting infinite execution, or more precisely CPCP, to checking lock-freedom and wait-freedom of the library.

Perhaps surprisingly, the same library can be used to show the undecidability of deadlock-freedom (resp., starvation-freedom), which requires that each infinite fair execution satisfies lock-freedom (resp., wait-freedom). This is because whenever a library execution simulates an accepting infinite execution of the lossy channel machine, we require library methods to collaborate and work alternatingly, and thus, such library execution must be fair and violates deadlock-freedom, and thus, violates starvation-freedom. Therefore, checking the existence of accepting infinite executions of the lossy channel machines is reduced to checking violations of deadlock-freedom and starvation-freedom.

Decidability Proof. We introduce a notion called *blocking pair*, coupling a process control state and a memory valuation, and capturing a time point from which we can generate an infinite execution on the SC memory model, for which eventually one process runs in isolation and does not perform any return. We reduce checking obstruction-freedom to the state reachability problem, a known decidable problem [3], for configurations that "contain a blocking pair" and have an empty buffer for each process. There are two difficulties here: firstly, the TSO concurrent systems of [3] do not use libraries; and secondly, the state reachability problem requires the buffer of each process to be empty for the destination configuration, while such configuration may not exist in an obstruction-freedom violation.

The first difficulty is addressed by making each process repeatedly call an arbitrary method with an arbitrary arguments for an arbitrarily number of times, while transforming each call and return action into internal actions. To solve the second difficulty, we show that each obstruction-freedom violation has a prefix reaching a configuration that "contains a blocking pair". By discarding specific actions of the prefix execution and forcing some flush actions to happen, we obtain another prefix execution reaching a configuration that both "contains a blocking pair" and has an empty buffer for each process.

Related Work. There are several works on the decidability of verification on TSO. Atig *et al.* [3] prove that the state reachability problem is decidable on TSO while the repeated state reachability problem is undecidable on TSO. Bouajjani *et al.* [5] prove that robustness is decidable on TSO. Our previous work [23] proves that TSO-to-TSO linearizability [6], a correctness condition of concurrent libraries on TSO, is undecidable on TSO. Our previous work [24] proposes a bounded versions of TSO-to-TSO linearizability and a bounded version of TSO linearizability [9], and prove that these two bounded linearizability, as well as a bounded version of TSO-to-SC linearizability [10], are decidable on TSO. None of these works address the decidability of concurrent library liveness on TSO.

Our approach for simulating executions of lossy channel machines with libraries is partly inspired by Atig *et al.* [3]. However, Atig *et al.* do not consider libraries, and their concurrent programs do not have call or return actions. Our library needs to ensure that, in each infinite library execution simulating an infinite execution of the lossy channel machine, methods are "fixed to process", in other words, the same method must run on the same process. The TSO concurrent systems of [3] do not need to "fix methods to processes" since they record the control states and transitions of each process. Both Atig *et al.* and our work store the lossy channel content in the store buffer. However, when simulating one lossy channel machine transition, methods of Atig *et al.* only require to do one read or write action, while methods of our paper require to read the whole channel content. It appears that we cannot "fix methods to processes" with methods in the style of [3], unless we use a specific command to directly obtain the process identifier.

Our previous work [23] considers safety properties of libraries. Both [23] and this paper use the collaboration of two methods to simulate one lossy channel machine transition. Our idea for simulating lossy channel machine transitions with libraries extends that of [23], since each library constructed using the latter contains executions violating liveness, which makes such libraries not suitable for their reduction to liveness. The library of [23] contains a method that never returns and thus, do not need to consider "fixing methods to processes".

Our previous work [24] verifies k-bounded TSO-to-TSO linearizability, k-bounded TSO-to-SC linearizability and k-bounded TSO linearizability by reducing them to another known decidable reachability problem, the control state reachability problem of lossy channel machines [3]. That work focuses on dealing with call and return actions across multiple processes, while our verification approach for obstruction-freedom considers call and return actions as internal actions.

2   Concurrent Systems

2.1   Notations

In general, a finite sequence on an alphabet Σ is denoted $l = a_1 \cdot a_2 \cdot \ldots \cdot a_k$, where $\cdot$ is the concatenation symbol and $a_i \in \Sigma$ for each $1 \leq i \leq k$. Let $|l|$ and $l(i)$ denote the length and the i-th element of l, respectively, i.e., $|l| = k$ and $l(i) = a_i$ for $1 \leq i \leq k$. Let $l(i, j)$ denote the string $l(i) \cdot \ldots \cdot l(j)$. Let $l \uparrow_{\Sigma'}$ denote the projection of l on the alphabet Σ', which is a subset of Σ. Given a function f, let $f[x \mapsto y]$ be the function that is the same as f everywhere, except for x, where it has the value y. Let $\_$ denote an item, of which the value is irrelevant, and ϵ the empty word.

A *labelled transition system* (LTS) is a tuple $\mathcal{A} = (Q, \Sigma, \rightarrow, q_0)$, where Q is a set of states, Σ is an alphabet of transition labels, $\rightarrow \subseteq Q \times \Sigma \times Q$ is a transition relation and q_0 is the initial state. A finite path of $\mathcal{A}$ is a finite sequence of transitions $q_0 \xrightarrow{a_1} q_1 \xrightarrow{a_2} \ldots \xrightarrow{a_k} q_k$ with $k \geq 0$, and a finite trace of $\mathcal{A}$ is a finite sequence $t = a_1 \cdot a_2 \cdot \ldots \cdot a_k$, with $k \geq 0$ if there exists a finite path $q_0 \xrightarrow{a_1} q_1 \xrightarrow{a_2} \ldots \xrightarrow{a_k} q_k$ of $\mathcal{A}$. An infinite path of $\mathcal{A}$ is an infinite sequence of transitions $q_0 \xrightarrow{a_1} q_1 \xrightarrow{a_2} \ldots$, and correspondingly an infinite trace of $\mathcal{A}$ is an infinite sequence $t = a_1 \cdot a_2 \cdot \ldots$ if there exists an infinite path $q_0 \xrightarrow{a_1} q_1 \xrightarrow{a_2} \ldots$ of $\mathcal{A}$.

2.2   Concurrent Objects and the Most General Client

Concurrent objects are implemented as well-encapsulated libraries. The *most general client* of a concurrent object is a program that interacts with the object, and is designed to exhibit all the possible behaviors of the object. A simple instance of the most general client is a client that repeatedly makes non-deterministic method calls with non-deterministic arguments. Libraries may contain private memory locations for their own uses. For simplicity, and without loss of generality, we assume that methods have only one argument and one return value (when they return).

Given a finite set $\mathcal{X}$ of memory locations, a finite set $\mathcal{M}$ of method names and a finite data domain $\mathcal{D}$, the set *PCom* of primitive commands is defined by the following grammar:

$$PCom ::= \tau \mid read(x, a) \mid write(x, a) \mid cas\_suc(x, a, b) \mid cas\_fail(x, a, b)$$
$$\mid call(m, a) \mid return(m, a)$$

where $a, b \in \mathcal{D}, x \in \mathcal{X}$ and $m \in \mathcal{M}$. Here τ represents an internal command. To use the commands as labels in an LTS we assume that they encode the expected values that they return (an oracle of sorts). Hence, for instance the read command $read(x, a)$ encodes the value read a. In general *cas* (compare-and-set) commands execute a read and a conditional write (or no write at all) in a single atomic step. In our case a successful *cas* is represented with the command $cas\_suc(x, a, b)$, and it is enabled when the initial value of x is a, upon which the command updates it with value b, while a failed *cas* command, represented with the command $cas\_fail(x, a, b)$ does not update the state, and can only happen when the value of x is not a.

A library $\mathcal{L}$ is a tuple $\mathcal{L} = (\mathcal{X}_{\mathcal{L}}, \mathcal{M}_{\mathcal{L}}, \mathcal{D}_{\mathcal{L}}, Q_{\mathcal{L}}, \rightarrow_{\mathcal{L}})$, where $\mathcal{X}_{\mathcal{L}}, \mathcal{M}_{\mathcal{L}}$ and $\mathcal{D}_{\mathcal{L}}$ are a finite memory location set, a finite method name set and a finite data domain of $\mathcal{L}$, respectively. $Q_{\mathcal{L}} = \bigcup_{m \in \mathcal{M}_{\mathcal{L}}} Q_m$ is the union of disjoint finite sets Q_m of program positions of each method $m \in \mathcal{M}_{\mathcal{L}}$. Each program position represents the current program counter value and local register value of a process and can be considered as a state. $\rightarrow_{\mathcal{L}} = \bigcup_{m \in \mathcal{M}_{\mathcal{L}}} \rightarrow_m$ is the union of disjoint transition relations of each method $m \in \mathcal{M}_{\mathcal{L}}$. Let $PCom_{\mathcal{L}}$ be the set of primitive commands (except call and return commands) upon $\mathcal{X}_{\mathcal{L}}, \mathcal{M}_{\mathcal{L}}$ and $\mathcal{D}_{\mathcal{L}}$. Then, for each $m \in \mathcal{M}_{\mathcal{L}}, \rightarrow_m \subseteq Q_m \times PCom_{\mathcal{L}} \times Q_m$.

The most general client $\mathcal{MGC}$ is defined as a tuple $(\mathcal{M}_{\mathcal{C}}, \mathcal{D}_{\mathcal{C}}, Q_{\mathcal{C}}, \rightarrow_{mgc})$, where $\mathcal{M}_{\mathcal{C}}$ is a finite method name set, $\mathcal{D}_{\mathcal{C}}$ is a finite data domain, $Q_{\mathcal{C}} = \{in_{clt}, in_{lib}\}$

is the state set, and $\rightarrow_{mgc} = \{(in_{clt}, call(m,a), in_{lib}), (in_{lib}, return(m,b), in_{clt}), | m \in \mathcal{M}_{\mathcal{C}}, a, b \in \mathcal{D}_{\mathcal{C}}\}$ is a transition relation. State in_{clt} represents that currently no method of library is running, and in_{lib} represents that some method of library is running.

2.3   TSO Operational Semantics

A concurrent system consists of n processes, each of which runs the most general client $\mathcal{MGC} = (\mathcal{M}, \mathcal{D}, \{in_{clt}, in_{lib}\}, \rightarrow_{mgc})$, and all the most general clients interact with a same library $\mathcal{L} = (\mathcal{X}_{\mathcal{L}}, \mathcal{M}, \mathcal{D}, Q_{\mathcal{L}}, \rightarrow_{\mathcal{L}})$. In this paper we follow the TSO memory model of [3] (similarly to [5,6,19]), where each processor is equipped with a FIFO store buffer. As explained in the introduction, in this TSO memory model, each process is associated with an unbounded FIFO store buffer. Fence commands are used to ensure order between commands before fence and commands after fence. The TSO memory model of [3] does not include fence commands, since fence commands can be simulated with *cas* commands.

The operational semantics of a concurrent system (with library $\mathcal{L}$ and n processes) on TSO is defined as an LTS $[\![\mathcal{L}, n]\!] = (Conf, \Sigma, \rightarrow, InitConf)$, with *Conf*, Σ, $\rightarrow$ and *InitConf* described below.

Configuration of *Conf* are tuples (p, d, u), where $p : \{1, \ldots, n\} \rightarrow \{in_{clt}\} \cup (Q_{\mathcal{L}} \times \{in_{lib}\})$ represents the control state of each process, $d : \mathcal{X}_{\mathcal{L}} \rightarrow \mathcal{D}$ is the valuation of memory locations, and $u : \{1, \ldots, n\} \rightarrow (\{(x,a) \mid x \in \mathcal{X}_{\mathcal{L}}, a \in \mathcal{D}\})^*$ is the content of each process's store buffer. The initial configuration *InitConf* $\in$ *Conf* is $(p_{init}, d_{init}, u_{init})$. Here p_{init} maps each process id to in_{clt}, d_{init} is a valuation for memory locations in $\mathcal{X}_{\mathcal{L}}$, and u_{init} initializes each process with an empty buffer.

We denote with Σ the set of actions defined by the following grammar:

$$\Sigma :: = \tau(i) \mid read(i, x, a) \mid write(i, x, a) \mid cas(i, x, a, b) \mid flush(i, x, a) \mid call(i, m, a) \mid$$

$$return(i, m, a)$$

where $1 \leq i \leq n, m \in \mathcal{M}, x \in \mathcal{X}_{\mathcal{L}}$ and $a, b \in \mathcal{D}$. The detailed definition of the transition relation can be found in Appendix A of our technical report [25]. Intuitively, a *write*(i, x, a) action puts an item (x, a) into the store buffer, and a *read*(i, x, a) action returns the latest value of x in the buffer if present, or returns the value in memory if the buffer contains no stores on x. Actions τ, *call* and *return* only influence the control state. A *flush* action is carried out by the memory model to flush the item at the head of the process's store buffer to memory at any time. A *cas* action atomically executes a read and a conditional write (or no write at all) if and only if the process's store buffer is empty.

3   Liveness

We use $T_{\omega}([\![\mathcal{L}, n]\!])$ to denote all infinite traces of the concurrent system $[\![\mathcal{L}, n]\!]$. Given an execution $t \in T_{\omega}([\![\mathcal{L}, n]\!])$, we say a call action $t(i)$ (the i-th step of execution t) matches a return action $t(j)$ with $i < j$, if the two actions are by the same process, and there are no call or return actions by the same process in-between. Here we assume that methods do not call other methods. Let *pend_inv(t)* denote the set of pending call actions of t, in other words, call actions of t with no matching return action in t.

We define the following predicates borrowed from [15]. Since we do not consider aborts, and we do not consider termination markers, we slightly modify the predicates definition of [15] by considering only infinite executions. Given an infinite execution $t \in T_\omega(\llbracket \mathcal{L}, n \rrbracket)$:

- *prog-t(t)*: This predicate holds when every method call in t eventually returns. Formally, for each index i and action e, if $e \in pend\_inv(t(1, i))$, there exists $j > i$, such that $t(j)$ matches e.
- *prog-s(t)*: This predicate holds when there is always some method return action which happens in the future if the system executes for a sufficient number of steps. Formally, for each index i and action e, if $e \in pend\_inv(t(1, i))$ holds, then there exists $j > i$, such that $t(j)$ is a return action.
  Note that *prog-t(t)* implies *prog-s(t)*, while the opposite direction does not hold. The reason is that, there exists executions where some process execute call and return for infinite times, and some process has a call action without matching return action. Such executions satisfy *prog-s* but do not satisfy *prog-t*.
- *sched(t)*: This predicate holds if t is an infinite trace with pending call actions, and at least one of the processes with a pending call action is scheduled infinitely many times. Formally, if $|t| = \omega$ and $pend\_inv(t) \neq \emptyset$, then there exists $e \in pend\_inv(t)$, such that $|t \uparrow_{pid(e)}| = \omega$. Here $t \uparrow_{pid(e)}$ represents the projection of t into the actions of the process of e. *sched* is used as basic requirement for good schedule in [15].
- *fair(t)*: This predicate describing fair interleavings requires that if t is an infinite execution, then each process is scheduled infinitely many times. Formally, if $|t| = \omega$, then for each process $proc$ in t, $|t \uparrow_{proc}| = \omega$. Here $t \uparrow_{proc}$ represents the projection of t into actions of process $proc$.
- *iso(t)*: This predicate requires that if t is an infinite execution, eventually only one process is scheduled. Formally, if $|t| = \omega$, then there exists index i and process $proc$, such that for each $j > i$, $t(j)$ is an action of process $proc$. *iso* is used to describe the situation where eventually only one process be scheduled.

With these predicates, we can present the formal notions of lock-freedom, wait-freedom, deadlock-freedom, starvation-freedom and obstruction-freedom of [15].

Definition 1. *Given an execution* $t \in T_\omega(\llbracket \mathcal{L}, n \rrbracket)$:

- *t satisfies lock-freedom whenever:* $sched(t) \Rightarrow prog\text{-}s(t)$,
- *t satisfies wait-freedom whenever:* $sched(t) \Rightarrow prog\text{-}t(t)$,
- *t satisfies deadlock-freedom whenever:* $fair(t) \Rightarrow prog\text{-}s(t)$,
- *t satisfies starvation-freedom whenever:* $fair(t) \Rightarrow prog\text{-}t(t)$,
- *t satisfies obstruction-freedom whenever:* $sched(t) \wedge iso(t) \Rightarrow prog\text{-}s(t)$

For library $\mathcal{L}$, *we parameterize the definitions above over* n *processes, and we define their satisfaction requiring that each execution of* $\llbracket \mathcal{L}, n \rrbracket$ *satisfies the corresponding liveness property.*

Petrank *et al.* [20] demonstrate how to formalize lock-freedom, wait-freedom and obstruction-freedom as LTL formulas. In Appendix B of our technical report [25] we state how to formalize deadlock-freedom and starvation-freedom for n processes as CTL* formulas. As explained in Sect. 6.2, concurrent system with n processes on SC can be expressed as finite state LTS, and LTL and CTL* model checking is decidable [7], we thus obtain that the above five liveness properties are decidable for SC.

4   Perfect/Lossy Channel Machines

A channel machine [2,3] is a finite control machine equipped with channels of unbounded size. It can perform send and receive operations on its channels. A lossy channel machine is a channel machine where arbitrarily many items in its channels may be lost non-deterministically at any time and without any notification.

Let CH be the finite set of channel names and Σ_{CH} be a finite alphabet of channel contents. The content of a channel is a finite sequence over Σ_{CH}. A channel operation is either a send operation $c!a$ sending the value a over channel c, a receive operation $c?a$ receiving a over c, or a silent operation nop. We associate with each channel operation a relation over words as follows: Given $w \in \Sigma_{CH}^*$, we have $[\![nop]\!](w, w)$, $[\![c!a]\!](w, a \cdot w)$ and $[\![c?a]\!](w \cdot a, w)$.

A channel operation over a finite channel name set CH is a mapping that associates, with each channel of CH, a channel operation. Let $Op(CH)$ be the set of channel operations over CH. The relation of channel operations is extended to channel operations over CH as follows: given a channel operation op over CH and two functions $u, u' \in CH \rightarrow \Sigma_{CH}^*$, we have $[\![op]\!](u, u')$, if $[\![op(c)]\!](u(c), u'(c))$ holds for each $c \in CH$.

A *channel machine* is formally defined as a tuple $CM = (Q, CH, \Sigma_{CH}, \Lambda, \Delta)$, where (1) Q is a finite set of states, (2) CH is a finite set of channel names, (3) Σ_{CH} is a finite alphabet for channel contents, (4) Λ is a finite set of transition labels, and (5) $\Delta \subseteq Q \times (\Lambda \cup \{\epsilon\}) \times Op(CH) \times Q$ is a finite set of transitions. When CM is considered as a perfect channel machine, its semantics is defined as an LTS $(Conf, \Lambda, \rightarrow, initConf)$. A configuration of $Conf$ is a pair (q, u) where $q \in Q$ and $u : CH \rightarrow \Sigma_{CH}^*$. $initConf$ is the initial configuration and all its channels are empty. The transition relation $\rightarrow$ is defined as follows: given $q, q' \in Q$ and $u, u' \in CH \rightarrow \Sigma_{CH}^*$, $(q, u) \xrightarrow{\alpha} (q', u')$, if there exists op, such that $(q, \alpha, op, q') \in \Delta$ and $[\![op]\!](u, u')$. When CM is considered as a lossy channel machine, its semantics is defined as another LTS $(Conf, \Lambda, \rightarrow', initConf)$, with transition relation $\rightarrow'$ defined as follows: $(q, u) \xrightarrow{\alpha}{}' (q', u')$, if there exists $v, v' \in CH \rightarrow \Sigma_{CH}^*$, such that (1) for each $c \in CH$, $v(c)$ is a sub-word of $u(c)$, (2) $(q, v) \xrightarrow{\alpha} (q', v')$ and (3) for each $c \in CH$, $u'(c)$ is a sub-word of $v'(c)$. Here a sequence $l_1 = a_1 \cdot \ldots \cdot a_u$ is a sub-word of another sequence $l_2 = b_1 \cdot \ldots \cdot b_v$, if there exists $i_1 < \ldots < i_u$, such that $1 \leq i_1 < \ldots < i_u \leq v$.

5   Undecidability of Four Liveness Properties

Abdulla *et al.* [2] reduce the cyclic post correspondence problem, a known undecidable problem, to checking whether some lossy channel machine $CM_{(A,B)}$ has a specific

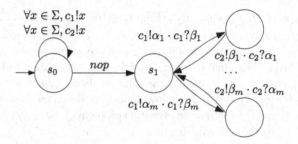

Fig. 1. The lossy channel machine $CM_{(A,B)}$.

infinite execution. In this section, we sketch a reduction from the cyclic post correspondence problem to a infinite execution problem of $CM'_{(A,B)}$, a lossy channel machine that is obtained from $CM_{(A,B)}$ and uses only one channel. Then, we propose a library $\mathcal{L}(A, B)$, and reduce checking such infinite execution problem of $CM'_{(A,B)}$ to checking lock-freedom, wait-freedom, deadlock-freedom and starvation-freedom of such library on TSO. Thus, such four liveness properties are undecidable on TSO.

5.1 The Lossy Channel Machine for CPCP of Abdulla et al. [2]

Given two sequences l and l', let $l =_c l'$ denote that there exists sequences l_1 and l_2, such that $l = l_1 \cdot l_2$ and $l' = l_2 \cdot l_1$. Given two collections of finite sequences $\alpha_1, \ldots, \alpha_m$ and $\beta_1, \ldots, \beta_m$, a solution of $\alpha_1, \ldots, \alpha_m$ and $\beta_1, \ldots, \beta_m$ is a nonempty sequence of indices $i_1 \cdot \ldots \cdot i_k$, such that $\alpha_{i_1} \cdot \ldots \cdot \alpha_{i_k} =_c \beta_{i_1} \cdot \ldots \cdot \beta_{i_k}$. The cyclic post correspondence problem (CPCP) [22], known to be undecidable, requires to answer given $\alpha_1, \ldots, \alpha_m$ and $\beta_1, \ldots, \beta_m$, whether there exists one such solution.

Given two collections $A = \alpha_1, \ldots, \alpha_m$ and $B = \beta_1, \ldots, \beta_m$ of finite sequences, Abdulla *et al.* [2] generate the lossy channel machine $CM_{(A,B)}$ shown in Fig. 1. Moreover, they prove that CPCP has a solution for A and B, if and only if $CM_{(A,B)}$ has an infinite execution that visits state s_1 infinite times. We point the readers to [2] for an explanation on how $CM_{(A,B)}$ solves CPCP.

$CM_{(A,B)}$ contains two channels c_1 and c_2. We use $c_1!\alpha_1$ to represent inserting the contents of α_1 into c_1 one by one, and use $c_1?\beta_1$ to represent receiving the content of β_1 from c_1 one by one. We use $c_1!\alpha_1 \cdot c_1?\beta_1$ to represent first do $c_1!\alpha_1$ and then do $c_1?\beta_1$. Each execution of $CM_{(A,B)}$ can be divided into (at most) two phases. The first phase, called the guess phase, is a self-loop of state s_0, and is used to guess a solution of CPCP. The second phase, called the check phase, goes from s_0 to s_1 and then repeatedly "checks the content of c_1 and c_2".

Based on $CM_{(A,B)}$ we generate the lossy channel machine $CM'_{(A,B)}$ which uses only one channel c and works in a similar way. To simulate one transition of $CM_{(A,B)}$, $CM'_{(A,B)}$ stores the content of c_1 followed by the content of c_2 (as well as new delimiter symbols) in its channel. Then it scans each symbol in its channel, modifies it (if necessary) and puts it back into its buffer, until the contents of c_1 and c_2 have all been dealt with.

We could depict $CM'_{(A,B)}$ similarly to Fig. 1, and each transition of $CM'_{(A,B)}$ is now a "extended version transition" as we discussed above. Therefore, there are "$CM'_{(A,B)}$'s versions" of s_0, s_1 and s_{trap}, and when no confusion is possible we also call them s_0, s_1 and s_{trap}, respectively. Note that if some new delimiter symbols are lost during transition, then such paths can not complete the simulation of one transition of $CM_{(A,B)}$, and thus, do not influence the proof of the following lemma. Based on above discussion, we reduce CPCP of A and B to an infinite execution problem of the lossy channel machine $CM'_{(A,B)}$, as stated by the following lemma.

Lemma 1. *There is a CPCP solution for sequences A and B of finite sequences, if and only if there is an infinite execution of $CM'_{(A,B)}$ that visits s_1 infinitely often.*

5.2   Libraries for Four Liveness Properties

In this subsection, we propose our library $\mathcal{L}(A,B)$ that is generated from $CM'_{(A,B)}$ and simulates the executions of $CM'_{(A,B)}$. This library contains two methods M_1 and M_2. Similarly to [3,23], we use the collaboration of two methods to simulate a lossy channel. Our library requires that each method be fixed to a single process when simulating infinite execution of $CM'_{(A,B)}$. Methods of our library work differently when simulating lossy channel machine transitions of different phases.

Let us now explain in detail the construction of $\mathcal{L}(A,B)$. $\mathcal{L}(A,B)$ uses the following memory locations: x_1, y_1, x_2, y_2, *phase*, *failSimu* and *firstM1*. *phase* stores the phase of $CM'_{(A,B)}$, and its initial value is *guess*. *failSimu* is a flag indicating the failure of the simulation of $CM'_{(A,B)}$, and its initial value is *false*. *firstM1* is used to indicate the first execution of M_1, and its initial value is *true*.

The pseudo-code of M_1 and M_2 are shown in Algorithms 1 and 2, respectively. $\perp_s$ and $\perp_e$ are two new symbols not contained in $CM'_{(A,B)}$. For brevity, we use the following notations. We use $writeOne(x,a)$ to represent the sequence of commands writing a followed by $\sharp$ into x. We use $writeSeq(x,a_1 \cdots a_k)$ to represent the sequence of commands writing $a_1 \cdot \sharp \cdot \ldots \cdot a_k \cdot \sharp$ into x. $\sharp$ is a delimiter that ensures one update of a memory location will not be read twice. We use $v := readOne(x)$ to represent the sequence of commands reading e followed by $\sharp$ from x for some $e \neq \sharp$ and then assigning e to v. Moreover, if the values read do not correspond with e followed by $\sharp$ we set *failSimu* to *true* and then let the current method return. This will terminate the simulation procedure. Similarly, $v := readRule(x)$ reads a transition rule followed by $\sharp$ from x, and assign the rule to v. We use $transportData(z_1, z_2)$ to represent repeatedly using $v = readOne(z_1)$ to read an update of z_1 and using $writeOne(z_2, v)$ to write it to z_2, until reading $\perp_e$ from z_1 and writing $\perp_e$ to z_2. Given a transition rule r, let $valueRead(r)$ and $valueWritten(r)$ be the value received and sent by r, respectively. The symbols s_0 and s_1 in the pseudo-code of M_1 represent the corresponding state of $CM_{(A,B)}$.

Figure 2 illustrates a possible execution of $\mathcal{L}(A,B)$. M_1 and M_2 work differently in the different phases. In the guess phase, M_1 and M_2 return after simulating one lossy channel machine transition, while in the check phase, M_1 and M_2 keep working until the simulation procedure fails.

Algorithm 1: M_1

Input: an arbitrary argument
1 **while** *true* **do**
2   If *failSimu*, then **return**;
3   **if** *firstM1* **then**
4   guess a transition rule r_1 that starts from s_0;
5          $writeSeq(x_1, r_1 \cdot \perp_s \cdot \perp_e)$;
6          $firstM1 = false$;
7   **else**
8          $r_1 := readRule(y_2)$;
9   let $z_1 := valueRead(r_1)$ and $z_2 := valueWritten(r_1)$;
10         $readOne(y_2, \perp_s)$;
11   if $z_1 \neq \epsilon$, then $readOne(y_2, z_1)$;
12   guess a transition rule r_2 starts from the destination state of r_1;
13         $writeSeq(x_1, r_2 \cdot \perp_s)$;
14   **while** *true* **do**
15             $tmp := readOne(y_2)$;
16   if $tmp = \perp_e$, then **break**;
17             $writeOne(x_1, tmp)$;
18         $writeSeq(x_1, z_2 \cdot \perp_e)$;
19   if *phase* = *guess* and the destination state of r_2 is s_1, then set *phase* to *check*;
20     $transportData(y_1, x_2)$;
21   if *phase* = *guess*, then **return**;

Algorithm 2: M_2

Input: an arbitrary argument
1 **while** *true* **do**
2   if *failSimu*, then **return**;
3      $transportData(x_1, y_1)$;
4      $transportData(x_2, y_2)$;
5   if *phase* = *guess*, then **return**;

Assume that M_1 (resp., M_2) runs on process P_1 (resp., process P_2). To simulate one lossy channel machine transition with channel content l, we first store $r_1 \cdot \perp_s \cdot l \cdot \perp_e$ in process P_2's store buffer as buffered items of y_2, where r_1 is the transition rule of this transition, and $\perp_s$ and $\perp_e$ are additional symbols indicating the start and end of channel content of $CM'_{(A,B)}$, respectively. Then, the procedure for simulating one lossy channel machine transition is as follows:

- M_1 reads the transition rule r_1 and channel content of $CM'_{(A,B)}$ by reading all the updates of y_2. After reading r_1, M_2 non-deterministically chooses a transition rule r_2 of the lossy channel machine. Such rule should begin from the destination state of r_1.
- There are four points for information update and transfer between M_1 and M_2: (1) According to transition rule r_1, M_1 modifies and writes all the updates of y_2 into x_1,

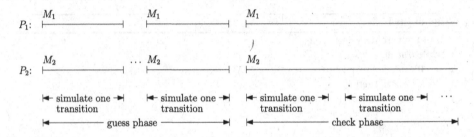

Fig. 2. One execution of $\mathcal{L}(A, B)$.

(2) then M_2 reads all the updates of x_1 and writes all the updates into y_1, (3) then M_1 reads all the updates of y_1 and writes all the updates into x_2, and (4) finally, M_2 reads all the updates of x_2 and writes all the updates into y_2. To read all the updates of a memory location, we need to repeatedly read until read $\perp_e$, which indicates the end of channel content.

Since there is no item in the buffer at the beginning of the simulation procedure, to simulate the first lossy channel machine transition M_1 directly writes $r \cdot \sharp \cdot \perp_s \cdot \sharp \cdot \perp_e \cdot \sharp$ to x_1 and does not need to read updates from y_2, where r is a transition rule from s_0. This is the reason for using *firstM1*.

– M_1 is also responsible for modifying the phase (stored in the memory location *phase*). If the last lossy channel machine transition simulated belongs to the guess phase and the destination state of r_1 is s_1, M_1 changes the memory location *phase* to check.

The reason why we need to update and transfer information between M_1 and M_2 is to deal with the case when an update of $\perp_e$ is not captured. Let us first consider a simple but infeasible solution: M_1 reads updates from y_2 (until reading $\perp_e$), and modifies and writes all the updates into x_1; while M_2 repeatedly reads an update of x_1 and writes it into y_2, until reading $\perp_e$. This solution can not deal with the case when updates of $\perp_e$ for y_2 is not seen by M_1, and will make M_1 and M_2 fall into infinite loop that violates liveness. This may happen in simulating each lossy channel machine transition, and thus, introduces "false negatives" to four liveness properties. To deal with this case, we need to break the infinite loop and avoid directly writing the updates of y_2 back into x_1. Instead, in our update and transfer points, we exhaust the updates of y_2, which are written to x_1, and later written to y_1 instead of y_2. Therefore, there is no infinite loop even if updates of $\perp_e$ for y_2 are lost.

Assume that we can successfully simulate one transition of $CM'_{(A,B)}$ with one M_1 running on process P_1 and one M_2 running on process P_2. Then the most general client on process P_1 (resp., on process P_2) can call M_1 and M_2. Perhaps surprisingly, the only possible way to simulate the second transition of $CM'_{(A,B)}$ is to let M_1 and M_2 to continue to run on processes P_1 and P_2, respectively. Let us explain why other choices fail to simulate the second transition: (1) If both processes run method M_1, then they both require reading updates of y_1. Since there is no buffered item for y_1, and none of them write to y_1, both M_1 fail the simulation. (2) If both processes run M_2, we arrive at a similar situation. (3) If M_1 and M_2 run on processes P_2 and P_1, respectively. M_1

requires reading the updates on y_2, and the only possible buffered y_2 items are in process P_2's buffer. According to the TSO memory model, M_1 always reads the same value for y_2 and thus fails to do $readOne(y_2, \_)$. Thus, M_1 fails the simulation. Therefore, we essentially "fix methods to processes" without adding specific commands for checking process id.

5.3   Undecidability of Four Liveness Properties

The following theorem states that lock-freedom, wait-freedom, deadlock-freedom and starvation-freedom are all undecidable on TSO for a bounded number of processes. Perhaps surprisingly, we prove this theorem with the same library $\mathcal{L}(A, B)$.

Theorem 1. *The problems of checking lock-freedom, wait-freedom, deadlock-freedom and starvation-freedom of a given library for a bounded number of processes are undecidable on TSO.*

Proof. (Sketch) For each infinite execution t of $[\![\mathcal{L}(A, B), 2]\!]$, assume that it simulates an execution of $CM'_{(A,B)}$, or it intends to do so. There are three possible cases for t shown as follows:

- Case 1: The simulation fails because some *readOne* does not read the intended value.
- Case 2: The simulation procedure succeeds, and t infinitely loops in the guess phase.
- Case 3: The simulation procedure succeeds, and t infinitely loops in the check phase and visits s_1 infinitely many times.

In case 1, since *failSimu* is set to *true*, each method returns immediately. Therefore, t satisfies wait-freedom and thus, satisfies lock-freedom. t can be either fair or unfair. In case 2, since each method returns after finite number of steps in the guess phase, t satisfies wait-freedom and thus, satisfies lock-freedom. In case 3, since M_1 and M_2 do not return in the check phase, t violates lock-freedom and thus, violates wait-freedom. Since M_1 and M_2 coordinate when simulating each transition of $CM'_{(A,B)}$, in case 2 and 3, t must be fair.

Therefore, we reduce the problem of checking whether $CM'_{(A,B)}$ has an execution that visits s_1 infinitely often to the problem of checking whether $\mathcal{L}(A, B)$ has an infinite execution of case 3 (which is fair and violates both wait-freedom and lock-freedom). By Lemma 1, we can see that the problems of checking lock-freedom, wait-freedom, deadlock-freedom and starvation-freedom of a given library for bounded number of processes are undecidable.

We remark here that [12] considers imposing liveness condition on store buffers, and requires buffered items to be eventually flushed. Our undecidability results on liveness properties on TSO still hold when imposing such liveness condition on store buffers, since in case 3 of the proof of Theorem 1, each item put into buffer will eventually be flushed.

6   Checking Obstruction-Freedom

6.1   The Basic TSO Concurrent Systems

Atig *et al.* [3] considers the following concurrent systems on TSO: Each process runs a finite control state program that can do internal, read, write and *cas* actions, and different processes communicate via shared memory. We use *basic TSO concurrent systems* to denote such concurrent systems.

Formally, let $\Sigma(proc, \mathcal{D}, \mathcal{X})$ be the set containing the τ (internal) action, the read actions, the write actions and the *cas* actions over memory locations $\mathcal{X}$ with data domain $\mathcal{D}$ and of process *proc*. A basic TSO concurrent system is a tuple $(P_1, \ldots, P_n)$, where each P_i is a tuple (Q_i, Δ_i), such that Q_i is a finite control state set and $\Delta_i \subseteq Q_i \times \Sigma(i, \mathcal{D}, \mathcal{X}) \times Q_i$ is the transition relation. They define an operational semantics similar to the one presented in Sect. 2. Each configuration is also a tuple (p, d, u), where p stores control state of each process, d is a memory valuation and u stores buffer content of each process. We refer the reader to [3] for a detailed description of the operational semantics on TSO which is unsurprising, and hence omitted here.

Given a basic TSO concurrent system $(P_1, \ldots, P_n)$, two functions p and p' that store control states of each process and two memory valuations d and d', the state reachability problem requires to determine whether there is a path from (p, d, u_{init}) to (p', d', u_{init}) in the operational semantics, where u_{init} initializes each process with an empty buffer. Atig *et al.* [3] prove that the state reachability problem is decidable.

6.2   Verification of Obstruction-Freedom

The definition of obstruction-freedom requires checking infinite executions, while the state reachability problem considers finite executions reaching specific configurations. To bridge this gap, we propose a notion called blocking pairs, which is defined on concurrent systems on the SC memory model and captures potential obstruction-freedom violations. Let $[\![\mathcal{L}, n]\!]_{sc}$ be the operational semantics of a concurrent system that runs on the SC memory model and contains n processes. The configurations of $[\![\mathcal{L}, n]\!]_{sc}$ coincide with the configurations of $[\![\mathcal{L}, n]\!]$ that preserve the buffer empty for each process. When performing a write action $[\![\mathcal{L}, n]\!]_{sc}$ does not put the item into the buffer, but directly updates the memory instead. $[\![\mathcal{L}, n]\!]_{sc}$ does not have flush actions, while other actions are unchanged from $[\![\mathcal{L}, n]\!]$. Since we use finite program positions, finite memory locations, a finite data domain, a finite method names and a finite number of processes, and since we essentially do not use buffers, we observe that $[\![\mathcal{L}, n]\!]_{sc}$ is a finite state LTS.

Let us now propose the notion of blocking pairs. Given a state $q \in \{in_{clt}\} \cup (Q_{\mathcal{L}} \times \{in_{lib}\})$ (recall that $Q_{\mathcal{L}}$ is the set of program positions of library, in_{clt} and in_{lib} are the states of the most general client) and a memory valuation d, (q, d) is a blocking pair, if in $[\![\mathcal{L}, 1]\!]_{sc}$ there exists a configuration (p, d, u), such that the state of process 1 of p is q $(p(1) = q)$, and there exists an infinite execution from (p, d, u) and such execution does not have a return action. This property can be expressed by the CTL* formula $E((G \, \neg P_{ret}) \wedge (G \, X \, P_{any}))$, where E is the usual modality of CTL*, P_{ret} is a predicate that checks if the transition label is a return action, and P_{any} returns true for any transition label. The following lemma reduces checking obstruction-freedom to the state reachability problem.

Lemma 2. *Given a library $\mathcal{L}$, there exists an infinite execution t of $[\![\mathcal{L}, n]\!]$ that violates obstruction-freedom on TSO, if and only if there exists an finite execution t' of $[\![\mathcal{L}, n]\!]$ and a process proc, such that t' leads to a configuration (p, d, u_{init}), where $(p(proc), d)$ is a blocking pair.*

The detailed proof can be found in Appendix C.1 of our technical report [25]. The *if* direction holds since we can obtain an obstruction-freedom violation $t' \cdot t_1$, in which t_1 is the specific infinite execution in the definition of blocking pairs. For the *only if* direction, there exists t_1, t_2 and process *proc*, such that $t = t_1 \cdot t_2$, and t_2 contains only actions of process *proc*. Let α_i be the last write action of process $i \neq proc$ in t_1 that has not been flushed. Dropping α_i in t yields a legal execution, since α_i does not influence the memory. Also, it is legal to clear buffer of process *proc* before executing t_2. With the approach above, we can generate an new execution that reaches a configuration, which has an empty buffer for each process and contains a blocking pair, before the execution of t_2.

Since the model checking problem for CTL* formulas is decidable for finite state LTSs [7], we could compute the set of blocking pairs by first enumerating all configurations of $[\![\mathcal{L}, 1]\!]_{sc}$, and then use model checking to check each of them. Thus, the configurations of the state reachability problem of Lemma 2 is computable. Since the the state reachability problem is decidable, we conclude that obstruction-freedom is decidable, as stated by the following theorem.

Theorem 2. *The problem of checking obstruction-freedom of a given library for bounded number of processes is decidable on TSO.*

7 Conclusion

Liveness is an important property of programs, and using objects with incorrect liveness assumptions can cause problematic behaviors. In this paper, we prove that lock-freedom, wait-freedom, deadlock-freedom and starvation-freedom are undecidable on TSO for a bounded number of processes by reducing a known undecidable problem of lossy channel machines to checking liveness properties of specific libraries. This library simulates the lossy channel machine $CM'_{(A,B)}$ and is designed to contain at most two kinds of executions: If methods collaborate in a fair way and the lossy channel machine execution being simulated visits state s_1 infinitely many times, then the library executions violate all four liveness properties; otherwise, the library executions satisfy all four liveness properties. Therefore, one library is sufficient for the undecidability proof of four liveness properties. Our undecidability proof reveals the intrinsic difference in liveness verification between TSO and SC, resulting from the unbounded size of store buffers in the TSO memory model.

Perhaps unexpectedly, we show that obstruction-freedom is decidable. Since each violation of obstruction-freedom eventually runs in isolation, from some time point the violation, running on TSO, has the same behavior as on SC. Therefore, checking whether a configuration contains a potential violation can be done by checking only this configuration itself, instead of checking all infinite executions from this configuration. Checking obstruction-freedom is thus reduced to a known decidable reachability problem.

Other relaxed memory models, such as the memory models of ARM and POWER, are much weaker than TSO. We conjecture that the undecidable liveness properties on TSO are still undecidable on ARM and POWER. As future work, we would like to investigate the decidability of obstruction-freedom on more relaxed memory models. Since the decidability result of obstruction-freedom on TSO has close connection to the state reachability problem of basic TSO concurrent system, and since Abdulla *et al.* prove that the control-state reachability problem is undecidable on POWER [1], thus, we conjecture that obstruction-freedom is also undecidable on POWER. There are variants of liveness properties, such as k-bounded lock-freedom, bounded lock-freedom, k-bounded wait-freedom and bounded wait-freedom [20]. We would also like to investigate the decidability of bounded version of liveness properties on TSO and more relaxed memory models.

References

1. Abdulla, P.A., Atig, M.F., Bouajjani, A., Derevenetc, E., Leonardsson, C., Meyer, R.: On the state reachability problem for concurrent programs under power. In: Georgiou, C., Majumdar, R. (eds.) NETYS 2020. LNCS, vol. 12129, pp. 47–59. Springer, Cham (2021). https://doi.org/10.1007/978-3-030-67087-0_4
2. Abdulla, P.A., Jonsson, B.: Undecidable verification problems for programs with unreliable channels. Inf. Comput. **130**(1), 71–90 (1996)
3. Atig, M.F., Bouajjani, A., Burckhardt, S., Musuvathi, M.: On the verification problem for weak memory models. In: Manuel, V., Hermenegildo., Palsberg, J. (eds.) Proceedings of the 37th ACM SIGPLAN-SIGACT Symposium on Principles of Programming Languages, POPL 2010, Madrid, Spain, 17–23 January 2010, pp. 7–18. ACM (2010)
4. Batty, M., Owens, S., Sarkar, S., Sewell, P., Weber, T.: Mathematizing C++ concurrency. In: Ball, T., Sagiv, M. (eds.) Proceedings of the 38th ACM SIGPLAN-SIGACT Symposium on Principles of Programming Languages, POPL 2011, Austin, TX, USA, 26–28 January 2011, pp. 55–66. ACM (2011)
5. Bouajjani, A., Derevenetc, E., Meyer, R.: Checking and enforcing robustness against TSO. In: Felleisen, M., Gardner, P. (eds.) ESOP 2013. LNCS, vol. 7792, pp. 533–553. Springer, Heidelberg (2013). https://doi.org/10.1007/978-3-642-37036-6_29
6. Burckhardt, S., Gotsman, A., Musuvathi, M., Yang, H.: Concurrent library correctness on the TSO memory model. In: Seidl, H. (ed.) ESOP 2012. LNCS, vol. 7211, pp. 87–107. Springer, Heidelberg (2012). https://doi.org/10.1007/978-3-642-28869-2_5
7. Clarke, E.M., Henzinger, T.A., Veith, H., Bloem, R. (eds.) Handbook of Model Checking. Springer (2018). https://doi.org/10.1007/978-3-319-10575-8
8. Intel Corporation. Intel 64 and IA-32 Architectures Software Developer's Manual (2021)
9. Derrick, J., Smith, G., Dongol, B.: Verifying linearizability on TSO architectures. In: Albert, E., Sekerinski, E. (eds.) IFM 2014. LNCS, vol. 8739, pp. 341–356. Springer, Cham (2014). https://doi.org/10.1007/978-3-319-10181-1_21

10. Gotsman, A., Musuvathi, M., Yang, H.: Show no weakness: sequentially consistent specifications of TSO libraries. In: Aguilera, M.K. (ed.) DISC 2012. LNCS, vol. 7611, pp. 31–45. Springer, Heidelberg (2012). https://doi.org/10.1007/978-3-642-33651-5_3
11. Herlihy, M., Shavit, N.: The art of multiprocessor programming. Morgan Kaufmann (2008)
12. Lahav, O., Namakonov, E., Oberhauser, J., Podkopaev, A., Viktor, V.: Making weak memory models fair. CoRR, arXiv preprint arXiv2012.01067 (2020)
13. Lamport, L.: How to make a multiprocessor computer that correctly executes multiprocess programs. IEEE Trans. Comput. **28**(9), 690–691 (1979)
14. Leijen, D., Schulte, W., Sebastian, B.: The design of a task parallel library. In: Arora, Shail., Leavens, G.T. (eds.) Proceedings of the 24th Annual ACM SIGPLAN Conference on Object-Oriented Programming, Systems, Languages, and Applications, OOPSLA 2009, 25–29 October 2009, Orlando, Florida, USA, pp. 227–242. ACM (2009)
15. Liang, H., Hoffmann, J., Feng, X., Shao, Z.: Characterizing progress properties of concurrent objects via contextual refinements. In: D'Argenio, P.R., Melgratti, H. (eds.) CONCUR 2013. LNCS, vol. 8052, pp. 227–241. Springer, Heidelberg (2013). https://doi.org/10.1007/978-3-642-40184-8_17
16. ARM Limited. ARM Architecture Reference Manual ARMv8 (2013)
17. Manson, J., Pugh, W., Adve, S.V.: The java memory model. In: Palsberg, J., Abadi, M. (eds.) Proceedings of the 32nd ACM SIGPLAN-SIGACT Symposium on Principles of Programming Languages, POPL 2005, Long Beach, California, USA, 12–14 January 2005, pp. 378–391. ACM (2005)
18. Michael, M.M., Vechev, M.T., Saraswat, V.A.: Idempotent work stealing. In: Reed, D.A., Sarkar, V. (eds.) Proceedings of the 14th ACM SIGPLAN Symposium on Principles and Practice of Parallel Programming, PPOPP 2009, Raleigh, NC, USA, 14–18 February 2009, pp. 45–54. ACM (2009)
19. Owens, S., Sarkar, S., Sewell, P.: A better x86 memory model: x86-TSO. In: Berghofer, S., Nipkow, T., Urban, C., Wenzel, M. (eds.) TPHOLs 2009. LNCS, vol. 5674, pp. 391–407. Springer, Heidelberg (2009). https://doi.org/10.1007/978-3-642-03359-9_27
20. Petrank, E., Musuvathi, M., Steensgaard, B.: Progress guarantee for parallel programs via bounded lock-freedom. In: Hind, M., Diwan, A. (eds.) Proceedings of the 2009 ACM SIGPLAN Conference on Programming Language Design and Implementation, PLDI 2009, Dublin, Ireland, 15–21 June 2009, pp. 144–154. ACM (2009)
21. Post, E.L.: A variant of a recursively unsolvable problem. Bull. Am. Math. Soc. **52**(1946), 264–268 (1946)
22. Ruohonen, K.: On some variants of post's correspondence problem. Acta Inf. **19**, 357–367 (1983)
23. Wang, C., Lv, Y., Wu, P.: TSO-to-TSO linearizability is undecidable. In: Finkbeiner, B., Pu, G., Zhang, L. (eds.) ATVA 2015. LNCS, vol. 9364, pp. 309–325. Springer, Cham (2015). https://doi.org/10.1007/978-3-319-24953-7_24
24. Wang, C., Lv, Y., Wu, P., Jia., Q.: Decidability of bounded linearizability on TSO memory model. Technical Report ISCAS-SKLCS-21-01, State Key Laboratory of Computer Science, Institute of Software, Chinese Academy of Sciences (2021). http://lcs.ios.ac.cn/~lvyi/files/ISCAS-SKLCS-21-01.pdf
25. Wang, C., Petri, G., Lv, Y., Long, T., Liu., Z.: Decidability of liveness for concurrent objects on the TSO memory model. Technical Report ISCAS-SKLCS-22-02, State Key Laboratory of Computer Science, Institute of Software, Chinese Academy of Sciences (2021). http://lcs.ios.ac.cn/~lvyi/files/ISCAS-SKLCS-22-02.pdf

Theorem Proving and SAT

Integration of Multiple Formal Matrix Models in Coq

ZhengPu Shi🆔 and Gang Chen$^{(\boxtimes)}$🆔

Nanjing University of Aeronautics and Astronautics, Nanjing 211106, China
zhengpushi@nuaa.edu.cn, gangchensh@qq.com

Abstract. Matrices are common tools in mathematics and computer science, and matrix formalization in proof assistants can provide strong support for verifying system behaviors related to matrix operations. The Coq community has proposed at least five formal matrix models, although the Coq standard library does not implement them. Developers who require a formal matrix library could have difficulty choosing what model to use. More importantly, once a choice is made, switching to another model later can be expensive. Although these matrix models have formalized matrix theory to a certain scale, demonstrating the ability to support the development of matrix theory, they have not identified the absolute advantages over other models, making it difficult for developers to choose. Moreover, the models have different data structures with completely different signatures of function and theorem, forcing developers to virtually completely rewrite matrix-related scripts when switching to a new matrix model. To address these problems, herein we undertake the following. First, we propose a unified matrix interface and integrate existing formal matrix models in the Coq community based on this interface. Secondly, we construct bijective functions between the different models to form isomorphisms, thus establishing connections between these models. We also provide technical comparison conclusions to help developers make choices. Hence, matrix formalization developers have a reference guide in the early stage and can switch to other models at a low cost at a later stage or use multiple models simultaneously with conversion assistance.

Keywords: Coq theorem prover · Formal matrix theory · Interface and implementation · Isomorphic mapping

1 Introduction

Matrix theory and linear algebra are important mathematical tools in science and engineering and are widely used in different fields such as control systems, signal processing, and neural networks [1]. For example, matrix theory is used to address kinematic and dynamic equations in flight control systems; optimization to improve the speed of matrix operations in deep learning also relies on matrix theory. Errors are easily introduced when writing matrix algorithms. Owing to

© The Author(s), under exclusive license to Springer Nature Switzerland AG 2022
W. Dong and J.-P. Talpin (Eds.): SETTA 2022, LNCS 13649, pp. 169–186, 2022.
https://doi.org/10.1007/978-3-031-21213-0_11

the large scale of the problem space to be verified, such errors are difficult to eliminate by software testing or automatic verification methods, whereas using theorem proving can fundamentally guarantee the reliability of matrix algorithms [2–4]. Currently, there are numerous theorem-proving platforms including Coq [5], Isabelle [6], Lean [7], and HOL [8], where each platform has its independent software ecosystem. Herein, we discuss the Coq theorem prover.

At least five formal matrix libraries are available for Coq community projects [9,11,12,14,15]. Note that we use the terms matrix model, matrix library, and matrix scheme interchangeably to refer to these different matrix libraries because each library has a unique model and scheme consisting of a set of related operations and properties. Each scheme implements a partial formalization of matrix theory, including basic matrix algebra; however, the majority of these schemes do not implement the difficult parts. For example, basic operations such as matrix addition, scalar multiplication, transposition, and multiplication have been implemented, but research on the matrix canonical form, factorization, matrix sequence, and generalized inverse matrix has not been implemented. This is partly because implementing complex matrix theories in a theorem prover requires long development circles. These models appear to compete with each other, forcing users to make choices.

For developers working on formal matrix theory, easily choosing a suitable matrix scheme from these schemes is difficult, and switching to another model at a later stage is costly. Matrix theory is broad and the upper-level verifications that rely on formal matrix libraries are more diverse, making the requirement for formal matrices a critical action item. However, these existing schemes cannot support multiple requirements. First, the full-featured matrix library expected by these upper-level applications currently does not exist, as mentioned previously. Secondly, we cannot predict what scheme will necessarily be optimal in the future. Because each scheme has unique technical characteristics, the progress of the verification process could be different. For example, a theorem A could be easy to be proven in Scheme 1 while a theorem B is easy in Scheme 2; however, A could be difficult to be proven in Scheme 2 or require a longer time. Again, switching costs can be high when the chosen model does not meet the actual requirements and one wants to appraise another model. Because different models have different types of matrices, with different function and theorem types, the scripts in these schemes are not portable. Hence, developers can be reluctant to choose a certain matrix model to meet long-term project requirements in the early stage; nor can they afford the huge costs of switching to new models in the later stage, resulting in slow verification progress.

We believe that the concept of interfaces and modularity in software engineering should be used to improve this situation. Coq is a theorem prover of higher-order logic with strong expressive ability and provides techniques such as module signatures and functors to realize interface programming. Moreover, the operations and properties of matrices are mathematically well defined; hence, concrete implementations of matrix theory should have strong similarities. These two aspects support our idea that the formalization of matrix theory in Coq can use the same interface. What is required is a method to abstract the matrix operations and properties implemented in these different models into a unified interface for external use. Because the research progress of these schemes is different, it would be helpful for these models to learn from each other by constructing transformations between themselves. In addition, because a matrix is a general concept, and its carrier can be a different type, we must also support polymorphic matrices. Hence, we have undertaken to complete the following.

1. Use Module Type to define a unified matrix interface.
2. Integrate five formal matrix schemes based on the interface.
3. Construct bijective conversion functions between these models.
4. Establish isomorphisms of certain operations between these models to provide another proof approach for certain properties.
5. Use a functor to implement polymorphic matrices and support different matrix element types such as rational numbers, real numbers, and functions.

Using this unified interface, the development of the underlying formal matrix library (FML) is effectively decoupled from the work of the upper-level matrix application (MApp), which facilitates multiteam collaboration. Matrix library developers gradually design the matrix library where multiple schemes can be performed in parallel based on a unified signature. MApp developers use this interface for matrix verification development. The relationship is shown in Fig. 1.

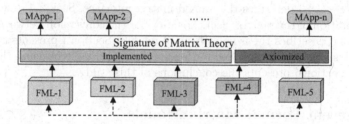

Fig. 1. Relationship between matrix interface, FML, and MApp.

The different sizes of *FML-1* to *FML-5* indicate that the existing scales of each library are different. The *Implemented* represents the formal matrix theory that has been implemented by at least one scheme. New matrix theory could be added to *Axiomized* in the form of abstract operations and axioms. After the formalization of this part, a complete verification result is obtained. The dashed lines at the bottom represent conversions between the FMLs.

Because matrices and vectors are mathematically transformable and vector theory has numerous applications, we also offer vector formalization. For example, a matrix with r rows and c columns can be viewed as either a column vector of length r or a row vector of length c. The design of the vector interface is similar to that of the matrix interface; it decouples the dependencies between the lower-level formal vector library (FVL) and upper-level vector application (VApp), as indicated in Fig. 2.

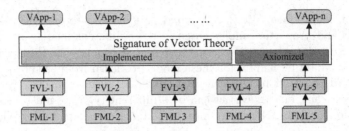

Fig. 2. Relationship between vector interface, FVL, and VApp.

FVL uses FML which is only a recommended practice. In fact, the vector signature does not force FVL to use FML because vectors and matrices are independent theoretically. In the current implementation, we define a vector of length n as an $n \times 1$ dimensional matrix followed mathematical conventions. Thus, vector theory reuses much of the matrix theory and avoids type conversions when operating between vectors and matrices. We do not overly discuss vector interfaces, which are not the focus of this paper.

The remainder of this paper is organized as follows. Section 2 presents the different existing formal matrix models. Section 3 describes the integration of the matrix library. In this section, Sect. 3.1 describes the mathematical properties used in this paper, Sect. 3.2 describes the polymorphism and hierarchy of matrix elements, Sect. 3.3 describes the unified matrix interface, Sect. 3.4 describes the implementation of the matrix, Sect. 3.5 describes the conversion between models, and Sect. 3.6 describes the isomorphism of models. Section 4 presents a comparative analysis of the models. Section 5 presents an example of using the matrix interface. Section 6 presents the conclusions of this study.

2   Different Formal Matrix Models

This section describes five formal matrix schemes presently available in the Coq community with a particular focus on matrix models. We analyze the definitions of the different matrix types that determine the type of all subsequent functions and theorems. Moreover, we briefly discuss the matrix functions implemented in the library and their technical characteristics.

2.1   DepList: Dependent List

Because this definition is similar to a list and is a dependent type, we call it *Dependent List* (*DepList* or *DL* for short). DepList is a formal matrix model used in the CoLoR project [14] and Nicolas Magaud's work [13]. CoLoR is a math library in Coq designed for theoretical research such as rewriting theory, lambda calculus, and termination; it was released in 2003 and remains valid today. The model is based on the vector type in the vector library provided by the Coq standard library. Matrix type is defined as follows:

```
Inductive vec (A : Type) : ℕ → Type :=
  | nil : vec A 0 | cons : A → ∀ n : ℕ, vec A n → vec A (S n).
Definition mat (r c : ℕ) := vec (vec A c) r.
```

Here, *Inductive* is a keyword in Coq that defines an inductive type. The vector type (called *vec*) has two cases: *nil* is a vector of length zero and *cons* is a vector of length $n + 1$ that is formed by a value of type A and a vector of length n. We use the notation $V[A]_n$ to represent a vector with a carrier of type A with n elements. Thus, a matrix type (*mat*) is regarded as a vector of vectors. Therefore, the operations on matrices are actually operations on vectors. The library implements the following: matrix definition on *setoid*, obtain the matrix elements, identity matrix, transposition, addition, multiplication, and related properties. A setoid is a set equipped with an equivalence relation, which is a general case of equality. In addition, the library supports polymorphic matrices using a *functor*. A functor is a *module* with a parameter called the *module type*; this *module* is a common technique in Coq for packaging a set of operations. The library requires the carrier to be *SemiRing*, meaning that a ring is not required to provide an additive inverse. Therefore, data types such as ℕ, ℤ, ℚ, and ℝ can be used as carriers to form a matrix. The features of this model are as follows.

- **Advantage**
  - Development based on the Coq standard library easily attracts developers.
  - Inductively defined data structures are easy to prove and list-like data structures are easier to understand.
  - The definition of setoid-based equality has wider applicability than Leibniz equality.
  - It is dimensionally scalable because higher-dimensional arrays can be defined by a nested vec structure.
- **Disadvantage**
  - The content of the vector library has not yet reached the maturity of the list library and requires significant development.
  - Proofs are roughly trickier than the ordinary list structures.

2.2 DepPair: Dependent Pair

Because this definition is similar to a pair and is a dependent type, we call it *Dependent Pair* (*DepPair* or *DP* for short). DepPair is a matrix model adopted in the Coquelicot project [12], a research project for real analysis funded by the French Foundation Centre. They proposed a compact representation of the matrices as follows:

```
Fixpoint Tn (A : Type) (n : ℕ) : Type :=
  match n with O ⇒ unit | S n ⇒ prod A (Tn A n) end.
Definition mat A (r c : ℕ) := Tn (Tn A c) r.
```

Here, the Tn function constructs a nested pair of length n of base type A. *Fixpoint* is a keyword for defining recursive functions in Coq, *unit* is a single-element set with only one member tt, and *prod* is product type with the constructor *pair*. Then, the Tn type represents a vector of length n, and the matrix type is defined as the Tn of Tn, i.e., a vector of vectors. This definition is similar to that of DepList in Sect. 2.1, except that the inductive definition is replaced by a recursive function. The library implements the following: construction of matrices, identity matrix, addition, multiplication, and related properties. In addition, the matrix carrier types are organized into a hierarchy in this scheme. For example, the carrier of matrix addition forms an abelian group, the carrier of matrix multiplication forms a monoid, and matrix addition and multiplication together form a ring. The features of this model are as follows.

- **Advantage**
  - Matrix construction is simple; only using a pair structure can create a matrix.
  - The structure is extensible because the carrier is carefully designed based on mathematical hierarchy.
  - Dimensionally scalable because higher-dimensional arrays can be defined by the nested Tn structure.
- **Disadvantage**
  - Not a significant amount of matrix theory has been implemented.
  - The skill for dependently typed proof is required to complete the proof.

2.3   DepRec: Dependent Record

Because the definition is in the form of a *Record*, and the fields of the record depend on the parameters and previous fields, we call it *Dependent Record* (*DepRec* or *DR* for short). In computer science, record is a data structure that can hold multiple named fields. The model was proposed by Zhenwei et al. [9].

Fixpoint *width* $\{A : \mathtt{Type}\}$ $(dl : list\ (list\ A))$ $(n : \mathbb{N})$: Prop :=
   match dl with $nil \Rightarrow True \mid cons\ x\ t \Rightarrow (length\ x = n) \land width\ t\ n$ end.
Record *matrix* $\{A : \mathtt{Type}\}$ $\{r\ c : \mathbb{N}\}$: Type := $mkMatrix\ \{$
   mdata: list $(list\ A);$ *matH: length mdata* $= r;$ *matW: width mdata c*$\}.$

Here, *length* returns the length of a list, and *width* indicates that each list item in the type *list(list A)* has a given length. A matrix is defined as a record with three fields: a data *mdata*, a proof *matH* indicating that mdata has r rows, and a proof *matW* indicating that mdata has c columns. The library implements the following: matrix construction, zero matrix, identity matrix, addition, scalar multiplication, transposition, multiplication, and related properties. Besides, a block matrix where the matrix elements are a matrix of a specified shape is also implemented [10]. This scheme separates the computation from the proof with clear logic. The matrix construction is divided into two parts. The first part is the computation, mainly based on list operations, which have a rich implementation in the standard library. The second part is the matrix row proof matH and column proof matW, which are easy to perform. In addition, when extracting functional programs such as OCaml, the model can obtain the most concise code that completely corresponds to the list type in OCaml and thus reduces the storage space overhead. The features are as follows.

- **Advantage**
  - Mature list libraries provide abundant support for matrix development.
  - The separation of computation and proof make the logic clear.
  - The extracted OCaml program has a concise data structure.
- **Disadvantage**
  - The script is longer because it requires separate construction of the data and provides two separate proofs.
  - It is marginally less scalable because it is currently fixed on two-dimensional arrays and cannot implement higher-dimensional arrays directly.

2.4   NatFun: Function with Natural Indexing

A matrix is defined as a function of two natural numbers (corresponding to the index of row and column) to a complex number; therefore, we call it a *Function with Natural indexing* (*NatFun* or *NF* for short). This scheme appeared in the quantum computing work of Rand et al. [15,16]. Because their work was oriented towards complex numbers, no other types of carriers were considered.

`Definition` *Matrix* $(r\ c : \mathbb{N}) := \mathbb{N} \to \mathbb{N} \to \mathbb{C}$.

Here, the function *Matrix* uses two arguments, r and c, as the number of rows and columns of the matrix, and returns a function. The problem is that these two arguments fail to constrain the shape of the matrix, which we address in Sect. 3.4. The library implements the following: conversion between list and matrix, zero matrix, identity matrix, addition, scalar multiplication, multiplication, transposition, trace, and related properties. Because the functional style does not have to maintain the storage structure, the matrix operations are extremely concise. Examples are defined as follows:

`Variable` *C0 C1* $: \mathbb{C}$.   `Variable` *Cplus Cmult* $: \mathbb{C} \to \mathbb{C} \to \mathbb{C}$.
`Infix "+"` := *Cplus*. `Infix "×"` := *Cmult*.
`Fixpoint` *Csum* $(f : \mathbb{N} \to \mathbb{C})\ (n : \mathbb{N}) : \mathbb{C} :=$
  `match` n `with` $O \Rightarrow$ *C0* $\mid S\ n' \Rightarrow$ *Csum* $f\ n'$ + $f\ n'$ `end`.
`Definition` *I* $(n : \mathbb{N}) :$ *Matrix* $n\ n :=$ `fun` $i\ j \Rightarrow$ `if` $(i =?j)$ `then` *C1* `else` *C0*.
`Definition` *Mmult* $\{r\ c\ s : \mathbb{N}\}$ $(A:$ *Matrix* $r\ c)$ $(B:$ *Matrix* $c\ s) :$ *Matrix* $r\ s :=$
  `fun` $x\ z \Rightarrow$ *Csum* $($ `fun` $y \Rightarrow A\ x\ y \times B\ y\ z)\ c$.

Here, *Csum* is the sum of the sequence, *I* is the identity matrix, and function *Mmult* is matrix multiplication. As can be observed, this definition is concise and expressive. The features of this model are as follows.

- **Advantage**
  - The definition of the function is concise.
  - The proof of the property is concise.

- **Disadvantage**
  - There are no corresponding structured data types. Although functions are first class in functional languages and have no impact on them.
  - The two parameters used to describe the shape in the matrix definition fail to constrain this type. However, a small improvement can fix this.

2.5   FinFun: Function with Finite Indexing

This definition is similar to NatFun in Sect. 2.4; just replaces the natural indexing with a finite set of elements; hence we call it *Function with Finite indexing* (*FinFun* or *FF* for short). This model appears in the *mathematical component library* (MC) [11], which forms the infrastructure for machine-checked proofs of the well-known four-color theorems. Although this scheme was introduced last, the MC library is the most complete and complex formalization of matrices. Following is the definition of the matrix.

From *mathcomp* Require Import *eqtype seq finfun fintype*.
Variant *matrix* $\{R : \text{Type}\}$ $\{m\ n : \mathbb{N}\}$: *predArgType* :=
  Matrix of $\{ffun\ 'I_m \times 'I_n \to R\}$.

It can be observed that the definition of the matrix introduces several types and notations. These are internally defined as follows:

Inductive *ordinal* $(n : \mathbb{N})$: Type := *Ordinal* $(m : \mathbb{N})$ $(\_ : (S\ m) \leq?\ n)$.
Notation " ''I_' n" := $(ordinal\ n)$.
Variant *phant* $(p : \text{Type})$: Prop := *Phant* : *phant* p.
Notation "$\{$ 'ffun' fT $\}$" := $(finfun\_of\ (Phant\ fT))$ (at level 0).
Variables $(aT : finType)$ $(rT : aT \to \text{Type})$.
Inductive *finfun_on* : *seq* $aT \to$ Type := | *finfun_nil* : *finfun_on* $[::]$
  | *finfun_cons* x s of rT x & *finfun_on* s : *finfun_on* $(x :: s)$.

Variant *finfun_of* $(ph : phant\ (\forall\ x,\ rT\ x))$: *predArgType* :=
  FinfunOf of *finfun_on* $(enum\ aT)$.

Here, *ordinal* n represents a set of ordinal numbers less than n. The *phant* type is used to generate constraints to maintain the consistency of the type. The *finfun_on* type wraps lists of different lengths into different types. The *funfun_of* type specifies funfun_on as the only source of construction. It can be observed that the internal structure of the matrix type is very complex.

The formal matrix theory of this library is extremely rich, covering virtually all schemes in previous sections, and adds the following: block matrix of different shapes, determinant, adjoint matrix, inverse matrix, and LU decomposition. In addition, proof scripts are typically short because of deep extensions to the *SSR* language. For example, the commutative law of matrix multiplication can be performed in only three lines, whereas schemes using lists require tens to hundreds of lines. In addition, the library creates an 11-level hierarchy that corresponds well with the mathematical concepts. However, the SSR language is not friendly to new users because of its large number of notations, and its complex hierarchy requires more mathematical knowledge and programming skills. A more important problem is that a number of the expressions cannot be reduced to a simple form; therefore, we cannot obtain the results of matrix operations intuitively. For example, obtaining matrix elements produces a complex expression instead of the expected value. The features of this model are as follows.

– **Advantage**
  - Implemented matrix theory is the most numerous of all schemes
  - The proof is concise owing to the SSR language extension.
  - It allows the careful organization of matrix operations and properties owing to a clear mathematical hierarchy.
– **Disadvantage**
  - Requires more math background to start; hence, it is not "newbie" friendly.
  - SSR extensions and too many notations are difficult to understand.
  - The inability to reduce to a simple form prevents symbolic computation.

3 Integrated Matrix Library

As can be observed from Sect. 2, each of these schemes has advantages and disadvantages, and not one can satisfy all cases. The first three schemes are more suitable for matrix symbolic computation, whereas the latter two are more suitable for verifying mathematical properties. Developers can make different choices based on the requirements such as technical difficulty, scalability of the design, or simplicity of the extracted functional code. As envisioned in Sect. 1, our next step is to integrate these disparate schemes to reduce the technical barriers. First, definitions of the mathematical properties used are provided. Subsequently, several approaches to polymorphic matrices and hierarchies are discussed. Then, we propose a matrix interface based on which of the above models are integrated. Furthermore, conversions and isomorphisms between the models are established.

3.1 Mathematical Properties

The mathematical properties used in this paper are as follows:

Variable $A\ B$: Type. Variable $a\ b\ c$: A.
Variable $Aop1\ Aop2$: $A \to A \to A$. Variable $Bop1$: $B \to B \to B$.
Infix "+" := $Aop1$. Infix "×" := $Aop2$. Infix "⊕" := $Bop1$.
Definition $eqdec$:= $\{a = b\} + \{a \neq b\}$.
Definition inj $(f: A \to B)$:= $\forall\ (a1\ a2 : A), f\ a1 = f\ a2 \to a1 = a2$.
Definition $surj$ $(f: A \to B)$:= $\forall\ (b : B), (\exists\ (a : A), f\ a = b)$.
Definition bij $(f: A \to B)$:= $inj\ f \wedge surj\ f$.
Definition $comm$:= $a + b = b + a$.
Definition $assoc$:= $a + (b + c) = (a + b) + c$.
Definition $distr\_l$:= $(a + b) \times c = a \times c + b \times c$.
Definition $homo$ $(f:A \to B)$:= $f\ (a + b) = (f\ a) \oplus (f\ b)$.

Here, *eqdec* indicates that the equality of set A is decidable; *inj*, *surj*, and *bij* indicate that the function f is injective, surjective, and bijective; *comm*, *assoc* indicate that the binary operation $+$ satisfies the commutative or associative law; *distr_l* represents the left distributive law of $\times$ over $+$; *homo* means that f is a homomorphic mapping between $\langle A, + \rangle$ and $\langle B, \oplus \rangle$.

3.2   Polymorphism and Hierarchy of Matrix Elements

A matrix is a generic data structure whose carrier can be of any type, such as a Boolean, natural, integer, real, complex, function, or matrix. In Coq, polymorphic functions can be defined directly, or the functor can be used to implement polymorphism at the module level.

Polymorphic matrices are overly flexible, and fewer type constraints can lead to redundant code, which can be avoided when the design follows a hierarchy of matrix carriers. For example, when proving the associativity law for matrix addition, the associativity of the carrier must be explicitly provided and can be omitted on *monoid* structure. There are at least three techniques in Coq to implement hierarchy.

1. *Type Classes*, which appear in the Coq standard library [5] and the work [18,19]. This is a method of generating abstract structures by overloading notations and contexts, allowing flexible combinations of different fragments to build complex theories. However, this approach causes system complexity to grow rapidly with the size [20,21].
2. *Canonical Structures*, which appear in the MC project [11] and Assia Mahboubi's work [22]. The idea is to use the hint database to extend the unification algorithm of the Coq system to solve type-inference problems from general to individual. In the MC, an 11-levels hierarchical structure was implemented in this manner with acceptable scalability and standardization.
3. Use the built-in module type in Coq. This method does not require significant skill to address type issues; however, the build process could not be sufficiently flexible. For example, when combining an additive group $\langle A, + \rangle$ and multiplicative semigroup $\langle B, * \rangle$ into a ring $\langle R, +, * \rangle$, the types of carriers A and B cannot be unified to R easily.

Although there has been related work on algebraic structures, they still cannot address our requirements. For example, in the CoLoR [14], MC [11], and Coquelicot projects [12], and the work of Herman Geuvers et al. [17], these implementations are overly complex for our matrix integration work. We consider primarily the realization of the matrix theory of rational, real, complex numbers and funtions which are commonly used in engineering, particularly automatically solving equations on matrix elements using the *ring* and *field* tactics in Coq. Therefore, we only consider the two-level structure of the ring and field; fine-grained algebraic structures have not yet been added, such as Group, Monoid, and Semi-Group. To maintain consistency, we manually built the *RingSig* and *FieldSig* module types based on the Coq standard library, as follows.

Require Import *Ring Field*.
Module Type *RingSig*.
Parameters (*A*: Type) (*A0 A1*: *A*) (*Aadd Amul*: *A* → *A* → *A*) (*Aopp*: *A* → *A*).
Notation *Asub* := (fun *x y* ⇒ (*Aadd x* (*Aopp y*))).
Parameter *Ring_thy* : *ring_theory A0 A1 Aadd Amul Asub Aopp eq*.
Add *Ring Ring_thy_inst* : *Ring_thy*.   End *RingSig*.

Module Type *FieldSig* <: *RingSig*.
Parameter *Ainv*: *A* → *A*.   Notation *Adiv*:= (fun *x y* ⇒ (*Amul x* (*Ainv y*))).
Parameters (*Field_thy*: *field_theory A0 A1 Aadd Amul Asub Aopp Adiv Ainv eq*).   Add *Field Field_thy_inst* : *Field_thy*.   End *FieldSig*.

We first import two libraries, *Ring* and *Field*, to enable ring and field theories in Coq. The keyword *Module Type* is used to create modules that can be used as arguments for other modules. *A* is the type of carrier; *Aadd, Amul, Aopp,* and *Asub* are addition, multiplication, additive inverse, and subtraction operations; *A0* and *A1* are the additive and multiplicative identities. *Ring_thy* is a proof for constructing a ring structure. Next, the syntax *Add Ring* registers this ring structure with Coq, enabling the ring tactic on A. FieldSig is similar to RingSig, adding more operations such as multiplicative inverse and division, and registering the field structure to Coq.

After building a concrete module that satisfies the signature of RingSig or FieldSig, a ring or field structure can be obtained. For example, the code for Qc (canonical rational number) is as follows:

Require Export *Qcanon*.
Module *RingQc* <: *RingSig*.   Definition *A*:= *Qc*.
Definition *A0*:= 0.   Definition *A1*:= 1.   Definition *Aadd*:= *Qcplus*.
Definition *Amul* := *Qcmult*. Definition *Aopp*:= *Qcopp*.
Lemma *Ring_thy*: *ring_theory A0 A1 Aadd Amul Qcminus Aopp eq*.
Add *Ring Ring_thy_inst* : *Ring_thy*.   End *RingQc*.

In this manner, we can define more ring and field structures for other data types such as real and complex numbers.

3.3 Matrix Interface

The matrix interface or matrix theory signature is defined in *MatrixThySig*. For simplicity, it is not organized based on a carrier hierarchy; rather, it adopts a field structure that meets general requirements, as follows.

Module Type *MatrixThySig*.
Parameter *A*: Type.   Variable *r c s t*: ℕ.
Parameters (*mat*: ℕ → ℕ → Type) (*meq_dec*: *eqdec* (@*mat r c*)
(*l2m*: *list* (*list A*) → *mat r c*)   (*m2l*: *mat r c* → *list* (*list A*)).
(*l2m_bij*: *bij l2m*) (*m2l_bij*: *bij m2l*) (*l2m_m2l_id*: ∀ *m*, *l2m* (*m2l m*) = *m*)
(*m2l_l2m_id*: ∀ *dl*, *length dl* = *r* → *width dl c* → *m2l* (*l2m dl*) = *dl*)
(*mat0 mat1* : *mat r c*)   (*madd* : *mat r c* → *mat r c* → *mat r c*)
(*mcmul* : *A* → *mat r c* → *mat r c*)   (*mtrans* : *mat r c* → *mat c r*)

$(mmul : mat\ r\ c \rightarrow mat\ c\ s \rightarrow mat\ r\ s)$.   Infix "×" := $mmul$.
Parameters $(mmul\_assoc : \forall\ (m1 : mat\ r\ c)\ (m2 : mat\ c\ s)$
$(m3 : mat\ s\ t),\ (m1 \times m2) \times m3 = m1 \times (m2 \times m3))$.
End $MatrixThySig$.

Here, A denotes the type of carrier, and matrix type mat is defined as a function determined by the number of rows and columns; $eqdec$ indicates that matrix equality is decidable; $l2m$ and $m2l$ denote conversion operations between matrices and lists (list A); $l2m\_bij$, $m2l\_bij$, $l2m\_m2l\_id$, and $m2l\_l2m\_id$ indicate that l2m and m2l are bijective functions and inverse functions of each other; $mat0$ and $mat1$ generate a zero matrix and unit matrix; $madd, mcmul, mtrans$, and $mmul$ are matrix addition, scalar multiplication, transposition, and multiplication. Owing to space limitations, other operations and properties of the matrices are not listed.

3.4 Matrix Implementation

We restructured or reimplemented all the schemes based on the MatrixThySig interface and finally combined them. Only the key issues are discussed below; the specific implementation is not introduced here.

Framework for Matrix Theory Implementation. A typical framework for matrix theory is a functor with a parameter of type $FiledSig$ as indicated below.
Module $MatrixThy$ $(E : FieldSig)$ <: $MatrixThySig$.
   Import X. Definition mat := @$matrix\ E.A$.   (* other things ... *)
End $MatrixThy$.

Here, X represents a specific scheme that should implement full matrix operations in its own style. The $MatrixThy$ module calls the content in X and completes it based on the unified interface MatrixSig.

Corrected Definition for NatFun. The definition of the matrix types in many schemes conforms to MatrixSig. However, the NatFun scheme must be modified because its two parameters cannot constrain the type, resulting in an inability to distinguish matrices of different shapes. See the code below.
Variable A : Type. Definition $Matrix$ $(r\ c : \mathbb{N})$:= $\mathbb{N} \rightarrow \mathbb{N} \rightarrow \mathbb{C}$.
Variable $mat1$: $Matrix$ 2 3. Check $mat1$: $Matrix$ 3 5.
Record mat $(r\ c : \mathbb{N})$:= $mkMat$ $\{mdata : \mathbb{N} \rightarrow \mathbb{N} \rightarrow A\}$.
Variable $mat2$: mat 2 3. Fail Check $mat2$: mat 3 5.

Here, $Matrix$ is the matrix definition used in NatFun. $mat1$ appears to be a 2×3 matrix; however, it also passes a type check as a 3×5 matrix. It seems the parameters r and c have no type constraints. If wrapped with a record type mat, it becomes a dependent type. Therefore, the shape parameters become part of the type, e.g., $mat2$ has a unique 2×3 matrix type.

Collection of All Matrix Implementations. After multiple matrix models are provided based on the same interface, we organize all these implementations; then, we can manage matrix module instances at the module level.

Module *MatrixAll* (*E* : *FieldSig*).
  Module *DP* := *DepPair.MatrixThy E.*   Module *DL* := *DepList.MatrixThy E.*
  Module *DR* := *DepRec.MatrixThy E.*   Module *NF* := *NatFun.MatrixThy E.*
  Module *FF* := *FinFun.MatrixThy E.*
End *MatrixAll.*
Module *MatrixR* := *MatrixAll FieldR.*   Module *MatrixR_DP* := *MatrixR.DP.*
Module *MatrixR_DL* := *MatrixR.DL.*   Module *MatrixR_DR* := *MatrixR.DR.*
Module *MatrixR_NF* := *MatrixR.NF.*   Module *MatrixR_FF* := *MatrixR.FF.*

Here, *MatrixAll* is the collection or entry of all matrix model implementations, *DP, DL, DR, NF*, and *FF* are shorthand for specific matrix models. Then, we take the real number field type *FieldR* as the module parameter and obtain *MatrixR* after instantiation. For concrete use, the specific name of the instantiated matrix model is also provided. For example, *MatrixR_DR* denotes the formal matrix theory, with *R* as the carrier and *DepRec* as the model.

Extract OCaml Code. The Formal matrix in Coq is not only used to verify abstract mathematical properties but also to obtain correct functional programs by program extraction. OCaml program extraction is used as an example to discuss the differences between these matrix models during extraction. First, all these schemes extract valid OCaml programs. Secondly, from the perspective of the simplicity of the extracted code, DepList and DepPair have more redundancy, mainly including the encoding of the matrix shape, whereas DepRec has virtually no redundancy because it directly corresponds to the list type. Again, the matrices resulting from NatFun and FinFun are defined as functions. Although the elements of the matrix are not available as a whole, each element can be accessed individually.

3.5   Conversion Between Matrix Models

After building multiple models that can perform the same function and have the same signature, we aim to create a connection between these models. In fact, the pair of conversion functions *l2m* and *m2l* and the properties associated with them given in *MatrisSig* were prepared for this purpose. This pair of functions are available for all five models. These functions can be used to convert between any of the models as indicated in Fig. 3.

Here, (a) displays all conversions between all models; (b) displays the detailed process for a pair of conversions. In the following section, we discuss the conversion between DepList and DepPair as an example. For example, *dl2dp* is the conversion of DepList to DepPair, which comprises *DL.m2l* and *DP.l2m*. Furthermore, we can demonstrate that dl2dp and dp2dl are bijective and their composition is an identity function.

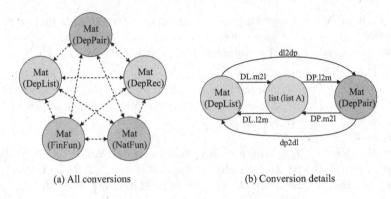

(a) All conversions   (b) Conversion details

Fig. 3. Conversion between different matrix models.

Variable r c: $\mathbb{N}$.
Definition $dp2dl$ $(m{:}DP.mat$ r $c)$: $DL.mat$ r $c := DL.l2m$ $(DP.m2l$ $m)$.
Definition $dl2dp$ $(m{:}DL.mat$ r $c)$: $DP.mat$ r $c := DP.l2m$ $(DL.m2l$ $m)$.
Lemma $dl2dp\_bij$: bij $(@dl2dp$ r $c)$.   Lemma $dp2dl\_bij$: bij $(@dp2dl$ r $c)$.
Lemma $dl2dp\_dp2dl\_id$: $\forall$ $(m{:}$ $DP.mat$ r $c)$, $dl2dp$ $(dp2dl$ $m)$ $=$ m.
Lemma $dp2dl\_dl2dp\_id$: $\forall$ $(m{:}$ $DL.mat$ r $c)$, $dp2dl$ $(dl2dp$ $m)$ $=$ m.

Here, the lemma $dl2dp\_bij$ means that $dl2dp$ is bijective, which is proved by the fact that both DP.l2m and DL.m2l are bijective functions. The lemma $dp2dl\_dl2dp\_id$ indicates that the composition of $dp2dl$ and $dl2dp$ yields an identity function, which can be proven by the following steps: 1). Unfolding dl2dp and dp2dl, we obtain DP.l2m (DL.m2l (DL.l2m (DP.m2l m))) = m; 2). Using DL.m2l_l2m_id to remove the middle part, we obtain DP.l2m (DP.m2l m) = m; 3). Completes the proof using DP.l2m_m2l_id.

3.6   Isomorphism of Matrix Models

Certain matrix operations form some algebraic systems under each matrix model, such as matrix addition, scalar multiplication, and square matrix multiplication. The structures of these algebraic systems are similar and we demonstrate the isomorphism between them. Isomorphic algebraic systems preserve certain properties such as associative and distributive laws, as follows:

Variable A B C: Type.   Variable fc: $C \to C \to C$.
Variable fa ga: $A \to A \to A$.   Variable fb gb: $B \to B \to B$.
Definition $isomor := \exists(\phi{:} A \to B)$, $homo$ fa fb $\phi \wedge bij$ ϕ.
Definition $isomor2 := \exists(\phi{:} A \to B)$, $homo$ fa fb $\phi \wedge homo$ ga gb $\phi \wedge bij$ ϕ.
Lemma $isoComm$: $isomor$ fa fb $\to$ $(comm$ $fa \leftrightarrow comm$ $fb)$.
Lemma $isoAssoc$: $isomor$ fa fb $\to$ $(assoc$ $fa \leftrightarrow assoc$ fb.
Lemma $iso2DistrL$: $isomor2$ fa ga fb gb $\leftrightarrow$ $distr\_l$ fa ga $\leftrightarrow$ $distr\_l$ fb gb.

Here, $isomor$ denotes the isomorphism between $\langle A, fa \rangle$ and $\langle B, fb \rangle$ and $isomor2$ denotes the isomorphism between $\langle A, fa, ga \rangle$ and $\langle B, fb, gb \rangle$. $isoComm$

indicates that the commutative law of fa and fb are equivalent. Similarly, associativity and left distributive laws are equivalent. We use matrix addition and square multiplication on DL and DP as examples; denoted as $\langle M_{dl}, +_{dl}, \times_{dl} \rangle$ and $\langle M_{dp}, +_{dp}, \times_{dp} \rangle$. Isomorphism theory can be applied to them.

Variable $r\ c\ n : \mathbb{N}$.

Lemma *isoMadd*: *isomor* (@*DL.madd r c*) (@*DP.madd r c*).

Lemma *isoMmul*: *isomor* (@*DL.mmul n n n*) (@*DP.mmul n n n*).

Lemma *addComm*: *comm* (@*DL.madd r c*) $\leftrightarrow$ *comm* (@*DP.madd r c*).

Lemma *addAssoc*: *assoc* (@*DL.madd r c*) $\leftrightarrow$ *assoc* (@*DP.madd r c*).

Lemma *distrL*: *distr_l DL.madd DL.mmul* $\leftrightarrow$ *distr_l DP.madd DP.mmul*.

Here, *isoMadd* denotes that $\langle M_{dl}, +_{dl} \rangle$ and $\langle M_{dp}, +_{dp} \rangle$ are isomorphic; *isoMmul* denotes that $\langle M_{dl}, \times_{dl} \rangle$ and $\langle M_{dp}, \times_{dp} \rangle$ are isomorphic; the remaining lemmas denote that commutative, associative, and distributive laws are separately equivalent on the two structures, which can be proved directly using isomorphism theory. The main task of the first two proofs is the homomorphic mapping between the operations, which is not discussed here due to space limitations.

4 Comparison of Different Matrix Models

Section 2 presents different matrix models with a separate analysis. Basically, the first three are "programming thinking" and the last two are "mathematical thinking". We provide ratings based on our current understanding and practical experience in the process of constructing the integrated library, see Table 1.

Table 1. Comparison of different matrix models.

Models	DepList	DepPair	DepRec	NatFun	FinFun
Maturity	⋆	⋆	⋆⋆	⋆⋆	⋆ ⋆ ⋆
Conciseness of the definitions	⋆	⋆	⋆	⋆ ⋆ ⋆	⋆ ⋆ ⋆
Conciseness of the proofs	⋆	⋆	⋆⋆	⋆ ⋆ ⋆	⋆ ⋆ ⋆
Conciseness of the extracted OCaml code	⋆	⋆	⋆ ⋆ ⋆	⋆⋆	⋆⋆
Simplicity of the syntax or skill	⋆⋆	⋆⋆	⋆ ⋆ ⋆	⋆⋆	⋆

Each rating is indicated by an asterisk from 1–3 stars, where a higher number is better. Note that there is a lack of quantifiable evaluation methods for theorem-proving libraries, and our ratings are subjective and one-sided. Nonetheless, these ratings can help developers to make certain choices.

5 Example of Using the Matrix Library

After a unified interface matrix library is built, verification projects using the matrix library are not required to consider the limitations of the underlying model. For example, in the application scenario of coordinate transformation, it is necessary to prove that the product of the three transposed matrices is equal to the given matrix. We can choose matrix library DL at will, and there is virtually no change in the code when switching to DP, DR, NF, or FF.

Import *MatrixR_DL*. (* *_DP/_DR/_FUN/_FF*. *)
Infix "×" := *mmul*. Notation "m^T" := (*mtrans m*). Variable ψ, θ, ϕ: $\mathbb{R}$.
Definition Rx := *mkMat33* 1 0 0 0 (*cos* ϕ) (*sin* ϕ) 0 (-*sin* ϕ) (*cos* ϕ).
Definition Ry := *mkMat33* (*cos* θ) 0 (-*sin* θ) 0 1 0 (*sin* θ) 0 (*cos* θ).
Definition Rz := *mkMat33* (*cos* ψ) (*sin* ψ) 0 (-*sin* ψ) (*cos* ψ) 0 0 0 1.
Lemma Rbe_ok := $(Rz)^T \times (Ry)^T \times (Rx)^T$ = *mkMat33*
 (*cos* θ × *cos* ψ) (*cos* ψ × *sin* θ × *sin* ϕ - *sin* ψ × *cos* ϕ)
 (*cos* ψ × *sin* θ × *cos* ϕ + *sin* ϕ × *sin* ψ) (*cos* θ × *sin* ψ)
 (*sin* ψ × *sin* θ × *sin* ϕ + *cos* ψ × *cos* ϕ) (*sin* ψ × *sin* θ × *cos* ϕ
 - *cos* ψ × *sin* ϕ) (-*sin* θ) (*sin* ϕ × *cos* θ) (*cos* ϕ × *cos* θ).

6   Conclusion

Matrices are important tools in mathematics and computer science, and numerous problems can be modeled and solved using matrix. However, owing to the complexity of matrix theory, typical system designs or programs related to matrices require the use of formal methods, particularly theorem proving, to ensure correctness. We focus on matrix formalization in the Coq theorem prover. We collected five existing matrix models from the Coq community. We found that these models varied widely, and none of them achieved the formalization of large-scale matrix theory. Therefore, developers face difficult choices and high switching costs when they want to switch between different models in later stages.

In this study, we made several contributions to solving this problem. First, a unified matrix interface was created. Subsequently, five models were integrated based on this interface. Then, bijection functions were created, thus establishing the isomorphism between certain matrix operations and providing a new method for proving the properties of these operations. Finally, evaluation ratings were provided for developer reference. In summary, we evaluated matrix models in the Coq community, which can assist developers when making choices at an early stage. Moreover, using the unified interface and implementation we provided significantly reduces the cost of switching models at a later stage.

Future work will be in the following direction. Regarding the hierarchy of matrices, we have explored techniques such as type classes, canonical structures, and modules; however, these have not yet been investigated sufficiently. We hope to build a more detailed hierarchy in the future. In addition, special tactic is defined with Ltac in matrix models; however, there is no unified design to date; this will be unified in the future. Furthermore, and most importantly, there is a large amount of matrix theory that has not yet been implemented in any matrix model; this will be our main task for future work.

Acknowledgments. I would like to thank ZhenWei Ma and YingYing Ma for their research on matrix formalization techniques, and my colleagues for their discussions and suggestions.

References

1. Zhang, X.D.: Matrix Analysis and Applications, 2nd edn. Tsinghua University Press, Beijing (2013)
2. Wang, J., Zhan, N.J., Feng, X.Y., Liu, Z.M.: Overview of formal methods. Ruan Jian Xue Bao/J. Softw. **30**(1), 33–61 (2019). (in Chinese with English abstract). https://doi.org/10.13328/j.cnki.jos.005652
3. Fisher, K., Launchbury, J., Richards, R.: The HACMS program: using formal methods to eliminate exploitable bugs. Philos. Trans. R. Soc. A, **375**, 20150401 (2017). https://doi.org/10.1098/rsta.2015.0401
4. Chen, G., Shi, Z.P.: Formalized engineering mathematics. Commun. CCF **13**(10) (2017). (in Chinese with English abstract)
5. Coq Development Team. The Coq Reference Manual 8.13.2. INRIA (2019)
6. Isabelle proof assistant. https://isabelle.in.tum.de
7. LEAN Theorem Prover: Microsoft Research. https://leanprover.github.io
8. The HOL Interactive Theorem Prover. https://hol-theorem-prover.org
9. Ma, Z.W., Chen, G.: Matrix formalization based on Coq record. Comput. Sci. **46**(7), 139–145 (2019). (in Chinese with English abstract). https://doi.org/10.11896/j.issn.1002-137X.2019.07.022
10. Ma. Y.Y., Ma, Z.W., Chen. G.: Formalization of operations of block matrix based on Coq. Ruan Jian Xue Bao/J. Softw. **32**(6), 1882–1909 (2021) (in Chinese with English abstract). https://doi.org/10.13328/j.cnki.jos.006255
11. Mathematical Components. https://math-comp.github.io
12. Boldo, S., Lelay, C., Melquiond, C.: Coquelicot (2015). https://coquelicot.saclay.inria.fr/
13. Magaud, N.: Programming with Dependent Types in Coq: a Study of Square Matrices (2004). https://hal.inria.fr/hal-00955444
14. Blanqui, F., Koprowski, A.: CoLoR: a Coq library on well-founded rewrite relations and its application to the automated verification of termination certificates. Math. Struct. Comp. Sci. **21**(4), 827–859 (2011). https://doi.org/10.1017/S0960129511000120
15. Hietala, K., Rand, R., Hung, S.-H., Xiaodi, W., Hicks, M.: A verified optimizer for quantum circuits. In: ACM SIGPLAN Symposium on Principles of Programming Languages (POPL (2021)
16. Rand, R., Quantum, V.: Computing. Software Foundations Inspired Volume Q. https://www.cs.umd.edu/~rrand/vqc/index.html
17. Geuvers, H., et al.: A constructive algebraic hierarchy in Coq. J. Symbol. Comput. **34**(4), 271–286 (2002)
18. Casteran, P., Sozeau, M.: A Gentle introduction to type classes and relations in Coq (2016)
19. Sozeau, M., Oury, N.: First-class type classes. In: Mohamed, O.A., Muñoz, C., Tahar, S. (eds.) TPHOLs 2008. LNCS, vol. 5170, pp. 278–293. Springer, Heidelberg (2008). https://doi.org/10.1007/978-3-540-71067-7_23
20. Jung, R.: Exponential blowup when using unbundled typeclasses to model algebraic hierarchies (2019). https://www.ralfj.de/blog/2019/05/15/typeclasses-exponential-blowup.html. Accessed 1 Feb 2022

21. Baanen, A.: Use and abuse of instance parameters in the lean mathematical library, 2 May 2022. arXiv, https://doi.org/10.48550/arXiv.2202.01629
22. Mahboubi, A., Tassi, E.: Canonical structures for the working Coq user (2013). https://hal.inria.fr/hal-00816703v1

On-The-Fly Bisimilarity Checking
for Fresh-Register Automata

M. H. Bandukara and N. Tzevelekos$^{(\boxtimes)}$

Queen Mary University of London, London, UK
{m.h.bandukara,nikos.tzevelekos}@qmul.ac.uk

Abstract. Register automata are one of the simplest classes of automata that operate on infinite alphabets. Each automaton comes equipped with a finite set of registers where it can store data values and compare them with others from the input. Fresh-register automata are additionally able to accept a given data value just if it is fresh in the computation history. The bisimilarity problem for fresh-register automata is known to be in NP, when empty registers and duplicate register content are forbidden. In this paper, we investigate on-the-fly algorithms for solving bisimilarity, which attempt to build a bisimulation relation starting from a given input configuration pair. We propose an algorithm that uses concise representations of candidate bisimulation relations based on generating systems. While the algorithm runs in exponential time in the worst case, we demonstrate through a series of benchmarks its efficiency compared to existing algorithms and tools. We moreover implement a translation from π-calculus processes to fresh-register automata, and use the latter to obtain a prototype (strong early) bisimilarity checking tool for finitary π-calculus processes.

Keywords: Automata over infinite languages · Nominal automata · Bisimulation equivalence checking

1 Introduction

Originally envisaged as acceptors of regular languages over infinite alphabets, register automata [11,25] are one of the simplest classes of automata that operate on such alphabets. To achieve this ability, each automaton comes equipped with a finite set of registers where it can store data values. Register automata can verify whether or not a given input[1] data value is currently stored in a register, and store it in a register overwriting its current value. Fresh-register automata [32] are an extension thereof where the automaton is able to accept a given data value just if it is *globally fresh*, that is, it has not appeared so far in the input. Global freshness captures generative behaviours in programming languages, like

---

[1] We view automata as accepting words from a given input alphabet.

M. H. Bandukara—Supported by EPSRC DTP EP/R513106/1.

creation of fresh references, objects, exceptions, etc. The notion is also present in languages for mobile processes, network protocols and secure transactions.

Automata over infinite alphabets are designed to capture scenarios which require unbounded data values. For example, they can be used for modelling mobile processes [27] and computation with variables [10,11], and for verifying XML query languages [30]. More recently, they have been applied to program and system modelling, leading to program semantics and verification tools [9,20,23] and, respectively, to learning algorithms for model learning [1,6,17].

Compared to finite-state automata, the complexity of decision algorithms for fresh-register automata is generally higher. For example, even for register automata, universality is undecidable [25], and hence so is equivalence, while reachability is NP-complete given a block-if-empty register discipline [28] (P-complete in the deterministic case). In contrast to equivalence, the bisimilarity problem for fresh-register automata is decidable, with its complexity being between P and EXPTIME, depending on the register discipline [21].

In this paper we concentrate on the bisimilarity problem for fresh-register automata and propose an algorithm, and an empirically fast implementation, by combining the *on-the-fly* approach [7] with representations and routines from computational group theory [21,22]. The latter consists of starting from the pair of configurations given as input to the bisimilarity problem, and attempt to build a bisimulation relation containing it. As mentioned above, the way registers are used in these automata can greatly affect the complexity of the bisimulation problem. For example, allowing for empty registers that can block if read from, can turn registers into write-once cells and thus lead to a PSPACE-hard bisimilarity problem [21]. Herein we choose a register discipline which avoids such complications while not conceding expressive power [22]. More specifically, our automata require all the registers to be initially filled, register content cannot be deleted, but registers may become inactive in given states. By a slight adaptation of the argument in [21], the bisimilarity problem we work on is in NP and also P-hard, though it is not known to be in P nor NP-hard. While our algorithm runs in exponential time, we show via extensive benchmarking that it is practically efficient compared to existing algorithms and implementations. As further evidence to the algorithm's practical efficiency, we implement a prototype bisimilarity checker for finitary π-calculus processes, by compilation to fresh-register automata, and benchmark that as well.

Overall, this work contributes an investigation of on-the-fly bisimulation algorithms for FRAs. While the ideas behind the algorithms have been presented before [7,21,22], ours are the first algorithms combining them and applying them to non-deterministic automata. This is accompanied with an implementation and extensive benchmarks which show our implementation to outperform existing approaches. We moreover provide time-complexity upper bounds for our algorithms (the problem previously only known to be in NP [21]). We finally implement a translation from π-calculus processes to FRAs and briefly benchmark it on a subset of our examples.

Related Work. Several automata models akin, or in fact equivalent, to register automata have been studied in the literature, such as *history-dependent* *automata (HDAs)* [27], *variable automata* [10] and *nominal automata* [5]. HDAs were designed for modelling π-calculus processes and have been studied intensively for bisimilarity [8,18,27]. They use states which contain *local names*, which can be seen as register indices, and their transitions encode instructions on how these names are propagated in the next state. With the use of *name symmetries*, HDAs can be minimised with respect to bisimilarity, and that fact yields a bisimilarity checking routine. The latter was implemented in the Mihda tool [8], though the complexity and efficiency of the tool were not examined further.

In the area of register automata, the first bisimilarity algorithm was given in [32] (for fresh-register automata). The complexity bounds of bisimilarity, for different register disciplines, was examined in [21]; while [19,22] presented a polynomial-time algorithm and implementation for deterministic automata. Register automata can be directly translated into nominal automata. For the latter, one can use the frameworks of LOIS [14] or NLambda [12] to implement standard bisimilarity checking algorithms. We implemented two such algorithms in LOIS (on-the-fly and partition refinement) and compared them with our implementation (cf. Sect. 5).

2   Background

We introduce the definitions that we will use in the paper. We begin by introducing bisimulation equivalence for labelled transition systems (cf. [3]), and then move to fresh-register automata.

Definition 1. *A Labelled-Transition System (LTS) is a tuple $\langle Q, A, \rightarrow \rangle$, where Q is a set of states, A is a set of actions and $\rightarrow \subseteq Q \times A \times Q$ is a transition relation. Given such an LTS, a* simulation *is a binary relation $R \subseteq Q \times Q$ which satisfies the following condition. For every $(q_1, q_2) \in R$ and every $a \in A$:*

– for every $q_1 \overset{a}{\rightarrow} q_1'$, there exists $q_2 \overset{a}{\rightarrow} q_2'$ with $(q_1', q_2') \in R$.

R is called a bisimulation *if both R and R^{-1} are simulations. We say that states q and p are* bisimilar, *and write $q \sim p$, if there is a bisimulation R with $(q, p) \in R$.*

Fresh-Register Automata (FRAs) are a class of automata that operate on infinite alphabets of input symbols. A useful convention is to assume input symbols contain elements from a finite set of atomic values called *tags*, and from infinite set of atomic values called *names* or *data values*. FRAs are based on register automata [25]: they utilize a finite set of registers where they store input names, which they can compare to, and replace with, new inputs. In addition, FRAs have access to the full name history of their runs and only accept an input if it is *fresh*, i.e. new in the current run.

Let us fix an input alphabet $\Sigma \times \mathbb{A}$, where Σ is a finite set of *tags* and $\mathbb{A}$ is an infinite set of *names* or *data values*. Moreover, let us use i, j, r to range over natural numbers and write $[i, j]$ for the set $\{i, i+1, \ldots, j\}$ (for $i \leq j$).

Definition 2. *An r-Fresh-Register Automaton (r-FRA) is a tuple $\mathcal{A} = \langle Q, q_0, \mu, \delta, F \rangle$ where r is the number of registers and:*

- Q is a finite set of states, $q_0 \in Q$ is initial, $F \subseteq Q$ are final;
- $\mu : Q \to \mathcal{P}([1, r])$ is the availability function which indicates which registers are filled at each state;
- $\delta \subseteq Q \times \Sigma \times \{i, i^\bullet, i^\circledast \mid i \in [1, r]\} \times Q$ is the transition relation;

subject to the following conditions (cf. Remark 3):

- if $(q, t, i, q') \in \delta$ then $\mu(q') \subseteq \mu(q)$;
- if $(q, t, i^\bullet, q') \in \delta$ or $(q, t, i^\circledast, q') \in \delta$ then $\mu(q') \subseteq \mu(q) \cup \{i\}$.

We shall write $q \xrightarrow{t, x} q'$ for $(q, t, x, q') \in \delta$. We call $\mathcal{A}$ an r-Register Automaton (r-RA) if there are no transitions of the form $q \xrightarrow{t, i^\circledast} q'$.

Remark 3. We note that there are three types of transitions in FRAs:

- $q \xrightarrow{t, i} q'$: a known transition that accepts an input containing a name that is already stored in register i.
- $q \xrightarrow{t, i^\bullet} q'$: a locally-fresh transition that only accepts an input containing a name not currently stored in any register, and writes this name to register i.
- $q \xrightarrow{t, i^\circledast} q'$: a globally-fresh transition that only accepts an input containing a name that has never appeared before, and writes this name to register i.

Our automata adhere to a certain register discipline, in that each state has a given set of active registers which need to be filled when the automaton is in that state, while non-active registers can be considered as dropped. This is done using an availability function, whereby each state is mapped to its set of active registers. Active registers help to directly represent certain scenarios where a register value is forgotten (e.g. during garbage collection). Finally, no two registers may contain the same name at any given point in the computation.

We next define FRA configurations and LTSs. Let ρ range over register assignments, i.e. injective $\rho : S \to \mathbb{A}$ for some $S \subseteq [1, r]$; and H range over histories, i.e. $H \subseteq_{\text{fin}} \mathbb{A}$. Given $S, \{j\} \subseteq [1, r], d \in \mathbb{A}$ and register assignment ρ, we write:

- $\rho \upharpoonright S$ for the restriction $\{(i, \rho(i)) \mid i \in S\}$, and
- $\rho[j \mapsto d]$ for the update $\{(i, \rho(i)) \mid i \in \text{dom}(\rho) \setminus \{j\}\} \cup \{(j, d)\}$.

Definition 4. Given an r-FRA $\mathcal{A} = \langle Q, q_0, \mu, \delta, F \rangle$, its set of configurations is:

$$\mathcal{C}_{\mathcal{A}} = \{(q, \rho, H) \mid q \in Q, \rho : \mu(q) \to \mathbb{A} \text{ injective}, \text{rng}(\rho) \subseteq H \subseteq_{\text{fin}} \mathbb{A}\}.$$

Moreover, we define the LTS $\langle \mathcal{C}_{\mathcal{A}}, \Sigma \times \mathbb{A}, \to_{\mathcal{A}} \rangle$, where $(q, \rho, H) \xrightarrow{t, d}_{\mathcal{A}} (q', \rho', H')$ if one of the following conditions are met:

- $d = \rho(i)$, $(q, t, i, q') \in \delta$, $\rho' = (\rho \upharpoonright \mu(q'))$ and $H' = H$;
- $d \notin \text{rng}(\rho)$, $(q, t, i^\bullet, q') \in \delta$, $\rho' = (\rho[i \mapsto d] \upharpoonright \mu(q'))$ and $H' = H \cup \{d\}$;
- $d \notin H$, $(q, t, i^\circledast, q') \in \delta$, $\rho' = (\rho[i \mapsto d] \upharpoonright \mu(q'))$ and $H' = H \cup \{d\}$.

We say that $\mathcal{A}$ makes a transition from (q, ρ, H) to (q', ρ', H') accepting (t, d).

Remark 5. FRAs require examining their configurations rather than individual states as each configuration differs based on which names have been previously seen. For example, given a state $q_1 \in Q$ and an input name d, it is not possible to verify whether the input (t, d) can be processed by a transition of the form $q_1 \xrightarrow{t, 1^\circledR} q_1'$, for some tag t, unless we know whether or not the name d has been previously seen. The role of component H in the configuration provides the automaton with this knowledge.

We are interested in testing bisimilarity of FRAs which, as we shall see, amounts to bisimilarity on the LTS produced by FRAs during their computation. Our analysis and our algorithms can be simplified if an additional convention is imposed in our FRAs, namely that locally and globally fresh transitions cannot be matched with each other. While this is a restriction, it is relatively harmless: (i) if tags are ignored, it leads to the same languages of names being accepted; (ii) it holds in practical applications of FRAs (e.g. for input/output π-calculus transitions (cf. Sect. 5.2), or Opponent/Proponent moves [20]); (iii) it does not alter the results in this paper, as we can implement our algorithms for non-normal FRAs modulo a polynomial time overhead (cf. [21]), but it simplifies the presentation considerably. This non-mixing convention is formalised as follows.

Definition 6. *Let us assume that the set of tags is partitioned as $\Sigma = \Sigma_1 \uplus \Sigma_2$. Given an r-FRA $\mathcal{A}$ as above, we call $\mathcal{A}$ a normal fresh-register automaton if:*

$$(q, t, i^\bullet, q') \in \delta \;\Rightarrow\; t \in \Sigma_1 \qquad and \qquad (q, t, i^\circledR, q') \in \delta \;\Rightarrow\; t \in \Sigma_2.$$

Henceforth, we assume that all the FRAs we are working with are normal.

We now establish the problem we are going to be working on.

Definition 7. *The problem $\sim$FRA is: given an r-FRA $\mathcal{A}$ and $\kappa_1, \kappa_2 \in \mathcal{C}_\mathcal{A}$ with common history components does $\kappa_1 \sim \kappa_2$ hold?*

Theorem 8. *([21]). The problem $\sim$FRA is in NP.*

3   Symbolic Reasoning

In this section, we discuss symbolic representations for bisimulation relations. When dealing with an infinite alphabet, making transitions explicit can lead to an infinitely sized LTS. For bisimulation purposes, this leads to an infinite space of configuration pairs $((q_1, \rho_1, H), (q_2, \rho_2, H))$. We can reduce this infinite state space to a finite abstract representation using *symbolic reasoning* [32], by replacing actual names in configuration pairs with a representation of the relationship between the names in each pair component. The names in the registers are abstracted as it does not matter which names are in which register, rather we are interested in which registers in the two configurations contain the same names.

The (common) history can be suppressed altogether. Thus, a configuration pair $((q_1, \rho_1, H), (q_2, \rho_2, H))$ is represented by a *symbolic triple* (q_1, σ, q_2), where σ is a partial permutation between register indices $(\sigma : \mathrm{dom}(\rho_1) \overset{\cong}{\rightharpoonup} \mathrm{dom}(\rho_2))$. Several pairs of configurations will map to the same triple in this abstract state space.

A partial permutation over $[1, r]$ is a bijection between two subsets of $[1, r]$. We write $\mathcal{IS}_r$ for the set of partial permutations over $[1, r]$. This is an inverse semigroup, with composition of $\sigma_1, \sigma_2 \in \mathcal{IS}_r$ written $\sigma_1; \sigma_2$. Note that we may use the same notation for relation composition: for instance, given register assignments ρ_1, ρ_2, we have that $\rho_1; \rho_2^{-1}$ is the relation (in fact, partial permutation) obtained by composing ρ_1 with ρ_2^{-1} as relations.

Definition 9. *Given an r-FRA $\mathcal{A} = \langle Q, q_0, \mu, \delta, F \rangle$, its set of* symbolic triples *is:*

$$\mathcal{U}_\mathcal{A} = \{(q_1, \sigma, q_2) \in Q \times \mathcal{IS}_r \times Q \mid \mathrm{dom}(\sigma) \subseteq \mu(q_1), \mathrm{rng}(\sigma) \subseteq \mu(q_2)\}.$$

Given configurations κ_1, κ_2, with $\kappa_i = (q_i, \rho_i, H)$, their symbolic representation is then: $\mathrm{symb}(\kappa_1, \kappa_2) = (q_1, \rho_1; \rho_2^{-1}, q_2)$.

Lemma 10. *The size of $\mathcal{U}_\mathcal{A}$ is $O(|Q|^2 \cdot \sum_{i=0}^r i! \binom{r}{i}^2)$, and thus $O(|Q|^2 r^{(1+\epsilon)r})$.*

Proof. The size of $\mathcal{IS}_r$ is $\sum_{i=0}^r i! \binom{r}{i}^2$ (e.g. [31]), which is upper bounded by $(r+1)^r$ using binomial expansion (and $i! \binom{r}{i}^2 = r \cdots (r-i+1) \binom{r}{i} \leq r^i \binom{r}{i}$). □

With the components defined, we now adapt the original notion of bisimulation to its symbolic counterpart, which we refer to as *symbolic bisimulation*. In bisimulation, the names accepted by each transition are compared to the names accepted by other transitions. If the accepted names were the same, we say that these transitions match. Symbolic bisimulation takes the abstracted names into account, and checks bisimulation based on which registers contain the same names. First, we must consider the possible transitions that could occur from one configuration, and all the ways they can be matched by another configuration:

- A known transition can be matched by a transition on a stored value or a locally-fresh transition, but not a globally-fresh one.
- A locally-fresh transition can be matched by a transition on a stored value or a locally-fresh transition, but not a globally-fresh one.
- A globally-fresh transition can only be matched by a globally-fresh one.

We proceed to formally defining the rules for symbolic bisimulation. The rules have been adapted from [32] to normal fresh-register automata. Given a partial permutation σ and states p, q, we write $\sigma \upharpoonright (p, q)$ for $\sigma \cap (\mu(p) \times \mu(q))$.

Definition 11. *Let $\mathcal{A} = \langle Q, q_0, \mu, \delta, F \rangle$ be an r-FRA. A symbolic simulation on $\mathcal{A}$ is a relation $R \subseteq \mathcal{U}_\mathcal{A}$, with $(q_1, \sigma, p_1) \in R$ written $q_1 \, R_\sigma \, p_1$, satisfying the following normal symbolic simulation conditions (NSYS). For all $(q_1, \sigma, p_1) \in R$:*

1. for all $q_1 \xrightarrow{t, i} q_2$:

(a) if $i \in \mathsf{dom}(\sigma)$, then there is some $p_1 \xrightarrow{t,\sigma(i)} p_2$ with $q_2 \, R_{\sigma'} \, p_2$ and $\sigma' = \sigma \upharpoonright (q_2, p_2)$,

(b) if $i \in \mu(q_1) \backslash \mathsf{dom}(\sigma)$, then there is some $p_1 \xrightarrow{t,j^\bullet} p_2$ with $q_2 \, R_{\sigma'} \, p_2$ and $\sigma' = \sigma[i \mapsto j] \upharpoonright (q_2, p_2)$,

2. for all $q_1 \xrightarrow{t,i^\bullet} q_2$:

(a) for all $j \in \mu(p_1) \backslash \mathsf{rng}(\sigma)$, there exists $p_1 \xrightarrow{t,j} p_2$ with $q_2 \, R_{\sigma'} \, p_2$ and $\sigma' = \sigma[i \mapsto j] \upharpoonright (q_2, p_2)$,

(b) there is some $p_1 \xrightarrow{t,j^\bullet} p_2$ with $q_2 \, R_{\sigma'} \, p_2$ and $\sigma' = \sigma[i \mapsto j] \upharpoonright (q_2, p_2)$,

3. for all $q_1 \xrightarrow{t,i^\circledast} q_2$, there is some $p_1 \xrightarrow{t,j^\circledast} p_2$ with $q_2 \, R_{\sigma'} \, p_2$ and $\sigma' = \sigma[i \mapsto j] \upharpoonright (q_2, p_2)$.

We call R a **symbolic bisimulation** if both R and R^{-1} are symbolic simulations, where $R^{-1} = \{(p_1, \sigma^{-1}, q_1) \,|\, (q_1, \sigma, p_1) \in R\}$. We let $\overset{s}{\sim}$ be the union of all symbolic bisimulations. We say that configurations κ_1, κ_2 with common history are symbolic bisimilar, written $\kappa_1 \overset{s}{\sim} \kappa_2$, if $\mathsf{symb}(\kappa_1, \kappa_2) \in \overset{s}{\sim}$.

Theorem 12. ([32]). For any κ_1, κ_2 with common history, $\kappa_1 \sim \kappa_2$ iff $\kappa_1 \overset{s}{\sim} \kappa_2$.

4   On-The-Fly Algorithms for Bisimilarity

Typical algorithms for bisimilarity checking such as partition refinement are based on a co-inductive approach whereby, starting from the set of all configuration pairs, the largest bisimulation is constructed by carving out non-bisimilar pairs [3]. For FRAs, such an approach is not immediately applicable as the set of configurations is infinite. Using symbolic triples we can finitise the state space but we are then met with new challenges, as the state space is exponentially large and therefore computing it in order to subsequently restrict it is inefficient. Moreover, partition refinement techniques require one to view configurations in isolation, which is incompatible with the symbolic triples representation.

4.1   Base On-the-fly Algorithm

We follow an alternative approach which starts from the configuration pair that one is testing for bisimilarity and tries to build *on-the-fly* a bisimulation containing it [7,15]. In the case of FRAs, instead of configuration pairs one has symbolic triples. Intuitively, an on-the-fly algorithm can be seen as producing an LTS where states are symbolic triples and represent a candidate bisimulation relation. Each transition in this LTS marks a common transition that a pair of configurations makes to another pair of configurations. These transitions are in fact pairs of transitions, whereby one configuration is making a transition (a *challenge*) and the other configuration is matching it. Since the FRA can be non-deterministic, there can be several transitions able to match a certain challenge. The algorithm tries each of them until either a bisimulation is built, or it is deemed that the examined configurations are not bisimilar.

```
1   onfly(u, V, A, B):
2     if u in B: return False
3     if u in V: A.add(u,u⁻¹); return True
4     save_state(V,A); V.add(u,u⁻¹)
5     if simulate(u,V,A,B) and simulate(u⁻¹,V,A,B): return True
6     if u in A: restore_state(V, A)
7     else: V.remove(u,u⁻¹)
8     B.add(u,u⁻¹); return False
9
10  simulate((q₁,σ,q₂), V, A, B):
11    for ((t,i,kind1), q₁′) in q₁.nexts():
12      matched = False; priv2 = ∅
13      match kind1:
14      case KNOWN:
15        if i∈ dom(σ): next2 = q₂.nexts(t,σ(i),KNOWN)
16        else: next2 = q₂.nexts(t,_,•)
17      case •:
18        next2 = q₂.nexts(t,_,•)
19        priv2 = μ(q₂) \ rng(σ)
20      case ⊛:
21        next2 = q₂.nexts(t,_,⊛)
22      for ((_,j,kind2), q₂′) in next2:
23        σ′ = σ.update(i,kind1,j,kind2)
24        if onfly((q₁′,σ′,q₂′),V,A,B): matched=True; break
25      if not matched: return False
26      for j in priv2:
27        matched = False
28        for ((t,j,kind2), q₂′) in q₂.nexts(t,j,KNOWN):
29          σ′ = σ.update(i,kind1,j,kind2)
30          if onfly((q₁′,σ′,q₂′),V,A,B): matched=True; break
31        if not matched: return False
32    return True
```

Fig. 1. Base on-the-fly algorithm.

The algorithm uses state in order to record the triples that it has *visited*, and therefore included in its candidate symbolic bisimulation relation: if a triple is visited twice by the LTS, in the second instance we do not need to analyse it again. The latter gives rise to a notion of dependency between visited triples, as a visited triple may be used to justify bisimilarity of later triples. In such a case, the former triple is recorded as an *assumption*, or *assumed* triple. Visited triples and assumptions may or may not be part of a bisimulation relation. If the algorithm realises that the latter is the case, it moves the offending triple from the set of visited triples to a set of *bad* triples. Bad triples represent configurations that are not bisimilar. In order for the algorithm to fully recover from a wrongly visited triple, say (q_1, σ, q_2), it also needs to check if that triple was used as an assumption for other triples. If that is the case, then the algorithm simply backtracks its visited and assumed triples to what they were when (q_1, σ, q_2) was first visited. Bad triples do not need backtracking: if a triple was shown non-bisimilar using generous assumptions, then it is non-bisimilar indeed.

We present our on-the-fly algorithm in Fig. 1. The algorithm has a main function onfly(u,V,A,B), where $u \in \mathcal{U}_{\mathcal{A}}$ is a triple tested for bisimilarity, and V, A, B $\subseteq \mathcal{U}_{\mathcal{A}}$ are sets of *visited, assumed* and *bad* triples respectively. These sets satisfy A $\subseteq$ V and V $\cap$ B = $\emptyset$, and are all initially empty. A call of onfly(u,V,A,B) proceeds as follows:

- We first check if u is in the sets of bad or visited triples; in the former case we know that u represents non-bisimilar configuration pairs, while in the latter we work under the assumption that it represents bisimilar pairs.
- We then add u (and its inverse) to the set of visited states and call simulate in order to check that the (NSYS) conditions can be satisfied for u and its inverse. Note that simulate in turn calls onfly, for checking that certain target configurations can be added (or are already in) the candidate symbolic bisimulation relation. In this process, the sets V, A and B may be altered.
- If the calls to simulate are not successful, we have established that u does not represent bisimilar pairs, so we can add it to B. Moreover, if u has passed into the assumed set A we need to restore V and A to their original values, as any additions performed on them by the calls to simulate may be based on the false assumption that u represents a bisimilar pair.

In Fig. 1, we also use a function q_i.nexts(tag, register, type). This function returns all transitions q_i can take using a transition of the form (*tag, register, type*). When called without any arguments, it returns every transition that the state can make.

Proposition 13. *Given an r-FRA* $\mathcal{A} = \langle Q, q_0, \mu, \delta, F \rangle$ *and* $u \in \mathcal{U}_{\mathcal{A}}$, onfly(u, $\emptyset$, $\emptyset$, $\emptyset$) *terminates in time* $O(|\mathcal{U}_{\mathcal{A}}|^2|\delta|^2)$ *and therefore in* $O(|Q|^4 r^{(2+\epsilon)r}|\delta|^2)$.

Proof. Let us set $\beta = $ B $\cup$ V and write fly_i for i-th *full call* of the onfly function, where a full call is one that goes beyond line 3. For economy, we write β_i for the β at the beginning of fly_i. We also define a size for β as $\|\beta\| = (|$B$|, |$V$|)$, so $\|\beta\|$ is bounded by $(|\mathcal{U}_{\mathcal{A}}|, |\mathcal{U}_{\mathcal{A}}|)$ (in the lexicographic order). Between fly_i and fly_{i+1}, we either have that at least the u (and u^{-1}) of fly_i has been added to V (and B has not decreased), or that fly_i failed and therefore its u was added to B. In either case, $\|\beta_i\| < \|\beta_{i+1}\|$, and hence the algorithm terminates in no more than $|\mathcal{U}_{\mathcal{A}}|^2/2$ full calls to onfly. Each such call may issue 2 calls to simulate, which in turn tries $O(|\delta|^2)$ possible matches. $\qquad\square$

Theorem 14. *If* onfly(u, $\emptyset$, $\emptyset$, $\emptyset$) *returns True then* $u \in \overset{s}{\sim}$, *and vice versa.*

4.2 Generator On-the-fly Algorithm

The on-the-fly algorithm explores an exponentially large state space $\mathcal{U}_{\mathcal{A}}$ and, because of backtracking, its complexity is proportional to the square of $|\mathcal{U}_{\mathcal{A}}|$. However, due to properties of bisimilarity, not all of the space needs to be explicitly explored. We have already applied this principle when, for each $u \in \mathcal{U}_{\mathcal{A}}$, we examine just one of u, u^{-1}: if $u \in \overset{s}{\sim}$ then we must also have $u^{-1} \in \overset{s}{\sim}$, and vice versa. But we can do much more.

As shown in [21,22], there is a polynomial-size way to represent symbolic bisimulations based on so called *generating systems*. This concise representation is based on group-theoretic notions and also allows us to take certain shortcuts in the exploration tree. We next present an adaptation of our base on-the-fly algorithm that uses generating systems in order to store visited triples.

We first note that symbolic bisimilarity is closed under certain operations.

Definition 15. *Given $R \subseteq \mathcal{U}_A$, we define the closure of R, written $Cl(R)$, to be the smallest $X \subseteq \mathcal{U}_A$ such that $R \subseteq X$ and X is closed under the following rules (where id_S is the identity on $S \subseteq [1, r]$):*

$$\frac{\sigma = id_{\mu(q)}}{(q, \sigma, q) \in X} \quad \frac{(q_1, \sigma, q_2) \in X}{(q_2, \sigma^{-1}, q_1) \in X} \quad \frac{(q_1, \sigma, q_2) \in X \ \sigma \subseteq \sigma'}{(q_1, \sigma', q_2) \in X} \quad \frac{(q_1, \sigma_1, q_2), (q_2, \sigma_2, q_3) \in X}{(q_1, \sigma_1; \sigma_2, q_3) \in X}$$

Theorem 16. ([22]). $Cl(\overset{s}{\sim}) = \overset{s}{\sim}$.

A generating system is a certain structure that, when closed under the above rules, yields a subset of $\mathcal{U}_A$. Below, we write $\mathcal{S}_S$ for the set of permutations on some set $S \subseteq [1, r]$.

Definition 17. *Given an r-FRA $A = \langle Q, q_0, \delta, \mu, F \rangle$, a generating system is a tuple $\mathcal{G} = \langle \diamond, \{(q_C, X_C, G_C) \mid C \in Q/\diamond\}, \{\sigma_q \mid q \in Q\} \rangle$ where:*

- $\diamond \subseteq Q \times Q$ *is an equivalence relation (write $[q]_\diamond$ for the equivalence class of q, and $Q/\diamond = \{[q]_\diamond \mid q \in Q\}$).*
- *For any $\diamond$-equivalence class C, q_C is a state from C (the class representative), $X_C \subseteq \mu(q_C)$ and $\emptyset \neq G_C \subseteq \mathcal{S}_{X_C}$.*
- *For any $q \in Q$ and $C = [q]_\diamond$, we have $\sigma_q \in \mathcal{IS}_r$ and $dom(\sigma_q) = X_C$. Finally, for any C, we have $\sigma_{q_C} = id_{X_C}$.*

Given such generating system $\mathcal{G}$, we define the subset of $\mathcal{U}_A$ generated by it as:

$$gen(\mathcal{G}) = Cl(\{(q_C, \sigma, q_C) \mid C \in Q/\diamond, \sigma \in G_C\} \cup \{(q_C, \sigma_q, q) \mid q \in Q, C = [q]_\diamond\}).$$

Thus, a generating system partitions the set of states into equivalence classes according to $\diamond$, and each class has a representative q_C which is "connected" to each element of the class via σ_q. Each representative q_C is also equipped with a set G_C of permutations (generators) from $\mathcal{S}_{X_C}$, for some $X_C \subseteq \mu(q_C)$.

Example 18. Let $R \subseteq \mathcal{U}_A$ be a symbolic bisimulation that is closed under Cl. We can construct a generating system representing R as follows. First, given a set X we define $id_X = \{(x, x) \mid x \in X\}$. We first set $\diamond = \{(q_1, q_2) \mid (q_1, \sigma, q_2) \in R\}$. For each $\diamond$-equivalence class C, we select a class representative q_C, and we take X_C to be the least X such that $(q_C, id_X, q_C) \in R$. For each equivalence class C, we define its set of partial permutations as $G_C = \{\sigma \mid (q_C, \sigma, q_C) \in R, dom(\sigma) = $

```
1   onflygen(u, G, B):
2     if u in B: return False
3     if u in G: return True
4     save_state(G)
5     G.update(u)
6     if simulate(u,G,B) and simulate(u⁻¹,G,B): return True
7     restore_state(G)
8     B.add(u,u⁻¹); return False
9
10  simulate((q₁,σ,q₂), G, B):
11    ... // same as Figure 1
```

Fig. 2. On-the-fly algorithm using generating systems.

$rng(\sigma) = X_C$}. Finally, for each C and member $q \in C$, we pick some σ_q such that $dom(\sigma_q) = X_C$ and $(q_C, \sigma_q, q) \in R$. In particular, the generating system:

$$\mathbf{1} = \langle \{(q,q) \mid q \in Q\}, \{(q, \mu(q), \{id_{\mu(q)}\}) \mid q \in Q\}, \{id_{\mu(q)} \mid q \in Q\}\rangle.$$

represents the identity bisimulation. represented   □

We can now present the on-the-fly algorithm using generating systems to represent the set of visited states. The algorithm is given in Fig. 2. We note that we do not use a set of assumed states anymore and we always restore our state when a simulation attempt does not go through. The reason is twofold: first, when updating a generating system G by adding a new triple, the relation represented by G is extended by possibly several more elements due to the used closure operation, and these elements could also be future flawed assumptions; on the other hand, removing a single u added to a generating system is not a uniquely defined operation (in the same way that there are several maximal subgroups one can obtain by removing an element from a group). The other two points to note is that in lines 3 and 5 the algorithm is checking whether the triple u is in $gen(G)$ and, respectively, updating G by adding u. These two operations were defined in [22] and have polynomial time complexity, which we can bound as follows.

Lemma 19. *Given a generating system $\mathcal{G}$ and $u \in \mathcal{U}_A$:*

1. we can check whether $u \in gen(\mathcal{G})$ in time $O(r^5)$,
2. we can construct the least extension of $\mathcal{G}$ containing u in time $O(r^5 + |Q|r)$.

Proof. We analyse the algorithms presented in [22] and use standard upper bound results from computational group theory. Firstly, checking if $u = (q_1, \sigma, q_2) \in gen(\mathcal{G})$. If q_1 and q_2 are in separate partitions, then we can deduce that $u \notin gen(\mathcal{G})$, in $O(1)$. If they are in the same partition, then we compute $\bar{\sigma} = \sigma_{q_1}; \sigma; \sigma_{q_2}^{-1}$, in $O(1)$, and check if $\bar{\sigma} \in Sub(G_C)$ ($Sub(G_C)$ is the subgroup generated by the elements in G_C), in $O(r^5)$ [13]. Next, for calculating the least extension of $\mathcal{G}$ containing u, there are three cases to consider. In the first case,

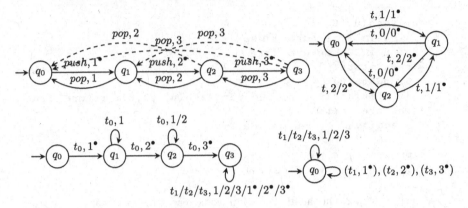

Fig. 3. Testing FRAs, clockwise from top left: (lossy) stacks, cliques, CPTs, flowers. Notation e.g. $q \xrightarrow{a/b, 1/2} q'$ denotes four transitions $q \xrightarrow{t,i} q'$ for $t \in \{a, b\}$ and $i \in \{1, 2\}$. All examples in this figure are taken to be for size 3.

we have $\bar{\sigma} \in S_{X_C} \backslash Sub(G_C)$, and it suffices to add $\bar{\sigma}$ to G_c. In the second one, $dom(\bar{\sigma}) \subsetneq X_C$ and we have to replace X_C with the set B_I, where $I = G_C \cup \bar{\sigma}$. B_I is the common domain of the inverse semigroup generated by I and is calculated using breadth-first search in a certain reachability graph, in $O(r^2)$. The next step is to set $G_C = \{\sigma \restriction B_I \mid \sigma \in I\}$, which is again $O(r^2)$ assuming that the set G_C remains linear in r. The final case involves merging the equivalence classes containing q_1 and q_2. For this, we again need to calculate a common-domain set B_I, in $O(r^2)$, but also update all connections σ_q in the merged equivalence class, which is done in time $O(|Q|r)$. Adding up, the update operation runs in $O(r^5 + |Q|r)$. $\qquad\square$

Proposition 20. *Given an r-FRA $\mathcal{A} = \langle Q, q_0, \mu, \delta, F \rangle$ and $\mathsf{u} \in \mathcal{U}_\mathcal{A}$,* $\mathtt{onflygen(u, 1, \emptyset)}$ *terminates in time* $O(|Q|^3 r^{2+(1+\epsilon)r}(r^5 + |Q|r + |\delta|^2))$.

Proof. The proof for termination is similar to that of the on-the-fly algorithm in Proposition 13. We use the same size measure $\|\beta\| = (|\mathtt{B}|, |\mathtt{V}|)$, where $\mathtt{V}$ is generated from $\mathtt{G}$, but note that the number of increases that $|\mathtt{V}|$ can have is bounded to $O(|Q|r^2)$: the length of subgroup chains over $\mathcal{IS}_r$ is $O(r)$ [4], the number of consecutive increases of a set X_C is $O(r)$, and the total number of consecutive equivalence class merges is $O(|Q|)$. Combining this with Lemma 19, we get an overall time complexity of $O(|\mathcal{U}_\mathcal{A}||Q|r^2(r^5 + |Q|r + |\delta|^2))$ and, therefore, $O(|Q|^3 r^{2+(1+\epsilon)r}(r^5 + |Q|r + |\delta|^2))$ using also Lemma 10. $\qquad\square$

5   Results

We implemented the two on-the-fly algorithms in Python[2] and ran a series of benchmarks, the results of which we present in Sect. 5.1. A natural application

---

[2] https://github.com/HamzaBandukara/FRABisim.

of bisimilarity checking in the presence of names is checking bisimilarity for π-calculus processes [16]. Following [32], we implemented a novel translation from the π-calculus to FRAs, and benchmarked the overall tool-chain for (strong early) bisimilarity checking of π-calculus processes (cf. Sect. 5.2). All experiments were carried out on a Windows 11 machine, equipped with an Intel Core i7-1165G7 at 2.80 GHz and 16 GB of RAM.

5.1 Benchmarks for On-the-fly Algorithms, and Existing Approaches

We ran tests on five family of examples, with tests parametric on the FRA sizes:

1. Stacks. These are finite stacks storing distinct names and using a set of tags $\{push, pop\}$ for stack operations (Fig. 3 top left, full lines). Each state q_i has registers $1, \ldots, i$ available. These were the only deterministic tests we used.
2. Lossy stacks. These are finite stacks which may "lose" names when popping and are therefore non-deterministic (Fig. 3 top left, full and dashed lines).
3. Cliques. In these automata each state has all registers available, and is connected to all other states with a pair of known/fresh transition on a corresponding register (Fig. 3 top right).
4. Flowers. In these automata we first fill in registers using tag t_0, until we reach a sink state from which we read and refresh all registers using a number of tags (Fig. 3 bottom left). Like cliques, these FRAs are highly non-deterministic, but from a single state.
5. CPTs *(compactly-presented partial permutations* [19]). These FRAs are compact but allow a large number of transitions and can form large bisimulation relations (Fig. 3 bottom right). In the single state, every known name can be read, but also refreshed. In our testing, different variants of fresh transitions were used (i.e. with different combinations of tags and register indices) so as to enforce the ensuing bisimulation relations to be large.

Thus, our tests included deterministic and non-deterministic FRAs, containing a single or more tags. For stacks, we examined bisimilarity between a stack as shown in Fig. 3 and a variant thereof where the registers available to state q_i are $r - i + 1, \ldots, r$ (and registers in transitions are adapted accordingly). For flowers we examined bisimilarity between a flower and a copy of itself. For cliques, we examined bisimilarity between a clique and a one-size-bigger one. For CPTs we examined bisimilarity between an FRA and a variant thereof with different tagging of its fresh transitions. In all cases, the initial triple examined was $(q_0, \{\}, p_0)$, where p_0 the initial state of the second copy of the examined FRA. While all these tests were indeed bisimilarities, we also examined non-bisimilarities on these examples. Versions with globally fresh transitions were also tested, but excluded from herein due to space constraints. In our tool repository we include the test results in full.

In Fig. 4 we present how our two algorithms perform in the last four example problems (i.e. the non-deterministic examples). We can see that the use of generating systems generally provides a significant speed up. The speed up is more

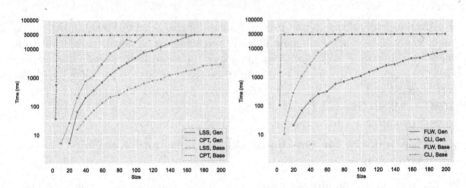

Fig. 4. Algorithm comparison. Timeout set to 30 s.

dramatic in the examples where the constructed bisimulation relation is larger, in particular in flowers and CPTs.

We also tested our algorithms against three alternative approaches (Fig. 5), two of which were based on the Looping Over Infinite Sets (LOIS) library [14]. LOIS is a C++ library that allows looping over infinite sets, and can be thus used in order to write standard bisimilarity algorithms albeit over register automata. For our benchmarks, we implemented two such algorithms: an on-the-fly one (LOIS-FW) and a partition refinement one (LOIS-PR). The other tool we benchmarked was DEQ [19], which is based on the same notion of generating systems as our second algorithm and is specialised for deterministic register automata; in fact, DEQ is a polynomial-time tool. As the DEQ tool only works with deterministic automata, and as the LOIS results were considerably slower in our initial tests, we restricted these comparisons to stacks only. We can see that our two algorithms have similar performance to DEQ, and outperform the LOIS-based implementations. Regarding the latter, we note that LOIS is a general-purpose library and addresses a wider problem than our algorithms. The fact that our generator-based algorithm has similar performance to DEQ is not surprising, as they use the same underlying theory. On the other hand, the good performance of our base algorithm is somewhat unexpected, but it is due to the fact that in the stack examples the bisimulations built are not exponentially large.

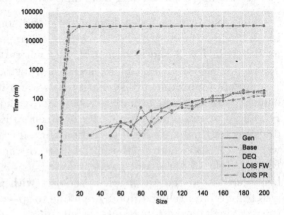

Fig. 5. Tool Comparison (Stacks). Timeout is 30 s.

$$\frac{}{\tau.P \xrightarrow{\tau} P} \quad \frac{}{\bar{x}y.P \xrightarrow{\bar{x}y} P} \quad \frac{}{x(y).P \xrightarrow{xz} P\{z/y\}} \quad \frac{P_1 \xrightarrow{\alpha} P'}{P_1 + P_2 \xrightarrow{\alpha} P'} \quad \frac{P \xrightarrow{\alpha} P'}{[x=x]P \xrightarrow{\alpha} P'}$$

$$\frac{P \xrightarrow{\alpha} P'}{\nu x.P \xrightarrow{\alpha} \nu x.P'} x \notin n(\alpha) \qquad \frac{P \xrightarrow{\bar{x}y} P'}{\nu y.P \xrightarrow{\bar{x}(z)} P'\{z/y\}} x \neq y, z \notin fn(\nu y.P)$$

$$\frac{P_1 \xrightarrow{\bar{x}y} P_1' \quad P_2 \xrightarrow{xy} P_2'}{P_1|P_2 \xrightarrow{\tau} P_1'|P_2'} \qquad \frac{P_1 \xrightarrow{\alpha} P'}{P_1|P_2 \xrightarrow{\alpha} P'|P_2} bn(\alpha) \cap fn(P_2) = \emptyset$$

$$\frac{P_1 \xrightarrow{\bar{x}(y)} P_1' \quad P_2 \xrightarrow{xy} P_2'}{P_1|P_2 \xrightarrow{\tau} \nu y.(P_1'|P_2')} y \notin fn(P_2) \qquad \frac{P\{y_1/x_1,\ldots,y_n/x_n\} \xrightarrow{\alpha} P'}{A(\vec{y}) \xrightarrow{\alpha} P'} A(\vec{x}) = P$$

Fig. 6. Early π-calculus semantics (symmetric versions of rules are omitted).

5.2 π-calculus Results

The π-calculus is a paradigmatic process language for concurrent interactions involving name passing [16,29]. The syntax of π-calculus processes is:

$$P, Q \ ::= \ 0 \,|\, \tau.P \,|\, \bar{x}y.P \,|\, x(y).P \,|\, \nu y.P \,|\, P|Q \,|\, P+Q \,|\, [x=y]P \,|\, [x \neq y]P \,|\, A(\boldsymbol{x})$$

where x, y range over *names* (taken from the set $\mathcal{D}$), and A ranges over *process variables*. Process variables allow for recursive processes, by means of definitions of the form: $A(\boldsymbol{x}) = P$. Names can be open or bound, with binding constructs being $x(y).P$ and $\nu y.P$ (for y). We write $bn(P)$ and $fn(P)$ for the bound and free names of P respectively.

The (early) semantics of π-calculus processes comprises the LTS in Fig. 6. Labels are given by the grammar: $\alpha \ ::= \ \tau \,|\, xy \,|\, \bar{x}y \,|\, \bar{x}(y)$. We write $n(\alpha)$ for the set of names included in α. These can be bound or free, with $bn(\bar{x}(y)) = \{y\}$ and $bn(\alpha) = \emptyset$ for any other α. We can now define the related notion of bisimilarity.

Definition 21. *A relation $\mathcal{R}$ between processes is called an* (early strong) *simulation if, for all $P \mathcal{R} Q$:*

- *if $P \xrightarrow{\alpha} P'$ and $bn(\alpha) \cap fn(P, Q) = \emptyset$ then there is some $Q \xrightarrow{\alpha} Q'$ with $P' \mathcal{R} Q'$.*

We call $\mathcal{R}$ an early bisimulation *if $\mathcal{R}, \mathcal{R}^{-1}$ are early simulations. Processes P, Q are* early bisimilar *(written $P \sim Q$) if $P \mathcal{R} Q$ for some early bisimulation $\mathcal{R}$.*

Let us call a π-calculus process *finitary* if the processes it can reduce to are bounded in length. In [32], it was shown that π-calculus processes can be translated to a variant of FRAs specifically designed for the π-calculus, in such a way that two finitary processes are bisimilar iff their FRA-like translations are.[3] We adapted that translation so that it maps directly into FRAs and implemented it as an extension to our tool. Thus, in order to test bisimilarity of π-calculus processes our tool first encodes each π-calculus process into an FRA, and then these FRAs are tested for bisimilarity by the generator-based algorithm.

---

[3] In fact, this holds for processes that are finitary up to *structural congruence* [16,29].

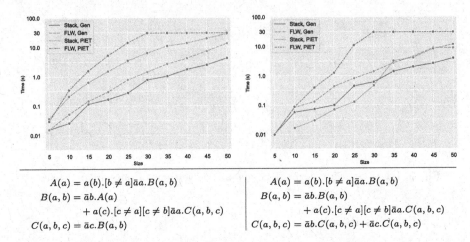

$$A(a) = a(b).[b \neq a]\bar{a}a.B(a,b)$$
$$B(a,b) = \bar{a}b.A(a)$$
$$\qquad + a(c).[c \neq a][c \neq b]\bar{a}a.C(a,b,c)$$
$$C(a,b,c) = \bar{a}c.B(a,b)$$

$$A(a) = a(b).[b \neq a]\bar{a}a.B(a,b)$$
$$B(a,b) = \bar{a}b.B(a,b)$$
$$\qquad + a(c).[c \neq a][c \neq b]\bar{a}a.C(a,b,c)$$
$$C(a,b,c) = \bar{a}b.C(a,b,c) + \bar{a}c.C(a,b,c)$$

Fig. 7. π-calculus tests: equivalences (top left), inequivalences (top right). Timeout set to 30 s. Stack (bottom left) and Flower (bottom right) translation.

We benchmarked our tool extension on π-calculus processes corresponding to stacks and flowers. While more elaborate examples are within reach (the tool can handle finite-control processes [32]), our approach can lead to bottlenecks in the translation phase, from π-calculus processes to FRAs, as the whole transition system needs to be produced for the examined (combined) process. Nonetheless, we compared our tool with PiET,[4] a π-calculus equivalence checker implemented in Fresh OCaML. PiET is a tool specialised for π-calculus processes and equipped to perform many types of equivalence checks. We chose it as it is the only tool that is complete for the finitary fragment and can check strong early bisimilarity. It is based on Lin's powerful symbolic-execution approach to checking process bisimilarity [15].

Example π-calculus encodings for size 2 stacks and flowers are shown in Fig. 7 (bottom). For instance, to encode stacks, we use a single channel a for both pushes (which are inputs) and pops (outputs). For flowers, we modified the transitions in the final states to be only on known names (we could not make PiET work in the original version). As we can see in Fig. 7 (top), our tool fares very well, even though it does not apply

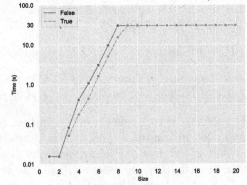

Fig. 8. Tests for $GEN|Stack$ (our tool), equivalences and inequivalences.

[4] http://piet.sourceforge.net/ implemented by Matteo Mio.

any π-calculus heuristics or optimisations. We also implemented a fresh-name generator $(GEN(a) = \nu b.\bar{a}b.GEN(a))$ which we composed in parallel with a stack to check how the tool responds to parallelism (Fig. 8). Our tool timeouts much sooner now (i.e. for smaller stacks). The bottleneck is the translation into FRAs, as the tool calculates the full (symbolic) LTS of the π-calculus processes – the automata that are finally fed to the FRA-bisimulation checker are not excessively larger than for plain stacks.

6   Conclusions

In this paper we proposed an algorithm for bisimilarity checking of FRAs, accompanied with a tool implementation and extensive benchmarking. We see several avenues for future research: (i) looking into Hennessy-Milner logics for FRAs (cf. [26]) capturing bisimilarity and devising model-checking routines; (ii) narrowing the current complexity gap in the bisimilarity problem (P-hard vs NP-solvable); (iii) using the techniques and tool to decide contextual equivalence of concurrent/non-deterministic higher-order programs [24]; (iv) adapting of the bisimilarity algorithm to operate directly on π-calculus processes (bypassing FRAs) and applying it to extensions of the π-calculus (e.g. the Spi Calculus [2]).

References

1. Aarts, F., Fiterau-Brostean, P., Kuppens, H., Vaandrager, F.: Learning register automata with fresh value generation. In: ICTAC Proceedings, pp. 165–183 (2015)
2. Abadi, M., Gordon, A.D.: A calculus for cryptographic protocols: the SPI calculus. Inf. Comput. **148**(1), 1–70 (1999)
3. Aceto, L., Ingólfsdóttir, A., Srba, J.: The algorithmics of bisimilarity. In: Advanced Topics in Bisimulation and Coinduction, pp. 100–172. CUP (2012)
4. Babai, L.: On the length of subgroup chains in the symmetric group. Comm. Algebra **14**(9), 1729–1736 (1986)
5. Bojanczyk, M., Klin, B., Lasota, S.: Automata theory in nominal sets. LMCS **10**(3), 1–14 (2014)
6. Bollig, B., Habermehl, P., Leucker, M., Monmege, B.: A robust class of data languages and an application to learning. LMCS **10**(4), 1–9 (2014)
7. Fernandez, J.-C., Mounier, L.: "On the fly" verification of behavioural equivalences and preorders. In: Larsen, K.G., Skou, A. (eds.) CAV 1991. LNCS, vol. 575, pp. 181–191. Springer, Heidelberg (1992). https://doi.org/10.1007/3-540-55179-4_18
8. Ferrari, G.L., Montanari, U., Raggi, R., Tuosto, E.: From co-algebraic specifications to implementation: The Mihda toolkit. In: FMCO Revised Lectures (2002)
9. Grigore, R., Distefano, D., Petersen, R.L., Tzevelekos, N.: Runtime verification based on register automata. In: TACAS Proceedings, pp. 260–276 (2013)
10. Grumberg, O., Kupferman, O., Sheinvald, S.: Variable automata over infinite alphabets. In: LATA Proceedings, pp. 561–572 (2010)
11. Kaminski, M., Francez, N.: Finite-memory automata. Theoret. Comput. Sci. **134**(2), 329–363 (1994)
12. Klin, B., Szynwelski, M.: SMT solving for functional programming over infinite structures. In: MSFP Proceedings, vol. 207, pp. 57–75 (2016)

13. Knuth, D.E.: Efficient representation of perm groups. Combinatorica **11**, 33–43 (1991)
14. Kopczynski, E., Torunczyk, S.: LOIS: syntax and semantics. In: POPL Proceedings, pp. 586–598. ACM (2017)
15. Lin, H.: Computing bisimulations for finite-control π-calculus. J. Comput. Sci. Technol. **15**, 1–9 (2008)
16. Milner, R., Parrow, J., Walker, D.: A calculus of mobile processes I and II. Inf. Comput. **100**(1), 1–40 (1992)
17. Moerman, J., Sammartino, M., Silva, A., Klin, B., Szynwelski, M.: Learning nominal automata. In: POPL Proceedings, pp. 613–625. ACM (2017)
18. Montanari, U., Pistore, M.: pi-calculus, structured coalgebras, and minimal HD-automata. In: Nielsen, M., Rovan, B. (eds.) MFCS Proceedings, pp. 569–578 (2000)
19. Murawski, A.S., Ramsay, S.J., Tzevelekos, N.: DEQ: equivalence checker for deterministic register automata. In: ATVA Proceedings, pp. 350–356 (2019)
20. Murawski, A., Ramsay, S., Tzevelekos, N.: A contextual equivalence checker for IMJ*. In: ATVA Proceedings, pp. 234–240 (2015)
21. Murawski, A.S., Ramsay, S.J., Tzevelekos, N.: Bisimilarity in fresh-register automata. In: LICS Proceedings, pp. 156–167 (2015)
22. Murawski, A.S., Ramsay, S.J., Tzevelekos, N.: Polynomial-time equivalence testing for deterministic fresh-register automata. In: MFCS Proceedings (2018)
23. Murawski, A.S., Tzevelekos, N.: Algorithmic nominal game semantics. In: ESOP Proceedings, pp. 419–438 (2011)
24. Murawski, A.S., Tzevelekos, N.: Algorithmic games for full ground references. Formal Methods Syst. Des. **52**(3), 277–314 (2018)
25. Neven, F., Schwentick, T., Vianu, V.: Finite state machines for strings over infinite alphabets. ACM Trans. Comput. Logic **5**(3), 403–435 (2004)
26. Parrow, J., Borgström, J., Eriksson, L., Gutkovas, R., Weber, T.: Modal logics for nominal transition systems. Log. Methods Comput. Sci. **17**(1), 1–14 (2021)
27. Pistore, M.: History-Dependent Automata. Ph.D. thesis, Università di Pisa (1999)
28. Sakamoto, H., Ikeda, D.: Intractability of decision problems for finite-memory automata. Theor. Comput. Sci. **231**(2), 297–308 (2000)
29. Sangiorgi, D., Walker, D.: The Pi-Calculus - a theory of mobile processes. Cambridge University Press, Cambridge (2001)
30. Schwentick, T.: Automata for XML-a survey. JCSS **73**(3), 289–315 (2007)
31. Sloane, N.J.A.: The On-Line Encyclopedia of Integer Sequences. https://oeis.org/A002720. Sep 2022
32. Tzevelekos, N.: Fresh-register automata. In: POPL Proceedings. ACM (2011)

LOGIC: A Coq Library for Logics

Yichen Tao and Qinxiang Cao[✉]

Shanghai Jiao Tong University, Shanghai, China
taoyc0904@sjtu.edu.cn, caoqinxiang@gmail.com

Abstract. LOGIC is a Coq library for formalizing logic studies, concerning both logics' applications and logics themselves (meta-theories). For applications, users can port derived rules and efficient proof automation tactics from LOGIC to their own program-logic-based verification projects. For meta-theories, users can easily formalize a standard soundness proof or a Henkin-style completeness proof for logics like classical/intuitionistic propositional logic, separation logic and modal logic with LOGIC's help. In this paper, we present how compositional and portable proof engineering is possible in LOGIC.

Keywords: Logic · Coq · Theorem proving

1 Introduction

Theorem provers like Coq [3] and Isabelle [19] have been used for formalizing sophisticated math proofs, including many important logic theorems [11,12]. Besides its own interests, formalized logics (especially program logics) have been widely used in program verification tools to guarantee big software systems' safety [7,9,15]. But for now, there was not yet a systematic, foundational and formalized library for general logic studies. In this paper, we present LOGIC[1] a Coq library for logic applications and logics' meta-theories. Specifically,

- we want to provide a foundational library so that more advanced results can be formalized on its basis, and proofs can be reused for similar conclusions;
- we want to export useful proof rules and proof automation tactics for proving assertion entailments in different program verification projects;
- we want to use one single "eco-system" to achieve both targets above.

One challenge of LOGIC is to formalize different logics and their meta-theories in a *uniform* way (for the purpose of maximum proof reuse). This seems straightforward since different logic studies share many technical notations and definitions. For example, "⊢ φ" usually means φ is provable and "$m \models \varphi$" describes a satisfaction relation between m and φ. Also, different logics and different semantics usually share some common parts. However, differences in subtle settings bring about many proof-engineering problems. For instance, different logic studies may choose different primitive connectives; thus it is even nontrivial to unify

---

[1] A link to the repository of LOGIC: https://github.com/QinxiangCao/LOGIC.

W. Dong and J.-P. Talpin (Eds.): SETTA 2022, LNCS 13649, pp. 205–226, 2022.
https://doi.org/10.1007/978-3-031-21213-0_13

different semantic definitions, which are usually defined by recursion over syntax trees. Also, different logics may choose different primitive judgements. Hilbert systems define *provability* ($\vdash \varphi$) by axioms and primary proof rules and define

$$\Phi \vdash \varphi \triangleq \text{exists a finite set } \Psi \subseteq \Phi, \text{ s.t. } \vdash \left(\bigwedge_{\psi \in \Psi} \psi \right) \to \varphi. \tag{1}$$

But sequent calculi use $\Phi \vdash \varphi$ (φ is derivable from Φ) as their primitive judgements and let $\vdash \varphi$ represent $\emptyset \vdash \varphi$. How to formalize a theory for both of them is not obvious.

Formalizing a uniform Henkin-style completeness proof is especially difficult. Different proofs may construct their canonical models differently, e.g. some proofs choose "maximal consistent sets" to be the canonical model's possible worlds while other proofs choose "derivable-closed sets". Moreover, different semantics have different additional structures in their models. For example, modal logics' Kripke model contains a binary relation for defining box modality's semantics. Intuitionistic logics' Kripke model has a preorder for defining implication's semantics. Henkin-style completeness proofs are different in detail due to the differences in these basic constructions and premises.

Another challenge of LOGIC is to generate *efficient* proof automation tactics. For generality, proofs in LOGIC should be parameterized over different languages and different proof systems. However, this parameterized setting will usually cause significant overhead for proof construction.

In the rest of this paper, we will explain how LOGIC addresses these formalization challenges. We will first introduce some background information about the Coq theorem prover in Sect. 2. We then give an overview of the whole framework of LOGIC in Sect. 3. After that, we describe our formalization of connectives, judgements, and proof rules, along with the meta-logic properties - soundness and completeness - in Sect. 4. In Sect. 5, we demonstrate how the logic generator in LOGIC can help us with exportable logic libraries. In the end, we discuss related work in Sect. 6, and conclude in Sect. 7.

2   Background: Coq Proof Assistant

Coq is a theorem prover whose logical objects are written in a Calculus of Inductive Constructions [6]. This underlying formal language enables Coq's users to define higher order functions and state high order propositions, i.e. one can quantify over a function, a predicate, or even a higher order function/predicate.

Type classes are a special kind of higher order objects in Coq, usually used to formalize abstract structures, like group, partial order, etc. For example, a common definition of group $\mathbf{G}$ is a tuple $(X_{\mathbf{G}}, +_{\mathbf{G}}, -_{\mathbf{G}}, 0_{\mathbf{G}})$ where $X_{\mathbf{G}}$ is the underlying set, $+_{\mathbf{G}}$ is an associative binary function, $-_{\mathbf{G}}$ is an inverse function and $0_{\mathbf{G}}$ is a unit element. In order to describe associativity, one usually writes: $\forall x\ y\ z \in X_{\mathbf{G}}, (x +_{\mathbf{G}} y) +_{\mathbf{G}} z = x +_{\mathbf{G}} (y +_{\mathbf{G}} z)$. Defining groups as a type class allows Coq's users to omit that $\mathbf{G}$ for conciseness if it is not ambiguous.

Besides higher order objects, Coq provides a *module system* for users to easily structure large developments and a means of massive abstraction. Specifically, a module is a collection of definitions and proofs; a module signature is a set of theorem statements; and a functor is a derivation from assumptions (represented by a module signature) to conclusions (represented by another signature).

The higher order logic system and the module system are two critical Coq infrastructure for modular development. In comparison, derivations using type classes are formal Coq proofs for parameterized instances, e.g. a theorem $\hat{P}$ for groups usually has a form of: for any group **G**, some property P holds for **G**. Functors are not Coq proofs but proof generators, e.g. given a *concrete* tuple **G**, a functor $\hat{P}$ for group theory will generate a proof of $P(\mathbf{G})$ from a proof that **G** is a group.

3   Overview

The major aim of LOGIC is to reuse definitions and proofs to automatically generate logic libraries based on users' demands, as well as providing flexible options on how the logic is constructed. For example, a logic language and its proof rules can be constructed in multiple ways. Specifically, if we want to formalize a propositional logic with the following connectives:

$$\rightarrow, \neg, \vee,$$

we can either follow Elliott Mendelson's approach [18], i.e. treating $\rightarrow$ and $\neg$ as primitive connectives and defining $p \vee q \triangleq \neg p \rightarrow q$, or adopt the method mentioned in Ebbinghaus *et al.*'s book [10], i.e. treating $\neg, \vee$ as primitive connectives and define $p \rightarrow q \triangleq \neg p \vee q$.

Besides, the proof system can be constructed in various ways. We often write $\vdash \varphi$ if φ is provable, and $\Phi \vdash \varphi$ if φ is derivable from a set of propositions Φ. When φ is derivable from a singleton proposition ψ, which is a rather common case, we write $\psi \vdash \varphi$. We wish to formalize these judgements by choosing any one of them as primitive, and deriving the others.

It seems a possible solution to construct with different modules and type classes including the parameterized definitions and proofs of different logics. There are indeed previous works done in this way, *e.g.*, VST-MSL [2], Iris [16,21], and Math Classes [22]. However, there are drawbacks of such an approach:

- The users need to be familiar with the entire framework to accomplish the construction. They would have to dig into our design details so that they can find the proper place-holder of each argument, and choose the classes that meet their requirements.
- Constructive proofs of proof rules would bring a large overhead. Suppose A, B and C are types, and we have a model defined as follows.

Definition model : Type := A * B * C.

We aim to build a separation logic on model, and need to instantiate the following classes:

```
Class Join (worlds : Type) := ...
Class Unit (worlds : Type) := ...
Class SepAlg (worlds : Type) {J : Join worlds} := ...
Class UnitJoin (worlds : Type) {U : Unit worlds}
    {J : Join worlds} {SA : SepAlg worlds} := ...
```

We can build instances on product types with the followings.

```
Instance prod_J (A B : Type) :
    Join A -> Join B -> Join (A * B) := ...
Instance prod_U (A B : Type) :
    Unit A -> Unit B -> Unit (A * B) := ...
Instance prod_SA (A B : Type) (J_A : Join A) (J_B : Join_B) :
    SepAlg A -> SepAlg B -> SepAlg (A * B) := ...
Instance prod_UJR (A B : Type) (J_A : Join A) (J_B : Join B)
    (U_A : Unit A) (U_B : Unit B)
    (SA_A : SepAlg A) (SA_B : SepAlg B) :
    UnitJoin A -> UnitJoin B -> UnitJoin (A * B) := ...
```

It is worth mentioning that there are implicit arguments in the instances. For example, the true Coq type of prod_SA A B J_A J_B is (@SepAlg A J_A) -> (@SepAlg B J_B) -> (@SepAlg (A * B) (prod_J A B J_A J_B)). The class UnitJoin on A * B * C can be instantiated as follows:

```
Definition UJR_ABC : UnitJoin (A * B * C) :=
    prod_UJR (A * B) C _ _ _ _ _ _
    (prod_UJR A B _ _ _ _ _ _ UJR_A UJR_B) UJR_C.
                      ⇑
```

The placeholder for the underscore pointed by the arrow should have type Join A, and we call it J_A. We can observe that the instance J_A may appear repeatedly during the process of the entire construction (*e.g.*, it may appear in the construction of SepAlg on A, A * B, A * B * C, *etc.*.). This phenomenon causes the size of the construction to be unacceptably large. If more classes need to be instantiated, the memory taken could be exponentially large.

In order to address the problems above, an automatized logic generator becomes indispensable. We designed a logic generator that accepts a configuration designated by the user, integrates the required classes of items, and presents an interface for the construction of logic. The users are not required to know how the entire class system works. Instead, with the help of the interface, the users can use the system compositionally and derive the demanded definitions and proofs. The logic generator frees them from the tedious work of searching for the correct class and constructing the proof terms themselves. All they need to do, is writing the configuration, and implementing the primitive items.

Furthermore, we observe that in most applications of program verification, we use a single logic, whose syntax and proof rules remain unchanged throughout the process. Since the composition of type classes has already been constructed by the generator in the whole procedure of use, there is no need to reconstruct the logic, and thus spares time and memory, which addresses the overhead problem.

4   Parameterized Definitions and Proofs

As previously mentioned, we will first build a type class based system, and then establish an auxiliary system on top of it to automatically build instances for users. However, due to the versatility of logic application scenarios, traditional applications of type classes do not suffice to solve the problems. Thus, we divide the type classes into four layers, and make different design choices based on their applications: (a) languages; (b) connectives and judgements (Sect. 4.1); (c) proof rules (Sect. 4.2); (d) soundness (Sect. 4.3) and completeness (Sect. 4.4).

Notations in Coq and in this paper. We use "andp x y" to represent the conjunction of x and y in the logic's proposition, where "p" stands for "proposition". Additionally, Coq's infrastructure allows us to define a notation for the connectives, judgements. For example, we use "x && y" as an object logics' notation to represent "andp x y" in LOGIC, which is distinguished from Coq's notation for its own logic, the meta-logic. In this paper, we choose not to use these notations for conciseness. We will use standard logic notations like $\land$, $\lor$, *etc..* for object languages and use informal English words "and", "or", *etc..* in the meta language. For consideration of readability, we will adopt this convention (but within a box container) when we present Coq code.

4.1   Connectives and Judgements

As mentioned before, we wish to enable various constructions of the same logic language. We illustrate our design choice using the previously mentioned example - formalizing a logic with connectives $\to, \neg, \lor$. We can either select $\neg, \to$ as primitive connectives and adopt Mendelson's approach, or select $\neg, \lor$ as primitive connectives and follow Ebbinghaus *et al.*'s approach.

```
Class Mendelson_Language := {
    expr : Type;
    negp : expr -> expr;
    impp : expr -> expr -> expr; }.
Definition Mendelson_orp := fun p q => ¬p → q .
```

```
Class Ebbinghaus_Language := {
    expr : Type;
    negp : expr -> expr;
    orp  : expr -> expr -> expr; }.
Definition Ebbinghaus_impp := fun p q => ¬p ∨ q .
```

However, since we wish to support both constructions (or even more sophisticated ones) simultaneously, neither of the above methods works. Instead, we define languages and connectives respectively with different type classes (see below), i.e., one type class for the language and one type class for each of the connectives. The type class does not assume if the connective is primitive or derived. They just indicate the existence and type of the corresponding connective.

The languages are defined by the following Coq type class. It says that, once the set of *expressions* (expr) is defined, the language is defined.

```
Class Language := {expr : Type}.
```

Some of the type classes for the connectives are listed as follows.

```
Class OrLanguage (L : Language) := {orp : expr -> expr -> expr}.
Class AndLanguage (L : Language) := {andp : expr -> expr -> expr}.
Class ImpLanguage (L : Language) := {impp : expr -> expr -> expr}.
```

It is worth mentioning that "OrLanguage L" does not assume disjunction to be a primitive connective. It can be either a primitive connective or a derived one. In order to reason about the derivation among connectives, we introduce *refl classes* in LOGIC, *e.g.*

```
Class OrDef_Imp_Neg (L : Language) {_ : ImpLanguage L}
  {_ : OrLanguage L} {_ : NegLanguage L} :=
{impp_negp2orp : for any φ ψ, φ ∨ ψ = ¬φ → ψ) }.
```

In LOGIC, we also have algebraic structures that do not rely on expressions. Instead, they work on the "model-level", directly showing the relationships between models. These are mostly used to derive higher connectives for expressions. For example, the algebraic structure join "⊕" is commonly used to define the separating conjunction "*".

```
Class Join (worlds : Type) : Type :=
  join : worlds -> worlds -> worlds -> Prop.
Class SepconLanguage (L: Language): Type :=
  { sepcon : expr -> expr -> expr }.
Instance worlds_L := Build_Language (worlds -> Prop).
Class SepconDef_Join {SepconL : SepconLanguage worlds_L} :=
{ join2sepcon : φ * ψ = fun w =>
  exists w_1 w_2, ⊕(w_1, w_2, w) and φ w_1 and ψ w_2 }.
```

In that sense, separating conjunction can be treated as a derived definition from join, which means that we do not need to distinguish logic connectives from algebraic structures of models in LOGIC. We put such derivations among connectives and algebraic definitions in one single type class system.

LOGIC supports 7 propositional connectives and constants ($\wedge, \vee, \rightarrow, \leftrightarrow, \neg, \top$, and $\bot$), separation logic connectives, and modalities in modal logics, as well as algebraic structures for defining semantics of intuitionistic propositional logic, separation logic, and modal logic. For brevity, we only demonstrate a part of them here.

Besides connectives, LOGIC also encompasses type classes formalizing judgements, built in an analogous manner. For example, provable is a meta-logic property of propositional expressions; thus, its Coq type is: expr -> Prop. We also define logic equivalence, which is useful for different applications.

```
Class Provable (L: Language) :=
  { provable: expr -> Prop }. (* |-- x *)
Class Derivable (L: Language) :=
  { derivable: set_of_expr -> expr -> Prop }. (* X |--- x *)
Class Derivable1 (L:Language) :=
  { derivable1: expr -> expr -> Prop }. (* x |-- y *)
Class LogicEquiv (L:Language) :=
  .{ logic_equiv: expr -> expr -> Prop }. (* x --||-- y *)
```

Again, "Provable L" does not assume $\vdash \varphi$ to be a primitive definition. Logicians may choose either $\vdash \varphi$ or $\varPhi \vdash \varphi$ as a primitive definition, and derive the other. Furthermore, computer scientists usually use $\varphi \vdash \psi$ as their primitive notation in formal program verification projects. LOGIC supports all these different choices and uses additional type classes to define transformation among them. The following is an example.

```
Class DerivableProvable
      (L: Language) (GammaP: Provable L)
      (GammaD: Derivable L) {_:ImpLanguage L} :=
{ derivable_provable:
```

for any $\varPhi\ \varphi,\ \varPhi \vdash \varphi$ iff.

there exists $\varphi_1, \varphi_2, \ldots, \varphi_n \in \varPhi$, s.t. $\vdash \varphi_1 \to \varphi_2 \to \cdots \to \varphi_n \to \varphi$ }.

4.2 Proof Rules

Like connectives and judgements, we also define type classes for proof rules, and portray the derivation between them using Coq lemmas. To illustrate how these type classes and Coq lemmas are designed, we take separation logic as an example. When constructing a separation logic, the following three rules regarding the separating conjunction "$*$" are often required:

- SEPCONCOMM: for any $\varphi\ \psi$, $\varphi * \psi \vdash \psi * \varphi$;
- SEPCONASSOC: for any $\varphi\ \psi\ \chi$, $\varphi * (\psi * \chi) \vdash (\varphi * \psi) * \chi$;
- SEPCONMONO: for any $\varphi\ \psi\ \varphi'\ \psi$, if $\varphi \vdash \varphi'$ and $\psi \vdash \psi'$, then $\varphi * \psi \vdash \varphi' * \psi'$.

If separating implication "$-*$" is present, we may have the following proof rule:

- WANDSEPCONADJOINT: for any $\varphi\ \psi\ \chi$, $\varphi * \psi \vdash \chi$ iff. $\varphi \vdash \psi -* \chi$.

It is known that SEPCONMONO can be derived from SEPCONCOMM, SEPCONAS-SOC, and WANDSEPCONADJOINT [8]. We then introduce how the type classes and Coq lemmas are designed with regard to the above example.

Primary Rule Classes for Internal Use. The followings are the two rule classes, SepconDeduction and WandDeduction, which serve the internal use of LOGIC. Notice that there is redundancy within these type classes, i.e. the third rule in SepconDeduction can be derived by the other three rules. However, it is still listed as a primary rule since some separation logic does not have separating implication "$-\!*$" in its language. Furthermore, as is the case in all primary rule classes for internal use, the dependency among them exhibits a clear hierarchy.

Class SepconDeduction (L : Language) (GammaD1 : Derivable1 L)
    {_ : SepconLanguage} :=
{ sepcon_comm : $\boxed{\text{for any } \varphi\ \psi,\ \varphi*\psi\vdash\psi*\varphi}$;

    sepcon_assoc : $\boxed{\text{for any } \varphi\ \psi\ \chi,\ \varphi*(\psi*\chi)\vdash(\varphi*\psi)*\chi}$;

    sepcon_mono : $\boxed{\text{for any } \varphi\ \psi\ \varphi'\ \psi',\ \text{if } \varphi\vdash\varphi' \text{ and } \psi\vdash\psi', \text{ then } \varphi*\psi\vdash\varphi'*\psi'}$ }.
Class WandDeduction (L : Language) (GammaD1 : Derivable L)
    {_ : SepconLanguage L} {_ : WandLanguage L} :=
{ wand_sepcon_adjoint : $\boxed{\text{for any } \varphi\ \psi\ \chi,\ \varphi*\psi\vdash\chi \text{ iff. } \varphi\vdash\psi-\!*\chi}$ }.

With the rule classes above, we can construct parameterized proofs of other rules. For example, the monotonicity of separating implication "$-\!*$" is derivable from the given context, including the basic properties of judgement BasicDeduction and WandDeduction shown above. This is formalized in the following lemma.

Lemma derivable1_wand_mono : forall {L : Language}
    {sepconL : SepconLanguage L} {wandL : WandLanguage L}
    {GammaD1 : Derivable L} {bD : BasicDeduction L GammaD1}
    {wandD : WandDeduction L GammaD1},
    $\boxed{\text{for any } \varphi_1\ \varphi_2\ \psi_1\ \psi_2,\ \text{if } \varphi_2\vdash\varphi_1 \text{ and } \psi_2\vdash\psi_1, \text{ then } \varphi_1-\!*\psi_1\vdash\varphi_2-\!*\psi_2}$

Rule Classes for Users' Construction. There are three type classes for users' construction concerning the above separation logic example, which are listed as follows. This allows users to be flexible in constructing the logics. If the desired logic does not involve separating implication "$-\!*$", the user can select SepconDeduction_Weak and SepconDeduction_Mono as the primary rule classes. Otherwise, SepconDeduction_Weak and WandDeduction can be selected as primary rule classes for the logic, so that the rule SEPCONMONO can be automatically derived. Among these type classes, there is no redundancy so that users can use whatever type class they demand without worrying about repetitive proofs.

Class SepconDeduction_Weak (L : Language) (GammaD1 : Derivable1 L)
    {_ : SepconLanguage} :=
{ __sepcon_comm : $\boxed{\text{for any } \varphi\ \psi,\ \varphi*\psi\vdash\psi*\varphi}$;

    __sepcon_assoc : $\boxed{\text{for any } \varphi\ \psi\ \chi,\ \varphi*(\psi*\chi)\vdash(\varphi*\psi)*\chi}$ }.
Class SepconDeduction_Mono (L : Language) (GammaD1 : Derivable1 L)
    {_ : SepconLanguage} :=
{ __sepcon_mono : $\boxed{\text{for any } \varphi\ \psi\ \varphi'\ \psi,\ \text{if } \varphi\vdash\varphi' \text{ and } \psi\vdash\psi', \text{ then } \varphi*\psi\vdash\varphi'*\psi'}$ }.
Class WandDeduction (L : Language) (GammaD1 : Derivable L)
    {_ : SepconLanguage L} {_ : WandLanguage L} :=
{ wand_sepcon_adjoint : $\boxed{\text{for any } \varphi\ \psi\ \chi,\ \varphi*\psi\vdash\chi \text{ iff. } \varphi\vdash\psi-\!*\chi}$ }.

Constructing Primary Rules from Inputs. In LOGIC, the derivation between rule classes is depicted using Coq lemmas, which allows constructing the primary rules with the input proofs of users. For example, the following lemma says that SEPCONMONO is derivable once SEPCONCOMM, SEPCONASSOC (given in type class SpeconDeduction_Weak), and WANDSEPCONMONO (given in type class WandDeduction) have been proved.

```
Lemma WeakAdjoint2Mono  :
    forall {L : Language} {GammaD1 : Derivable1 L}
    {_ : SepconLanguage L} {_ : WandLanguage L}
    {_ : SepconDeduction_Weak L GammaD1}
    {_ : WandDeduction L GammaD1},
  SepconDeduction_Mono L GammaD1.
```

Rules for Derived Connectives. Another use of Coq lemmas in LOGIC lies in the syntactic sugars of connectives and judgements. As is described in Sect. 4.1, LOGIC supports using syntactic sugars to define new connectives (judgements) from primitive ones. We show that we can use these derived connectives and judgements when proving inner theorems or derived rules as if they are primitive concepts. For example, OrFromDefToAx_Imp_Neg proves that disjunction will have its introduction rule and elimination rule if it is defined as $\varphi \vee \psi \triangleq \neg\varphi \rightarrow \psi$.

4.3   Semantics and Soundness

Double turnstile "$\cdot \vDash \cdot$" usually describes a satisfaction relation, while its left side may vary in accordance with the semantics. Thus, we use Coq type classes to parameterize over different possibilities.

```
Class Model := {model : Type}.
Class Semantics (L : Language) (MD : Model) :=
   {denotation : expr -> model -> Prop}.
```

That is: a semantics is defined as long as a denotation function maps every propositional expression to a subset of "models", the set of models where it is satisfied. Here, the "model" set, which may be different in different semantics, is defined by type class Model. Based on Model and Semantics, we can define semantics of different connectives. For example, "AndSemantics L MD SM" says SM is a semantics defining on language L and models MD; this language has at least one connective, conjunction; and $\varphi \wedge \psi$ is satisfied if and only if both φ and ψ is satisfied for any φ and ψ.

```
Class AndSemantics (L: Language) {_: AndLanguage L}
   (MD: Model) (SM: Semantics L MD) :=
   {denote_andp : for any m φ ψ, m ⊨ φ ∧ ψ iff. m ⊨ φ and m ⊨ ψ }.
```

Typically, a logic's soundness is proved by induction over proof trees and it suffices to prove that all primary proof rules preserve validity. We achieve proof reuse in LOGIC by formalizing these validity preservation lemmas, under parameterized assumptions over semantic definitions. For example, the validity preservation of MODUSPONENS is formalized in the following lemma.

```
Lemma sound_modus_ponens:
  forall {L: Language} {MD: Model} {kMD: KripkeModel MD}
         {M: Kmodel} {SM: Semantics L MD}
         {__:ImpLanguage L} {__:IL.Relation (Kworlds M)}
         {__:KripkeIntuitionisticSemantics L MD M SM}
         {__:KripkeImpSemantics L MD M SM},
```

for any $\varphi\ \psi$, if $\varphi \to \psi$ and φ are valid on M, then ψ is valid on M .

4.4   Completeness

Completeness proofs are usually more complicated than simple inductions on proof trees. In LOGIC, we leverage a Henkin-style completeness proof, which consists of the following steps.[2]

– Proof by contradiction: assume $\Phi \nvdash \varphi$.
– Lindenbaum construction: find a "good" set Ψ such that $\Psi \supseteq \Phi$ and $\Psi \nvdash \varphi$.
– Canonical model construction: define a Kripke model $\mathcal{M}^c$ whose possible worlds are all "good" sets.
– Truth lemma: prove that for any Θ and θ, $\mathcal{M}^c, \Theta \vDash \theta$ if and only if $\theta \in \Theta$.
– Achieving contradiction: $\Phi \nvDash \varphi$, since $\mathcal{M}^c, \Psi \vDash \Phi$ but $\mathcal{M}^c, \Psi \nvDash \varphi$.

Parameterized Lindenbaum Construction. The target of Lindenbaum construction is to find a super set $\Psi \supseteq \Phi$ (given Φ) such that $\mathcal{F}(\Psi)$. Lindenbaum constructions always follow this routine:

$$\begin{aligned} &\Phi_0 = \Phi, \Psi = \bigcup_n \Phi_n \\ &\Phi_{n+1} = \Phi_n \cup \varphi_n \quad \text{if } \Phi_n \cup \varphi_n \text{ has property } \mathcal{G} \\ &\Phi_{n+1} = \Phi_n \quad\quad\ \text{if } \Phi_n \cup \varphi_n \text{ does not have property } \mathcal{G} \\ &\text{where } \{\varphi_n | n \in \mathbb{N}\} \text{ are all propositions.} \end{aligned} \quad (2)$$

In LOGIC, we first formalize the Lindenbaum construction process in (2) as: $\Psi = \mathrm{LC}(\Phi, \mathcal{G})$. Then all Lindenbaum construction lemmas share the same format: for any Φ, if $\mathcal{G}(\Phi)$, then $\mathcal{F}(\mathrm{LC}(\Phi, \mathcal{G}))$. We call it $\mathrm{LLS}(\mathcal{F}, \mathcal{G})$, where LLS stands for *Lindenbaum Lemma Statement*. It is worth clarifying that $\mathrm{LLS}(\mathcal{F}, \mathcal{G})$'s definition only depends on languages but does not depend on proof theories or semantics. Only when instantiating $\mathcal{F}$ and $\mathcal{G}$ with concrete sets of propositions, a proof theory would be needed in their definitions. We prove in Coq that $\mathrm{LLS}(\mathcal{F}, \mathcal{G})$ is compositional on $\mathcal{F}$ (Lindenbaum_by_conj). Additionally, we prove some general lemmas like Lindenbaum_self_by_finiteness and Lindenbaum_derivable_closed for $\mathcal{F}$'s common conjuncts.

---

[2] There has been previous work formalizing completeness of first-order logic [11]. We partially base our work on [8]. We significantly improve proof reuse and support more completeness proofs.

Lemma `Lindenbaum_by_conj` {L: Language }:

> for any $\mathcal{F}_1$, $\mathcal{F}_2$, and $\mathcal{G}$, if LLS($\mathcal{F}_1, \mathcal{G}$) and LLS($\mathcal{F}_2, \mathcal{G}$), then LLS($\mathcal{F}_1$ and $\mathcal{F}_2, \mathcal{G}$) .

Lemma `Lindenbaum_self_by_finiteness` {L: Language }:

> for any $\mathcal{G}$, if $\mathcal{G}$ is finite-captured and subset-preserved, then LLS($\mathcal{G}, \mathcal{G}$) .

Lemma `Lindenbaum_derivable_closed` {L: Language} {Gamma: Derivable L}:

> for any $\mathcal{G}$, if $\mathcal{G} \circ \partial$ is subset-preserved and LLS($\mathcal{G}, \mathcal{G}$), then LLS(derivable-closed, $\mathcal{G}$) .

Corollary `Lindenbaum_cannot_derive` {L: Language} {Gamma: Derivable L}:

> for any $\mathcal{G}$ φ, if $\mathcal{G}(\Phi)$ has form $\Phi \nvdash \varphi$ for any Φ, then LLS(derivable-closed, $\mathcal{G}$) .

Here, a property $\mathcal{G}$ is finite-captured means: for any Φ, if Φ's every finite subset has property $\mathcal{G}$, then Φ itself has property $\mathcal{G}$; a property $\mathcal{G}$ is subset-preserved means: for any $\Phi \supseteq \Psi$, if $\mathcal{G}(\Phi)$ then $\mathcal{G}(\Psi)$; and ∂ is a function from proposition sets to proposition sets such that $\partial(\Phi) = \{\varphi \mid \Phi \vdash \varphi\}$. Based on Coq's higher order feature, we are able to define concepts like finite-captured and use them in the lemmas above. As a result, we do not need to duplicate proofs in Coq for different Lindenbaum constructions.

Parameterized Well-Definedness. In Henkin-style proofs, we need to prove that the canonical model is indeed a legal model. For example, in separation logic's completeness proof, we should check whether the join relation is commutative in the canonical model, i.e. $\text{join}^c(\Phi, \Psi, \Theta)$ if and only if $\text{join}^c(\Psi, \Phi, \Theta)$ for any "good" sets Φ, Ψ and Θ. Here, join^c is the join relation in the canonical model, which is usually defined as:

$$\text{join}^c(\Phi, \Psi, \Theta) \text{ iff. } \Phi * \Psi \subseteq \Theta.$$

According to the definition of $\Phi * \Psi$, its proof is very straight forward since $\vdash \varphi * \psi \leftrightarrow \psi * \varphi$. However, its formalization is nontrivial since different separation logics' completeness may choose different definitions of "good". For classical separation logics, a "good" set is a maximal consistent set. For intuitionistic separation logics without disjunction ($\vee$) or false ($\bot$), a "good" set is a derivable-closed set. For intuitionistic separation logics with disjunction ($\vee$) and false ($\bot$), a "good" set is a derivable-closed, disjunction-witnessed, consistent set. In LOGIC, we prove the following general statement of join^c's commutativity.

Lemma `canonical_comm`:
> forall {L: Language} {GammaD : Derivable L} {__: SepconLanguage L}
> {__: BasicSequentCalculus L GammaD}
> {__: SepconSequentCalculus L GammaD},

> if every "good" set is derivable-closed, then join^c is commutative .

The main idea is: we do not prove a theorem for a specific definition of "good" sets; instead, we consider a general class of "good" sets. We use this method in many places in LOGIC for proving canonical model well-formed.

Parameterized Truth Lemma. Truth lemmas are usually proved by induction over propositions' syntax trees. For proof reuse, we formalize different induction steps separately for proof reuse as we do in soundness proofs (see Sect. 4.3). For example, the induction step of conjunction is to prove:

$$\text{If} \quad \text{for any } \Theta, \mathcal{M}^c, \Theta \vDash \varphi \text{ iff. } \varphi \in \Theta$$
$$\text{and for any } \Theta, \mathcal{M}^c, \Theta \vDash \psi \text{ iff. } \psi \in \Theta,$$
$$\text{then for any } \Theta, \mathcal{M}^c, \Theta \vDash \varphi \wedge \psi \text{ iff. } \varphi \wedge \psi \in \Theta.$$

Of course, the conclusion above is true only under some specific assumptions about "good" sets and canonical model's structures. We prove these lemmas based on relaxed classes of "good" sets again as we do before.

In summary, we decompose Henkin-style completeness proofs into small steps so that these intermediate conclusions can be proved in a parameterized way. We heavily use Coq's higher order logic in these generalized proofs. Readers can check our Coq development and see how we can easily combine components together and achieve formalized completeness proofs for concrete logics.

5 Logic Generator

We have in LOGIC a logic generator, which uses the parameterized definitions and proofs to support generating and exporting the desired logic libraries, so as to untangle the problems mentioned in Sect. 3. In Sect. 5.1, we introduce how users can leverage the logic generator to generate an exportable library of logic according to their requirements. In Sect. 5.2, we explain how the logic generator is implemented to perform the desired features.

5.1 Features of Logic Generator

In order to build a logic system (including its connectives, judgements, and proof rules) based on LOGIC's generator, one needs to take the following three steps. First of all, a *configuration* file is set up by the user indicating their logic's primitive connectives, judgements, and primary proof rules, as well as how the other primitives and judgements are derived. For example, if we want to formalize Mendelson's propositional logic, the configuration should be written as follows.

```
Definition how_connectives :=
[ primitive_connective impp;
  primitive_connective negp;
  FROM_impp_negp_TO_orp ].
Definition how_judgements :=
[ primitive_judgement provable;
  FROM_provable_TO_derivable1 ].
Definition primitive_rule_classes :=
[ provability_OF_impp;
  provability_OF_classical_logic_by_contra ].
```

The configuration above specifies the followings about the desired logic.

- There are three connectives in the logic's language: implication "$\rightarrow$", negation "$\neg$", and disjunction "$\vee$", where the first two are primitive, and the third one is derived by $\varphi \vee \psi \triangleq \neg\varphi \rightarrow \psi$.
- There are two judgements in the logic's proof system: provable "$\vdash \cdot$" and derivable1 "$\cdot \vdash \cdot$", where the former is primitive, and the latter is derived by $\varphi \vdash \psi \triangleq \vdash \varphi \rightarrow \psi$.
- The primitive proof rules of the logic include the followings, where the first three are basic proof rules for implication "$\rightarrow$", and the fourth is the contradiction rule.
  - MODUSPONES: for any $\varphi \; \psi$, if $\vdash (\varphi \rightarrow \psi)$ and $\vdash \varphi$, then $\vdash \psi$.
  - AXIOM1: for any $\varphi \; \psi$, $\vdash (\varphi \rightarrow (\psi \rightarrow \varphi))$.
  - AXIOM2: for any $\varphi \; \psi \; \chi$, $\vdash ((\varphi \rightarrow \psi \rightarrow \chi) \rightarrow (\varphi \rightarrow \psi) \rightarrow (\varphi \rightarrow \chi))$.
  - BYCONTRADICTION: for any $\varphi \; \psi$, $\vdash (\neg\varphi \rightarrow \psi) \rightarrow (\neg\varphi \rightarrow \neg\psi) \rightarrow \varphi$.

Then the logic generator takes the configuration as input, and outputs an *interface* file, which includes Coq module types illustrating primitive connectives, judgements and rules that users need to provide, and Coq functors that derive derived connectives, derived judgements and derived proof rules. The primitive types, connectives and judgements are included in the module type LanguageSig, which only indicates the types, and is to be implemented by the user.

```
Module Type LanguageSig.
  Parameter Inline expr : Type .
  Parameter provable : (expr -> Prop) .
  Parameter impp : (expr -> expr -> expr) .
  Parameter negp : (expr -> expr) .
End LanguageSig.
(* Automatically generated *)
```

Analogously, the primary rules are included in another module type PrimitiveRuleSig, also to be proved by the user.

```
Module Type PrimitiveRuleSig (Names: LanguageSig).
Include DerivedNames (Names).
```

Axiom by_contradiction : $\boxed{\text{for any } \varphi \; \psi, \vdash (\neg\varphi \rightarrow \psi) \rightarrow (\neg\varphi \rightarrow \neg\psi) \rightarrow \varphi}$.

Axiom modus_ponens : $\boxed{\text{for any } \varphi \; \psi, \text{ if } \vdash (\varphi \rightarrow \psi) \text{ and } \vdash \varphi, \text{ then } \vdash \psi}$.

Axiom axiom1 : $\boxed{\text{for any } \varphi \; \psi, \vdash (\varphi \rightarrow (\psi \rightarrow \varphi))}$.

Axiom axiom2 : $\boxed{\text{for any } \varphi \; \psi \; \chi, \vdash ((\varphi \rightarrow \psi \rightarrow \chi) \rightarrow (\varphi \rightarrow \psi) \rightarrow (\varphi \rightarrow \chi))}$.

```
End PrimitiveRuleSig.
(* Automatically generated *)
```

All the proof rules that can be derived using the primary ones are included in the module LogicTheorems. To give a taste of what are the rules that can be derived, we list some of the rules included in LogicTheorems.

- DERIVABLE1REFL: for any φ, $\varphi \vdash \varphi$;
- DERIVABLE1TRANS: for any $\varphi \; \psi \; \chi$, if $\varphi \vdash \psi$ and $\psi \vdash \chi$, then $\varphi \vdash \chi$;
- IMPP2ORP1: for any $\varphi \; \psi$, $\vdash (\varphi \rightarrow \psi) \rightarrow (\neg\varphi \vee \psi)$;

– PEIRCELAW: for any $\varphi\ \psi, \vdash ((\varphi \to \psi) \to \varphi) \to \varphi$.

The first two of the above are included because the judgement derivable1 is derived by provable according to LOGIC's internal type classes. The third follows from an analogous reason. The fourth is included because we have the primary rule class provability_OF_classical_logic_by_contra making the given logic a classical logic, and there are internal lemmas that ensure such derivation is valid.

Guided by the interface file, the users need to provide concrete definitions of primitive connectives and judgements, and proofs of primary rules. These are done in an *implementation* file. LOGIC supports implementation of both deep embeddings (defining propositions by syntax trees) and shallow embeddings (defining propositions as the set of worlds where it is satisfied, without using syntax trees). If shallow embedding is employed, the implementation of primitive connectives and judgements can be written as follows.

```
Module NaiveLang.
    Definition expr := worlds -> Prop.
    Definition impp (x y : expr) : expr := fun m => if x m, then y m .
    Definition negp (x : expr) : expr := fun m => not x m .
    Definition provable (x : expr) : Prop := for any m, x m .
End NaiveLang.
```

Alternatively, if the user chooses to apply a deep embedding, the proposition (expr) should be defined as a syntax tree, as shown below. Here, an expr can be constructed in three different ways, corresponding to the two primitive connectives and the atom var, and provable can be derived in three different ways, corresponding to the four primitive rules.

```
Inductive expr: Type :=
  | impp : expr -> expr -> expr
  | negp : expr -> expr
  | varp : var -> expr.
```

```
Inductive provable: expr -> Prop :=
  | modus_ponens: for any φ ψ, if ⊢ (φ → ψ) and ⊢ φ, then ⊢ ψ
  | axiom1: for any φ ψ, ⊢ (φ → (ψ → φ))
  | axiom2: for any φ ψ χ, ⊢ ((φ → ψ → χ) → (φ → ψ) → (φ → χ)) .
  | by_contradiction: for any φ ψ, ⊢ (¬φ → ψ) → (¬φ → ¬ψ) → φ .
```

```
Module NaiveLang.
    Definition expr := expr.
    Definition impp := impp.
    Definition negp := negp.
    Definition provable := provable.
End NaiveLang.
```

No matter what kind of embedding is used, the primary rules need to be proved.

```
Module NaiveRule.
  Include DerivedNames (NaiveLang).
  Lemma by_contradiction : ... Proof. ... Qed.
  Lemma modus_ponens : ... Proof. ... Qed.
  Lemma axiom1 : ... Proof. ... Qed.
  Lemma axiom2 : ... Proof. ... Qed.
```

Once these are done, an exported library is ready. We have many examples of using the logic generator, which we list in the appendix.

5.2 Design of Logic Generator

Here is a brief sketch of our design: we put all connectives, judgements and primary proof rules that we support in LOGIC into a built-in list; we record dependencies among them with a dependency graph; and we compute all derivable connectives, judgements and rules from user's input (the configuration file) based on this graph. The dependencies we document in the dependency graph involve the followings:

- The dependency between connectives, judgements. For example, specifying FROM_impp_negp_TO_orp in the list how_connectives depends on the connectives injunction "→" and negation "¬".
- The dependency between rules. This is computed internally in the logic generator. For example, the derived rules of some connectives' properties depend on the users' input rules and the derivation of the connectives.

It is worth mentioning that the dependency graph is not typed into our source code manually, we develop a Coq tactic to analyze dependent types of Coq terms and use that tactic to generate the graph automatically. With the dependency lists and computations mentioned above, we are ready to generate and print the interface according to the configuration given by the users.

6 Related Work

We are not the first one to formalize logic studies in theorem provers. Blanchette *et al.* formalized FOL completeness in Isabelle/HOL using its codata type. Foster *et al.* formalized FOL completeness [11] and undecidability [12] in Coq. Tews [23] formalized cut elimination for propositional multi-modal logics in Coq. There are many other works that we do not have space to enumerate here. Comparing to these previous work, we do not yet support first order quantifiers but we are the first one who systematically support different choices of primitive connectives (not fixing the set of connectives), logic extension (not fixing the set of primary proof rules) and compositional proof formalization (especially for completeness).

If using shallow embeddings in formalization, logics are extensible since there is no limitation on which connectives can/cannot be involved. Jensen [14] formalized soundness theorems for a wide range of separation logic and their semantics. Benzmüller and Paleo [5] formalized shallowly embedded modal logics in Coq and formalized Gödel's ontological argument based on that. Henz and Hobor [13] taught propositional modal using a formalization in Coq. The famous formalized text book *Software Foundations* [20] uses shallow embeddings to formalize assertions and Hoare logics. However, these works limit themselves in using shallow embedding, thus completeness proofs cannot be formalized in their framework.

Many research groups have developed different program verification tools based on theorem provers. Benzmuller and Claus [4] formalized higher-order multi-modal logic in Isabelle using shallow embedding and provide a proof automation library in Isabelle. VST [1,7] enables users to prove C programs correct using a shallowly embedded impredicative higher-order concurrent separation logic with a semi-automatic tactic library. Bedrock [9] are designed for low level program verification. Iris proof mode (IPM) [17] provides a tactic library for building interactive separation logic proofs. None of these verification projects can be applied to different (but similar) logics like LOGIC if not causing any overhead. For example, IPM's users should provide instances for IPM's BI type class and affined-BI type class, which causes some overhead. VST uses a rich enough memory model for C so that it can use a fixed Coq type "environ −> mpred" for C programs' assertion language. However, some of its proof rules are proved sound using a general separation logic framework VST-MSL. Thus, this generalization-instantiation process causes overhead in some of its proof automation. In comparison, LOGIC supports parameterized reasoning for internal proofs and exports proof libraries with no efficiency overhead.

7   Conclusion

In this paper, we present LOGIC which formalizes logics' meta-theories and can be used to generate exportable logic libraries. For formalized meta-theories, LOGIC is the first to support different logic settings (like primitive connectives and primary proof rules) in one uniform system. It also provides support for compositionally building completeness proofs. For logic applications, LOGIC aims to provide multi-scenario support with proof automation tactics and related proof rules. For example, users would like to have a rich language, a powerful logic and efficient proof construction commands in real program verification. But for educational purpose, a teacher may prefer to use a simple logic to explain the key ideas involved. LOGIC can export libraries for both scenarios according to users' configuration.

Acknowledgement. This research is sponsored by National Natural Science foundation of China (NSFC) Grant No. 61902240.

A   Sample Use Cases of Logic Generator

A.1   Demo1: Intuitionistic Propositional Logic

Primitive connectives: $\rightarrow, \wedge, \vee, \perp$.
Syntactic sugar for connectives: $\varphi \leftrightarrow \psi \triangleq (\varphi \rightarrow \psi) \wedge (\psi \rightarrow \varphi)$, $\neg \varphi \triangleq \varphi \rightarrow \perp$, $\top \triangleq \perp \rightarrow \perp$.

Primitive judgements: provable ($\vdash \varphi$).
Syntactic sugar for judgements: for any $\Phi\,\varphi$, $\Phi \vdash \varphi$ iff. exists $\varphi_1, \varphi_2, \ldots, \varphi_n \in \Phi$, s.t. $\vdash \varphi_1 \to \varphi_2 \to \cdots \to \varphi_n \to \varphi$.
Primary rules:

- PEIRCELAW: for any $\varphi\,\psi$, $\vdash ((\varphi \to \psi) \to \psi) \to \psi$;
- FALSEPELIM: for any φ, $\vdash \bot \to \varphi$;
- ORPINTROS1: for any $\varphi\,\psi$, $\vdash \varphi \to (\varphi \vee \psi)$;
- ORPINTROS2: for any $\varphi\,\psi$, $\vdash \psi \to (\varphi \vee \psi)$;
- OPRELIM: for any $\varphi\,\psi\,\chi$, $\vdash (\varphi \to \chi) \to (\psi \to \chi) \to ((\varphi \vee \psi) \to \chi)$;
- ANDPINTROS: for any $\varphi\,\psi$, $\vdash \varphi \to \psi \to (\varphi \wedge \psi)$;
- ANDPELIM1: for any $\varphi\,\psi$, $\vdash (\varphi \wedge \psi) \to \varphi$;
- ANDPELIM2: for any $\varphi\,\psi$, $\vdash (\varphi \wedge \psi) \to \psi$;
- MODUSPONES: for any $\varphi\,\psi$, if $\vdash \varphi \to \psi$ and $\vdash \varphi$, then $\vdash \psi$;
- AXIOM1: for any $\varphi\,\psi$, $\vdash \varphi \to (\psi \to \varphi)$;
- AXIOM2: for any $\varphi\,\psi\,\chi$, $\vdash (\varphi \to \psi \to \chi) \to (\varphi \to \psi) \to (\varphi \to \chi)$.

A.2   Demo2: A Very Small Logic

Primitive connectives: $\to$.
Primitive judgements: provable ($\vdash \varphi$).
Primary rules:

- MODUSPONES: for any $\varphi\,\psi$, if $\vdash \varphi \to \psi$ and $\vdash \varphi$, then $\vdash \psi$;
- AXIOM1: for any $\varphi\,\psi$, $\vdash \varphi \to (\psi \to \varphi)$;
- AXIOM2: for any $\varphi\,\psi\,\chi$, $\vdash (\varphi \to \psi \to \chi) \to (\varphi \to \psi) \to (\varphi \to \chi)$.

A.3   Demo3: Intuitionistic Propositional Logic

Primitive connectives: $\to, \wedge, \vee, \bot$.
Syntactic sugar for connectives: $\varphi \leftrightarrow \psi \triangleq (\varphi \to \psi) \wedge (\psi \to \varphi)$, $\neg\varphi \triangleq \varphi \to \bot$, $\top \triangleq \bot \to \bot$, $\bigwedge_{i=1}^{n} \varphi_i \triangleq \varphi_1 \wedge \ldots \wedge \varphi_n$.
Primitive judgements: derivable $\Phi \vdash \varphi$.
Syntactic sugar for judgements: for any φ, $\vdash \varphi$ iff. $\emptyset \vdash \varphi$.
Primary rules:

- DEDFALSEPELIM: for any $\Phi\,\varphi$, if $\Phi \vdash \bot$, then $\Phi \vdash \varphi$;
- DEDORPINTROS1: for any $\Phi\,\varphi\,\psi$, if $\Phi \vdash \varphi$, then $\Phi \vdash \varphi \vee \psi$;
- DEDORPINTROS1: for any $\Phi\,\varphi\,\psi$, if $\Phi \vdash \psi$, then $\Phi \vdash \varphi \vee \psi$;
- DEDORPELIM: for any $\Phi\,\varphi\,\psi\,\chi$, if $\Phi \cup \varphi \vdash \chi$ and $\Phi \cup \psi \vdash \chi$, then $\Phi \cup (\varphi \vee \psi) \vdash \chi$;
- DEDANDPINTROS: for any $\Phi\,\varphi\,\psi$, if $\Phi \vdash \varphi$ and $\Phi \vdash \psi$, then $\Phi \vdash \varphi \wedge \psi$;
- DEDANDPELIM1: for any $\Phi\,\varphi\,\psi$, if $\Phi \vdash \varphi \wedge \psi$, then $\Phi \vdash \varphi$;
- DEDANDPELIM2: for any $\Phi\,\varphi\,\psi$, if $\Phi \vdash \varphi \wedge \psi$, then $\Phi \vdash \psi$;
- DEDMODUSPONENS: for any $\Phi\,\varphi\,\psi$, if $\Phi \vdash \varphi$ and $\Phi \vdash \varphi \to \psi$, then $\Phi \vdash \psi$;
- DEDIMPPINTROS: for any $\Phi\,\varphi\,\psi$, if $\Phi \cup \varphi \vdash \psi$, then $\Phi \vdash \varphi \to \psi$;
- DEDWEAKEN: for any $\Phi\,\Psi\,\varphi$, if Φ is included in Ψ and $\Phi \vdash \varphi$, then $\Psi \vdash \varphi$;
- DEDASSUM: for any $\Phi\,\varphi$, if φ belongs to Φ, then $\Phi \vdash \varphi$;
- DEDSUBST: for any $\Phi\,\Psi\,\psi$, if (for any φ, if φ belongs to Ψ, then $\Phi \vdash \varphi$) and $\Phi \cup \Psi \vdash \psi$, then $\Phi \vdash \psi$.

A.4   Demo4: Separation Logic, Without Separation Conjunction

Primitive connectives: $\wedge, \vee, \bot, \top, *, \mathbf{emp}$.
Syntactic sugar for connectives: $\bigwedge_{i=1}^{n} \varphi_i \triangleq \varphi_1 \wedge \ldots \wedge \varphi_n$, $*_{i=1}^{n} \varphi_i \triangleq \varphi_1 * \ldots * \varphi_n$.
Primitive judgements: derivable1 $\varphi \vdash \psi$.
Primary rules:

- FALSEPSEPCONLEFT: for any φ, $\bot * \varphi \vdash \bot$;
- ORPSEPCONLEFT: for any $\varphi\ \psi\ \chi$, $(\varphi \vee \psi) * \chi \vdash (\varphi * \chi) \vee (\psi * \chi)$;
- SEPCONEMPLEFT: for any φ, $\varphi * \mathbf{emp} \vdash \varphi$;
- SEPCONEMPRIGHT: for any φ, $\varphi \vdash \varphi * \mathbf{emp}$;
- DER1SEPCONCOMM: for any $\varphi\ \psi$, $\varphi * \psi \vdash \psi * \varphi$;
- DER1SEPCONASSOC1: for any $\varphi\ \psi\ \chi$, $\varphi * (\psi * \chi) \vdash (\varphi * \psi) * \chi$;
- DER1SEPCONMONO: for any $\varphi_1\ \varphi_2\ \psi_1\ \psi_2$, if $\varphi_1 \vdash \varphi_2$ and $\psi_1 \vdash \psi_2$, then $(\varphi_1 * \psi_1) \vdash (\varphi_2 * \psi_2)$;
- DER1TRUEPINTROS: for any φ, $\varphi \vdash \top$;
- DER1FALSEPELIM: for any φ, $\bot \vdash \varphi$;
- DER1ORPINTROS1: for any $\varphi\ \psi$, $\varphi \vdash \varphi \vee \psi$;
- DER1ORPINTROS2: for any $\varphi\ \psi$, $\psi \vdash \varphi \vee \psi$;
- DER1ORPELIM: for any $\varphi\ \psi\ \chi$, if $\varphi \vdash \chi$ and $\psi \vdash \chi$, then $\varphi \vee \psi \vdash \chi$;
- DER1ANDPINTROS: for any $\varphi\ \psi\ \chi$, if $\varphi \vdash \psi$ and $\varphi \vdash \chi$, then $\varphi \vdash \psi \wedge \chi$;
- DER1ANDPELIM1: for any $\varphi\ \psi$, $\varphi \wedge \psi \vdash \varphi$;
- DER1ANDPELIM2: for any $\varphi\ \psi$, $\varphi \wedge \psi \vdash \psi$.

A.5   Demo5: Separation Logic, with Separating Conjunction

Primary connectives: $\rightarrow, \wedge, \vee, \bot, *, -\!*, \mathbf{emp}$.
Syntactic sugar for connectives: $\varphi \leftrightarrow \psi \triangleq (\varphi \rightarrow \psi) \wedge (\psi \rightarrow \varphi)$, $\neg \varphi \triangleq \varphi \rightarrow \bot$, $\top \triangleq \bot \rightarrow \bot$, $\bigwedge_{i=1}^{n} \varphi_i \triangleq \varphi_1 \wedge \ldots \wedge \varphi_n$, $*_{i=1}^{n} \varphi_i \triangleq \varphi_1 * \ldots * \varphi_n$.
Primitive judgements: provable ($\vdash \varphi$).
Syntactic sugar for judgements: for any $\Phi\ \varphi$, $\Phi \vdash \varphi$ iff. exists $\varphi_1, \varphi_2, \ldots, \varphi_n \in \Phi$, s.t. $\vdash \varphi_1 \rightarrow \varphi_2 \rightarrow \cdots \rightarrow \varphi_n \rightarrow \varphi$.
Primary rules:

- SEPCONEMP: for any φ, $\vdash (\varphi * \mathbf{emp}) \leftrightarrow \varphi$;
- SEPCONCOMM: for any $\varphi\ \psi$, $\vdash (\varphi * \psi) \leftrightarrow (\psi * \varphi)$;
- SEPCONASSOC: for any $\varphi\ \psi\ \chi$, $\vdash ((\varphi * \psi) * \chi) \leftrightarrow (\varphi * (\psi * \chi))$;
- WANDSEPCONADJOINT: for any $\varphi\ \psi\ \chi$, $\vdash ((\varphi * \psi) \rightarrow \chi) \leftrightarrow (\varphi \rightarrow (\psi -\!* \chi))$;
- PEIRCELAW: for any $\varphi\ \psi$, $\vdash ((\varphi \rightarrow \psi) \rightarrow \psi) \rightarrow \psi$;
- FALSEPELIM: for any φ, $\vdash \bot \rightarrow \varphi$;
- ORPINTROS1: for any $\varphi\ \psi$, $\vdash \varphi \rightarrow (\varphi \vee \psi)$;
- ORPINTROS2: for any $\varphi\ \psi$, $\vdash \psi \rightarrow (\varphi \vee \psi)$;
- OPRELIM: for any $\varphi\ \psi\ \chi$, $\vdash (\varphi \rightarrow \chi) \rightarrow (\psi \rightarrow \chi) \rightarrow ((\varphi \vee \psi) \rightarrow \chi)$;
- ANDPINTROS: for any $\varphi\ \psi$, $\vdash \varphi \rightarrow \psi \rightarrow (\varphi \wedge \psi)$;
- ANDPELIM1: for any $\varphi\ \psi$, $\vdash (\varphi \wedge \psi) \rightarrow \varphi$;
- ANDPELIM2: for any $\varphi\ \psi$, $\vdash (\varphi \wedge \psi) \rightarrow \psi$;
- MODUSPONES: for any $\varphi\ \psi$, if $\vdash \varphi \rightarrow \psi$ and $\vdash \varphi$, then $\vdash \psi$;
- AXIOM1: for any $\varphi\ \psi$, $\vdash \varphi \rightarrow (\psi \rightarrow \varphi)$;
- AXIOM2: for any $\varphi\ \psi\ \chi$, $\vdash (\varphi \rightarrow \psi \rightarrow \chi) \rightarrow (\varphi \rightarrow \psi) \rightarrow (\varphi \rightarrow \chi)$.

A.6   Demo6: Separation Logic, Without Separating Implication

Primitive connectives: $\rightarrow, \wedge, *, \mathbf{emp}$.
Syntactic sugar for connectives: $\varphi \leftrightarrow \psi \triangleq (\varphi \rightarrow \psi) \wedge (\psi \rightarrow \varphi)$.
Primitive judgement: provable ($\vdash \varphi$).
Syntactic sugar for judgements: for any $\Phi \varphi$, $\Phi \vdash \varphi$ iff. exists $\varphi_1, \varphi_2, \ldots, \varphi_n \in \Phi$, s.t. $\vdash \varphi_1 \rightarrow \varphi_2 \rightarrow \cdots \rightarrow \varphi_n \rightarrow \varphi$;
for any $\psi \varphi$, $\psi \dashv\vdash \varphi$ iff. $\vdash \psi \rightarrow \varphi$ and $\vdash \varphi \rightarrow \psi$.
Primary rules:

- SEPCONEMP: for any φ, $\vdash (\varphi * \mathbf{emp}) \leftrightarrow \varphi$;
- SEPCONCOMM: for any $\varphi \psi$, $\vdash (\varphi * \psi) \leftrightarrow (\psi * \varphi)$;
- SEPCONASSOC: for any $\varphi \psi \chi$, $\vdash ((\varphi * \psi) * \chi) \leftrightarrow (\varphi * (\psi * \chi))$;
- SEPCONMONO: for any $\varphi_1 \varphi_2 \psi_1 \psi_2$, if $\vdash \varphi_1 \rightarrow \varphi_2$ and $\vdash \psi_1 \rightarrow \psi_2$, then $\vdash (\varphi_1 * \psi_1) \rightarrow (\varphi_2 * \psi_2)$;
- ANDPINTROS: for any $\varphi \psi$, $\vdash \varphi \rightarrow \psi \rightarrow (\varphi \wedge \psi)$;
- ANDPELIM1: for any $\varphi \psi$, $\vdash (\varphi \wedge \psi) \rightarrow \varphi$;
- ANDPELIM2: for any $\varphi \psi$, $\vdash (\varphi \wedge \psi) \rightarrow \psi$;
- MODUSPONES: for any $\varphi \psi$, if $\vdash \varphi \rightarrow \psi$ and $\vdash \varphi$, then $\vdash \psi$;
- AXIOM1: for any $\varphi \psi$, $\vdash \varphi \rightarrow (\psi \rightarrow \varphi)$;
- AXIOM2: for any $\varphi \psi \chi$, $\vdash (\varphi \rightarrow \psi \rightarrow \chi) \rightarrow (\varphi \rightarrow \psi) \rightarrow (\varphi \rightarrow \chi)$.

A.7   Demo7: Separation Logic, Constructed from Model Level

Primitive connectives: $\oplus, \mathbf{unit}$.
Syntactic sugar for connectives: define $\rightarrow, \wedge, \vee$ directly from model level, using Coq's meta-logic; $(\varphi * \psi)\, m \triangleq$ exists $m_1\, m_2$, $\oplus(m_1, m_2, m)$ and $\varphi\, m$ and $\psi\, m$; $\mathbf{emp}\, m \triangleq \mathbf{unit}\, m$.
Syntactic sugar for judgements: define provable ($\vdash \varphi$) and derivable1 ($\varphi \vdash \psi$) with Coq's meta-logic.
Primary rules:

- JOINCOMM: for any $m_1\, m_2\, m$, if $\oplus(m_1, m_2, m)$, then $\oplus(m_2, m_1, m)$;
- JOINASSOC: for any $m_1\quad m_2\quad m_3\quad m_{12}\quad m_{123}$, if $\oplus(m_1, m_2, m_{12})$ and $\oplus(m_{12}, m_3, m_{123})$, then (there exists m_{23}, $\oplus(m_2, m_3, m_{23})$ and $\oplus(m_1, m_{23}, m_{123})$).

A.8   Mendelson's Propositional Logic

Primitive connectives: $\rightarrow, \neg, \top$.
Syntactic sugar for connectives: $\varphi \vee \psi \triangleq \neg\varphi \rightarrow \psi$, $\bot \triangleq \neg\top$.
Primitive judgements: provable ($\vdash \varphi$).
Syntactic sugar for judgements: for any $\Phi \varphi$, $\Phi \vdash \varphi$ iff. exists $\varphi_1, \varphi_2, \ldots, \varphi_n \in \Phi$, s.t. $\vdash \varphi_1 \rightarrow \varphi_2 \rightarrow \cdots \rightarrow \varphi_n \rightarrow \varphi$.
Primary rules:

- BYCONTRADICTION: for any φ ψ, $\vdash (\neg\varphi \to \psi) \to (\neg\varphi \to \neg\psi) \to \varphi$.
- MODUSPONES: for any φ ψ, if $\vdash \varphi \to \psi$ and $\vdash \varphi$, then $\vdash \psi$;
- AXIOM1: for any φ ψ, $\vdash \varphi \to (\psi \to \varphi)$;
- AXIOM2: for any φ ψ χ, $\vdash (\varphi \to \psi \to \chi) \to (\varphi \to \psi) \to (\varphi \to \chi)$.

We have proved in Coq the completeness of this logic.

A.9 Minimum Separation Logic

Primitive connectives: $\to, \wedge, *$.
Primitive judgements: provable ($\vdash \varphi$).
Syntactic sugar for judgements: for any Φ φ, $\Phi \vdash \varphi$ iff. exists $\varphi_1, \varphi_2, \ldots, \varphi_n \in \Phi$, s.t. $\vdash \varphi_1 \to \varphi_2 \to \cdots \to \varphi_n \to \varphi$.
Primary rules:

- SEPCONCOMMIMPP: for any φ ψ, $\vdash (\varphi * \psi) \to (\psi * \varphi)$;
- SEPCONASSOC1: for any φ ψ χ, $\vdash (\varphi * (\psi * \chi)) \to ((\varphi * \psi) * \chi)$;
- SEPCONMONO: for any φ_1 φ_2 ψ_1 ψ_2, if $\vdash \varphi_1 \to \varphi_2$ and $\vdash \psi_1 \to \psi_2$, then $\vdash (\varphi_1 * \psi_1) \to (\varphi_2 * \psi_2)$;
- ANDPINTROS: for any φ ψ, $\vdash \varphi \to \psi \to (\varphi \wedge \psi)$;
- ANDPELIM1: for any φ ψ, $\vdash (\varphi \wedge \psi) \to \varphi$;
- ANDPELIM2: for any φ ψ, $\vdash (\varphi \wedge \psi) \to \psi$;
- MODUSPONES: for any φ ψ, if $\vdash \varphi \to \psi$ and $\vdash \varphi$, then $\vdash \psi$;
- AXIOM1: for any φ ψ, $\vdash \varphi \to (\psi \to \varphi)$;
- AXIOM2: for any φ ψ χ, $\vdash (\varphi \to \psi \to \chi) \to (\varphi \to \psi) \to (\varphi \to \chi)$.

We have proved in Coq the completeness of this logic.

A.10 Demo for Bedrock2's Separation Logic

Primitive connectives: $\to, \wedge, *, \mathbf{emp}$.
Syntactic sugar for connectives: $\varphi \leftrightarrow \psi \triangleq (\varphi \to \psi) \leftrightarrow (\psi \to \varphi)$.
Primitive judgements: provable ($\vdash \varphi$).
Syntactic sugar for judgements: for any ψ φ, $\psi \vdash \varphi$ iff. $\vdash \psi \to \varphi$;
for any ψ φ, $\psi \dashv\vdash \varphi$ iff. $\vdash \psi \to \varphi$ and $\vdash \varphi \to \psi$.
Primary rules:

- SEPCONEMP: for any φ, $\vdash (\varphi * \mathbf{emp}) \leftrightarrow \varphi$;
- SEPCONCOMM: for any φ ψ, $\vdash (\varphi * \psi) \leftrightarrow (\psi * \varphi)$;
- SEPCONASSOC: for any φ ψ χ, $\vdash ((\varphi * \psi) * \chi) \leftrightarrow (\varphi * (\psi * \chi))$;
- SEPCONMONO: for any φ_1 φ_2 ψ_1 ψ_2, if $\vdash \varphi_1 \to \varphi_2$ and $\vdash \psi_1 \to \psi_2$, then $\vdash (\varphi_1 * \psi_1) \to (\varphi_2 * \psi_2)$;
- ANDPINTROS: for any φ ψ, $\vdash \varphi \to \psi \to (\varphi \wedge \psi)$;
- ANDPELIM1: for any φ ψ, $\vdash (\varphi \wedge \psi) \to \varphi$;
- ANDPELIM2: for any φ ψ, $\vdash (\varphi \wedge \psi) \to \psi$;
- MODUSPONES: for any φ ψ, if $\vdash \varphi \to \psi$ and $\vdash \varphi$, then $\vdash \psi$;
- AXIOM1: for any φ ψ, $\vdash \varphi \to (\psi \to \varphi)$;
- AXIOM2: for any φ ψ χ, $\vdash (\varphi \to \psi \to \chi) \to (\varphi \to \psi) \to (\varphi \to \chi)$.

References

1. Appel, A.W.: Verified software toolchain. In: Barthe, G. (ed.) ESOP 2011. LNCS, vol. 6602, pp. 1–17. Springer, Heidelberg (2011). https://doi.org/10.1007/978-3-642-19718-5_1
2. Appel, A.W.: Verifiable C, chap. 5–17, 21, 35–39 (2016)
3. Barras, B., et al.: The coq Proof Assistant reference manual. Technical report, INRIA (1998)
4. Benzmüller, C., Claus, M., Sultana, N.: Systematic verification of the modal logic cube in Isabelle/Hol. In: Kaliszyk, C., Paskevich, A. (eds.) Proceedings Fourth Workshop on Proof eXchange for Theorem Proving, PxTP 2015, Berlin, Germany, 2–3 August 2015. EPTCS, vol. 186, pp. 27–41 (2015), https://doi.org/10.4204/EPTCS.186.5
5. Benzmüller, C., Woltzenlogel Paleo, B.: Interacting with modal logics in the coq proof assistant. In: Beklemishev, L.D., Musatov, D.V. (eds.) CSR 2015. LNCS, vol. 9139, pp. 398–411. Springer, Cham (2015). https://doi.org/10.1007/978-3-319-20297-6_25
6. Bertot, Y., Castéran, P.: Interactive Theorem Proving and Program Development - Coq'Art: The Calculus of Inductive Constructions. Texts in Theoretical Computer Science. An EATCS Series, Springer, Heidelberg (2004). https://doi.org/10.1007/978-3-662-07964-5
7. Cao, Q., Beringer, L., Gruetter, S., Dodds, J., Appel, A.W.: VST-FLOYD: a separation logic tool to verify correctness of C programs. J. Autom. Reason. 61(1–4), 367–422 (2018). https://doi.org/10.1007/s10817-018-9457-5
8. Cao, Q., Cuellar, S., Appel, A.W.: Bringing order to the separation logic jungle. In: Chang, B.-Y.E. (ed.) APLAS 2017. LNCS, vol. 10695, pp. 190–211. Springer, Cham (2017). https://doi.org/10.1007/978-3-319-71237-6_10
9. Chlipala, A.: The bedrock structured programming system: combining generative metaprogramming and Hoare logic in an extensible program verifier. In: Morrisett, G., Uustalu, T. (eds.) ACM SIGPLAN International Conference on Functional Programming, ICFP 2013, Boston, MA, USA - 25–27 September 2013, pp. 391–402. ACM (2013). https://doi.org/10.1145/2500365.2500592
10. Ebbinghaus, H., Flum, J., Thomas, W.: Mathematical Logic. Undergraduate Texts in Mathematics, vol. 291, 2nd edn. Springer, Cham (1994). https://doi.org/10.1007/978-3-030-73839-6
11. Forster, Y., Kirst, D., Wehr, D.: Completeness theorems for first-order logic analysed in constructive type theory. J. Log. Comput. 31(1), 112–151 (2021). https://doi.org/10.1093/logcom/exaa073
12. Forster, Y., Larchey-Wendling, D.: Certified undecidability of intuitionistic linear logic via binary stack machines and Minsky machines. In: Mahboubi, A., Myreen, M.O. (eds.) Proceedings of the 8th ACM SIGPLAN International Conference on Certified Programs and Proofs, CPP 2019, Cascais, Portugal, 14–15 January 2019, pp. 104–117. ACM (2019). https://doi.org/10.1145/3293880.3294096
13. Henz, M., Hobor, A.: Teaching experience: logic and formal methods with coq. In: Jouannaud, J.-P., Shao, Z. (eds.) CPP 2011. LNCS, vol. 7086, pp. 199–215. Springer, Heidelberg (2011). https://doi.org/10.1007/978-3-642-25379-9_16
14. Jensen, J.B.: Techniques for model construction in separation logic. Ph.D. thesis, IT University of Copenhagen, March 2014. https://public.knef.dk.s3-website-us-east-1.amazonaws.com/research/sltut.pdf

15. Jung, R., Jourdan, J., Krebbers, R., Dreyer, D.: RustBelt: securing the foundations of the rust programming language. Proc. ACM Program. Lang. **2**(POPL), 66:1–66:34 (2018). https://doi.org/10.1145/3158154

16. Jung, R., et al.: Iris: Monoids and invariants as an orthogonal basis for concurrent reasoning. In: Rajamani, S.K., Walker, D. (eds.) Proceedings of the 42nd Annual ACM SIGPLAN-SIGACT Symposium on Principles of Programming Languages, POPL 2015, Mumbai, India, 15–17 January 2015, pp. 637–650. ACM (2015). https://doi.org/10.1145/2676726.2676980

17. Krebbers, R., et al.: Mosel: a general, extensible modal framework for interactive proofs in separation logic. PACMPL. **2**(ICFP), 77:1–77:30 (2018). https://doi.org/10.1145/3236772

18. Mendelson, E.: Introduction to Mathematical Logic, 3rd edn. Chapman and Hall, London (1987)

19. Paulson, L.C. (ed.): Isabelle. LNCS, vol. 828. Springer, Heidelberg (1994). https://doi.org/10.1007/BFb0030541

20. Pierce, B.C., et al.: Software foundations. Webpage: https://wwwcis.upenn.edu/bcpierce/sf/current/index.html (2010)

21. Sieczkowski, F., Bizjak, A., Birkedal, L.: ModuRes: a COQ library for modular reasoning about concurrent higher-order imperative programming languages. In: Urban, C., Zhang, X. (eds.) ITP 2015. LNCS, vol. 9236, pp. 375–390. Springer, Cham (2015). https://doi.org/10.1007/978-3-319-22102-1_25

22. Sozeau, M., Oury, N.: First-class type classes. In: Mohamed, O.A., Muñoz, C., Tahar, S. (eds.) TPHOLs 2008. LNCS, vol. 5170, pp. 278–293. Springer, Heidelberg (2008). https://doi.org/10.1007/978-3-540-71067-7_23

23. Tews, H.: Formalizing cut elimination of coalgebraic logics in COQ. In: Galmiche, D., Larchey-Wendling, D. (eds.) TABLEAUX 2013. LNCS (LNAI), vol. 8123, pp. 257–272. Springer, Heidelberg (2013). https://doi.org/10.1007/978-3-642-40537-2_22

Diversifying a Parallel SAT Solver
with Bayesian Moment Matching

Vincent Vallade[1(✉)], Saeed Nejati[4], Julien Sopena[1,2], Souheib Baarir[1,3],
and Vijay Ganesh[5]

[1] Sorbonne Université, CNRS, 75005, Paris, France
vincent.vallade@lip6.fr
[2] Sorbonne Université, Inria, 75005, Paris, France
[3] Paris Nanterre University, CNRS (Now at EPITA), 75005 Paris, France
[4] Amazon Web Services, Seattle, USA
[5] University of Waterloo, Waterloo, Canada

Abstract. In this paper, we present a Bayesian Moment Matching
(BMM) in-processing technique for Conflict-Driven Clause-Learning
(CDCL) SAT solvers. BMM is a probabilistic algorithm which takes as
input a Boolean formula in conjunctive normal form and a prior on a possible satisfying assignment, and outputs a posterior for a new assignment
most likely to maximize the number of satisfied clauses. We invoke this
BMM method, as an in-processing technique, with the goal of updating
the polarity and branching activity scores. The key insight underpinning
our method is that Bayesian reasoning is a powerful way to guide the
CDCL search procedure away from fruitless parts of the search space of
a satisfiable Boolean formula, and towards those regions that are likely
to contain satisfying assignments.

1 Introduction

Modern Conflict-Driven Clause-Learning (CDCL) SAT solvers have been used
successfully to solve a wide variety of real-world problems, coming from a variety
of domains such as hardware and software verification/testing [3,5], security [2],
cryptography [11], and resolving mathematical conjectures [4].

In their paper [7], Duan et al. present a Bayesian Moment Matching (BMM)
based probabilistic learning algorithm that was used as a pre-processor to a
CDCL SAT solver with the aim of providing an initial assignment for the solver's
search to start from (the problem of finding an optimal initial assignment to start
a solver's search from is often referred to as the initialization problem). The
BMM method for the Boolean SAT problem takes as input a Boolean formula
in Conjunctive Normal Form (CNF) and a probability assignment $P(x = T)$
for every variable x that captures the likelihood of that variable x being true
according to the method (where the corresponding joint probability distribution
over the value assignment to the variables of the input formula is referred to as
the *prior*), and outputs a joint probability distribution or posterior that is most

W. Dong and J.-P. Talpin (Eds.): SETTA 2022, LNCS 13649, pp. 227–233, 2022.
https://doi.org/10.1007/978-3-031-21213-0_14

likely to maximize the number of satisfied clauses. The BMM method repeatedly applies Bayesian inference update rule on the input distribution and uses each clause in the input formula as evidence in order to compute the output posterior. The learned probabilities collectively represent an assignment that most likely satisfies most of the clauses (if not all). While Dual et al. report excellent results of using BMM as a pre-processor to solve the initialization problem, they didn't use it in any other way in their solver.

In this paper, we propose a BMM-based in-processing technique to update the polarity and branching scores of a CDCL solver. The choice of the prior distribution can affect the quality of the learned posterior distribution, and BMM uses Bayesian inference starting from a random prior. Therefore, running the same solver with different initial seeds could lead to different performance results. However, this behavior can be exploited in parallel portfolio settings, where the solvers are run with different priors. Therefore, in this paper we also evaluate the use of BMM approach for diversification of parallel portfolio solvers.

2   Algorithm Description

We refer the reader to [7] for a full description of the BMM method. We use the same methodology by applying the BMM method as a preprocessing mechanism to initialize the polarity and branching order (or activity) of the variables. In this paper, we go further and use the BMM method as an in-processor to update these same metrics. Algorithm 1 gives an overview of CDCL, along with the BMM update technique (see the shaded instructions).

We recall that the CDCL algorithm is based on a main loop that first applies unitPropagation[1] on the formula $\mathcal{F}$ simplified by the current assignment $\mathcal{A}$ (Line 6). If the formula is empty, the algorithm returns $true$ (Line 9), and $\mathcal{A}$ is the model. If the formula implies an empty clause, then two scenarios are possible: (i) we are at level 0 and the algorithm returns $false$ (Line 13); (ii) otherwise we deduce the reasons for the empty clause and a backjump point is computed (Lines 15–18). Otherwise, a new literal is selected to make progress in the resolution of $\mathcal{F}$ (Lines 23–24). Note that lvl represents the number of decisions in the current branch, often called $decision$ $level$.

We augment the aforementioned algorithm with the BMM procedure as a pre-processor, as well as an in-processing search re-initializer of variable polarities and activities (guiding the algorithm at key points of its progression). The shaded instructions in Algorithm 1 implement both the pre-$processing$ and in-$processing$ steps. These steps are described in the following paragraphs.

Pre-processing Step: BMM is called to initialize the polarity and activity of the variables (Line 4). During pre-processing, the input to BMM are the input clauses and a randomly-generated prior distribution for each variable. Because this step is executed once, we can afford more computational cost to get to a

---

[1] The unitPropagation function implements the Boolean constraint propagation (BCP) procedure that forces (in cascade) the values of variables in unit clauses [6].

Algorithm 1: Conflict-driven clause learning algorithm with Bayesian Moment Matching (CDCL + BMM).

```
1 function CDCL(F: CNF formula)
     /* returns true if F is SAT else false (UNSAT)              */
2      A ← ∅                                    // Current assignment
3      lvl ← 0                                  // Current decision level
4      bmmUpdate()                              // Call BMM with K = 100
5      forever
6          (F', A') ← unitPropagation(F|_A)
7          A ← A ∪ A'                           // Add propagated literals in A
8          if F' = ∅ then
9          |   return true                                  // F is SAT
10         end
11         if ∅ ∈ F' then            // There is a conflict to be analysed
12             if lvl = 0 then
13             |   return false                             // F is UNSAT
14             end
15             C ← conflictAnalysis(F, A)
16             F ← F ∪ {C}
17             lvl ← backjumpAndRestart(lvl, C, ...)
18             A ← {ℓ ∈ A | δ(ℓ) ≤ lvl}
19         else
20             if threshold limit is reached then
21             |   bmmUpdate()                      // Call BMM with K = 10
22             end
23             A ← A ∪ {pickBranching()}    // Pick a new decision literal
24             lvl ← lvl + 1
25         end
26     end
27 end
```

---

more accurate posterior distribution. Therefore the number of passes over the set of input clauses is set to $K = 100$.

In-Processing Step: When the unit propagation reaches a fix point (Line 21), i.e. no unit clauses left to propagate and there is no conflict, BMM procedure is called to re-evaluate the probabilities for all variables. The difference here is that the prior distribution given to BMM is determined by the assignment trail (probability of variables on the trail is set to zero or one according to their polarity), and the rest of the variables are updated based on this prior. Moreover, a subset of the learnt clauses is considered as evidence by BMM (those learnt clauses that have a LBD [1] value less than or equal to 3). Unlike the pre-processing step, this step is executed several times during the search process, therefore we limit the number of passes over the set of clauses to $K = 10$.

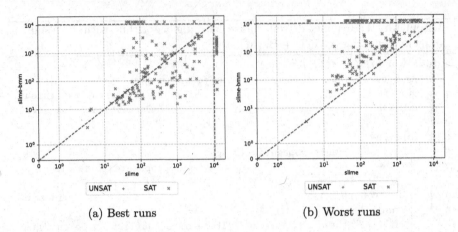

(a) Best runs   (b) Worst runs

Fig. 1. Scatter plot showing the performance of the `slime-bmm` vs `slime` sequential solvers on the 2021 SAT Competition Crypto benchmark.

The BMM update process has a considerable overhead, therefore we only call the update whenever a certain threshold is reached. This threshold is crossed when the solver has restarted 50 times and whenever the number of variables in the "current" assignment trail exceeds 40% of the total number of variables in the input formula or the current trail size is larger than 90% of the largest trail seen so far[2]. The learned posterior distribution over all variables together with the trail are used in the `pickBranching()` of the CDCL to further extend the search tree.

The pre-processing step is similar to the pre-processing component in [7], however, the in-processing step has a novel design. In the original BMM paper, authors only update the BMM probabilities when a unary or binary clause is learned, and use those clauses as new evidence. Learning unary and binary clauses mean that solver can learn valuable information from the search subspace that it is exploring. However, it is equally important to help guide the search of the CDCL solver whenever the BCP has reached a fix-point (i.e., is not making progress) by modifying the polarity and activity prior to branching. Therefore, we designed this BMM update method to be called to guide the solver's search whenever the BCP is not making progress (i.e., there are no prospects of further learning without making decisions).

3   Evaluation of slime and bmm Sequential Solvers

We chose to compare the efficacy of our BMM technique in the context of crypto benchmarks, given its previous success in this domain [11]. We chose the winner of the crypto track of the SAT competition 2021[3], called `slime` [12], as the base

---

[2] These magic numbers are borrowed from the base solver that we used for our implementation.

[3] https://satcompetition.github.io/2021/.

Table 1. This table shows performance of `p-slime` and `p-slime-bmm` on the 2021 Crypto Track.

Solvers	PAR2	UNSAT	SAT	TOTAL (200)
p-slime- bmm-50%	133H36	13	147	160
p-slime-bmm-75%	136H05	13	145	158
p-slime-bmm-90%	138H39	13	144	157
p-slime	142H03	13	142	155
p-slime-bmm-25%	147H42	13	140	153

CDCL engine for our implementation[4], and evaluated it on the crypto track benchmarks from the same competition.

It is worth noting that slime uses an in-processing approach similar to ours: a Stochastic Local Search (SLS) engine is used when the BCP reaches a fix point to guide the search. So, we replaced this component by our BMM procedure along with the removal of all heuristics related to the SLS sub-routine. It is this version that we refer to as `slime-bmm`.

Since the initialization of the BMM component induces randomness, we ran `slime-bmm` 10 times on each instance. As the `slime` configuration that won the competition was deterministic [12], a simple run of this latter was sufficient.

The scatter plots of Fig. 1 show the results of our experiment. Plot of Fig. 1a (respectively Fig. 1b) highlights the scores of solvers with respect to the best (respectively worst) runs. The axis are running time in seconds on a logarithmic scale. If both solvers timeout for an instance, it is not represented in the figures. So we can focus on the instances where one of the two solvers stands out. Even though the timeout is fixed at 5000 s, for readability, a timeout run is shown with a point beyond the grey dotted line, above 10^4 s.

Here we can observe that in the case of the best runs, `slime-bmm` is more effective than `slime`, solving 6 more instances. On the other hand, when looking at the worst case, `slime` is more stable and outperforms `slime-bmm`.

There are two main takeaways from the experimental results we observed in this section. First, BMM is a good candidate for an in-processing component that can help guide the CDCL search. Compared to other solving engines that are used for in-processing component (e.g. SLS), our experience was that BMM performs well right out of the box, without too much tuning of the heuristics. Second, running sequential solvers with different random priors given to BMM makes the solver explore different solutions (for satisfiable instances), which is a great opportunity for parallel portfolio solvers. Thus, in the next section we explored the possibility of using BMM with different priors as a means of diversifying the set of worker solvers in a parallel portfolio setting.

---

[4] https://github.com/lip6/painless/tree/bmm.

3.1   Architecture of the `p-slime-bmm` Parallel Portfolio Solver and Results

We named the resulting parallel solvers `p-slime` and `p-slime-bmm`. To implement these solvers, we used Painless infrastructure [9], a framework that eases the implementation of parallel SAT solvers for many-core environments. The parallelization and sharing strategies we implemented are the same as the one used by the winner of the parallel track of the SAT competition 2021 `p-mcomsps` [13]. Both `p-slime` and `p-slime-bmm` are portfolio solvers [8]. Therefore each instance of a CDCL engine (thread) is launched on the entire formula. The sharing strategy is based on the Literal Block Distance (LBD) measure: the LBD of a clause is the number of decision levels represented in that clause [1]. Initially the thread responsible for sharing receives every clause with a LBD inferior or equal to 2. This distribution happens in an asynchronous manner between the solver threads and the sharing threads. After some predetermined round of sharing, if the sharing threads received too much/not enough clauses from a particular solver, it will dynamically decrease/increase the LBD limit for this solver. In `p-slime-bmm`, the cdcl engines are either `slime` or `slime-bmm` and we make the proportion of `slime-bmm` vary between the different versions of the solver from 25% to 90%. The aim here is to ensure a total collaboration between the solvers (of the portfolio) to get a maximum of solved instances. As a deterministic solver would not make sense in the parallel context, we use `slime` diversification mechanism, which consists in fixing a random polarity to each variable, for each `slime` in the portfolio.

Both solvers were run on a cluster of 12-core Intel Xeon CPU E5645, with 64 GB of RAM, a timeout of 5000 s,s setting the framework to launch 10 sequential solvers. In this performance study, we use the following success metrics: penalized average runtime (PAR-2) sums the execution time of a solver and penalizes the executions that exceed the timeout with a factor 2; the number of instances solved. As observed in Table 1, it seems that having both algorithms in equal proportion is the sweet spot, as `p-slime- bmm-50%` solves 5 more SAT instances than `p-slime`, resulting in a much better PAR-2. Hence, the new proposed solver proves to be more efficient than the state-of-the-art `p-slime`.

4   Conclusion

In this paper, we presented a Bayesian Moment Matching (BMM) in-processing technique for CDCL SAT solvers. We invoked this BMM method, as an in-processing technique after Boolean Constraint Propagation and before branching is called in a CDCL SAT solver, with the goal of updating the polarity and branching activity scores. Bayesian reasoning has proven to be a powerful way to guide the CDCL search procedure away from fruitless parts of the search space of a satisfiable Boolean formula. We experimented massively our approach on cryptographic instances and under sequential settings. The outputs were positives for some random seeds and not others (given the probabilistic nature of BMM). This led us to develop a portfolio parallel solver using our new algorithm as a back-end engine along with the standard engines. The resulting derived hybrid parallel solver showed good performances with respect to the vanilla solver. Using an incremental approach, we found that 50% of `slime-bmm` is a good proportion but it may not be the most optimal solution. The next step will be to fine-tune the proportion of `slime-bmm` in the portfolio based on the work done in [10] using a Multi-Armed Bandit approach.

References

1. Audemard, G., Simon, L.: Predicting learnt clauses quality in modern sat solvers. In: Proceedings of the 21st International Joint Conferences on Artificial Intelligence (IJCAI), pp. 399–404. AAAI Press (2009)
2. Avgerinos, T., Cha, S.K., Hao, B.L.T., Brumley, D.: AEG: Automatic exploit generation. In: Network and Distributed System Security Symposium (2011)
3. Bradley, A.R.: SAT-based model checking without unrolling. In: Jhala, R., Schmidt, D. (eds.) VMCAI 2011. LNCS, vol. 6538, pp. 70–87. Springer, Heidelberg (2011). https://doi.org/10.1007/978-3-642-18275-4_7
4. Bright, C., Kotsireas, I., Ganesh, V.: The science of less-than-brute force: when satisfiability solving meets symbolic computation. In: Communications of the ACM (CACM). ACM (2022)
5. Cadar, C., Ganesh, V., Pawlowski, P.M., Dill, D.L., Engler, D.R.: EXE: automatically generating inputs of death. ACM Trans. Inf. Sys. Secur. (TISSEC) **12**(2), 10 (2008)
6. Davis, M., Logemann, G., Loveland, D.: A machine program for theorem-proving. Communun. ACM **5**(7), 394–397 (1962)
7. Duan, H., Nejati, S., Trimponias, G., Poupart, P., Ganesh, V.: Online bayesian moment matching based sat solver heuristics. In: International Conference on Machine Learning, pp. 2710–2719. PMLR (2020)
8. Hamadi, Y., Jabbour, S., Sais, L.: ManySAT: a parallel sat solver. J. Satisfiability Boolean Model. Comput. **6**(4), 245–262 (2009)
9. Le Frioux, L., Baarir, S., Sopena, J., Kordon, F.: PaInleSS: a framework for parallel SAT solving. In: Gaspers, S., Walsh, T. (eds.) SAT 2017. LNCS, vol. 10491, pp. 233–250. Springer, Cham (2017). https://doi.org/10.1007/978-3-319-66263-3_15
10. Liang, J.H., Oh, C., Mathew, M., Thomas, C., Li, C., Ganesh, V.: Machine learning-based restart policy for CDCL SAT solvers. In: Beyersdorff, O., Wintersteiger, C.M. (eds.) SAT 2018. LNCS, vol. 10929, pp. 94–110. Springer, Cham (2018). https://doi.org/10.1007/978-3-319-94144-8_6
11. Nejati, S., Ganesh, V.: CDCL (crypto) SAT solvers for cryptanalysis. arXiv preprint arXiv:2005.13415 (2020)
12. Riveros, O.: Slime SAT solver. In: Proceedings of SAT Competition 2021: Solver and Benchmark Descriptions, p. 37. Department of Computer Science, University of Helsinki, Finland (2021)
13. Vallade, V., et al.: New concurrent and distributed painless solvers: P-MCOMSPS, P-MCOMSPS-com, P-MCOMSPS-MPI, and P-MCOMSPS-com-MPI. In: Proceedings of SAT Competition 2021: Solver and Benchmark Descriptions, p. 40. Department of Computer Science, University of Helsinki, Finland (2021)

Author Index

Printed in the United States
by Baker & Taylor Publisher Services